The Royal Dragon Court- INBRED BRITAIN Dragon Bloodlines.
By Abbe De Vere

Copyright to Abbe De Vere/ Abbe Brooks-Weir, The Royal Dragon Court 1981-2025,©.
Inherited owner of all Copyright and royalties regarding the books: The Dragon Legacy and The Dragon Cede by Nicholas de Vere, Previously but now terminated Published by The Book Tree, No part of this book should be copied or reconstructed using this methodology as is part of Abbe De Vere's intellectual property and owned under The Royal Dragon Court and Dragon Publishing. All Idea's for the basis of this book The Royal Dragon Court "Inbred Britain", Dragon Bloodlines, is original, and authentically owned by Abbe De Vere, spanning 16 Years of research,

However, the author has used collated essays in a paraphrased, academic style to convey the message. All authors of the original essays and work have been acknowledged, All work is cited using the Chicago style. The Author has used Grammarly to assist with spelling, punctuation, grammar and fluency of the text. The author has used Bing AI and Chat GPT for visual presentation of images, Photographs by Abbe De Vere along with citation from source.
This book has been published under Dragon Publishing
ISBN 978-1-9193098-1-1
Date of Publishing Oct 2025

Preface

This book is the culmination of years of focused historical research, legal training, and a deep personal commitment to uncovering the untold and unrecorded parts of our shared human story. I am not a scientist or an anthropologist, and I do not pretend to be. I am a historical researcher — one who approaches the past with the same critical thinking and investigative discipline that my degree in law has instilled in me. Law teaches you to question, to demand evidence, to notice the gaps in the record, and to follow the trail others have overlooked. Those skills have been essential in building the foundation of this work.

At its heart, this book is about connection — the undeniable fact that through millions of years of migration, movement, and intermarriage, we are all related. The bloodlines that weave through history, binding families, nations, and dynasties together, also bind every one of us. Marriage alliances, royal unions, and clan ties were not only political or economic arrangements; they are the recorded evidence of a truth far deeper — a truth that science, genetics, and even ancient traditions now echo.

I believe that in ages past, humanity possessed abilities that today seem almost mythical: a natural telepathy, a hive-like connection akin to that of bees, and a deep intuitive awareness of each other and of the world around us. These were not supernatural gifts, but part of our natural inheritance — capacities diminished over centuries by the erosion of our freedoms, the control of our knowledge, and the dumbing-down of our awareness. Yet traces remain. We see them in the way prayer has now been scientifically shown to have measurable effects, in the proven benefits of mindfulness and meditation, and in the rising awareness of principles like affirmation and the law of attraction. These are not new inventions; they are the remnants of a lost mastery.

This book is not about providing all the answers. It is about giving you a map. For some, this will be enough. For others — those with the curiosity to dig deeper — it will be the start of their own investigations. My role is to lay down the historical, genealogical, and contextual groundwork so that you can see the patterns for yourself. I have traced marriages, bloodlines, and migrations to show that the idea of separation — between peoples, classes, or nations — is an illusion. We are one extended human family, and the recognition of that truth may be the first step in reclaiming our sovereignty.

In a time when governments and systems work tirelessly to keep us divided, controlled, and distracted, remembering who we are — and what we are capable of — is an act of quiet rebellion. If we can begin to reconnect with our natural gifts, our shared heritage, and our rightful place in the world, we may yet reclaim the abilities that once made us whole.

This is not simply a history book. It is an invitation: to think critically, to question deeply, and to rediscover the parts of yourself that history tried to erase.

As you move into the Introduction, you will see how these ideas take shape through the stories, records, and connections I have uncovered. The following pages lay out not only the historical framework but also the personal journey that led me to question accepted narratives, to search beyond the obvious, and to follow the threads of truth wherever they might lead.

Foreword

The origins and psychology of humanity have long been a deep fascination of mine. What began as a simple question — who are we, and where do we come from? — evolved over time into a broader inquiry: why do certain individuals exhibit particular traits and behaviours? What sets us apart, and what binds us together?

Through over a decade of research in ancestry, DNA, and my work as a genealogist, one truth repeatedly emerged: we are far more connected than we often realise. As I traced countless family bloodlines, I found that most were intricately linked — through marriage, shared ancestry, or both. The further I delved, the more compelling and interconnected the picture became.

This book reflects that journey. It explores not only the historical and genetic ties that link us, but also the psychological and neurological traits that travel down family lines. In studying criminal law, for instance, we encounter the concept of *mens rea* — the mental capacity for accountability. Are traits such as sociopathy, ADHD, or narcissistic personality disorder inheritable? Can we trace these through generational patterns?

Similarly, I examine whether traits like telepathy, extrasensory perception (ESP), and psychic sensitivity could also be inherited. The deeper you go into these subjects, the more the lines between science, genetics, and the unexplained begin to blur — and the more intriguing the human story becomes.

None of this knowledge would have been of interest, had I of not read my late fathers' books. After taking over The Royal Dragon Court back in 2013 when my father died, I wanted to write this book to clarify some of the misunderstandings that arose from my dad's books, "The Dragon Legacy and The Dragon Cede". Using my research to connect the dots to provide evidence to why or how my father's books and his natural instincts were actually correct, Looking back to when he published his books, it was all very new information, showing how he was ahead of his years with knowledge.

Some people have labelled my father a "fictional- pseudo-historian" for a number of reasons, primarily due to the lack of references in his books. Over the years, this has raised questions about the authenticity of his research, which I have been able to verify.

Many have attempted to defame my father because his work is considered alternative. They often call him a pseudo-historian, trying to categorise him as part of the "tin foil hat" crowd in order to boost their own sales. I assume that most readers of this book have also read my father's works; if not, I encourage you to do so, as it will foster a productive dialogue about the information presented here.

I want to acknowledge a few individuals who have been instrumental in helping me write this book. Firstly, I want to thank my father, Nicholas De Vere, for equipping me with the tools necessary to continue his work in preserving The Royal Dragon Court. His love and intellectual brilliance shaped my understanding of the subjects he discussed and taught me throughout my upbringing. I also want to express my gratitude to my mother, Susan Weir, for her perseverance in raising me, though times were extremely difficult, she taught me how to be a better mother and to always prioritize my children's needs above my own.

I am thankful to Iona Miller for her kind words, unwavering support, along with her dedication to my father over the years. During the time of my father's passing, she was the only person I could truly trust.

I also reach out and acknowledge my cousins, Kaaron De Vere and Mandy De Vere, who have been a tremendous source of support and humour over the years. These two women welcomed me back into the family, along with my beloved cousin Wilma, who has taken me on many adventures around Scotland, back to my ancestral lands—the real family. I extend my heartfelt thanks to my ever-supportive friends, Thomas Kelly, Jim Debussey, and my cousin Matthew Collison, who have stood by me during some of the toughest times in my life, showing me unconditional love. I also want to thank my beautiful confidant, Ian, who helped me navigate through the challenges and provided me with information that was lost or stolen, while others were preoccupied with The Games of Dungeons and Dragons, conducting round table meetings to take over the Dragon Court for their own financial gains. Ian helped me discern who was genuine and who was leading me astray.

My devotion to Amanda Radcliffe for her friendship and dedication to enlightening her followers with the spiritual growth, her support toward myself and the work I do with The Royal Dragon Court.

Lastly, I want to thank my children for their love and support. They have patiently listened to my ramblings about The Royal Dragon Court and allowed me to teach them about their heritage while enjoying the many wonderful road trips we have taken together. My everlasting gratitude goes to all of these people.

Additional thanks to people who have requested interviews with myself over podcast, This isn't my cup of tea, so I have tended to thrust others members into the lime light to take my place, Thank you to Clyde Lewis at Ground Zero radio station for his interview with Thomas Kelly on my behalf, Massive appreciation to Robert Sepehr for his many videos about the Serpent Seed and Royal Dragon Court, Along with the inclusion of work from the books The Dragon Legacy and The Dragon Cede on my behalf, I really enjoyed my time getting to know Robert and showing him dads work, in order to create these videos and collaborate, ensuring that the correct information was put forward. Much thanks to Andy Rouse at Deep Share podcast for his friendship over the years and work he has uploaded in regard to the Royal Dragon Court. Along with One Sip Sunday for the interview they did with our Jim Debussey. For more information, please go to the Royal Dragon Court YouTube channel and website[1]

Declaration of intent due to copyright laws.

Most of the information presented is my own life story and interpretation of research over the last decade of promoting my father's book, where I have used other essays to combine my narrative of inbreeding and defects due to this.
I use the right of fair use when information is in the public domain in terms of copyright law, This is especially the case for when information has been used many times over and is available on multiple websites. I also point to notice to part owning some of the history written as being a blood relative of such information and is my right to use it.
Authors and their work has been cited within the text and footnote to acknowledge their contribution either in books or from website's (public domain) or YouTube channels, Some of which I have paraphrased, or improved, to the point that it actually becomes my own however, Most authors have gathered and also paraphrased this information from as above, the public domain, or work accumulated from sources that are over 70 years old. My work is a story of how we are all interbred using snippets of essays gathered. If anyone feels that their work has not been acknowledged then please contact myself at royaldragoncourt@gmail.com, so that I can publicly acknowledge your work, No harm or plagiarism in meant by the publishing of this book. If anything, it aids towards promotion of your efforts, Your're Welcome.

---

[1] *The ROYAL DRAGON COURT – YouTube, research further on the playlists or go to the original source.*
www.royaldragoncourt.com

Contents

Picture denoting the Royal Dragon Court, copyright, and publishing information, Pg 1
Preface, Pg 2
Foreword, Pg 4
Introduction, Pg 12
Small Biography, From Hippy communes to castles, Pg 16
Includes: Lady Olivia Durden Roberts — The Fellowship of ISIS.
The Story Of The Drakenberg Dragon Bloodline, Pg 21
Abbe De Vere — My Ancestry Journey: Genealogy, Pg 37
History of The Sinclair's, Pg 40
Freemason Connections, Pg 46
History of Clan Logan
Includes: The Logan's are from the Scottish Clan Logan from Restalrig and Logan Manor, Logan of that Ilk, Pg 48
History of Clan Macdonald, Pg 52
Queen Victoria's Servants, Pg 60
Tales from The Royal Dragon Court, Pg 64
Includes: The Nicholas De Vere confirmation letters of authenticity, Argument about Laurence Gardiner plagiarising his work
Understanding the Law of Succession,
Pretenders to the Throne,
DNA Markers and Migrations, Pg 80
The Tree of Life — DNA Bridge, Pg 82
The Origins of Humanity, Hybridization, and the Foundations of Social Structure, Pg 85
Migration and the Paradox of Inbreeding: A Deep Human History, Pg 90
Origins of the Picts and Scots, Pg 96
Pict DNA R1B, Pg 102

Bloodlines and Echoes — Genetic Clues to Nobility and Ancestral Identity, Pg 105

De Vere DNA Markers — Royal and Scottish Clan DNA Markers,
My DNA Matches Through Susan Wright, Pg 112
My DNA Matches Through Nicholas de Vere, Pg 117
High Kings of Ireland DNA Markers, Pg 121
How Our DNA Reveals We're All Related, Pg 130
How to Begin: A Reader's DNA Starter Guide, Pg 135
JRR Tolkien and the origins of The Lord of the Rings Pg 138
The Tuatha-de-Danann, Pg 141
Brian Boru, High King of Ireland, Pg 145
The Tale of King Arthur and Tintagel Castle, Pg 147
The King of the Road — Gypsy Origins and the Myth of Memory, Pg 151
The Gypsy Royal Family, Pg 155
The Arrival of the Romani: Gypsies in Scotland, Pg 160
Scotland: Scota, Sovereignty, and the Shadow of Migration, Pg 162
The Bruce Dynasty: True Kingship Rooted in Blood and Legend, Pg 164
Includes: Scottish Royalty — King Robert the Bruce.
Rollo The Viking, Pg 171
The De Vere's of Hedingham Castle, Includes:
De Vere Genealogy: Principal Line of Descent, Pg 173
The Magna Carta, Pg 184
Major Thomas Weir — The Wizard of West Bow, Pg 192
It's a Family Affair — The Connection with the De Vere's and The De Courtenay's (Nicholas De Vere and Susan Wright Genealogy), Pg 199
The History of Torquay — Tor Mohun, Pg 211
Includes: Mohun of Tor Mohun and Dunster Castle.
Cockington — The Cary Family, Pg 216
The Scrope Family, Pg 231

The De Clare Line, Pg 237
A Witches Craft, Pg 245
Royal Witches and 'Love Magic', Pg 258
One in a Million, Pg 273
Historical Factors in Genetic Proliferation, Pg 275
The World's Largest Family Trees, Pg 277
DNA Research — Dangers of Royal Inbreeding
Questioning the Links Between Hereditary Illnesses, Pg 280
The Queen's Hidden Cousins, Pg 292
Royal Genetically Inherited Autism, Pg 295
What Gene Causes Red Hair?, Pg 299
Deep Dive into R Negative Blood, Pg 302
What Is Pseudo History, Pg 307
Includes: Original sources from Mythology
Defining Dragons and Serpents Throughout History and Mythology.
The Meaning of the Serpent, Pg 322
The Dragon of the Orient, Pg 332
Includes: European Dragons, Pg 333
Geography of the Sacred Serpent: Myths of Wadjet, Pg 339
Etymology of Quetzalcoatl, Pg 343
Jehoiakim in the Old Testament, Pg 351
Snakes on Staffs in Egypt, Pg 357
Snakes on Staffs in Mesopotamia, Pg 358
My Spiritual Journey, Pg 361
Spiritual Consciousness, Pg 367
Body Wisdom & Natural Senses Pg 368
The Relativity of Body and Soul, Pg 373
Creation of the False Self, Pg 375
The Memory Beneath the Veil, Pg 378
Appendix, Pg 383
The CIA Files Pg390
Bibliography, Pg 398

Includes: Further reading for information relating to *The Dragon Legacy* by Nicholas de Vere
Index, Pg 419

INTRODUCTION

Let me introduce myself and my father, I am Abbe de Vere,
I have been a professional Genealogist since 2009, taking on clients to help them with their ancestral and DNA journey.
I have a passion for researching history, with the love of road trips to lands and castles owned by my family, using this information to continue to promote and sell the books of my late father. I am also a self-made Farmer, owning four acres of land containing 70 animals and livestock, from Horses, Goats and Poultry, I have a humble egg supplying business.
I do all of this whilst being a full-time carer for my Autistic children.

My Father is or was Nicholas Thomas Logan Weir (RIP), AKA Nicholas De Vere,
(Prince Nicholas de Vere Von Drakenberg)
He was the author of the books "The Dragon Legacy" and "The Dragon Cede."
The Dragon Legacy invites readers on a fascinating journey into the ancient and sacred bloodlines that have quietly shaped history, culture, and spirituality across Europe and beyond. Written by Nicholas de Vere, this work uncovers the extraordinary heritage of the "Dragon Bloodlines"—noble families whose lineage carries not only royal roots but a deep well of spiritual wisdom and power.

At it's core, the dragon is much more than a mythical creature—it is a timeless symbol of strength, wisdom, and transformation, woven into the stories and beliefs of countless civilizations, from the ancient Egyptians and Biblical traditions to Celtic legends and Medieval heraldry. Through these stories, the dragon connects us to a living legacy of knowledge and identity passed down through generations.

"The Dragon Legacy" is a work that guides people from our bloodline back to our roots, taking readers on a journey to the beginning of human creation, through the story of the Anunnaki Gods, traces the origins of these bloodlines back to ancient tribes like the Tuatha Dé Danann, whose remarkable gifts—both physical and spiritual—continue to shine in their descendants today. Combining history, myth, and esoteric insight, The Dragon Legacy offers a unique perspective on who we are and where we come from.

More than just a tale of ancestry, this book encourages readers to awaken to their own heritage of strength, intuition, and sovereignty—and to embrace the powerful destiny that flows through the blood of the Dragon.

However, one might wonder how we can ascertain the truth of these claims or whether they are merely an amalgamation of information gathered from various sources, Myths, The Bible, and ancient texts like the Dead Sea Scrolls and Sumerian cuneiform. What solid evidence do we have to uncover the true origins of the Royal Dragon Court?
In his research, Dad aimed to explore the discrepancies within the etymology of words we use in the English language to describe mystical beings like fairies, dragons, pixies, and vampires. He discovered that we belonged to a unique bloodline, one that set us apart from others. He found out that he descended from Royalty, and with that came certain characteristics and abilities that most people lack—specifically, a sense of clarity or, in other words, clairvoyance and magical Skills. Some may refer to these abilities as witch craft, the law of attraction or a means of mastering one's own creation. All is in the mind.

My own research into our bloodline started in 2009, recalling many earlier visits to my father and grandparents in Wales. Dad would share stories about our ancestry, while Nan would gather us to sift through old family history, showing us photographs from a century ago. At that time, as teenagers, we often brushed off their stories. I distinctly remember having an argument with my father when he recounted how the Weirs were once connected to royalty, including a figure named Major Thomas Weir, who was once a priest but was labelled as a witch and ultimately burned at the stake, for various reasons we wouldn't be proud of. As a historian, I strive to remain objective in my research and seek out the truth. Following that heated exchange regarding Major Thomas, Dad mentioned a man named "Sandy," or Alexander Weir, who he claimed provided our connections. As we talked, it felt as if he was piecing things together on a whim. I replied that there was no way to know for sure, to which he counters, "Well, who knows?" I retorted, "I know, and I don't believe you. I'll either prove you right or prove you wrong."

That's how it all began: a disgruntled teenager challenging her father in a fit of frustration, However, I have steadfastly embraced these words, uncovering both truths and falsehoods within my father's work. The problem arises when some fans/ Critics, having caught wind of my insights, took it upon themselves to spotlight alleged inaccuracies. Yet, as I delved deeper, I found ample evidence that solidly supports my father's findings. Many have misdirected their focus, jumped to conclusions, and opportunistically boarded the Nicholas de Vere bandwagon for clickbait on their YouTube channels, which I find to be utterly distasteful. In order to write this book, I conducted rigorous research on my own, intentionally steering clear of my father's work. I pursued a law degree with a specialization in Copyright Law, The Corruption of the Police and Government, learning all aspects of Criminal and Business Law, equipping myself to research and reference properly—Something my father did not do as thoroughly.

My objective was to align the genealogy with my late father's findings to establish indisputable truths, while also discerning which aspects were fiction or mythology. My mission is clear: to demonstrate, How the Dragon Court is connected to royalty and to answer the pressing questions about my own royal lineage. How many ancestral lines are enriched with spiritual gifts, magic, and witchcraft?

I have engaged with numerous individuals who share my heritage, and I demand answers: Are we all interconnected? not just those who can trace their lineage but every person in the world today. Are we all linked to royalty? Has migration impacted or enhanced the amalgamation of certain bloodlines.

How do our genetics shape our spiritual abilities and mental capacity? Is the autism spectrum prevalent within just our bloodline, and does it serve as a catalyst for these unique abilities? This is precisely why I titled the book "Inbred Britain." After a decade of thorough research, I am confident that we are all fundamentally related. Removing the once was elitist ideology of just a certain few to how many of us lead humble lives and still have these gifts.

I am deeply invested in the genealogy and anthropological aspects of this work, and I share the same vital questions that humanity has posed throughout history: Who are we, and where do we come from?

From Hippy Communes to Castles

My Dad was in the Army and Mum was a nurse in the local hospital, Before I was born, they both lived in Omagh in Northern Ireland, Dad served in the battles against the IRA to which is my Elder sister was born, They all returned to Sussex after dad decided to go AWOL due to mental health issues because of the bombings.

I was bought up in Haywards Heath in Sussex, which I thought I would have a long history lying there, I thought I was a Sussex girl through and through. I did not know that my Weirs were really Scottish, In fact I always hated Scotland, unbeknown to the reason, I just thought it was boring and had nothing about it," It's all just mountains". I felt that being from Sussex made me the well-spoken lady I am.

We lived in an estate, which I'm sure we owned our house, But at the same time it could well have been a council estate. We used to have huge wooden Victorian dolls houses and all the toys you could ask for. Summoned every week to Sunday school, We wore what you could called little house on the prairie outfits, hand sewn sweet identical little dresses. It was the 80's, the kind of neighbourhood where everybody knew each other, all go out on our bikes first thing in the morning, with a backpack full of food and drinks, and come home when the streetlight went off and our mother bellowed from the doorsteps.
We would holiday in the caravan to the New Forest with my grandparents, often go the Isle of Wight and Cowes, which I later found out why and will go into later on. My grandparents were very well known in the area, pillars of society, As grandad was best friends with the local police force, He also served as the highest ranking leader to the Boy scouts, Once building a huge log cabin within the Boscombe Weald and giving it to the scouts, many people will have known John Brooks, as I have seen many articles about him during my research a lot of people reminiscing on what a kind man he was, He would be in every single pantomime and play at Clare Hall in Haywards Heath, along with his sister Aunty Liz.

Along with his 25-year service as Bishop and organiser to the Famous Lewes Bonfire nights, This was a massive part of our lives and still today Johns family lead the procession and are a big part of the bonfire nights.

Grandad John was my step grandfather as my grandfather James Weir had died in 1978, John was always in love with my nan, Natalie (again I later found out that her name was not even Natalie it was Eunicia). John was a bachelor and stayed that way all his life as he waited for my nan, When grandad James Weir, passed, John took over to look after her, This is probably one of the most beautiful love stories I have come across and I endeavour to have a love like that in my life. They married the year I was born, Grandad wanted to give mum a special pram for me, it was beautiful Victorian black pram, a proper one, Mum said to John that she wanted him to be part of the family, so she took his surname to add to ours and we became Brooks-Weir. (I may add That I am one of the very few Brooks-Weirs in the world, We have an extremely rare surname). I have however along with my father adopted the Surname of deVere for my written work to follow suit.

Growing up became a weird series of events that I could only describe as adventure to enlightenment and truth, it was not all fancy and sometime pushing us as a family to our limits, however it's what has made me and gotten me to have the perseverance, strength and independence I have today.
Now to start, I will say that dad had Asperger syndrome which back then was not understood to its entirety, autism did not exist, it was called naughty boy syndrome. He was given the choice of going into the Army or Borstal, Dad chose the Army.

Later on in life, he would have Hyper focus fixations now this is when it gets a bit much, but dad started to research who he was and ended up getting involved in the occult, A thirst for knowledge, He started having an affair with one of the neighbours, Mum obviously didn't want to loose her family unit and went along with it, before

you know it dad had a wife and a girlfriend. Thank god it didn't last long; it was a very unusual situation especially for that time.
Some things went on and one night we were all whisked away in a truck, Me, my sister and mum, and then dad's girlfriend and her kids, there was nine of us in a hippy truck bought from some Chinese woman, before we knew it, we ended up in Tee pee village, Tally Valley in the Brecon Beacons.
I have good and bad memories of that time, so I tend to focus on what good came from it, We would learn to live off the land, tread the hot coals and I had a fixation on fire and became somewhat of a pyromaniac.
We lived in the truck and fed the goats daily, fetch the water from the river and go about our daily lives in the commune playing with a little girl called Plum, Whilst looking after the other kids. One night we had to leave due to farmers and police forcing us to leave with petrol bombs.[2]

We then moved on to **Bally Healy Castle** and lived there for a few months.[3]

---

[2] TIPI *Valley – TV First Tuesday, aired 1985, YouTube video, uploaded by "TV First Tuesday Archive," https://www.youtube.com (accessed [Feb 2025).*
[3] *Ballyhealy Castle – The Norman Way," The Norman Way, accessed August 4, 2025, https://thenormanway.com/ballyhealy-castle*

We were told as children that we owned the castle, we certainly lived there for a short while, my sibling and I would play ball games with ghosts and see baby crows nesting in the tiny tower window, one day I fell through the floorboards and that was the end of our time there. It needed far too much refurbishment than what we could handle.

Clonegal Castle

We ended up at **Huntington Castle**, We called it Clonegal Castle,
When meeting Olivia Robertson and we were told to call her Aunty Olivia.
However, after recent research she is my18th cousin 1x removed, sharing Elizabeth Carew and Joan Courtenay of Haccombe as cousins, therefore Hugh Courteney as a grandfather, I am related to Aunty Olivia through my mother's lines. Which would come as a surprise to my late father, I am yet to discover if I share ancestry with Olivia through my father.

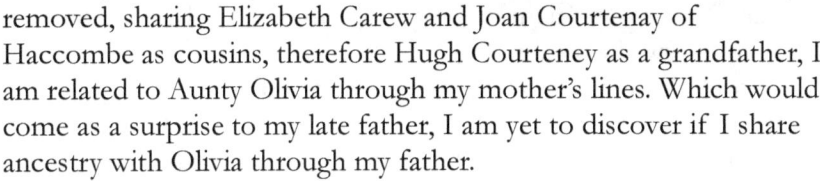

I think about Aunty Olivia a lot and the weird castles we lived in and owned for a short time. She took us to the dungeons, around the gardens, we would make her cups of tea in her library, looking in awe at all of her art and paintings.
Olivia was eccentric and scary in the kindest way, extremely posh and well spoken.

She had a kind nature but at the same time a sense of authority over us kids, I remember playing hide and seek in the gardens and courtyard with Alexander, I remember his blonde hair, He is now the current owner, he was a few years older than me, not by much. He remembers this as well as I wrote to him when Olivia died, we laughed how Olivia would shout, "those bloody children". This is when she knighted my father Nicholas De Vere and Clonegal sometimes named as Huntington became our home for a few short months.

Olivia Robertson
Apr. 13, 1917 - Nov. 14, 2013

They would have meetings of all sorts of people, whilst hiding in the trees, we would see people all dressed in white, we thought they were ghosts but turned out to be some druid gatherings, now that rational thought takes over. Olivia took us all one day into the dungeons where she anointed myself and sibling, under the fellowship of ISIS (Please do not get confused with terrorist groups under the same name, LOL) and told us that we would forever be protected, She said to me, be careful what you wish for Abbe, as it will always come true. Inside the Dungeon there would be alters with Zodiac symbols, she told us to stand by our alter and wish for something, I wished to go home and see my grandparents, my wish came true, and grandad sent for us or rather collected us. Dad stayed with his Girlfriend, and we departed, I will always remember the long journey back from Ireland, The rampant sea swishing, the boat tipping us from side to side, going through the Sussex hills, Seeing the chalk man (The long man of Wilmington) knowing we were home.

What a bizarre life I have experienced.

In the footnotes I direct my readers to the fellowship of ISIS on YouTube so that they can see what life was like for me back then.[4] I later got back in contact with the fellowship of ISIS and rejoined with a woman in Devon, however I got lots of bad entities surrounding me and I can't be sure if they were sent by this person of not, I did have to get baptised and have exorcisms performed to remove these entities from my environment. Note to self, do not join a cult, LOL.

Either way it was and still is pretty cool to know that I once owned a castle and lived at Clonegal, It is not a normal part of life that most people experience, Looking back it was a very supernatural and magical time.

The Story Of The Drakenberg Dragon Bloodline

Then we moved from Sussex to Teignmouth in Devon, When my grandparents moved to Wales, but stayed in touch with them and would visit them and dad during the half term holidays.
My dad would write to me, a letter I still have today telling me about who I am, he said I was a princess and not in the normal daddy dearest darling you are a princess but a true blood royal.

After he showed me his passport whilst going on a trip to Devils Bridge in the Hafod Estate in Wales, He made the remark of ensuring that I read what the words on the back,

---

[4]*The Royal Dragon Court*, YouTube channel, accessed August 4, 2025,
https://www.youtube.com/@theroyaldragoncourt1228
Fellowship of Isis – Lady Olivia, YouTube channel, accessed August 4, 2025, https://www.youtube.com/@FellowshipofIsis.

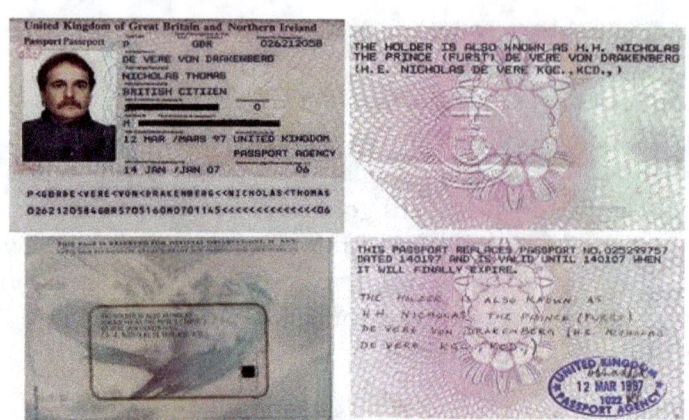

THE HOLDER OF THIS PASSPORT IS ALSO KNOWN AS HH NICHOLAS PRINCE (FURST) DE VERE VON DRAKENBERG (H.E NICHOLAS DE VERE KGC., KDC.,)

Dad told me that I was to declare myself Princess Abbe De Vere Von Drakenberg and bestowed the titles onto me from the family inheritance, As a teenager and again later on in 2009, However, this was under Drakenberg, so the first question was,
What was Drakenberg? How did he get his titles? who gave them to him? He told me that he had gotten into aristocratic circles around the world, That Drakenberg came from an allowance or warrants from relatives of ancient rulers, albeit in exile. He laughed about aristocratic lunches and how Princess Margaret being drunk at the time, He had given the impression from the way he spoke that he knew her and had been in some form of contact, I thought this could have been dad tugging my chain so to speak, Like I say he had a funny sense of humour and would lead the horse to water even if there was no water. I even asked my step mother about this after he passed away and she told me that we owned one of the Galapagos Islands, she laughed and said what if you did own an island and it was mostly full of bird poop, Again we laughed it off, who wants to be a Queen to an island of bird poop?, although it's the most expensive bird poop around, makes amazing fertilizer and was mined to be used as gunpowder, It gives the phrase explosive shit a whole new meaning.

Well, it turns out that The manuscript that my dad gave me when I was 14 held the key to all of this information that I will divulge. The manuscript was about the Ten High Kings of Ireland, along with the letters dad wrote to me telling me how he was helping this lady Margaret Sheil with her genealogy, Now I have been holding onto this information for over 30 years as he told me that I wasn't allowed to tell ANYONE about it, Until now, the non-disclosure has been lifted and someone has written about it in their blog about my father and how he came about getting his title of PRINCE and name changed to de Vere Von Drakenberg, So here is the official and very legally binding statement of truth of who, what, how, when, where and why.

The Kingdom of Redonda holds a unique place in the world's tapestry of symbolic monarchies. Though uninhabited and tiny in size, Redonda has become a storied title intertwined with literary tradition, aristocratic heritage, and secretive bloodlines. For over a century, the throne of Redonda has passed through various hands, often accompanied by controversy and disputed claims. However, through the efforts of my father, Prince Nicholas de Vere von Drakenberg, and the legitimising actions of Queen Margaret Parry, the crown has been restored and its succession firmly anchored in modern legal frameworks. This essay details the journey from Nicholas's recognition as Prince of Drakenberg, through Margaret Parry's lawful investiture as Queen of Redonda, to my own rightful inheritance as Princess Abbe de Vere von Drakenberg, custodian of the Dragon Court and Drakenberg legacy..

Historical and Symbolic Context of Redonda
Redonda, a small uninhabited Caribbean island, first gained literary fame through the works of Matthew Phipps Shiell, whose fantasy novels imbued the island with mythic significance. Over time, the title of "King of Redonda" became a cherished symbolic monarchy passed through an informal lineage of writers, artists, and eccentric nobility. While largely ceremonial, the throne was held in high regard among its holders and those who valued its romantic legacy. However, prior to the 1990s, the succession was often contested

and lacked formal legal recognition. The island's monarchs had no official status under any government, and claims to the throne were often viewed as whimsical or purely honorary. It was in this context that my father sought to restore and solidify the legitimacy of the Dragon Court and the Redondan monarchy—not merely as symbolic titles but as legally recognized and protected estates.

Nicholas de Vere and the Dragon Court Legacy

Nicholas de Vere (born Nicholas Thomas Logan Weir) inherited a deep interest in genealogy, mythology, and royal bloodlines. Drawing upon historical Vere and Merovingian dynasties, he styled himself the Sovereign Grand Master of The Royal Dragon Court, a hereditary order tracing its origins back to medieval and even ancient times. His seminal book, The Dragon Legacy, chronicles this lineage and sets forth his vision of restoring ancient royal traditions in the modern era. In the early 1990s, Nicholas pursued the legal formalisation of his titles and those associated with the Dragon Court. Recognizing the symbolic power and historicity of the Redondan monarchy, he sought to establish a legal covenant that would solidify the succession of titles under English law.

Margaret Parry and the Legal Foundation of the Crown of Redonda

A pivotal figure in this restoration was Margaret Parry, granddaughter of Matthew Phipps Shiell and rightful heir to the Redondan throne. In 1993, she executed a Statutory Declaration under the UK Statutory Declarations Act 1885, a formal legal instrument declaring her hereditary right to the throne and her intent to uphold its legacy. Alongside this, she issued Letters Patent—a formal legal document used historically to confer titles and privileges. These documents legally recognised Margaret Parry as Queen of Redonda and empowered her to grant titles and privileges under the traditional laws of primogeniture. This legal recognition marked a watershed moment in the history of Redonda, moving it from an informal literary title to a legally acknowledged sovereignty with hereditary succession.

The Granting of the Title Prince de Vere von Drakenberg Under Margaret Parry's authority, Nicholas de Vere was formally granted the title Prince de Vere von Drakenberg. This was not merely a stylistic choice, but a legally binding act supported by statutory declarations and Letters Patent. The significance of this is underscored by the British government's acceptance of these titles in official documents. Nicholas's UK passport includes an OBTO observation (also known as) section which states:
> "HH Nicholas the Prince de Vere von Drakenberg, and H.E."

This entry demonstrates that the Passport Office regarded the claim as more than a simple alias or assumed name. Rather, it recognised it as a title supported by legal instruments, granting Nicholas a formal status acknowledged by the Home Office. This level of administrative recognition is rare and significant, placing the Dragon Court and Redondan succession on a much firmer legal footing.

The Lineage and Succession: Legal Precedents Craig Brewin's recent research further elucidates the legal basis of Redondan succession. In his blog post, "How Prince Nicholas de Vere made the Queen of Redonda a Legal Title (Part 1). His work affirms the continuity of Redonda's monarchy under English law and establishes a clear, uncontested hereditary succession from Margaret Parry to current heirs. This evidence is crucial not only in historical terms but also in safeguarding the lineage from false claims or attempts to undermine its legitimacy. The declaration is a formal covenant and legal charter recognized by UK authorities.

My Inheritance and Role as Princess Abbe de Vere von Drakenberg

Upon my father's passing—though intestate—I was appointed as the main executor of his estate and inherited 99% ownership of the Sovereign Grand Duchy of Drakenberg, along with all intellectual property connected to The Royal Dragon Court and The manuscript concerning Margaret Parry's information relating to the Redondan legacy. My siblings voluntarily renounced claims to these titles and works, leaving me as sole custodian. A personal letter written by my father in the 1990s explicitly names me Princess Abbe de Vere von Drakenberg, affirming my role as successor and guardian of our family's heritage. This letter, alongside official documents such as my father's birth and death certificates (which list his royal titles), strengthens my claim and provides irrefutable proof of my position.

The Manuscript and Future Publications
I am also custodian of a vital manuscript written by my father, detailing Margaret Parry's investiture as Queen of Redonda and tracing the bloodline back through the Ten High Kings of Ireland. This manuscript is currently being published through Dragon Publishing Ltd as a follow-up volume to my current work. Publication of this manuscript will not only preserve historical and legal knowledge but also serve as a testament to the continuity of The Royal Dragon Court, The Sovereign Grand Duchy of Drakenberg and the Redondan monarchy history under the association my father had to it.

Corporate Reinstatement and Legacy Preservation
Currently, I have re-registered the Sovereign Grand Duchy of Drakenberg Ltd at Companies House. This company serves as the parent holding entity for Dragon Publishing Ltd, which manages all literary works, copyrights, and royalty streams. Additionally, my agricultural enterprise, de Vere Farm, operates under this corporate umbrella, further solidifying our families economic and cultural legacy. By including my full title in the company registration documents, I reinforce the legitimacy and continuity of The Royal Dragon Court in official UK records. This structure also allows me to place land assets into trust for my children, ensuring long-term stewardship.

The journey from a symbolic island kingdom to a legally recognised hereditary monarchy is complex and filled with both historical and legal nuance. As Princess Abbe de Vere von Drakenberg, I carry the responsibility to safeguard and expand this legacy. By protecting critical documents, re-establishing corporate legitimacy, and preparing key publications, I ensure that The Royal Dragon Court and The Sovereign Grand Duchy of Drakenberg endure—not just as symbols but as living, legally acknowledged institutions[5].

 Life has a funny way of giving you what you need and when, I had literally just finished writing this book, scanning the internet for bits about how our ancestors used oral stories as a way of recording lost history, Still bleary eyed, I woke up to a message from Thomas Kelly, who has passed on this information via James Robert Wright, Sending me links to some random guys blog who says he's going to write about my dad, Makes you wonder really, what people's obsession is about writing books that literally have nothing to do with them, So I thought it were best if you got the information here from me. Dad kept this a secret, he continued with the fact that he was a De Vere and had adopted the name through finding that he was related to an Aubrey de Vere, along with his findings that it is a variant of Weir. Off the top of my head, It was the 20th Earl of Oxford, The de Vere's held the seat of Hedingham Castle in Essex, upon asking how he would send me his extensive genealogy research.
Being in two minds and always critically thinking, I went on to research his information. I went to Burke's Peerage and Debrett's to get confirmation, I wanted our lines added to their records, I was

---

[5].*Abbe de Vere von Drakenberg, The Restoration of Redonda's Crown: From Prince Nicholas de Vere to Princess Abbe de Vere von Drakenberg (London: Dragon Publishing Ltd, 2025).*
UK Statutory Declarations Act 1885, c. 55,
https://www.legislation.gov.uk/ukpga/Vict/48-49/55.
Margaret Parry, "Statutory Declaration of Hereditary Claim to the Crown of Redonda," 1993. Private archive of the Dragon Court.   UK Home Office Passport Entry for Nicholas de Vere von Drakenberg, OBTO observation, issued c. 1990s. Copy held by Princess Abbe de Vere von Drakenberg.
Nicholas de Vere, The Dragon Legacy and associated genealogical records.
Craig Brewin, How Prince Nicholas de Vere made the Queen of Redonda a Legal Title (Part 1), March 16, 2025. (*livinginmontserrat.wordpress.com*) Declaration of Legal Succession to the Throne of Redonda, Craig Brewin, March 2025.

told by both that this information was incorrect and that it was a mixture of fact and fictitious lines from us the Weirs to the de Vere's. This was due to the inclusion of the descent from Melusine and the ancient Angevin House of Vere.[6]

Melusine was a "mermaid", half fish (or rather Water Serpent) and half woman.[7] Emperor Sigismund (as he was styled from 1410) was a son of the House of Luxembourg—dynasts who flagrantly altered their genealogy in order to be able to claim a fraudulent descent from this Dragon Dynasty of Maelasanu and Anjou. It is from this descent—from Maelasanu or Melusine—and upon her British, later Angiers-Angevin, Dragon Court, that Sigismund claimed the right to base Societas Draconis as a bloodline continuation of this ancient, prehistoric, anti-Christian, pre-Catholic, British Elven Institution[8].

As far as my research goes, it is forever being updated, I have Sigismund of Luxembourg (15 February 1368 – 9 December 1437) was a monarch who reigned as king of Hungary and Croatia from 1387 [9] as my 8th cousin through Margaret of bar onto king Louis VI (late 1081 – 1 August 1137), called the Fat (French: le Gros) or the Fighter[10], However when you read the Dragon Legacy is show that the Dragon Bloodline included a much earlier descent, from Egypt.

I wanted to pause for a moment to evaluate an issue that has surfaced many times over, due to this Melusine information, My next statement will allow others to understand further to why we could not get into Debrett's or Burkes peerage with this lineage:

---

[6] *Nicholas de Vere, The Dragon Legacy: The Secret History of an Ancient Bloodline (San Diego: The Book Tree, 2004)*, **16**

[7] *Nicholas de Vere, The Dragon Legacy: The Secret History of an Ancient Bloodline (San Diego: The Book Tree, 2004)*, **69**

[8] *Nicholas de Vere, The Dragon Legacy: The Secret History of an Ancient Bloodline (San Diego: The Book Tree, 2004)*, **16**

[9] *Sigismund of Luxembourg (15 February 1368 – 9 December 1437)," Ancestry.com*, accessed August 4, 2025, https://www.ancestry.com

[10] *King Louis VI Ancestry.com , Ibid accessed on 4th August 2025*

Discussion to separate fantasy and fact where titles land, and laws are concerned

From time to time a message arrives from someone convinced that blood alone entitles them to revive a manor or redeem a crown. The modern script is surprisingly consistent: a fragment of Tudor succession doctrine discovered on a family website; a coat of arms "aligned" with a supposed *de jure* line; and a promise to come to England to "reclaim" property that a family once held in the Middle Ages. A typical specimen reads: "I have aligned myself with the current *de jure* descendants who own the current coat of arms, who are already in office to the seat of the king." It sounds authoritative to the untrained ear. But *de jure* ("by law") in England is not defined by a website's table of descent; it is defined by Parliament, the courts, and the Crown's recognised officers. Today's law—not a sixteenth-century memorandum—governs estates, dignities, offices, and arms.[1]

The enduring magnet in these claims is the de Vere story. In 1133 Henry I made Aubrey (Alberic) de Vere II hereditary royal chamberlain; later the family held the earldom of Oxford, and with it the aura of old nobility.[2] His son, Aubrey de Vere III—"the Grim" in some later chronicles—received the earldom in the civil war of the 1140s, and the line held it for generations.[3] Even the heraldry feels talismanic: the famous mullet (star), quarterly gules and or, and, in later tradition, the blue boar crest.[4] The prestige of the office and the earldom attracted myths and forgeries and romances in equal measure. But the legal history is prosaic and decisive: when Henry de Vere, 18th Earl of Oxford, died without a male heir in 1626, the House of Lords adjudged the hereditary office of Great Chamberlain not to a collateral male de Vere but to the heir general, Robert Bertie, Lord Willoughby de Eresby (later Earl of Lindsey).[5] If one hears that "Edward de Vere had his entitlement removed," the law is simpler than the gossip: Edward, 17th Earl (d. 1604), held the office in his lifetime, but on later succession the right went with the heir general—out of the male de Vere line—by adjudication of the Lords. That is how *de jure* actually works: by authoritative decision, not by incantation.

Confusion multiplies because England has both a modern Lord Chamberlain of the Household (an appointed court official who oversees ceremonial and royal household business) and the hereditary Lord Great Chamberlain (an ancient office now shared in moieties among families descended from the 1626 award). The former is an appointment of the Crown; the latter is a hereditary dignity constrained by Lords' decisions and partition. Conflating the two—reading an appointment as if it were a hereditary investiture—feeds precisely the sort of "already in office to the seat of the king" rhetoric that misleads enthusiasts into thinking they have discovered a live constitutional lever.[6]

Local memory around Great Addington and Drayton (Northamptonshire) provides another lure. The medieval de Vere footprint is real: All Saints' at Great Addington preserves twelfth-century fabric; parish history records a late-medieval Henry de Vere, a county justice and sheriff, commemorated in church; and manorial holdings in the district passed on over the centuries to other families by settlement and sale.[7] That is how English land changes hands: by conveyances, marriage portions, parliamentary forfeitures, mortgages, dissolutions—and not, in the twenty-first century, by the appearance of a far descendant who announces that "it is still in the blood." When an estate has been transferred by lawful deeds and descents for five hundred years, the law presumes continuity of title, not a sleeping right waiting for a modern claimant to breathe life into it.

Mythic ancestry often rides in tandem with these mistakes. The Vere/Weir materials that circulate in family circles sometimes braid the medieval French tale of Melusine—the water-spirit ancestress of the house of Lusignan—with Pictish and Strathclyde king-lists, then telescope that legendary antiquity into medieval English and Scottish lines. In literature, Melusine is a fountain-fey, a "dragon princess," that great old story of enchanted noblesse as literary history it is powerful and beautiful. But in law it is immaterial. Medieval romance is not evidence of modern entitlement.[8] A handsome chart is not a deed; a well-told saga is not a writ.

Three stubborn facts frame the present law. First, "abandoned" property is almost never truly abandoned. Where land or goods are ownerless in England and Wales, they fall to the Crown as *bona vacantia*, administered by the Government Legal Department.[9] Where a company is dissolved, its property similarly escheats to the Crown; where a person dies intestate without heirs, the estate becomes Crown property. If a building has been left derelict, the problem is practical—disrepair—not legal; it still belongs to someone, or to the Crown if truly ownerless. The route to recover land is not to show "blood" but to prove title (conveyance or inheritance) or, in narrow cases, to rely on adverse possession of registered land: ten years' factual possession with intention to possess, without the owner's consent, after which an application can be made—but the registered proprietor may usually defeat that application by counter-notice unless strict exceptions apply.[10] ,Second, heraldry is regulated. In England, a personal right to bear arms comes by descent from a lawful grantee or by new grant from the College of Arms, in Scotland, by grant or matriculation under the Lord Lyon. The College publishes its scale of fees (a personal grant currently in the four figures), but the full process—research, artistry, optional supporters, illumination—often rises into the low tens of thousands.[11] The folklore that "a coat of arms costs £24,000" reflects the all-in spend many families reach once vellum, painting, and display are added. Third, peerage is a dignity, not a thing you "find" in a ruin. Claims to abeyant baronies in England proceed by petition to the Crown through the Lord Chancellor and are often referred to the House of Lords' Committee for Privileges. Modern practice is cautious: abeyances of very long standing are rarely terminated; petitioners usually must show a substantial fractional entitlement; and the Sovereign's decision is informed by law officers and evidence, not online pedigrees.[12]

The romance of "*de jure*" also collides with Parliament's absolute control over the succession to the Crown. Whatever medieval writers thought, the Bill of Rights (1689) and the Act of Settlement (1701) placed the succession under statutory control; later statutes—most recently the Succession to the Crown Act (2013)—altered rules on gender preference and marriage to Roman Catholics.[13] In short: Parliament made and unmade the line of succession. A person who claims "the Stewart line makes me king" is in the wrong century. The lawful heir is whoever Parliament says it is, as recognised by the courts and the Privy Council.

History supplies the classic remedies to the dreamers. Lambert Simnel—paraded as Edward, Earl of Warwick—was crowned "Edward VI" by his supporters in Dublin in 1487 and marched to Stoke; after defeat he was spared and consigned to the royal kitchens.[14] Perkin Warbeck—presented as Richard of Shrewsbury, one of the Princes in the Tower—was hanged at Tyburn in 1499 after years of theatre backed by foreign courts.[15] The moral is not that claimants never had pedigrees; it is that pedigree without lawful recognition is theatre, and power without Parliament is revolt.

Modern versions are tamer but no less revealing. An Australian, Simon Dorante-Day, has for decades claimed to be the son of the present King and Queen; his petitions—including requests for DNA testing—have not obtained judicial recognition of royal status.[16] Another figure, remembered as "Gerald," sought to read royal gestures as legal acts: when a prince removed his tie, Gerald argued, it signified the King undressing himself of entitlement. This is not law; it is word-association theatre posing as hermeneutics.

Then there is the Stuart afterlife in the 1990's and 2000's, when alternative histories and private courts briefly flourished. Michel Roger Lafosse—"Prince Michael of Albany"—(Which dad discusses later) published baroque genealogies purporting to establish him as the living Stuart heir; reporting later alleged irregular documentation, and heraldists dismissed the claims as fantasy royalty[7], Around the margins of these circles, writers and genealogists crossed paths; when my father realised that a central plank of one collaborator's genealogy was unsound, he disengaged. That is what one should do when evidence fails. But having once been in the room with claim-culture, he was sometimes lumped—unfairly—with those who wanted to be obeyed as kings. The confusion deepened because, elsewhere, he helped Margaret Shiel (later Parry) in the Redonda succession saga, creating the title "Prince of Drakenberg" and guiding that micronation "in exile." There was even a United Nations web page at one point, for which I briefly had login access. Micronations are performance and ritual, not sovereignty; and in any case, as of now, my own position is simple and verifiable: I am the director of the Sovereign Grand Duchy of Drakenberg as a UK-registered company. That is not a claim against the British Crown; it is an entry at Companies House.

My cousin's experience illustrates a better instinct. She once wondered whether we held a right to an historic office. She did not act on it; when I sent her an academic source showing that the hereditary element had been abolished, she accepted it and actually joked about it seeing who would take the bait. Twenty years ago, I too was susceptible to the charm that a medieval thread might be pulled through to the present. The law disabused me. Precedent (*stare decisis*) binds courts until a higher court or Parliament changes the rule; judicial review is a public-law remedy for unlawful administrative acts, not a mechanism for private citizens to procure castles.[18] If a person insists on litigating in that register, costs follow. And so does disappointment.

People often ask why, if I can trace descent, I do not "take back" what is "mine." The honest answer is that in law it is not mine. Through my mother I can document a pathway to the abeyant Barony of Cobham; the correct road is a petition in the Crown Office with evidence. Likewise, I can point to a seventeenth-cousin link to Haccombe and sometimes joke that I ought to be "Lady of Haccombe"—and my neighbours have their own private jest, calling the present lay holder "Lord F***wit," their joke, not mine—but the title passed to the Carew's centuries ago and was later transferred to or sold, which I don't think is the legal route to this new unrelated person. Long chains of conveyance break romantic links. A village wink is not a writ.

The same sobriety governs coats of arms. If my father bore arms and the grant or confirmation exists in the proper registers, then I may lawfully display them with the appropriate cadency. If I wished to alter them, I would petition the College of Arms (or in Scotland, matriculate with the Lord Lyon) and pay the requisite fees for research, design, and painting—costs that explain why families recall "twenty-four thousand" as the total for the whole experience, even though the institutional base fee is lower[9]. If a family spent around that sum in a given period and a patent exists, the verification path is direct: write to the College or consult the Lyon Register. If it does not exist, the remedy is not a Facebook post; it is a petition.

There is one last distinction that will save many good people much money. Titles, offices, manors, and arms are different species. A peerage is a dignity that gives precedence and, historically, a summons to Parliament; it is not the same thing as a "lordship of the manor," which is an incorporeal hereditament and, post-2002, registrable only in particular ways. HM Land Registry is explicit: a manorial lordship does not equate to ownership of the soil; it is a separate species of property⁰, The National Archives add the common-sense gloss: you can buy a manorial lordship, but you have not thereby become a peer of the realm, and the manor's historic lands remain wherever the title deeds put them now.[21], Once that is understood, an extraordinary portion of online claim-culture simply falls silent.

Why, then, do people persist? Because lineage is a story, and stories are how we recognise ourselves. The goal here is not to sneer at anyone who has felt that tug. In many old families the archives also hold a few fairy-threads: a Melusine here, an Arthurian echo there. They are part of culture. The challenge is keeping them in their proper place. Between a moving family myth and a legal right stands the awkward, necessary world of Acts of Parliament, House of Lords reports, practice directions, and fees. The rule of law is decidedly unromantic in its methods; but it is precisely that quality that preserves everyone's rights. The village joke lives beside the statute book; both have their uses. The only danger is when a joke hardens into a plan to "take back" a house or a throne. If this chapter saves one reader the price of a doomed filing fee, a needless flight, or a bruising public embarrassment, it will have done its work. I think it is better to honour your lineage by visiting our once own castles and just be happy and take pride in that, best not to get ahead of ourselves and think we are the next in line to the throne, and in all honesty, I have had a friend along the way make such assertion and he did end up in a mental hospital for a year or so, Let that sink in, What we feel is our inheritance can come across as lunacy, grandeur and then may lead to criminal accusations[11].

I had found this information confusing, I thought well if you're a royal, then you will have other lines that give the information, so Dad sent me his book, The Dragon Legacy which he signed with love from dad. I started to read it but gotten myself further discombobulated with the influx of information.
Along the way, dad would give us some little snippets, never the full picture, One time when discussing all of this, Dad gave us a document detailing the Royal Imperial Dragon Court Order and its origins. He gave that to one sibling and to myself a manuscript about the Sechnaill Kings of Ireland, who were related to the Ten High Kings of Ireland, I did not look at this manuscript for many years, as at the time I was not ready, I had to connect all the dots. This took me a very long time, I had disassociated myself with that manuscript, read it very few times, until this year, when I fully invested myself into the research and finding out why he had given me this manuscript, I had assumed at the time that it was for me to write a book about, which I am now in the process of editing and publishing on his behalf.

After reading information on the internet with some of the people dad had been associated with, certain pretenders, it didn't make me feel so great about it all, so I decided to start fresh from the beginning, I remember back when I was 14, Dad told me my future and said, "Abbe you will try to help me but you won't be able to". Then he got sad because he saw that he would not be around when I had. He told me to do Law, Copyright Law, but at that age, I had no brains at all, to even comprehend thinking about that.

---

[11] *See appendix.*

He said, You will find the information through the Glens, being sat right in the Valleys in Wales, I did not click that it was the surname Glen and not the physical hills, Glens, but in a way it's both.

My Ancestry Journey

My ancestry journey started, He said it would be more difficult for me as if you are to be fully royal then you have to have the lines through both sides of your family, mother and father, However my mother was adopted and tried to find her family with no success, it almost brings you to an absolute stop. Mum knew who she was, she knew her surname, she actually got contact at one point to her long-lost brother, but didn't tell us, instead she kept it to herself as she was upset with the fact that her brother Peter was hurt by their circumstances, and he rejected her. The poor woman would be in tears and torment due to this, I wish she spoke to us and told us what she knew, however she kept it to herself. It was a random message from a person on Ancestry that gave me answers to my mother's family lines from her mother's side, I found all of her family and half siblings, it's very unfortunate that this was only for me to find out many years later after her death. Still being able to connect the dots and have a fully complete family tree that leads to royalty on both my mother and my father's lines allows me to complete the work that my father said I would not be able to. Although I have this information, it is extremely important to add that I have alongside over 150 separate Noble and royal elites, I have ancestors whom were Land Army Girls, War hero's, Warrant Officers, Sargents, Farmers, Blacksmiths, Thatchers, Engineers, Servants, Photographers, Some have been home-makers not in work at all, some sent to the workhouses or asylums along with some whom were admirals, pirates, gypsies and travellers. The story of each individual makes the research more enticing.

Most people are able to research their genealogy back to around the 1500's, However due to the lack of records, they hit the brick wall, Parish records only began in the 1500's, when Thomas Cromwell ordered churches to start recording births, deaths and marriages, Before this, records were sparse, were not well preserved and often kept orally and told through the family. There was a lack of records for common people, Nobles or landowners appear in charters, deeds, or heraldic visitations, sometimes going back to the 1100-1200's. Also due to a loss of records via fires (such as the four courts fires, which my father said was the reason to why we could not ascertain certain people in our tree that connected us and fully verified us to Major Thomas Weir), wars, floods and religious reformations like the dissolution of the monasteries which destroyed vast amounts of information. It is only that I have managed to research the following information for over a decade, through peerage books, the doomsday book, parish records, historical references ancestry and DNA that I have been able to discover a wealth of information which as I have already mentioned in my aims for the book, is not just my family but perhaps yours too. With this I encourage the reader to venture on your own ancestral journey to discover your roots and the many stories they have left behind.

I therefore set on an adventure for all of us, showing those people who were prevalent within history, enough for it to be highly documented in books and show how we are all connected.

Abbe De Vere Genealogy
From Susan Wright,

Through Lillian Breeze, I am related to the De Courtenay's and Baron's of Cobham

Baron John Cobham born 1320 died 1407 married to Margaret Courtenay Born 1326 and died 1385

17th great-grandfather

Catherine Cobham
Daughter of Baron John Cobham born 1320 died 1407 married to Margaret Courtenay Born1326 and died 1385

John Seyliard born 1388 married to Ellen Pawlyn Seyliard
Son of Catherine Cobham

Robert Seyliard born 1415 and died 1464 Married to Eleanor Gabriall Seyliard
Son of John Seyliard born 1388 married to Ellen Pawlyn Seyliard

Sir Thomas Seyliard 1476-1535
Son of Robert Seyliard born 1415 and died 1464 Married to Eleanor Gabriall Seyliard

Nicholas Seyliard 1504-1583
Son of Sir Thomas Seyliard

Nicholas Seyliard 1547-1625
Son of Nicholas Seyliard

Dorothy Seyliard 1589-1642
Daughter of Nicholas Seyliard

George Antrobus 1631-1708
Son of Dorothy Seyliard

Mary Antrobus 1675-
Daughter of George Antrobus

John PARKER 1708-1764
Son of Mary Antrobus

Samuel Parker 1735-1800
Son of John PARKER

Thomas Parker 1767-1837
Son of Samuel Parker

William Parker 1805-1883
Son of Thomas Parker

Susannah Parker 1852-1919
Daughter of William Parker

William Bird 1873-1940
Son of Susannah Parker

Melissa Maud Bird 1907-1974
Daughter of William Bird

Lillian Edith breeze 1930-
Daughter of Melissa Maud Bird

Susan J Wright 1953-2006
Daughter of Lillian Edith breeze

Abbe Brooks-weir
You are the daughter of Susan J Wright

This line from myself to the Baron Cobham and the De Courtenay's verified by multiple sources, shows why I have included this information later on in the book, the intertwined, interconnected family lines.

From Nicholas De Vere
Abbe De Vere, Daughter of **Nicholas De Vere,**
Son of **James Weir** and **Natalie Hopgood,**
Son of **Thomas Logan Weir** and **Annie Macdonald.**
The Weir descent and genealogy is detailed in this book and also in 'The Dragon Cede' By dad, Nicholas De Vere.

Thomas Logan Weir's son of **John Weir** and **Mary Logan** Mary Anne Logan's Parents were **Thomas Logan** and **Anne McColm**, Through this line the **McColms** are descendants of the **Sinclair**, The Sinclair's are married into Scottish Royalty and nobility: The family is surrounded by mystery.

SIR JOHN SINCLAIR, KNIGHT,

The first of this family, was third son of John, Master of Caithness and was styled of Greenland, but his descendants have been designed of Rattar. He married Janet Sutherland, who was probably of the Sutherland of Forse, Since his nephew, Francis, son of his brother, James of Murkel, married also a lady of that family. From his brother George, the fifth Earl, he obtained, in 1609 (26th January and 16th May 1609) the farms of the lands of Rattar and others, by charter to himself in life rent and to his son, William, and in 1613 he got a disposition from the Earl of the lands of Rattar, Corsbach, Lieurary, Reaster, Murrsay, and Hailand, which are described to be pertinence of the Barony of Achergill, sometime pertaining to George, Earl Marischal, and William, Lord Keith, his son, and acquired by the Earl from them. In 1612 he occupied the Castle of Ormlie, near Thurso. He died in 1622, and had five sons and a daughter (Peerage case): -

    1.   William, who died before his father. Of him Sir Robert Gordon writes: "This year of God, 1620, the eldest son of Sir John Sinclair of Greenland perished in the water

of Risgill, as he was riding that river in a great speat and storm of weather. He was a young gentleman of good expectation". This event must have occurred earlier than 1620, for in 1618 his immediate younger brother, Alexander, obtained a precept as his heir.

2.   Alexander, who in 1618 obtained from his uncle, Earl George, a precept of Clare as heir to William. He died without issue

3.   John, who obtained in 1623 a precept of Clare as heir to Alexander. He also died without issue, and was succeeded by -

4.   James of Reaster, who obtained a precept on 16th December 1634, and was afterwards of Rattar.

5.   Francis, who died without issue.

6.   There is mention of a son, Thomas, as alive about 1630, but there is no trace of any of his descendants.

1.   Elizabeth, Sir John's only daughter, married John Cunningham of Geise and Brownhill. In November 1630, her brother, James, borrowed from Sir John Sinclair of Geanies and Dunbeath £3000 "for payment of his sister Elizabeth's tocher to John Cunningham of Geise, her spouse". In Douglas's accounts of the Cunningham's there is much confusion and error as to this lady and her marriage.[12]

The Sinclair line go back to William Sinclair of Ravencraig Castle, Kirkcaldy in Fife Scotland. James II acquired the lands of

---

[12] *The Sinclair's of Greenland and Rattar. Fiona Sinclair Genealogy. Accessed August 4, 2025.* https://www.fionasinclair.co.uk/Genealogy/cathness/rattar.htm.

Ravenscraig Castle in 1460. Work immediately began on construction of a residence for his wife, Queen Mary of Guelders.

Within five months, James II was killed by one of his own guns at the siege of Roxburgh. Mary pressed on with the castle's construction regardless, and in 1461 it was completed to such a state where her house staff were able to stay there for 25 days.

It's unclear whether Mary herself stayed at the castle before her death in 1463. She never saw a finished castle at Ravenscraig – the only parts completed by her death were the east tower and foundations of a central range.

Mary's son, James III, granted the still-unfinished castle to William Sinclair in 1470. It was compensation for resigning the earldom of Orkney and lordship of Shetland to the Crown. He became earl of Caithness at the same time.

Household to Stronghold

As a royal household, Ravenscraig was certainly built with defence in mind. It is situated on a promontory into the Firth of Forth, fronted by a large rock-cut ditch.

But the Sinclair transformed it into the well-defended fort we see today. Over the central vaults, where Mary would have built her great hall, the Sinclair's instead installed a gun platform in the mid-1500s[13]

The Sinclair surname is also known as St Clair of Rosslyn Chappel

---

[13] *Ravenscraig Castle Statement of Significance. Historic Environment Scotland. Accessed August 4, 2025.*
Ravenscraig Castle. The Douglas Archives. Accessed August 4, 2025

Rosslyn Chapel

In the heart of Midlothian, Scotland, on a hill overlooking what is claimed to be one of the largest remaining areas of ancient woodland known as Roslin Glen, is a lovely little collegiate church referred to as Rosslyn Chapel. The chapel has suffered the effects of the Reformation and been the inspiration of many writers and painters. It played a prominent part in the best-selling book by Dan Brown, The Da Vinci Code and went on to be featured in the movie inspired by said book. Filled with a delicious assortment of mysterious stonework and surrounded by a plethora of (sometimes inaccurate) history, the chapel houses over five hundred years of inspiration and enlightenment.

The interior of Rosslyn Chapel, looking toward the altar.

A Worthy Endeavour
Construction on Rosslyn began in 1446. William St. Clair, Earl of Orkney and Caithness commissioned it, with the intentions that it would be used to offer prayers for his ancestors and descendants

and provide a place of worship for generations to come. It was also to aid in the spread of intellectual and spiritual knowledge. Referring to Sir William's idea for Rosslyn, Father Richard Hay, author of *A Genealogy of the Saint Claire's of Rosslyn* said, "*It came into his mind to build a house for God's service, of most curious work, the which that it might be done with greater glory and splendour...*"

When St. Clair died in 1484 construction on the chapel was halted. Sir William was buried under the unfinished choir section and the chapel was left as it was. Sir William's son, Oliver, either didn't want to spend the money, or lost interest in the chapel construction, for he simply put a roof over the choir section and that became what we now know as Rosslyn Chapel. The larger portion of the building that was planned was never finished.

A hundred years later the winds of Reformation would blow through Scotland wreaking havoc on Catholic chapels such as Rosslyn. Another Oliver St. Clair would be commanded to tear down the altars within the chapel as it was reputed as a "house and monument of idolatry." After the altars were destroyed, the chapel was left to ruin.

There are over 100 carvings of the Green Man at Rosslyn Chapel. Some claim the Green Man is pagan in origin as the sprouting vines that protrude from the figure's mouth represent nature's growth and fertility. Others claim this is a good representation of the Christian's belief in the rebirth.

The Mystery and Symbolism of the Stonework

According to Father Hay, when Sir William St. Clair began the building of the Rosslyn, "he caused artificers to be brought from other regions and foreign kingdoms and caused daily to be abundance of all kinds of workmen present as masons, carpenters, smiths, barrow men and quarriers…"

Rosslyn is filled with symbols cut into the stonework of the interior. The result of many artisans, most are of a Biblical nature (it is a church after all). However, not all the Biblical carvings are saintly, as there are several symbols of the devil, fallen angels, sin and death. There are other symbols that have no apparent Biblical reference, and some appear to refer to objects that were not even known to Scotland at the time of the construction. Some stonework and etchings refer to the St. Clair family, and others appear to be pagan in nature.

The Knights Templar Connection

Although Rosslyn Chapel plays a role in Dan Brown's book The Da Vinci Code, some historians claim that there really are no connections with the Knights Templar to Rosslyn Chapel. The chapel was not built by the Knights Templar and although many of the men in the St. Clair family were known to be knights, they were not Templar Knights. According to Rosslyn historian, Michael Turnbull, Templar Knights took a vow of poverty, chastity, and loyalty to their order. The St. Clair family knights were men of wealth, married and had children and were loyal to their king.

The St. Clair family had roots that grew deep in religious and royal loyalty. Several of Sir William's ancestors were friends of Robert the Bruce. Two of his ancestors, brothers by the names of William and John Logan were chosen to accompany Sir Robert Douglas to carry the heart of Bruce to Jerusalem. All three of these men were killed in one final service to their dead king.

Robert the Bruce was said to have been aided by the Knights Templar during the Battle of Bannockburn. Since the St. Clair family were strongly associated with Bruce, some historians believe there has been some confusion pertaining to the St. Clair family and the Knights Templar.

Although the Knights Templar were disbanded over one hundred years earlier, other researchers tend to believe that the four altars on the east wall of the Lady Chapel are a symbolic reference to the four final Templars who had been tried after the dissolution of the Knights Templar. They would be Jacques de Molay (Grand Master of the Order), Geoffrey de Charney (Grand Commander of Normandy), Geoffrey of Goneville (Grand Commander of Aquitaine, & Poitou), and Hugh Peraud (Grand Commander of the Isle de France). Just as one of the altars is elevated higher than the other three, could these altars represent the four Templars, one (the Grand Master) ranked higher than the other three (Grand Commanders)[14]

The Freemason Connection

It is a common belief that with the abolishment of the Knights Templar came the birth of the Freemasons. In keeping with the Templar/Freemason connection there is one very intriguing story about the Rosslyn stonework which pertains to two intricately carved columns within the chapel. These are known as the Mason's Pillar and the Apprentice Pillar. Legend says that while the master mason was away researching the design that had been requested for the pillar, his apprentice had a dream in which it was revealed to

---

[14] *Rosslyn Chapel. Masonic Source Book. Accessed August 4, 2025.*
http://www.masonicsourcebook.com/rosslyn_chapel_freemasonry.htm

him what the design of the pillar should be. Upon the master's return, he found that his apprentice had finished the beautiful carving of the pillar. In a fit of jealousy, the master flew into a rage and struck the apprentice over the head with a hammer, killing him. Both men are forever commemorated within the walls of the chapel. One head carved into the stone with a gash on its forehead, looking across the way at another, the head of his master and killer. This story closely resembles the murder of Hiram Abif, the master mason involved in the building of Solomon's Temple. The Freemasons, who have ties with these ancient stonemasons view this event as symbolic and tie them to the construction of Rosslyn Chapel.

According to Freemason historian and scholar, Dr. Albert Mackie, Sir William St. Clair, the Earl of Orkney, and Caithness was appointed the title of Patron and Protector of the Freemasons of Scotland in 1441 by King James II. This became a hereditary title that would be passed down through the St. Clair generations. However, when King James VI failed to exercise his prerogative of nominating office-bearers, the Freemasons found themselves without a Protector. Therefore, the Freemasons themselves appointed William St. Clair of Roslin (too many Williamses! Lol) as their Protector around 1600. Then, in 1630, a second charter was granted, giving William's son, Sir William St. Clair the same power his father had been given. He was given the title the first Grand Master of the Grand Lodge of Scotland. St. Clair assumed the administrative role and the office continued to be passed down for more than one hundred years, until the final Saint Clair, recognizing he would have no heir, offered to let the office be appointed by election.[15]

---

[15] *Masonic Dictionary*, Accessed August 4, 2025. http://www.masonicdictionary.com/sinclair.html)

Some of the imagery carved into Rosslyn is said to have hints of Masonic rites. However, in spite of the Freemasons' claims on the founder of Rosslyn Chapel, the New World Encyclopaedia claims that the earliest records of Freemasonic lodges date back only to the late sixteenth and early seventeenth centuries..[16] Thus, we are left to wonder if the images we see carved in stone were pieces to a Masonic puzzle, or are people only seeing what they want to see?[17]

The Logan's are from the Scottish Clan Logan from Restalrig and Logan Manor.

Thomas Logan Weir, Had the middle name Logan, which all male heirs inherited, They did this to ensure that they kept the name Logan prevalent, this was due to The Clan Logan, being one of the oldest Scottish clans. The history of the Logan's is up for interpretation, Having researched what is available in the public domain, many website's attempt to say that the Logan's came from a Sir Robert Logan who married Robert the Bruce's great granddaughter, He was a companion to the king and carried his heart to the Holy lands with a 'Walter Logan', However other sources say that this Robert married a Katherine De Lastalrig, whom inherited the Restalrig lands and titles. I do think there is some misunderstanding with dates from this reference as it was in the 1300's that Robert the Bruce died, so it could be a later Robert Logan below. I personally traced through ancestry the Logan Line to Logan Manor, then fast castle of Berwickshire and back to

---

[16] *New World Enclyopedia*, Accessed August 4, 2025.
https://www.newworldencyclopedia.org/entry/Rosslyn_Chapel

[17] *St Clair Family - The Official Rosslyn Chapel Website*
_Rosslyn Chapel – The Rose and the Thistle Accessed August 4, 2025.

Restalrig, Information is found in the Gowry Conspiracy, Along with the History of the Logan family.[18]

Logan of that Ilk

The leading Logan family's principal seat was in Lastalrig or **Restalrig**, near Edinburgh. Sir Robert Logan of Restalrig married Katherine Stewart, daughter of Robert II of Scotland and later in 1400 Sir Robert was appointed Admiral of Scotland. Sir Robert Logan was one of the hostages given in 1424 to free James I of Scotland from being held as a prisoner in England. Robert's son or grandson, John Logan of Restalrig, was principal sheriff of Edinburgh by James II of Scotland. In 1555 Logan of Restalrig sold the superiority of **Leith** (the principal seaport of Edinburgh) to the queen regent Mary of Lorraine, also known as Marie de Guise.
The last Logan to possess the barony was Robert Logan of Restalrig, who was described by contemporaries as "Ane godless, drunkin, and deboshit man". Sir Walter Scott described him as "one of the darkest characters of that dark age".

HUGH LOGAN, of LOGAN, was lineally descended from the ancient and once powerful Barons of Restalrig, whose wide-spread domains were forfeited in the reign of James VI. In the year 1660, Sir Robert Logan, a grandson of the fore mentioned Baron, effected a purchase of a substantial portion of the barony of Cumnock, to which he gave the family name. This extensive and valuable property descended through a line of respectable ancestry to the subject of our present notice, who was born at Logan House in 1739.

From his earliest years, Hugh Logan was of a quick, volatile, and somewhat irritable disposition and although every facility was affordable to him for acquiring that education becoming his rank in society, yet either from his unmanageable temper, or the want of a

---

[18] *The Story of Leith - V. The Logans*, Electric Scotland. Accessed August 4, 2025

proper system of discipline on the part of his teachers, it was found impossible to obtain even the slightest degree of application to his academic exercises. While his boyish years were passing away in this unprofitable manner, being the youngest of three sons, his father frequently urged him to adopt some useful profession. On these occasions his uniform answer was, "I've made up my mind, Laird, to follow nae trade but your ain." "Weel, weel, Hughie," the good natured old gentleman would say, "I was the youngest o' three myself." and, strange as it may appear, the coincidence was realized – his elder brothers both died in early life-and on the decease of his father, which took place soon after, Hugh succeeded to the estate under the control of tutors or guardians, who do not appear to have been more successful in forwarding his instruction than those who had formerly been entrusted with it; for although he was sent to Edinburgh for the purpose of repairing the defects which his own aversion to study and the negligence of his father had occasioned in his education, yet he returned to his country pursuits with literary acquirements scarcely superior, if even equal, to those of the meanest mind upon his estate. Though the cultivation of the young Laird's mind had been thus neglected, it was not so with those external qualities which he possessed. In all field sports he was considered an adept, while in doing the honours of the table he was acknowledged to have been almost without a rival, and such was his natural quickness and ingenuity that when the errors of his education chanced to make their appearance few of his companions would venture to notice them, as they well knew he would either turn the laugh in his favour by some humorous palliation of his ignorance or render them ridiculous by making them the butts of his wit for the time being – a distinction seldom considered as very enviable. There is one well-known anecdote which, as it illustrates this part of his character, our readers may perhaps excuse our noticing. Logan had occasion one day to write a letter in the presence of a school companion, who, on looking over it, expressed his surprise at the singularity of the orthography. "It is strange, Logan," said he, "that you cannot manage to spell even the shortest word correctly." "Spell! " cried the Laird, with a look of well-feigned pettishness, "man, what are you haverin' about? look at that!" holding up the stump of a quill to him; " would ony man that kens ony thing about spelling ever attempt to spell wi' a pen like that? " This anecdote is, though erroneously, ascribed to the late eccentric Laird of McNab.

As another instance of the archness peculiar to our uneducated wit, we may mention the following. The plantations of Coilsfield having been much injured by the wanton depredations of some evil-disposed vagrants, Mr Montgomerie, the proprietor, brought the case before a meeting of the Justices, of which Sir Andrew Ferguson and the Laird of Logan formed part. On investigating the case the damage had been the work of children, and in consequence the complainer could obtain little or no redress. Sir Andrew, feeling the hardship of the case, and by way of soothing a brother proprietor, observed with some warmth that he would have a Bill brought into Parliament for making parents liable for the misdeeds of their children, and constituting such offences as the above felony in law. At this declaration, Logan broke out into a loud laugh; and, being asked the cause of his merriment, replied, "Sir Andrew, when your bill is made law, we shall soon have few old lairds among us." "Why?" demanded the other. "Because," said the wit, "their eldest sons will only require to cut their neighbours' young plants to become lairds themselves."

New Statistical account 1845 - Rev-Ninian-Bannatyne,

Hugh Logan, Esquire of Logan, the famous Ayrshire wit, resided during the greater part of his life, on his estate in this parish; and there is a stone, near to the house or Logan, which goes by the name of Logan's pillar, where, it is said, he was much in the habit of sitting, and cracking his jokes with those around him. His numberless witticisms and sarcasms, which were oftentimes pregnant, not only with the most genuine humour, but likewise marked by an eagle-eyed discrimination, as well as an unsparing dissection of character, and conduct, are generally current among the people of this district, and form an unfailing source of amusement at their jovial meetings. But, from the frequent mixture or coarseness and profanity that interlard them, they have by no means contributed to promote the interests, either of religion or morality, in the neighbourhood.[19] Hugh Logan was the last chief of Clan Logan, The clan is currently searching for the rightful heir.

The Clan Donald (or Clan MacDonald)

Scottish roots run deep – being the oldest and largest of all Scottish clans. For nearly four hundred years, Clan Donald ruled the West Highlands and the Hebrides – their land and power stretched so wide that it was only second to the Kings of Scotland and England.[20]

"Ceannas Ghaidheal do Chlann. Cholla, 's còir fhogradh" – (The sovereignty of the Gael to Clan Colla, it is right to proclaim it); so, wrote the bard, O'Henna in his poem on John of Isla, last Lord of the Isles.

Clan Donald was indisputably the largest and most renowned of all the Highland clans of Scotland controlling, at one time, virtually the whole western seaboard from the Butt of Lewis in the north to the Mull of Kintyre in the south, almost a third of the Kingdom with possessions in

---

[19] *Cumnock History Group - Country Houses, Villas and Castles Accessed August 4, 2025*
[20] *Clan MacDonald: History, Tartan & Battles. Highland Titles. Published March 26, 2019. Last updated October 9, 2024. Accessed August 4, 2025. www.highlandtitles.com/blog/clans-scotland-macdonald*

Northern Ireland as well.

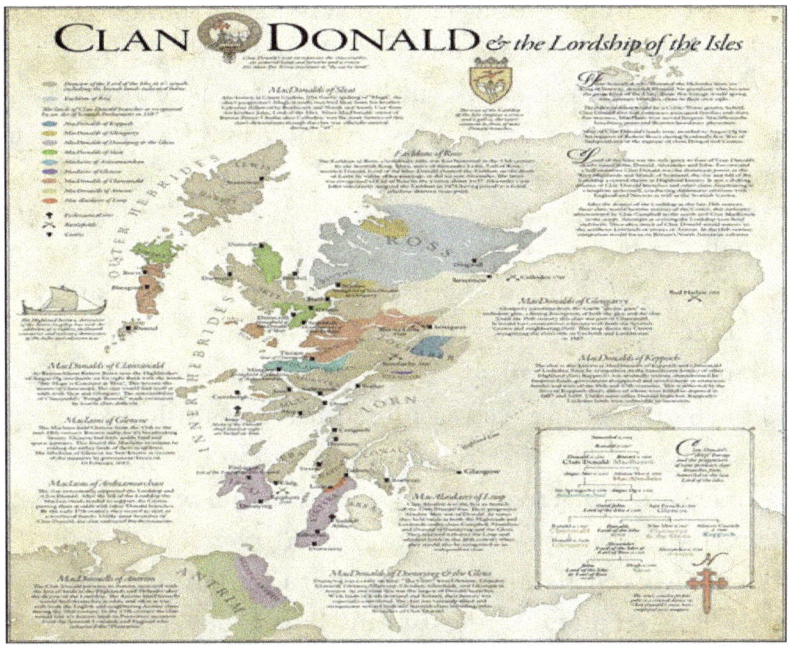

Figure 1: Map: Clan Donald & Lordship of the Isles Archival prints are available from McMillen Design

The Clan claims descent from Conn of the Hundred Battles, Ard-Righ or High-King of Ireland in the 1st century A.D., through Colla Uais, the first of the family to settle in what is now the Hebrides, and from whom the Clan took its earlier designation of "Clan Cholla" i. e. the Children of Coll, down to Somerled, Lord of Argyll, in the 12th century who, after defeating the Norsemen, was proclaimed King of the Isles, Righ Innsegall, or Rex Insularum. Somerled's grandson, Donald of Isla(y) is the progenitor of CLAN DONALD, in Gaelic rendered Clan Dhomhnaill, i.e., the Children of Donald.

Donald had, among other children, two sons, Angus Mór and Alasdair or Alexander. Mór means in Gaelic, Big or Great. From Alasdair are descended the CLAN ALISTER or MACALISTERS OF LOUP in Kintyre. Angus Mór had three sons, Alasdair Òg, Angus Òg and John Sprangach. Òg means young and Sprangach means Bold.

Alasdair Òg chose to serve the English after the deposition of John Balliol, King of Scots, by Edward I of England and was killed in 1299 in a battle with his distant cousin, Alexander MacDougall of Argyll and Lorn, with whom he had been at feud. Angus Òg joined forces with Robert the Bruce, whom he is said to have sheltered in the Castle of Dunaverty in Kintyre and later played a vital part with his followers in Bruce's signal victory over the mighty army of Edward II of England at Bannockburn, on Midsummer's Day, 1314 – Scotland's finest hour! For his loyal services to his King and Country, Angus received from the grateful monarch many of the vast territories in the Western Highlands and Isles formerly held by the Comyns and MacDougall's, who were forfeited for their opposition to The Bruce. By the addition of these lands to those already in his possession, Angus became the most important and powerful magnate in Argyll and the Isles south of Ardnamurchan Point.

From John, or Iain Sprangach are descended the CLAN IAIN (MacDonald's or MacIAINS) OF ARDNAMURCHAN.

Angus Òg had two sons, both named John or Iain, one legitimate, the other natural. From the natural son, known as Iain Fraoch, i.e., John of the Heather, or Iain Abrach, from his having been fostered in Lochaber, are descended the CLAN IAIN ABRACH or MacDonald's of GLENCOE, whose Chief was known by the patronymic MacIAIN.

Angus Òg's elder, legitimate son, also named John, added greatly to the already vast possessions of the family, largely through his marriage to his distant cousin Euphemia (Amie) MacRuairi, whose only brother Ranald was murdered by the Earl of Ross at Elcho Nunnery in 1346: and left no heirs.

John of Isla, as the family were now designated, was the first of his line to assume the title of LORD OF THE ISLES which although not at that time recognised by the Scottish Crown, almost accurately reflected his position in the Gaelic-speaking Western Highland and Isles. John held court, appointed his own heralds, ran the government of his domains through the Council of the Isles, built monasteries and generally acted in the manner of an independent prince, whose authority was absolute.

He patronised the Gaelic bards and thereby preserved the culture of the Gael. For his benevolence to the Church, John earned the soubriquet of "Good John". It is probable that John's first wife, Amie MacRuairi, whom he had married in 1337, died, perhaps in childbirth, sometime prior to his second marriage in 1350 to Margaret, daughter of Robert, the High Steward of Scotland, who succeeded his uncle, David II as King of Scots in 1371 by the title of Robert II and adopted the surname of Stewart, derived from his former "office".

One of the first acts of the new king was to grant to his son-in-law, John of Isla, a charter of the former MacRuairi lands, which comprised the Lordship of Gamoran in western Inverness-shire, the Isle of Eigg and the Outer Hebrides. The following year, 1372, John granted to Ranald, the eldest surviving son of his first marriage to Amie MacRuairi, a charter of most of the former MacRuairi lands to be held of the eldest son of John's second royal marriage with the Princess Margaret Stewart.

Ranald, whose principal seat was Castle Tioram in Loch Moidart, became the progenitor of the MacDonald's of CLAN RANALD, descended from his eldest son, Allan and the MacDonnell's of GLENGARRY, descended from his second son, Donald.

This is my particular line, I went to Moidart with my cousin Wilma and Castle Tioram.

By his second wife, John had several sons. The eldest son, Donald, succeeded him as Lord of the Isles and fought the Battle of Harlaw, in Aberdeenshire, against the Government forces, under the Earl of Mar, in 1411; the second son, Iain Mòr Tanaistear, i.e. Big John the Heir, founded the CLAN IAIN MHOIR or MacDonald's of DUNYVAIG, with lands in Isla, Kintyre and Antrim, sometimes known as the CLAN DONALD SOUTH to distinguish them from the MacDonalds of Sleat who were also known as the CLAN DONALD NORTH; the third surviving son, Alexander was granted the Lordship of Lochaber and it is from his natural son, Alasdair Carrach (Mangy) that the MacDonald's or Macdonell's of KEPPOCH, also known as the CLAN RANALD of LOCHABER, from Ranald Mór, the 7th Chief of that branch, descend.

Donald of Harlaw was succeeded as Lord of the Isles and High Chief of Clan Donald by his eldest son, Alexander, who inherited, through his mother, the Earldom of Ross — the reason why the Battle of Harlaw was fought by his father. Alexander had three sons. The eldest, John, by his wife Elizabeth Seton, succeeded him as Lord of the Isles and Earl of' Ross.

The second, Celestine, by a daughter of MacPhee of Glen Spean, became the progenitor of the MacDonald of LOCHALSH, the larger part of whose lands passed, in the sixteenth century to Glengarry.

The third son, Uisdean, or Hugh, by a daughter of Gilpatrick, grandson of the Green Abbot of Applecross, became the progenitor of the CLAN UISDEAN or MacDonald's of SLEAT.

The weakness of John, the fourth Lord of the Isles and his reliance on the advice of persons out with his own family on how to govern his vast territories, which led to his defeat by his son Angus Òg, in the naval engagement off Mull, known as the Battle of Bloody Bay, his intrigues with the English Government and his failure to match the duplicity of the Campbells, resulted in his final forfeiture by the Crown in 1493.

The title of Lord of the Isles was annexed to the Crown as had been the Earldom of Ross in 1475, due to John, the last Lord's intrigues with England, and bestowed on the Dukes of Rothesay, heirs to the Kings of Scots and has ever since been retained among their principal titles by the British Crown Princes.

With the fall of the MacDonald dynasty in the Western Highlands and Isles, Gaelic culture fell into rapid decline. The Scottish monarchs and their Lowland-dominated Governments had no sympathy for what they regarded as an alien and barbaric way of life. A political vacuum was created which the Government agents, the Campbell Earls of Argyll, largely due to their policy of self-aggrandisement and intrigue, were unable to fill.

Several vigorous attempts were made by various Clan Donald leaders to re-establish the old order and were supported by most of the old vassals of the Isles e.g. the MacLean's, MacLeod's and MacPhees, who all despised the Campbells but they were eventually forced to yield to the stronger forces sent against them and when the 17th century dawned, the various branches of Clan Donald, e.g. Sleat, Clan Ranald, Glengarry, Keppoch and Glencoe, had become independent clans, each with its own Chief, none of whom could claim to be MAC DHOMHNAILL.

This situation pertained through the troublesome times of the 17th century and the Jacobite risings of the 18th century till after the Battle of Culloden in 1746 and the end of the Clan System.

Not until 1947, was Clan Donald again to have a High Chief, when the Rt. Hon. Alexander Godfrey Macdonald, 7th Lord Macdonald, was granted by the Lord Lyon, King of Arms, the undifferenced ARMS of MACDONALD. His elder son, the Rt. Hon. Godfrey James Macdonald of Macdonald, 8th Lord MacDonald, is the present High Chief of the Clan.

The principal branches of the Clan are represented at the present time by Sir Ian Godfrey Macdonald, 17th Baronet and 24th Chief of Sleat; Ranald Alexander Macdonald, Captain and 24th Chief of Clan Ranald; Aeneas Ranald Euan MacDonnell, 23rd Chief of Glengarry; The Rt. Hon. Alexander Randal Mark McDonnell, 14th Earl of Antrim, and William St. John Somerville McAlester, 25th Chief of Loup.[21]

---

[21] *Noman H. MacDonald, F.R.S.A., F.S.A.Scot., Clan Donald: An Introduction into History. The High Council of Clan MacDonald. Accessed August 4, 2025. highcouncilofdonald.com/clan-donald-an-introductory-history. /*

Queen Victoria's Servants

After researching My dad and grandfathers' line, I decided to look at my Grandmother, Eunicia Hopgood. Her Father was George Collison Hopgood and Mother was Julia Harding. Julia's Mother was Julia Martha Butcher, her father was Arthur George Butcher who is mentioned in the household of Queen Victoria's servants.

Dad would always joke about Nan having been born with a silver spoon in her mouth and how her family lived with Queen Victoria. I found her butchers where actually living in Victoria house on the Isle of Wight, this is why she would take us there, this is why she would talk about being a proper lady and making us walk her living room with books on our head, etiquettes darling,

I found that her mother was called Julia Martha Butcher and she married Charles Harding, the Harding's were artists, lithographers, portrait photographers and architects, again loved working in the theatre as actresses. Her father was called Arthur George Butcher, He married Julia cooper, They both worked at Windsor Castle and Osbourne house for Queen Victoria, Arthur was a tapissier, a person who worked on the tapestries with the castle and Osbourne house, it is stated in many census records and on the household list of the queen's palace.[22]

---

[22] *Queen Victoria, Household Staff, 1853, p. 146. Royal Collection Trust. Accessed August 4, 2025. www.rct.uk/collection/search.*

In 1851 My 3rd great grandfather Arthur George Butcher, St Johns Place, Upton Cum Chalvey in Slough/ Windsor as a tapisseir for Queen Victoria at OLD WINDSOR TAPESTRY MANUFACTORY (1876-1890) (1880 ROYAL WINDSOR TAPESTRY MANUFACTORY), [23]

In 1881 He was living with the rest of my family at Victoria cottage in Whippingham. Worked at Osbourne House as Lord of Chamberlain department 2nd Class of the civil list.[24]

In 1881 he was a lodger at 13 Medway street Stockwell Lambeth now known as Brixton, He worked as the Groom Of The Great Chamber In Ordinary To Her Majesty (C S O O F)
How did he get to work for Queen Victoria?
His father was a Captain in the army and was in many battles, gaining a Victoria cross for the battle of Waterloo, He also was written about in a book
and saved a woman called Ethel Grimwood The heroine of Manipur[25]

His Daughter Julia married Charles Harding who was an architect to the Holborn Viaduct and many churches, His sons went on to be well known photographers, Lithographers. Adrian Harding was a photographer; his work is on display at Godalming Museum.

---

[23] *Ibid*

[24] *Victoria Cottage. On The Market. Accessed August 4, 2025.* media.onthemarket.com/.../612487423/document-0.pdf

[25] *History of Ethel Grimwood. The Royal Dragon Court. Accessed August 4, 2025.* digital.library.upenn.edu/.../manipur/manipur.html., Dragon Court Genealogy. The Royal Dragon Court. Accessed August 4, 2025. royaldragoncourt.com/dragon-court-genealogy.

Adrian Harding, Godalming Photographer,
Adrian Francis Harding (1882-1968) was born in Clapham and grew up in Guildford. In the 1901 census he is listed as a photographer's assistant. By 1910 he had set up in business at the Barn Studio in Godalming and that same year he married Dora Taylor. During the First World War he served with the Royal Flying Corps in Canada, documenting planes and aircrew. Adrian Harding was also an artist. He painted scenery and designed costumes for local amateur dramatic productions, in which he also acted. He and Dora had two sons, Adrian and John, and lived in Busbridge, moving to Milford when Adrian Francis Harding retired in 1939. These photos are of Adrian Harding's advert in the 1914 Godalming street directory, showing the Barn Studio, and the entrance to the studio, alongside Clarke's on the High Street[26]

---

[26] *Adrian Francis Harding, Godalming Photographer, Godalming Museum, Facebook video, accessed August 4, 2025. facebook.com/GodalmingMuseum/videos/2321583594812143/.*

For a year or so, I had given up on ancestry, as I could not find anything other than being servants to Queen Victoria. Which for me, I was rather deflated, so I went back to the MacDonalds side and as dad told me look through the Glen's which turned out to be a family line. This is where I journey truly started.
Going back Through the Scottish line of Weirs, Macdonald and Logan were attached to my great Grandmother's side, Through these people I found The Glens who were the descendants of aristocrats who intermarried with the Montgomery lines, This information helped me to connect to other researchers in the USA, which also assisted in confirming our lines.

Tales from The Royal Dragon Court, Old and New

When dad died in 2013, I managed to sort out the affairs through probate and give each of his children and my siblings what was their fair share of the remains of the money from my grandparents' house, This was always my grandparents wishes, The siblings said I could take on the book for myself as they did not want anything to do with The Royal Dragon Court or dads work, and because of this, having taken over and being the head of what is today.

Since taking over from the promotion of the sales of the books written by my father, I had made friends with some of dad's old friends. The first person I made contact with was a lady called Iona Miller, she was what I would call a confidant, a friend, teacher, a pearl of wisdom whom gave me much inspiration, Iona was the person who put up all of the information on The Royal Dragon Court onto a free Weebly site, she did this because she wanted it to always be in the domain, had she of paid for a domain name then she would have had to keep updating the payment fee however, giving it a subdomain allowed it to be set in stone, online for as long as possible, she recommended that I use this site as a source of information to teach me history and relevant information that I had not already been made aware of, Such things like Hermetics, psychology , alchemy, the universal laws, all things governed by the ethereal. It made me wiser and gave me a thirst to ask more questions. Iona did not like many people who stated that they were friends with father, and she taught me to be wise and keep my distance from many, like a wise old owl, perched in a tree, watching and observing those below. In order to see who a friend or foe was truly. Many pretenders came, stalked me online and watched me also.

This was weird, cringe and made me feel somewhat in danger, who were all of these people that were saying they knew my dad?, many tried to friend me but I was very choosy, some I allowed to pour their show of egotistical poppycock upon me to see who was fake and who was real, and mostly what hilarious stories I could find out. Bearing in mind what Iona told me and that she said she will be there for me if it gotten to much, we would go back on confer about most of these people, so I would know the truth.

I started reading the books again which enlightened me to who I was, were I came from and gave me the strength to see clearly what was actually going on in my personal life that was not right. I would speak to the in laws who would laugh at me, saying that I am not royal, they picked up the book and went to the pages, the rite of the vampire and read little paragraphs, they decided it was fictional and scoffed at me. It was almost like well where's your proof, So along with this and the online stalkers, I had to give it a break again, to sort out my own affairs of being domestically abused.
About a year later, I had been made homeless by my ex-partner after years of abuse and had to start my life again, building everything up from scratch, It was 2016 and the first person I found was Thomas Kelly, He became my friend and brother, He inspired

me, taught me so much history as he is a walking encyclopaedia, spend many nights chatting on face-time building our friendship, he saw me through my darkest day and nights, seen me at my worst and now sees me at my best.

Thomas encourage me to start promoting the books and gave me ideas of what we could do.
This was the start of the new Royal Dragon Court. Thomas would tell me funny stories about all the people that dad was friends with, the ones he gotten into arguments with. We discussed what really happened between dad and Laurence Gardner and how dad wrote most of the books, The bloodline of the Holy Grail, The realm of the Ring Lords, most of this was based from the research dad had done and collaborated with Laurence at the time, however sometime only receiving small acknowledgements on the book and no royalties. Dad did many massive rants about this which is still publicly available today, he would get extremely annoyed about the amount of people who wanted to steal his intellectual property with the information he shared, Still to this day many people jump on The Dragon Court band wagon to use as click bait to gather more followers. So, overexerting the copyright laws of public use without firstly asking myself for the usage of our works. I address many and some are not even worth my time, They say that any publicity is publicity.

Here is dads rant about all of those who attempted to redo their own version of The Royal Dragon Court Order for their own monetary gains. This is why I never say that people can join The Court, honestly if you want a 2ft plot of land with a tree, go and be a lady of Glencoe, or a lord of Sealand, which means absolutely nothing. Most of these titles' companies are frauds. If you want to read the rant in full, please see my Facebook page.
This letter also tells the reader his intentions where it comes to memberships, which I am constantly being asked for, People saying they want to be part of a secret society for their own spiritual growth, being part of anything that takes money from you is not

spiritual growth, its ego and if we were a secret society, you certainly would not know about us.

Extract from 'The Dragon Cede' by Nicholas de Vere. Page 87 et sub.
Having defended Laurence from David Icke, I must regrettably add, as a cautionary public addendum, my own criticisms, and my reply to his libels of 16th May 2000 onwards. This reply has been a long time coming, and previously I considered any reaction to be beneath my dignity. Now however, such a response, though reluctant, appears to be absolutely necessary in order to restore my good name, my honour and integrity, and that also of the true Imperial and Royal Dragon Court.
Under Hungarian constitutional law ALL royal or noble; courts or orders are actually banned in Hungary; this is a well-known fact throughout Europe. A Catholic Monseigneur (remember the "Donation of Constantine!") and a nondescript, minor baron, registered "Sarkany Rend" (Ordo Draconis: The Dragon Order?) in the High Courts in Budapest as Gardner asserts, but as nothing more than a social club. Certainly NOT as "The Imperial and Royal Dragon Court." Laurence Gardner and Michael La Fosse, were dismissed by me from the Vere Dragon Court, so they then STOLE the Imperial and Royal Dragon Court and Sovereignty names from us and hurriedly decamped to this Hungarian Social Club, claiming that I was a fraud and that this Glorified Hungarian Boy Scout Troop they had joined was actually the REAL Dragon Court. However, I had registered the Vere "Imperial and Royal Dragon Court" years before, as a royal and noble organisation, in a British Court of Law. I then passed all the documentation to the Home Office who acknowledged it by bestowing me
With Passport documents, within which were included my royal and ambassadorial titles, dated 12th March 1997. Lawrence had inspected these Government documents three years prior to the schism and subsequent libels concerning me.
 (See Appendix C, pages See index pages for full bibliography) 446-7: "H.H. Nicholas the Prince [Furst] de Vere von Drakenberg.... H.E. Nicholas de

Vere KGC., KCD.").

The present Hungarian Pseudo-Dragon Order never existed as an "Order" originally, it isn't Hungarian in Origin and despite Laurence's assertions to the contrary, it NEVER was registered as a Court of Nobility or Chivalry in the High Courts in Hungary. It has no legitimate Fons honorum and no right to bestow noble rank or title. It is that organisation which is fraudulent, thieving and usurping, not mine. Its original leaders have no bloodline descents or genealogical connections with any of the original 1408 membership, whilst I have numerous. So, on all levels, it is simply an insubstantial, baseless and illegal artifice, embellished largely after the fact by Lawrence to cover his tracks, after his dismissal from the real Imperial and Royal Dragon Court of the House of Vere.

Mrs. Angela Gardner told me on 8th October 1999 that she and Lawrence were only in the Dragon Tradition for the money.; By that time, I had had enough of him, his literary impertinences, the petty political hubris of his faux prince, and the boorishness of his equally faux and untalented lift-music writer chum. That, and the fact that he plagiarised me repeatedly by failing to credit my research and writing (Realm of the Ring Lords).

Lawrence proceeded to libel me in order to keep his gravy train rolling along nicely and cover up the fact that I had very politely kicked him and his awful cronies out of the Dragon Court. On May 16th, 2000, he publicly announced that the name on the 1997 passport he had seen was Nicholas Weir and that this name appeared on all my official documents.

Not so.

As for he is suggesting that the name De Vere that I bear is a fraud, that is hilarious, laughable in the extreme and sadly pathetic. There are about 15 different, clearly historically recorded spelling variants for this name, including de Vere, Vere, Weir, Were, Wier, Ver, Uerre, Wer, Vir, Mhaior, Muir, Vor, Fir, Fer and so on.

Whether Laurence likes to admit it or not, he knows full well that my titles are legitimate, as is my genealogy (which he inspected thoroughly and helped to fine tune in research and collation) and both are recognised by governments in their numerous strata, and by those governments' numerous administrative departments. I have published herein the documentary proofs along with my recognised right of Fons honorum.

King Sigismund changed his family tree fraudulently in order to be descended from Princess Melusine Vere, a REAL Dragon Royal, and in any event the Society of the Dragon never was and is NOT Hungarian, it is Angevin French. Like Sigismund I am descended from the House of Luxembourg in numerous lines, I am his descendant cousin on both sides of my family and my right to hold the Dragon Court is legitimate, far more so than that of a bunch of contemporary Magyar arrivistes and a dubious Catholic Priest.

Societas Draconis was NEVER founded as a Catholic body, it had no Chapel or Cathedra, no Patron Saint and no Chaplain. It's Inner Spiritual Guide – Ibrahim Eleazar – was a Muslim! Its Sacred day was Friday, the Holy Day of Venus-Lucifer in whose honour members would wear black, hence the modern Gothic and Hollywood association of vampires with that colour. My Family Seals bore the double Dragon Motif 100 years before Sigismund was even born.

Laurence Gardner knows full well that 12 years ago I confirmed my Imperial and Royal lineage by genetic testing, and I do indeed have 127 recorded Imperial, Royal and Noble descents stemming from antiquity. Finally, most of the secret, central genealogical, spiritual and biochemical knowledge he received, he obtained from me and from my family's archives, so the foreword I wrote in Genesis of the Grail Kings concerning his having inside, initiated access to hidden wisdom, was actually only through me. I trust This statement will settle the matter finally. It has not been easy to publish these criticisms of Lawrence, I once considered him to be a friend.

In 2002 The Dragon Court went into abeyance and all titles, honours and memberships formerly bestowed were rescinded and annulled. In 2009 the Dragon Court was revised and re-opened to Family Members, Seneschals and Companions. Entry to the Inner Family Court is permitted when an application is accompanied with a verifiable royal genealogy and/or a comprehensive genetic profile compiled by FTDNA. Entry as a Seneschal is at the discretion of Family Members and entry as a Companion is Open to all who support the aims of the Dragon Tradition. We do not bestow titles, rather, we recognise the individual's rights to bear such, and we do not charge any monies whatsoever for membership. As a Scythian, Dragon Family and Court, Yr Llys Y Draig Ymerodrol ac Brenhinol, we adhere to "Yr Cyfraithau Am Anrhydeddei Cymraeg" in all matters concerning heraldry and honours.

The foregoing excerpt from my Book 'The Dragon Cede' was written in 2005-6. Clearly, if there were any confusion, it is apparent that Dufton et al were kicked out of the IRDC in 2002, and Johnson whom I had never heard of NEVER supplied a verifiable genealogy nor genetic test paper after 2009.
Johnson's genealogy was obtained from a Mr. William King without a bibliography, and therefore Johnson was accepted as a Companion of The Family who would serve as a probationer for a year and a day or until I and the rest of us were satisfied that he was acceptable, and a genetic test was forthcoming. He was not and the gene test never turned up, nor did a verifiable genealogy, instead he has now simply copied mine, which appears in full in my Notes Section on Facebook. Unfortunately, I was a little too generous with people back then. No matter. Not anymore.
Who rightfully owns the IRDC?
The world-famous Dragon Princess Melusine de Vere (Milouziana An Mhaior) decamped from Caledonia to Anjou in 746, taking her entourage with her as the legitimate Fairy Dragon Court of a universally accepted Elven Witch Queen and Dragon Princess who is ubiquitously recorded in European history as such. Subsequently and consequently, some centuries later, the House of Luxembourg and King Sigismund altered their genealogical descent in order to be able to claim Dragon Blood from our Melusine and add legitimacy to their usurpation of The Imperial and Royal Dragon Court of the House of Vere. Melusine's Vere name in Gaelic is spelled Mhaior. This has corrupted down the ages to become spelled in many variant ways, including Muir and most significantly 'Murray'.

The Murrays are members of the 'Pictish Clan of Mar' of Caledonia, which in modern terms is 'The Pictish Clan of Vere. We all still bear the Pictish/elven/fairy/ Scythian armorial of the 'three stars argent/or on either a field or fesse azure'. Domiciled for centuries around The Moray Firth (Murray or Mhaioray or Vere-ay Firth), the Vere's – as the Murray's – still own vast swathes of north-eastern Scotland today and bear the name of the Fairy King who first settled there – King Vere – ancestral grandson of Cait, Last King of the Tuatha de Danaan. In Iron Age terms, from 400 bc onwards, the Kingdom of Vere became vast, stretching from Great Eastern Caledonia in the north, to the Western Isles, and beyond the contemporary Scottish Border in the south. It was probably the largest single northern European kingdom of its age and the Dragon King Vere was the first sovereign high king of Scotland in its unified form.

The name Vere – through adaptation - contemporarily means 'Officer' in Gaelic. This actually is recorded historically as being derived from an earlier Gaelic term meaning 'Keeper of the Knowledge', clearly and distinctly encapsulating the Vere family's role in society as Bhruidhes (Bh = V. Ergo sometimes pron. Breeths or more properly 'Vrees') and Archdruid Kings, the ancient custodians of the history and wisdom of their elven species. Such a state of affairs pertains and is indeed pertinent today. I am still the Hereditary Keeper of the Wisdom of my Vere family, My Dragon race and species, and thereby I still hold the Keys of The Kingdom.

Two hundred years prior to the birth of Sigismund, our family were already using the Double Dragon Motif as supporters in their heraldry denoting Dragon ancestry in both the patrilineal and matrilineal descents. Following on from this, Richard de Vere, 11th Earl of Oxford became recognised as a Dragon Court Member by Emperor Sigismund when both were installed as Princes of the Order of the Garter at St. George's Chapel in Windsor Castle. We founded the first Dragon Court in Europe in 749 ad. The Luxembourg's misappropriated it, now we have it back again. In Summary and closure: Instances of the exclusive Vere ownership of the IRDC appear numerously in history. In 749 a.d. it moved from Scotland and was re-established in Anjou by Melusine de Vere, heiress of the largest kingdom of Alba (Scotland): The Scythian Kingdom of The Calle Daouine or Caledonia. She had previously completed the rites of Chronos/Arachne to become the head of our House, prior to her removal to Gaul. In 1200 a.d. it was still in the hands of Hugo de Vere Earl of Oxford, who displayed the alchemical dragons of the IRDC in his arms appended to which was the Archdruidic Crest of the Blue Boar.

By 1066 the Vere Dukes of Angiers and Anjou had become the Vere Earls of Guisnes in Flanders, following the usurpation and theft of Anjou by the faux "count" Fulk the Red, descendant grandson of a common woodcutter 'Tortulf the woodman of Nide de Merle' (a dhamphyr) and were forced to accompany William the Bastard to England, he having taken our children hostage to ensure our complicity in his crimes of usurpation; the rightful king of England being, neither Harold Godwinsson or Guillaume le Batarde, but Eustache de Vere, count of Boulogne and the elected Atheling of the Witan, who was the husband of the sister of Edward the Confessor. Consequently, the IRDC had returned to these Isles in those days, and by 1640 it had removed again to it's original birthplace Scotland in the form of the Royal Dragon Court and it's 13 Covens of the Lallan headed by Major Thomas Weir of Vere, King of Witches and Laird of Kirkton. Following the Covenant Wars and our escape to Ireland to avoid persecution for "witchcraft" in 1670; the senior, premier IRDC contemporarily originates from him and subsequent to the family's homecoming to Scotland in 1840, the IRDC descended directly in the unbroken senior bloodline to me as the eldest surviving scion of The Vere Race. All the time that I and the senior heirs bearing de sanguine, de jure et de facto the Vere name are still alive, no man nor woman may claim to own the IRDC by virtue of any obscure, tenuous, irrelevant blood link to the family in dim and distant centuries past. Simple.

Today the IRDC and The Sovereign Grand Duchy of Drakenberg indivisible are recognised under British and International Law as a corporate entity with its own rights and duties; and it is registered with, and recognised by the British Government as a Corporate 'Membership Organisation', rather than any form of common or garden trading outfit. It is also registered as an NGO within the United Nations and is a member of both their Civil Society Organisation and The U.N. Global Compact.

Within all these registrations I am the recorded, recognised hereditary Prince, the Head of the Grand Duchy and Sovereign of the Imperial and Royal Dragon Court. In none of these International Legal recognitions or registrations are the names of Mr. Charles Dean Johnson, Mr. Mark Pinkham or Mr. Richard Anthony Dufton mentioned in any sense......not even in passing, and they NEVER WERE. They are simply not IRDC members and have absolutely no rights or claims whatsoever over The Sovereign Grand Duchy of Drakenberg or the Vere IRDC in any way shape or form.

After the problems caused by associates in mid to late 2011, I discontinued those associations and closed the IRDC on the 6th of January 2012 and posted the closure publicly. This document now follows:

"NOTICE Given on the 6th of January 2012. To all persons whomsoever:
All those declaring an official interest in the matters proceeding, may write formally to me by letter to: HI&; RH Prince Nicholas Tarnawa de Vere-Sachsenstein von Drakenberg,
Rathdragun Mor, SY23 4BA, United Kingdom.
Personal and unofficial correspondence may be directed to 'His Imperial and Royal Highness Prince Nicholas de Vere' at the email address devere@drakenberg.eu
Unless otherwise directed, all future correspondents whomsoever, will adhere to the prescribed protocols and address me as indicated. Alas, my generosity has led to

familiarity, and familiarity has led to contempt it seems. If the accepted protocols are ignored, so too will be any correspondence. On behalf of myself and the Family of the Imperial and Royal House of Tarnawa-de Vere including certain selected adoptees and named cousins, The Sovereign Grand Duchy of Drakenberg therein, The Imperial and Royal Dragon Court, The International Council of Princes, Dragon Heritage and the International Dragon Corporation, I hereby give notice of the following. Henceforth our association with this social facility is terminated. All memberships, formerly enjoyed by Individuals, of any of the foregoing institutions, corporations or bodies derived during the sojourn of these corporate entities on the Facebook social networking facility, are herein declared null and void. Whilst we have never given any noble or royal titles but have only ever recognised a person's right to such titles, or have only bestowed title purely as a form of specific job description, such recognitions and all or any executive directorships whatsoever are now rescinded forthwith and in their entirety.

The right to use the de Vere and Drakenberg Titular-Nominatives by others not directly related by blood as a first, second or third cousin of the name, unless otherwise indicated by sealed letter, is also banned. These proscriptions in their entirety shall pertain to all persons unless otherwise indicated by letter. As none have ever received signed and sealed warrants of membership from either myself or my family, this being a legal requirement, no person may consider themselves to have been members of these bodies other than as Companions by verbal consent. The name; The Imperial and Royal House of Tarnawa-Vere including certain selected adoptees, The Sovereign Grand Duchy of Drakenberg therein, The Imperial and Royal Dragon Court, The International Council of Princes, Dragon Heritage and the International Dragon Corporation remain the property of myself and the House of Tarnawa -Vere and are registered as such with and under the United Nations, The European Union and the United Kingdom Companies House, with all legal articles and penalties pertaining.

The registration with both the United Nations and the European Union are under my name alone and are not transferable. Unless an individual has specific written authority from me bestowing ownership of any or all parts of these institutions, which no other person actually does, or ever will have, any attempt to obtain the latter by any persons, either on Facebook or elsewhere, will be deemed by the U.N. and the E.U as criminal acts of fraud, and the perpetrators will face Federal Prosecution in the United States and European International Courts. Furthermore, my rights and those of my family by heritable extension concerning my sole irrefutable and unassailable ownership of The Imperial and Royal House of Tarnawa-Vere & The Sovereign Grand Duchy of Drakenberg therein, The Imperial and Royal Dragon Court and The International Council of Princes; singularly or plurally as a titular government in exile; are recognised, supported and protected by International Sovereign Law. Consequently, any attempt by any persons whomsoever to wrest ownership of the foregoing by any means is considered by International Sovereign Law to be both illegal and an act of aggression. Whilst it was formerly considered tenable, the cessation of all or any of these foregoing bodies has been suspended. We have returned to our position prior to being placed on Facebook without our knowledge or consent, two years ago. Any persons encountering the use of any of the foregoing names, titles or institutions associated with myself or my family or company on Facebook may consider such to be fraudulently usurped and perpetrated by individuals who have been dismissed from these organisations in disgrace. You know who you are. These individuals will be reported to the appropriate authorities and retributive action will be taken in full.

Under Flemish Law only those persons having parents who are both noble, may be considered to be noble themselves. Other than myself, as it stands at present, with certain exceptions, no person who was formerly associated with the IRDC on Facebook has any noble blood Whatsoever. This is why we did not give out titles.

PLEASE…. do your research and come to your own conclusions[27]

Notice in bold, I now have this right as I have both parents' ancestry that traces to exactly this over a hundred time over. Basically, if your names not Weir, you're not getting in, how can people called themselves or add our surname or Vere, Weir, De Vere onto themselves if they are not actually a Weir. Many people have tried in the past and continue to do so now to attempt to sell their own books about dragon cultures which they have nothing to do with us, so show me your proof, if your dad or grandad was not a Weir then they are frauds, please do not part with any money to these charlatans. Their surname will get changed multiple times to suit the book they are writing at the time. Pure lies and not the way of the dragon, Vero Nihil Verius. Mote it be.
There are many of the fake friends that remain, as attempt of fraud and defamation to my dad, especially after he died. I called the grave diggers, and said many times, " There's no gold in them there mountains", Now they call themselves Reverends and make up silly little religious sects, take our surname and apply dads work as their own in their books written under the Imperial and Royal Dragon Court, and still they are nothing but the spewtrum of the lowest forms of life, That should have been spat out by their mother.

They are still and have never had association with The Royal Dragon Court, as much as they try with their many attempts at self-publishing books under my name De Vere Von Drakenberg.
I know many people who know that the real Royal Dragon Court will avoid these people like the plague and to others that are gullible enough to part their money to read such tripe, that's on you. There are multiple fake ROYAL DRAGON COURTS, ORDO DRACONIS', Many pretenders whom make out they are the original Court.

---

[27]: *May Also be cited in The Dragon Cede, NicholasDevere, The Book Tree This was sent personally to Abbe Devere as an email from Nicholas Devere before his death, Several other people also sent it via email -SEE END NOTE AND INDEX FOR REFERENCES CONCLUDING NICHOLAS DEVERE'S STATEMENT AND WORK.*

Back then dad would find associates and then quickly end up butting heads with them over these matters regarding The Dragon Court and his genealogy, It was a time online where people argued a lot, all to be seen on social media, and some almighty takes downs.

Lucrencia Plantagenet became a house hold name in some men's lives, which, those who know what happened here, know, before the times of honey pots and catfishes we had Lucrencia would make men fall in love with her and ruin relationships and lives, She was in fact 3 or 4 men who set out to diminish anyone that stood in my father's way, for all the snowflakes out there or anyone that was affected by her charms, you only have yourselves to blame. Arkm inkhamp you will see with your own research that this one is still digging for gold amongst the gullibility that are willing to part with it, thinking they are part of The official Dragon Court, Alas they are not.
I will say I had nothing to do with this but again saw the show unravel online years later, It certainly was a popcorn moment!!!

For me personally, this is what I had to unravel and bring back to some sort of normal order, it was literally Chaos, Fighting, Ego's, Still having some of the names above continue to pursue me, friend me, for many years I refused and then gave in, some I found hilarious but still the damage they have done to my associates when they didn't get their own way was horrendous. Many of these people are a danger to themselves and others.
I had one guy stalk me for years, after many attempts of trying to pursue a friendship I gave in and let him in, years later he tells me that he had the log in detail to dads information held by the United Nations, Dads NGO, The Royal Duchy of Drakenberg in Exile, that he had rebirthed as the leader of his own sovereign government, this guy was trying to dangle it on a stick, like a carrot, assuming that I was some sort of donkey that would take the bait for his requests. Luckily for me as mentioned already, the first thing I did was to remove the Drakenberg entity from the UK government companies house, this was to stop any further fraud being committed in my dead dads name, or trying to pursue

anything that remotely had anything financial that would lead back to us, I had 99% share of Drakenberg but as all money had been stolen from it or withheld from the accounts, what's 99% of nothing? NOTHING. So when I was told 5 years after I had taken over information, inheritance that I should have been made aware of, I was fuming, how dare people try to use me in this way and not be as forthcoming with this information as they all said they had been, I felt betrayed.

Luckily, I had a friend whom I was very close to who told me everything, I will never forget this man, he was a true dragon and showed integrity, honesty, and friendship where other said they had before him but didn't. He found the log in details of the NGO listed at the United Nations and told me everything I should have been told, this was a new friend as many people tried to stop us from connecting, which lead me to believe they had other motives to keep this information for themselves.
So, I logged into the United Nations account and what did I see??

Nothing, no one had done anything with it, It had gone dormant, had they of had any brain cells in their attempt to steal this from me then I would have imagined them to work and make some changes in the world for good, This made me laugh, all those who threatened to take The Royal Dragon Court from me and did absolutely nothing, This became a regular thing, threats and then nothing, so I used to say to these foes, or people with big dreams, if you don't like what I'm doing and think you can do better go for it, lets see what you can do, I've seen you types many times before and its all a game of blowing smoke up their behinds. The most funniest thing is, people would not know about The Royal Dragon Court, Dragon Bloodline's or The Sovereign Grand Duchy of Drakenberg if it were not for my father's work, So they cannot inherit what my father left to me due to many protecting laws or commence a hostile takeover as they will only be promoting my books that I get royalties to anyway.

I took over completely and started to sort all of this out, I created the Facebook page, an idea which I never wanted to do and ran away from for many years, but in order to stop the chaos and pretenders I had no choice. I thought how I can present this in a way that is informative, shows history and genealogy in its entirety, but for me it needed facts. I loved going to various places and decided to start blogging about the history and connection to our family, in the beginning it was more about spiritual growth and loving the road trips with my kids.
I built a website to promote dads works to better the sales of the book. When I started the sales were literally in their hundreds, now I have sold over 10k copies of the books on my own through working with my publishers at the Book Tree and sheer determination of promoting the books to keep them relevant, At the same time ensuring that I preserved my father's intellectual property.

We move on and find ourselves in 2020. My ancestry journey previously had hit many stops and I decided that I would never carry the de Vere surname or pertain to be something I am not without the evidence to back up my claims, I didn't want to lead of dads coats tails, the information that was left to me, by dad in our chats, genealogy timelines and tree he had sent me in 2009, I still didn't believe, at the time when he was alive I would write letters to Debrett's and Burke's peerage to clarify dads line and was told by them, that it was a mix of fact and fiction, so you can understand why I would think that I needed the evidence for myself. I took a DNA test and uploaded it to My True ancestry; The evidence came back conclusive of the genealogy I had researched. Albeit I still wonder if this site is a bit scammy and say's the same information to all persons who add their DNA.

However, a vital part of this research to conclude my own associations with the Dragon Bloodline through my mother and my father. As the main issue with genealogy sites is that some people fudge their lines, add certain people, make mistakes, as I have literally found out today, a line and marriage I thought had happened and added it to this book, I found I hadn't had all the records to verify it, further research has lead me now to believe that it is incorrect information and have removed and deleted that information, the last thing I need is for people to copy any of my work and it be wrong, so humbly I take that, we are not always perfectly correct, even if we do get 10/10 for our customers tree's, mine still has discrepancies that need cleaning up, that being said all that I have added is correct as far as I am aware, with my DNA as absolute confirmation. Not only am I related to the de Vere's thorough my father, but at the same time, my mother was also related to them, a repetitive synchronicity with most of the families I am related to.

DNA Markers and Migrations

My maternal haplogroup is T1b. As our ancestors migrated out of eastern Africa, they split into numerous groups that travelled and mingled across the globe over tens of thousands of years. These ancient journeys can often be traced through haplogroups—families of related maternal lineages that share a common ancestor.

Haplogroup L, 180,000 Years Ago
If every person alive today could trace their maternal line back through countless generations, they would all converge on a single woman who lived in eastern Africa between 150,000 and 200,000 years ago. Although she was just one among thousands of women at that time, only the branches descending from her maternal haplogroup survive in people today. My maternal lineage begins with this ancestral woman.

Haplogroup T1, 16,500 Years Ago
Haplogroup T originated in the Middle East roughly 45,000 years ago, shortly after humans left Africa. For many millennia, this group remained mostly stationary. Then, around 15,000 years ago, as the

Ice Age glaciers covering much of Eurasia began to retreat and the climate warmed, people started migrating northward into regions like the Alps and beyond. My maternal line belongs to the T1 branch of haplogroup T. All individuals within T1 trace their maternal ancestry back to a woman who lived approximately 16,500 years ago when haplogroup T was still largely confined to the Middle East. Following the rise of agriculture in that region, some groups travelled westward around 9,000 years ago, bringing their crops and livestock into Europe. Among these migrants were women from haplogroup T1, whose descendants today span from Britain in the west to Turkey and Syria in the east.

Haplogroup T1b, 6,000 Years Ago
My specific maternal haplogroup, T1b, traces back to a woman who lived roughly 6,000 years ago—about 240 generations ago. Although T1b is relatively rare among 23andMe customers, sharing this haplogroup means I am connected to all maternal descendants of that ancient woman. Approximately 1 in every 1,500 23andMe users carry this lineage[28].

DNA Marker through Nicholas de Vere
My Fathers Marker is R1B1A.
I uploaded my raw data to my true ancestry and the results showed that I am related to every royal family throughout history, knowing that my lines have over time intertwined in many ways with my father and mother we started to question whether the dragon bloodline holds certain traits.

We have many times spoken about the gifts and magical abilities we have, is this something that only the dragon DNA holds? What is the DNA marker for our bloodline as many share variations that also match ours. Who was the first dragon? again we have discussed that it came from Egypt, but as with the Jesus bloodline theory, how many of us can truly insist that the research we have done is correct and not in a biased way in order to find the conclusion that you

---

[28] *23 and me, Ancestry and DNA research for Abbe De Vere. 2020*

want?, this goes with most theories, statistics and recording of data. as with theories or the works by Sitchen and others that has been debunked·

The Tree Of Life

THE DNA BRIDGE: Paternal & Mitochondrial Dragon DNA explains the importance of the female decent. Mitochondrial DNA is passed only through the female line. Mitochondria is a living sentient and separate life form from ourselves. The mitochondria are dependent on us for life; we live in a symbiotic relationship. Mitochondrial DNA can live 15 generations. 15 generations of living mitochondria live inside you. Your 15 generation grandparents living cells are in you. A mutant mtDNA will drift to fixation in a human matriline in 15 generations. Recently an attempt was made to estimate the age of the human race using mitochondrial DNA.

This material is inherited always from mother to children only. By measuring the difference in mitochondrial DNA among many individuals, the age of the common maternal ancestor of humanity was estimated at about 200,000 years. It remains implausible to explain the known geographic distribution of mtDNA sequence variation by human migration that occurred only in the last ~6,500 years.

Mitochondrial DNA (mtDNA) (by virtue of its maternal, non-recombining mode of inheritance, rapid pace of evolution, and esraspecific polymorphism) permits and even demands an extension of phylogenetic thinking to the microevolutionary level. Many species exhibit a deep and geographically structured mtDNA phylogenetic history. Study of the relationship between genealogy and geography constitutes a discipline that can be termed intraspecific phylogeography. 'alien genes' in human DNA.

The (Central Asian) Khazar name is derived from Turkic *qaz-, meaning "to wander." The Ashina was considered a sacred clan of quasi-divine status. Q1 actually refers to the subclade Q-P36.2. The Ashina clan, a noble caste, carry the 16q24.3 "red gene" inherited from the Sumerian Anunnaki, the root of the Dragon seed that permeates royal lines: Merovingian, Carolingian, Tudor, Plantagenet, Stuart, Hapsburg, Hanoverian, Saxe-Coburg-Gotha, Guelph, Bowes-Lyon, Battenberg (Mountbatten), Guise, and Savoy families - and Transylvanian lineages. The Davidic House of Judah married into the descent of the Merovingian Kings of the Franks. They are connected by a shared bloodline. The dragon archetype rests within the Dragon blood, passed on through the genes.

According to Nicholas de Vere, "Briefly, the Dragon lineage starts in the Caucasus with the Anunnaki, descending through migrating proto-Scythians to the Sumerians while branching off also into the early Egyptians, Phoenicians and Mittani. A marriage bridge back to Scythia infused the Elvin line of "Tuatha de Danaan" and the Fir Bolg, which branched into the Arch-Druidic, Priest-Princely family to the Royal Picts of Scotland and the ring kings of the Horse Lords of Dal Riada, through the Elven dynasty of Pendragon and Avallon del Acqs, and down to a few pure bred families today." The Royal Court of the Dragon was founded by the priests of Mendes in about 2200 BC and was subsequently ratified by the 12th dynasty Queen Sobekneferu. This sovereign and priestly Order passed from Egypt to the Kings of Jerusalem; to the Black Sea Princes of Scythia (Princess Milouziana of the Scythians) and into the Balkans - notably to the Royal House of Hungary, whose King Sigismund reconstituted the Court just 600 years ago. Sigismund's assumed descent from Melusine. Her ancestry actually can be traced back to the Scythian Dragon Princess Scota, Queen Sobekneferu and the Egyptian Cult of the Dragon. Vlad Dracul was a minion of Sigismund of Luxembourg and was educated at the Emperor's court in Nuremberg. Dracul was invested into Societas Draconis. The Byzantine Emperor Constantine was a Dragon King. The Byzantine emperor Leo III married his son Constantine (V) to the Khazar princess as part of the alliance between the two empires. Princess Tzitzak was baptized as Irene. Their son Leo (Leo IV) was known as "Leo the Khazar", emperor of the Eastern Roman (Byzantine) Empire from 775 to 780.

The re-expansion of paternal group R1b and maternal group H from the Basque Ice Age refuge spread up the coasts of all the countries facing the Atlantic, after the ice melted. The British Isles retained higher rates than the other countries, for several reasons related specifically to early movements directly from the Basque country rather than from general diffusion from western Europe. First, as a result of lower sea levels, the British Isles, in particular Ireland, were connected and at the furthest edge of the extended Ice Age European continent, and thus received the bulk of early coastal migration. Then, as sea levels rose, first Ireland then Britain became islands, relatively insulated from further migration from elsewhere in Europe, thus preserving their high rates of R1b and similarity to the initial settlements. The means by which I could separate the R1b types in the British Isles from those on the other side of the channel is by the use of "Founder Analysis." That is, looking at the detail of their gene types (so-called STR haplotypes). These revealed 21 founding clusters, which could only have arrived direct from the Basque country. Their descendant twigs are unique to the British Isles.[29]

Seeing how the same forces that shaped royal bloodlines—alliances, unions, and the blending of distinct peoples—were mirrored in far older, prehistoric migrations was a turning point in my research. The union of Byzantine and Khazar dynasties was, in its own way, a reflection of what had already occurred for millennia: the meeting and merging of different genetic and cultural streams. The story carried in the DNA of the British Isles was not simply one of survival after the Ice Age, but of deliberate crossings, chance encounters, and enduring legacies. Realising this, I was drawn to

---

[29] *Iona Miller on behalf of Nicholas De Vere, https://drakenberg.weebly.com/dragon-family-tree.html*

Rb1 - http://www.familytreedna.com/public/r1b1b2/default.aspx

Royal Red Dragons - http://www.youtube.com/watch?v=OnYpMcaHCFI&feature=related accessed on Aug 2025

King Tut was a Celt , Accessed on Aug 2025- http://wn.com/King_Tut_was_a_Celt

look further back—beyond written history—into the origins of humanity itself..

The Origins of Humanity, Hybridization, and the Foundations of Social Structures

My work under the Royal Dragon Court has led me to profound discoveries about the origins of humanity. The traditional linear view of human evolution—progressing simply from primitive ancestors to modern Homo sapiens—is outdated. Instead, research now reveals a far richer story of multiple hominin species living simultaneously, interbreeding, and contributing to the genetic fabric of modern humans. ^1 For centuries, mythologies, ancient texts, and oral traditions hinted at beings beyond ordinary humans—giants, elves, and "hobbit" people—stories that modern science is beginning to validate. This expanded understanding challenges what we have been taught and forces a re-evaluation of who we are, where we came from, and why our social structures exist.

Ancient sources like the Book of Enoch, part of the Dead Sea Scrolls and dated to around the 3rd century BCE, recount the Watchers—celestial beings who descended to Earth, mated with humans, and produced the Nephilim, giants considered corruptors of mankind.^2 While these texts have theological origins, they may encode distant memories of interbreeding between modern humans and other archaic hominins, remembered through mythological language.^3 The Sumerian Anunnaki, often portrayed as gods or extraterrestrials who engineered humanity, may similarly reflect ancestral narratives of hybrid beings.^4 Though some interpretations venture into pseudoscience, these ancient records preserve fragments of cultural memory, providing context to the genetic evidence emerging today.^5

Genomic research firmly establishes that modern humans are the result of complex hybridization events involving several archaic human species. Present-day non-African humans carry approximately 1–4% Neanderthal DNA, while certain Oceanian populations have up to 6% Denisovan ancestry.^6 In 2018, a remarkable discovery of a 90,000-year-old individual—dubbed "Denny"—who was a first-generation offspring of a Neanderthal mother and Denisovan father, provided direct proof of interspecies mating.^7 This overturned previous assumptions that such species were reproductively isolated. Instead, multiple interbreeding events occurred across Eurasia, facilitated by overlapping habitats during climatic changes. ^8

Further fossils and genomic evidence from East Asia, including ancient teeth from China, suggest admixture between archaic Homo erectus, Denisovans, and early Homo sapiens ancestors as far back as 300,000 years ago.^9 These complex gene flows conferred adaptations, such as enhanced immune responses and high-altitude tolerance, illustrating the evolutionary advantage of hybridization.^10 Among these discoveries is the Harbin skull, or "Dragon Man," from northeastern China, dated to approximately 146,000 years ago, exhibiting robust features distinct from both Neanderthals and modern humans, attributed to the Denisovan lineage.^11–^13 This find expands the geographic and morphological understanding of Denisovans, whose range extended beyond Siberia into the vast East Asian interior.^14 A jawbone from Taiwan's Penghu Channel has also been identified as Denisovan, indicating their presence on islands previously thought inaccessible to archaic humans.^15

The "hobbit" people, or Homo floresiensis, discovered in 2003 on the Indonesian island of Flores, measured about one meter tall with a brain size about one-third that of modern humans.^16,^17 Their small stature and primitive tools suggest island dwarfism, an evolutionary adaptation seen in other insular species.^18 Additional archaic species like Homo luzonensis from the Philippines and Homo naledi from South Africa coexisted with modern humans well into the late Pleistocene, displaying diverse morphologies and behaviors.^19,^20 While no direct genetic evidence links these dwarfed hominins to contemporary humans, their existence complicates linear evolutionary models and highlights the genus Homo's adaptability.^21

The disappearance of Neanderthals roughly 40,000 years ago and Denisovans about 30,000 years ago likely resulted from a combination of climatic fluctuations, competition with expanding Homo sapiens populations, and possibly pathogen transmissions.^22 Island dwarfs like Homo floresiensis vanished without genetic contribution to modern humans.^23 These dynamics illustrate how Homo sapiens absorbed advantageous archaic genes while outcompeting others demographically.^24

Looking further back, early hominins such as Australopithecus afarensis ("Lucy," ~3.2 million years ago) evidence upright walking preceding brain enlargement.^25 Ardipithecus ramidus (~4.4 million years ago) shows mixed arboreal and terrestrial adaptations, revealing the complex path to modern humans.^26 Homo erectus, emerging around 1.9 million years ago, was the first to migrate out of Africa and utilize Acheulean tools.^27 Fossilized footprints in Kenya indicate multiple hominin species coexisted 1.5 million years ago, supporting the idea of sympatry and potential interactions.^28 These ancestral species laid the groundwork for anatomically modern humans, who emerged in Africa roughly 300,000 years ago and later dispersed worldwide, interbreeding with archaic populations en route.^29

Linguistic and mythological studies reinforce these biological findings. Indo-European proto-deities such as Dyēus ph₂ter (sky father) manifest across cultures—Sanskrit's Dyaus Pita, Greek Zeus, and Latin Jupiter—reflecting shared ancestral heritage and possibly memories of early migrations and interactions.^30 Similarly, Eurasian steppe tribes preserved oral histories of divine ancestry and giants, blending historical and mythic elements.^31 These cultural motifs suggest that ancient peoples encoded knowledge of hybridization and coexistence into their myths and social identities.^32

Human physical diversity today, including stature differences from over seven feet tall individuals to those of smaller frame like my own 4ft 10in height, may echo archaic admixture combined with environmental and genetic factors.^33 Certain craniofacial traits, metabolic variations, and disease susceptibilities have roots in Neanderthal and Denisovan ancestry.^34 Conditions such as dwarfism, traditionally seen purely as genetic disorders, may sometimes reflect ancient evolutionary processes like insular dwarfism or population bottlenecks, though further research is needed to clarify this link.^35

Understanding the biological reality of hybridization is only one side of the coin. Equally important is the social and cultural impact. How did prehistoric communities perceive hybrids? What social roles did they occupy, and how did these interactions shape early human identity, social cohesion, and exclusion?

Modern genomes show that archaic admixture was not rare but frequent, suggesting hybrids lived within early Homo sapiens populations.^36 Anthropological theories propose that in small prehistoric bands, where cooperation was vital for survival, differences in appearance or behaviour could lead to suspicion or exclusion.^37 Hybrids, possessing traits from archaic species, may have been "othered," leading to marginalization or persecution.^38 Archaeological evidence of ritual burial practices and artifact diversity within sites hints at social stratification and identity negotiation, possibly reflecting hybrid status.^39

Cognitive archaeology indicates that symbolic thought and language allowed early humans to conceptualize self and other, creating social categories that both unified and divided groups. ^40 Myths of giants, supernatural hybrids, and "other" peoples found worldwide may encode ancestral memories of real hybrid individuals, providing both explanations and justifications for social exclusion. ^41

The recurring nature of interbreeding events implies that societies developed evolving cultural responses, including rituals to integrate or exclude hybrids. Ethnographic parallels show "mixed" individuals often face ambivalent social roles, revered yet stigmatised. ^42 These dynamics likely laid foundations for later historic persecutions of witches, pagans, and other marginalized groups, echoing deep-seated human fears of difference and threats to social order. ^43

In sum, archaic-modern human hybridization was a biological and social crucible, shaping human evolution, cultural complexity, and behavioural responses to difference. Studying these early interactions helps us understand the origins of prejudice, inclusion, and the social mechanisms that continue to influence humanity. ^44

The story of uncovering these truths has unfolded over more than a century. The 1856 Neander Valley discovery marked the start of palaeoanthropology when Johann Carl Fuhlrott and Hermann Schaffhausen recognized the unique morphology of Neanderthal fossils.^45 For decades, Neanderthals were misunderstood as brutish and separate from modern humans. Advances in genetics revolutionized this view.

DNA's structure was elucidated in 1953, but extracting ancient DNA remained challenging until the 1990s when Svante Pääbo succeeded in sequencing Neanderthal DNA.^46 His team's 2010 publication of the Neanderthal genome draft demonstrated archaic DNA persistence in modern humans, overturning previous paradigms.^47 Shortly after, DNA from Denisova Cave revealed a new archaic human group—the Denisovans—extending knowledge of human diversity.^48 The discovery of "Denny," a hybrid individual, further confirmed interbreeding.^49

Fossil finds worldwide, like Homo floresiensis in 2003 and the Harbin skull recently, have expanded our understanding of human diversity. ^50, ^51 Advances in sequencing and computational biology, driven by researchers like David Reich, Matthias Meyer, and Kay Prüfer, have enabled detailed population histories integrating fossil and genetic data.^52,^53

While many fossil discoveries are well documented, some remain unpublished or lost due to natural erosion and uneven archaeological coverage. The fossil record is inherently incomplete, and ongoing research continues filling gaps in our understanding. ^54

In addition to tracing ancestry, research explores how archaic gene flow aided adaptation, such as high-altitude tolerance in Tibetans. ^55 The synthesis of genetics, archaeology, anthropology, and linguistics paints a complex mosaic of human history.

The social response to hybridization likely drove the development of social leadership. Managing difference, ensuring cooperation, and maintaining group cohesion required social mechanisms that evolved into governance and nobility. Clan chiefs, elders, and councils arose to mediate conflicts and unify groups under shared identities. ^56 Hereditary power structures and royal bloodlines emerged from this need for social order. ^57

Governance was not merely political but a social adaptation to manage diversity and perceived threats. Control and identity negotiation fostered stability but also exclusion and persecution, patterns echoed in later historical episodes. ^58 Groups like the Picts illustrate how social structures both divided and united communities. ^59

Understanding the origins of nobility as an outgrowth of early human social adaptation enriches our grasp of lineage and power's deep roots in human history. ^60[30]

Migration and the Paradox of Inbreeding: A Deep Human History

The story of human migration is one of movement, adaptation, and intermingling, yet paradoxically, it is also a story of isolation, fragmentation, and inbreeding. From the earliest dispersals out of Africa to the complex patchwork of populations across Eurasia, the Caribbean, and beyond, migrations have not only enabled cultural and genetic diversity but have also often resulted in founder effects and small isolated gene pools. These circumstances, especially when repeated across generations in regions where migration ceased or localised, have fostered conditions ripe for inbreeding—genetic bottlenecks where close-kin reproduction becomes inevitable or culturally normalized. By examining ancient DNA, archaeological patterns, and anthropological evidence from across the globe—including Africa, Persia, the Black Sea steppes, Russia, Jamaica, and beyond—one begins to understand how human movement both prevented and paradoxically seeded the conditions for genetic isolation.

---

[30] *This essay has been inserted at the end of writing the book therefroe as there are over 60 citations they will be added in the appendix and bibliography, to ensure the flow of the book.*

The cornerstone of understanding this duality lies in recent breakthroughs in genomics, most notably the work of **David Reich** and his colleagues, who, through the analysis of ancient DNA, have radically transformed our understanding of human ancestry. Reich's work shows that virtually no present-day population is a direct descendant of the people who lived in the same place thousands of years ago. Instead, today's populations are the result of complex waves of migration, admixture, and disappearance of ancient groups— "ghost populations"—that left traces only in our genes. Reich writes, "Not only are all human beings mixed, but our intuitive understanding of the evolution of the population structure of the world around us is not to be trusted." [1] This complexity challenges the assumption that stable, continuous human populations ever truly existed. It also implies that periods of intense admixture were often followed by local isolation—conditions under which inbreeding could arise.

Consider our earliest ancestors: **Homo sapiens** who left Africa approximately 60,000 years ago encountered and interbred with archaic humans such as **Neanderthals** and later with **Denisovans**. Genetic analysis reveals that all non-African humans today carry roughly 1-4% Neanderthal DNA, with Melanesians and some South Asians carrying up to 6% Denisovan DNA.[2] This interbreeding was not merely incidental; it occurred in contexts of small, migrating groups where reproduction was largely endogamous out of necessity.[3] These early Eurasian populations were genetically vulnerable, and genomic studies show evidence of high levels of inbreeding in some Neanderthal —particularly the Altai Neanderthal genome, which suggests a child born of closely related parents.[4] In short, the earliest human migrations exposed Homo sapiens to new gene pools but also placed them in environments conducive to genetic isolation.

As migrations continued, new cultures and peoples emerged across the vast Eurasian steppe. One such group were the **Scythians**, nomadic Indo-European horse warriors who dominated the Black Sea region from roughly the 9th century BCE to the 1st century CE. Recent archaeogenetic research from Scythian burial mounds (kurgans) reveals complex genetic signatures: a mix of West Eurasian, East Asian, and steppe ancestry. [5] Yet despite this broad intermixture, Scythian tribes themselves were relatively isolated once established in certain regions. In-group marriage was common among noble lines, as evidenced by genetic clustering in elite burials. [6] A similar pattern can be seen among the **Yamnaya culture**, precursors to Indo-Europeans, who spread rapidly from the Pontic-Caspian steppe across Europe about 5,000 years ago. While their migrations seeded genetic change across the continent, their own group was highly patrilineal and homogenous, suggesting repeated reproduction within elite male lines—a pattern linked to both cultural preference and limited exogamy. [7]

Meanwhile, in the cradle of civilisation—**Persia and Iran**—archaeological and DNA evidence indicates extensive human movement through ancient trade networks, yet many local populations remained genetically consistent over millennia. The **Elamites** of southwestern Iran, for example, are genetically distinct from Indo-European speakers who later entered the Iranian plateau.[8] Reich's findings show that modern Iranians have ancestry from multiple waves of steppe migrations, but also harbour deeply local ancestry from ancient farming and hunter-gatherer groups who had, at points, minimal contact with outsiders.[9] The mountainous geography of Iran created pockets of isolation where kin-based marriage structures, including cousin marriage, became embedded in tradition, further compounding the effects of genetic drift and inbreeding.[10]

In **sub-Saharan Africa**, often mischaracterised as a genetic monolith, ancient DNA reveals extraordinary diversity—and complex patterns of both admixture and isolation. Africa's deep-time genetic history includes multiple hominid lineages and extensive internal migration, particularly the **Bantu expansion**, which swept across central and southern Africa beginning around 3000 BCE. Yet, even amid this movement, isolated hunter-gatherer groups such as the **San** of southern Africa maintained distinct genetic lineages for tens of thousands of years, occasionally mixing with others but largely reproducing within small communities.[11] In regions like Ethiopia and the Horn of Africa, mountainous terrains similarly facilitated genetic separation.[12] Social customs—including marriage within clan or religious lines—ensured continued endogamy, reinforcing patterns akin to inbreeding without outright familial reproduction.

The history of **Jamaica** provides a modern colonial case of genetic isolation through forced migration. With the transatlantic slave trade, enslaved Africans—primarily from West and Central Africa—were transported to the Caribbean, where they were subjected to plantation slavery and stripped of their original ethnic identities. The result was not only cultural fragmentation but also genetic bottlenecks. Jamaican populations were founded by small, forcibly displaced gene pools. Over generations, intermarriage among descendants of these survivors, especially in rural or maroon communities, created conditions where distant relatives may unknowingly intermarry.[13] Though not "inbreeding" in a classical sense, the effect of founder population dynamics and limited mate pools is similar. Moreover, the European and later South Asian indentured influences added layers of complexity, creating a genetic landscape marked by admixture layered over constrained reproductive networks.

Modern population genetics also highlights **Ashkenazi Jews** and **Roma people** in Europe as examples where historical migration and isolation intertwined. Ashkenazi Jews experienced multiple bottlenecks—after leaving the Levant, settling in Europe, and being confined to specific communities. This isolation produced high rates of recessive genetic disorders traceable to in-group marriage.[14] Similar patterns are evident in **the Roma**, whose ancestors left north-west India over a thousand years ago and subsequently experienced centuries of reproductive isolation and social marginalization in Europe.[15] Reich's work confirms these narratives: the Roma genome reflects both Indian ancestry and admixture with European host populations, but genetic drift and inbreeding are visible due to repeated population contractions.[16]

The idea that white Europeans have existed only for about 4000 years, as discussed by Reich, arises from the understanding that skin lightening genes entered Europe relatively late. The earliest Homo sapiens in Europe were dark-skinned hunter-gatherers. Farming populations from the Near East migrated into Europe about 9000 years ago, bringing new genes, but only later—around 4000 to 5000 years ago—did populations carrying variants for light skin and hair spread widely, likely via the Yamnaya migrations.[17] This means that the phenotype associated with "whiteness" is recent, and also resulted from intense population replacement rather than continuity. Ironically, this replacement was itself often followed by reproductive isolation within new social groups, again introducing the risk of genetic homogeneity.

What becomes clear through this lens is that **migration** often sets the stage for **admixture**, but that admixture is not the final state—many migrating populations, once settled, develop cultural, geographic, or socio-political mechanisms of reproductive isolation. Whether through caste, clan, ethnicity, religion, or geographic boundaries, these structures foster inbreeding over generations. The paradox is that human movement and mixing do not inherently eliminate inbreeding risk—in fact, by creating new groups in new lands with limited partners, migration frequently leads to it. And these conditions, repeated over millennia, shaped not only our genetics but the very frameworks of human society.[31]

---

[31] *David Reich, Who We Are and How We Got Here (Pantheon, 2018).*

Green et al., "A Draft Sequence of the Neandertal Genome," Science 328, no. 5979 (2010): 710-722.

Sankararaman et al., "The Date of Interbreeding between Neandertals and Modern Humans," PLoS Genetics 8, no. 10 (2012).

Prüfer et al., "The Complete Genome Sequence of a Neanderthal from the Altai Mountains," Nature 505, no. 7481 (2014): 43–49.

Damgaard et al., "137 Ancient Human Genomes from Across the Eurasian Steppes," Nature 557 (2018): 369–374.

Unterländer et al., "Ancestry and Demography and Descendants of Iron Age Nomads of the Eurasian Steppe," Nature Communications 8 (2017): 14615.

Haak et al., "Massive Migration from the Steppe Was a Source for Indo-European Languages in Europe," Nature 522 (2015): 207–211.

Lazaridis et al., "The Genetic Structure of the World's First Farmers," Cell 157, no. 3 (2014): 656–667.

David Reich, Who We Are and How We Got Here, 169.

Tadmouri et al., "Consanguinity and Reproductive Health Among Arabs," Reproductive Health 6, no. 1 (2009): 17.

Schlebusch et al., "Southern African Ancient Genomes Estimate Modern Human Divergence to 350,000 to 260,000 Years Ago," Science 358, no. 6363 (2017): 652–655.

Pagani et al., "Ethiopian Genetic Diversity Reveals Linguistic Stratification and Complex Influences," The American Journal of Human Genetics 91, no. 1 (2012): 83–96.

Bryan Sykes, DNA USA: A Genetic Portrait of America (W.W. Norton, 2012).

This cyclical pattern—migration, mixture, and eventual isolation—can be traced in both genetics and history, offering a framework for understanding the rise of distinct peoples. Just as the Yamnaya migrations reshaped the genetic and social landscape of Europe, earlier movements and subsequent inbreeding would have forged the unique identities of ancient tribes. It is within this interplay of movement and consolidation that the origins of specific cultural groups emerge, and nowhere is this more intriguing than in the case of the Picts and Scots. Their story, preserved in the writings of classical authors and the echoes of archaeology, begins in the same crucible of shifting populations and defined boundaries that has shaped so many peoples before and since.

Origins of the PICTS AND SCOTS

Who did the Picts descend from?

Tacitus, who wrote a biography of his father-in-law, the Roman governor of Britain from AD 77 to 84, Agricola, the whole of Britain north of the Forth-Clyde isthmus was "Caledonia".

Carmi et al., "Sequencing an Ashkenazi Reference Panel Supports Population-Targeted Personal Genomics and Illuminates Jewish and European Origins," Nature Communications 5 (2014): 4835.

Mendizabal et al., "Reconstructing the Population History of European Romani from Genome-wide Data," Current Biology 22, no. 24 (2012): 2342–2349.

David Reich, Who We Are and How We Got Here, 211.

Mathieson et al., "Genome-wide Patterns of Selection in 230 Ancient Eurasians," Nature 528, no. 7583 (2015): 499–503.

However, Tacitus never calls the inhabitants of the country Caledonians, only "Britons". The geographer Ptolemy, writing in the mid-2nd century (but apparently using data gleaned during Agricola's tenure), lists the Caledonians (Caledonii) as just one of several tribes living beyond the isthmus. So, although the whole country was called Caledonia, the Caledonians were but one tribe inhabiting that country.

Cassius Dio, discussing events in northern Britain during the period 197–211, notes:

There are two principal races of the Britons, the Caledonians and the Maeatae, and the names of the others have been merged in these two. The Maeatae live next to the cross-wall which cuts the island in half, and the Caledonians are beyond them. Roman History (Epitome, Xiphilinus) LXXVI, 12

It is generally believed that Dio's "cross-wall" is the Antonine Wall (on the Forth-Clyde line), in which case, the tribes of Caledonia had amalgamated to produce two major groups: the Maeatae, to the immediate north of the Wall, and to the north of them the Caledonians.

Almost a century later, in a panegyric delivered in 297, appears the earliest extant mention of the Picts. The anonymous author makes a poetic reference to Julius Caesar having had a relatively easy task invading Britain, since his opponents were:

… an uncivilised nation and accustomed to no enemies except the Picts [Picti] and the Irish [Hiberni], still half-naked …Panegyrics Latini 'VIII. Panegyric on Constantius Caesar'

A little later, in 310, another panegyric, also anonymous, refers to the:

… forests and marshes of the Caledonians [Caledon's] and other Picts

…Panegyrici Latini 'VI. Panegyric on Constantine'

Appended to the Verona List – a list of Roman provinces, dating from about 314 (it survives in a 7th-century manuscript at Verona) – is a catalogue of forty "barbarian peoples that have sprung-up under the emperors", which begins with the Scots, the Picts and the Caledonians. This is apparently the earliest historical reference to the Scots (Scot or Scott), and also the last reference to the Caledonians.

Amianthus Marcellian, writing about the, so-called, <u>Barbarian Conspiracy</u> of 367:

… at that time the Picts, divided into two tribes, called Dictaphones and Overtures, as well as the Attraction, a warlike race of men, and the Scots, were ranging widely and causing great devastation …Res Gestae XXVII, 8

Presumably, the Caledonians (Caledonii/Caledones) had evolved into the Dicalydones – the similarity of name is clear – and the Maeatae had metamorphosed into the Verturiones. It would seem, then, that by the early-4th century all the tribes beyond the Forth-Clyde line had come to be known, collectively, as Picti by the Romans. Scoti also seems to be a new name for an old foe – in this instance Irish raiders. The 'Panegyric on Constantius Caesar' of 297 linked the Picts with the Hiberni, but thereafter they are always linked with the Scoti. The poet Claudian (Claudius Claudianus), writing in 398, confirms that the Scots are indeed Irish: ice-bound Hibernia [Ireland] wept for the heaps of slain Scots. Panegyricus de Quarto Consulatu Honorii Augusti, line 33

(Panegyric on the Fourth Consulship of Honorius)

The etymology of the word Scoti is uncertain – it does not have a Latin root, nor has any proposed <u>Goidelic</u> derivation gained wide acceptance. According to one legend the Scots were named from, Pharaoh's daughter, Scota – wife of the man who led their forebears from Egypt at the time of Moses.

The origins of the name Pict has been much debated (along with many other aspects of the Picts, who thrived for over five hundred years but about whom remarkably little is known). What they called themselves is not known – the Picts left no literature – but the Latin word Picti would appear to mean 'painted people' (pictus = 'painted', hence the English word 'picture').

Septimius Severus arrived in Britain, to campaign against the tribes of Caledonia (the Maeatae and the Caledonians), in 208. Herodian, a contemporary of Severus, writes:

Most of the regions of [northern] Britain are marshy, since they are flooded continually by the tides of the ocean; the barbarians are accustomed to swimming or wading through these waist-deep marsh pools; since they go about naked, they are unconcerned about muddying their bodies. Strangers to clothing, they wear ornaments of iron at their waists and throats; considering iron a symbol of wealth, they value this metal as other barbarians value gold. They tattoo their bodies with coloured designs and drawings of all kinds of animals; for this reason they do not wear clothes, which would conceal the decorations on their bodies. Extremely savage and warlike, they are armed only with a spear and a narrow shield, plus a sword that hangs suspended by a belt from their otherwise naked bodies. They do not use breastplates or helmets, considering them encumbrances in crossing the marshes. History of the Empire after Marcus III, 14

Almost a century after Severus' campaigns, the name Pict first appears (297). Another century onwards, in 400, the poet Claudian talks of Britain (in female personification) being:

... clothed in the skin of some Caledonian beast, her cheeks tattooed, and an azure cloak,

rivalling the swell of Ocean, sweeping to her feet ...De Consulatu Stilichonis II, lines 247–249

(On the Consulship of Stilicho)

And, in 402, of:

... the strange devices tattooed on dying Picts. De Bello Gothico, lines 417–418

(On the Gothic War)

And he had, in 396, referred to:

... the well-named Picts ...Panegyricus de Tertio Consulatu Honorii Augusti, line 54

(Panegyric on the Third Consulship of Honorius)

Possibly, then, it was their tendency to decorate themselves with extravagant body-art that caused the Romans to nickname the inhabitants of northernmost Britain Picti: 'painted people'. On the other hand, maybe the association of tattooing with these British "barbarians" was based not on reality, but on a stereotyped notion of those distant savages. In other words, perhaps it was a myth that the Picts tattooed their bodies. The British cleric Gildas, writing in about 545(?), likens "the terrible hordes of Scots and Picts" to "dark swarms of worms", and says of them:

Differing partly in their habits, yet alike in one and the same thirst for bloodshed – in a preference also for covering their villainous faces with hair rather than their nakedness of body with decent clothing ...De Excidio Britanniae.

It is difficult to believe that Gildas would have passed-up the opportunity to make disparaging remarks about tattoos if the Picts were particularly noted for them. Perhaps Picti was simply a Latinization of their native name (which could have had a completely different meaning). Nevertheless, the Spanish bishop and encyclopaedist, Isidore of Seville, in the early-600s, wrote:

Some nations lay claim to distinguishing marks not only in clothing but also on their bodies: as we see the curly hair of the Germans; the whiskers and red pigment of the Goths; the tattoos of the Britons. The Jews cut around their foreskin; the Arabs bore holes in their ears; the Getae have yellow hair which they do not cover; the Albanians are resplendent with white hair. Black night possesses the bodies of the Moors; the Gauls have white skin; without horses the Alans are idle. The race of the Picts is not absent from this list, for their name is from their body, which an artisan abuses with tiny needle pricks and the juice of native grass, so it bears things which look like scars – their nobility is spotted with painted limbs. Etymology (or Origines) XIX, 23.7

The image of the highly decorated, naked, Pict still seems to be stuck in the public imagination. Whatever its derivation, it is apparent that the Picti was a new collective name for the disparate tribes already living beyond the Forth-Clyde isthmus. According to the mythology that developed, however, the Picts were a migrant race of people who eventually settled in Britain. In the 8th century, the Anglo-Saxon monk and historian, Bede, wrote:

... at first this island had no other inhabitants but the Britons, from whom it derived its name, and who, coming over into Britain, as is reported, from Armorica, possessed themselves of the southern parts thereof. Starting from the south, they had occupied the greater part of the island, when it happened, that the nation of the Picts, putting to sea from Scythia, as is reported, in a few ships of war, and being driven by the winds beyond the bounds of Britain, came to Ireland and landed on its northern shores. There, finding the nation of the Scots, they begged to be allowed to settle among them. The Scots answered that the island could not contain them both; but "We can give you good counsel," said they, "whereby you may know what to do; we know there is another island, not far from ours, to the eastward, which we often see at a distance, when the days are clear. If you will go thither, you can obtain settlements; or, if any should oppose you, we will help you." The Picts, accordingly, sailing over into Britain, began to inhabit the northern parts thereof, for the Britons had possessed themselves of the southern. Now the Picts had no wives, and asked them of the Scots; who would not consent to grant them upon any other terms, than that when any question should arise, they should choose a king from the female royal race rather than from the male: which custom, as is well known, has been observed among the Picts to this day.[32]

---

[32]*Translations:*
Bede the Venerable. Historia Ecclesiastica Gentis Anglorum. Translated by A.M. Sellar.
Bede the Venerable. Historia Ecclesiastica Gentis Anglorum. Free Download, Borrow, and Streaming. Internet Archive. Accessed August 4, 2025.
Claudian. Works of Claudian. Translated by Maurice Platnauer.
Cassius Dio. Roman History. Translated by Earnest Cary.
Jerome. Adversus Jovinianum. Translated by Philip Rance.
Gildas. De Excidio Britanniae. Edited and translated by Hugh Williams.
Julius Caesar. The Gallic War. Translated by T. Rice Holmes.
Isidore of Seville. Etymologiae. Translated by Priscilla Throop.
Ammianus Marcellinus. Res Gestae. Translated by John C. Rolfe.
Herodian. History of the Empire after Marcus. Translated by Edward C. Echols.
The Picts: DNA and Origins. Accessed August 4, 2025. dot-domesday.me.uk/picts.htm

Pict DNA R1B.

3% of Irish men hold Pictish DNA, r1b. Who were the ancestors of the Picts?

Three percent of men in Northern Ireland and roughly one in 200 men in Ireland carry the Scotland DNA, an ancestry testing company, discovered a DNA marker that strongly suggests that ten percent of Scotsmen are directly descended from the Picts, the Gaels' fierce neighbours who battled the Romans. The company's chief scientist, Dr. Jim Wilson, found a Y chromosome marker among direct descendants of the Picts in 2013. The Scotsman.com reported he said this marker is the "first evidence that the heirs of the Picts are living among us." The marker is labelled R1b-S530.

Scotland DNA's managing director Alistair Moffat said about the discovery, "These findings were probably one of the biggest surprises we've had in our research. The Picts seem kind of exotic, and different and quite colourful and so I was personally, really, really rather taken with this." Dr. Wilson tested this marker in more than 3,000 British and Irish men and he found it was 10 times more common in those with Scottish grandfathers than with English grandfathers. 170 Scottish men have been found to carry this marker, though the real number is likely higher. More than 10 percent of 100 Scotsmen tested carried R1b-S530. He said, "As you go up your family tree, there are all sorts of paths. But if we can see that about 10 percent of father-lines look to have a Pictish origin, then we can make the prediction that probably a lot of other lines do too."

Only 0.8 of English men carry this marker and about 3 percent of men in Northern Ireland carry it. The presence in Northern Ireland may be due to the Scottish plantation in the 16 and 17 centuries. Only 1 of 200 men carried the marker in the Republic of Ireland. Dr. Wilson commented on these differences, "The finding just popped out of the analysis. While there have been hints of this from previous data, what was surprising was the really huge difference between Scotland and England." Irish people have far more Viking DNA than was suspected Dr. Wilson is also a senior lecturer in population and disease genetics at the University of Edinburgh. He said, "It is a clear sign that while people do move around there remains a core who have remained at home. Perhaps this was due to farming or that moving around would have to be done on foot." The Picts were a group of tribes living in the Forth and Clyde beyond the reach of the Romans. They lived near the Britons, Gaels, Angeles, and the Vikings. The Romans called them the "Picti" which means "the painted ones." They were first mentioned by a Roman chronicler in 300 AD. They fought with the Romans and the Angles, and the Picts had overrun the northern frontier of the Roman empire on several occasions by the late 200's. Previously thought to have "disappeared," scholars now believe they became assimilated by invading Scots from Ireland[33]

Scientists and archaeologists were making huge leaps forward in the understanding of our ancient ancestors before the lockdown began. Here, Writer at Large Neil Mackay, uncovers what we know today about the mysterious and very misunderstood Picts.

We think of the Picts as an almost mythological people – mystical, mysterious, barbarian and pagan – lost to us in the mists of time. But nothing could be further from the truth. Before the coronavirus lockdown began, archaeologists were making rapid advances in our understanding of these ancient ancestors. A standing stone carved by Pictish hands some 1,200 years ago was recently discovered near Dingwall, shedding new light on their art and culture. A 1,400-year-old Pictish cemetery was located on the Black Isle, giving us an insight into their religious beliefs and social rituals. In recent years, scholars have been revolutionising how history views the Picts – a people who, until the 1950s, were seen as a subject too fanciful for serious academic study. Who really were the Picts? The broad answer is that they were the inhabitants of Scotland long before the idea of Scotland even existed. They withstood the Roman occupation of Britain, maintaining their own distinct culture while

---

[33] *Neil Mackay. The Picts: Who Really Were Our Mythical Ancestors? Irish Central. April 26, 2020. Accessed August 4, 2025 .*

other cultures were subsumed by the Empire. By the Dark Ages, the Picts emerged as a culture just as sophisticated as any other on the British isles at the time. The Picts helped shape modern Britain – and without them Scotland wouldn't exist. Nor were they stubbornly pagan – they embraced Christianity. Their greatest failing, though, is that they left us no written records beyond the strange hieroglyphics carved onto their standing stones. We still don't understand what these symbols mean. Other contemporary cultures, however, like the Irish Gaels and the Anglo-Saxons, left plenty of written records. So, the void in our understanding of the Picts was filled with either accounts by their neighbours and their enemies, or myths and legends. And so, a faulty understanding of the Picts has existed right up to the present day. Origin story The ancestors of the Picts were the tribes who lived in the north of Scotland, beyond the River Tay. In the first century AD, the Romans called these people Britanni, today we think of them as the Caledonii or Caledonians. These Caledonians defended their land with guerrilla attacks against the legions of Rome. Roman chroniclers such as Tacitus tell us that these tribes forged alliances against Rome – and finally took on the might of the Empire in a huge set piece battle at Mons Graupius in 83AD. The exact location of the battle is unknown, but it was probably in Aberdeenshire and gave rise to the name of the Grampian Mountains. The battle was a defeat for the Caledonians but at least two-thirds of their army survived. Resistance, weather, and landscape all made it impossible for Rome to complete its conquest of the entire island of Britain. The north remained free, and the Caledonian ancestors of the Picts continued their hit-and-run campaign against Roman forces[34]

The legacy of the Caledonians did not vanish with the retreat of the Romans; it endured in the bloodlines of their descendants. Over centuries, these northern tribes evolved into the Picts, their identities shaped by defiance, isolation, and the forging of tight-knit kinship groups. Such histories are not just recorded in chronicles—they are carried within the people themselves. The very resilience

---

[34] *Ibid*

that kept these tribes free from Roman conquest left its imprint in the genetic signatures passed down through the ages, threads that can still be traced today in the DNA of their modern heirs. It was this idea—that history survives within us—that drew me deeper into the study of my own genetic heritage.

Bloodlines and Echoes—Genetic Clues to Nobility and Ancestral Identity

The past speaks in echoes—sometimes through bone and stone, sometimes through stories passed down, and increasingly, through the microscopic language written in our DNA. When I uploaded my genetic data to My True Ancestry, I was struck by what came back. The results didn't just suggest regional connections or migrations; they carried the names of clans, dynasties, and noble houses. Scottish and Irish clans. Medieval nobility. Royal families with lineages that shaped the political, cultural, and military history of entire continents. What does it mean when your genome aligns with the rulers of the past? And more importantly—how can others trace the same roots?

To begin answering this, we need to understand how these links are made. My True Ancestry and similar platforms rely on **ancient DNA comparisons**, connecting modern genetic profiles with excavated remains of people who lived hundreds or thousands of years ago. These samples come from burial mounds, battlefields, royal crypts, and forgotten cemeteries. Each genome is extracted, sequenced, and placed into a comparative framework that spans both time and geography. When you upload your DNA, the platform doesn't just assign you to regions; it matches you with actual **historical genomes**, often tied to named cultures, clans, or individuals from archaeological reports.[1]

When my results connected me to Scottish clans such as the **MacLeod's**, **Campbells**, or **McDonald's**, and Irish nobility descended from the **Uí Néill** or **Eóganachta**, I was intrigued. These weren't vague regional guesses—they were based on tangible genetic similarity to samples from burial sites in the British Isles. The science behind this uses **shared IBD (identity by descent)** segments, **haplogroups**, and **allele frequency patterns**. In particular, **Y-DNA haplogroups** like **R1b-L21** and subclades like **R1b-M222** are prevalent among men with deep ancestry in Ireland and Scotland, especially those connected to historical ruling classes. [2] These markers are associated with patrilineal dynasties—male-line descendants that pass not just names and lands, but also tightly linked genetic sequences.

The story deepens when one considers that many royal lineages—especially in medieval Europe—were deeply endogamous. Royalty often married within narrow circles to preserve power, territory, and bloodline purity. Ironically, this made their genetic markers easier to track. In fact, **haplogroup studies on famous royal remains**, such as the analysis of **Richard III of England** or **members of the Bourbon dynasty**, have shown distinct Y-DNA signatures that can now be compared with modern individuals.[3] So when someone today is shown to match the same rare subclades found in royal or noble remains, it's not just coincidence—it's a historical echo encoded in DNA.

But nobility wasn't always confined to palaces. Across **Celtic** and **Nordic** regions, clan-based societies often merged governance with kinship. In Scotland, clans were extended families with chiefs who governed their people through tradition and loyalty. Clans like **MacGregor**, **Fraser**, and **Douglas** played vital roles in wars, land disputes, and royal politics. Many of them trace their origins back to medieval kings, Viking settlers, or Norman invaders. In Ireland, high kingship and tribal rule revolved around descent from legendary figures like **Niall of the Nine Hostages**, a supposed 5th-century warlord whose real genetic legacy may be visible in **haplogroup**

R1b-M222, found disproportionately among Irish men in the north-west. [4]

In my case, My True Ancestry also revealed links not only to Gaelic royalty but also to **continental European nobility**—points of overlap with samples identified as part of the **Merovingian**, **Carolingian**, and even **Byzantine** elite. While some of this may reflect shared ancient Indo-European roots, some may be due to **later admixture via Norman conquest**, Habsburg expansion, or Crusader movement—times when elite lineages intermarried across borders and cultures. These trans-regional connections show how genetic identity doesn't always stay local. In fact, it often rides the same currents of migration, empire, and conquest we examined in the previous chapter.

The value in this kind of testing isn't only in what it tells us about ourselves, but also in what it invites others to explore. Anyone curious about their ancestral roots can start by taking a **DNA test from a service that provides raw data downloads**—such as 23andMe, Ancestry DNA, or Living DNA. After obtaining your raw DNA file (a simple text format of hundreds of thousands of SNPs), you can upload it to **MyTrueAncestry**, or **GEDmatch Genesis**—sites that specialize in deep-time or ancient genome comparison. They'll scan your DNA for genetic similarity to samples from Viking Age warriors, Iron Age Celts, Roman aristocrats, Slavic chieftains, and more.

You may be surprised at what emerges. You might find yourself genetically linked to **Thracian nobles**, **Scythian horsemen**, **Visigothic kings**, or **Coptic clerics**. Or your DNA might connect to ancient **Berber**, **Sarmatian**, or **Phoenician** groups who were part of trade networks, slave routes, and migrations that made their way into the bloodlines of modern populations.

And while these matches don't mean you're directly descended from a king or queen in any linear genealogical sense, they do mean you **share ancestry from the same population pool**—from the same gene flow that made that lineage possible. In that sense, **genetic nobility is less about titles and more about time-travelled kinship**. The genome democratizes the story: you don't need a castle or a coat of arms to carry royal blood.

Perhaps more importantly, this process reshapes identity. For people from colonised, enslaved, or displaced ancestries—especially from the **African diaspora, indigenous Caribbean nations**, or **dispossessed European minorities**—these genetic platforms can restore what history erased. They can help reconstruct belonging when paper trails vanish. They can reconnect fragmented lineages and give names, places, and histories back to people who were denied them.

For readers following this path, I offer encouragement and caution. Your results will be surprising—sometimes affirming, sometimes disorienting. Embrace them as a beginning, not a verdict. Remember that while **DNA is a powerful tool**, it is not a complete biography. Your story is shaped by migration and memory, but also by language, tradition, and self-definition.

In the coming pages, we'll dive deeper into **specific genome markers**, explore **haplogroup interpretations**, and explain how your **ethnicity estimates, admixture components**, and **historical matches** reveal the hidden architecture of your family's past. You'll learn how to read your own report, trace your paternal and maternal lines, and begin to tell your own ancestral story with confidence. But this story—of DNA, of ancient peoples, of bloodlines—is not just about those who descend from Highland clans or royal houses. It is not only for those with surnames etched in coats of arms. That would be a mistake, and an injustice. The deeper I've gone into my own ancestry, the more clearly, I've seen that **our genomes don't obey the boundaries history imposed**. The tools I used to uncover links to Picts and Celts can be used by anyone—from **Ghana to Jamaica to Ethiopia or Israel**, or any point in between—to begin reclaiming stories that were lost, stolen, or silenced.

One of the greatest myths of genealogy is that only certain lineages "matter." Often, when people of African, Indigenous, or diasporic descent enter these spaces, they are confronted with a sense of exclusion—either due to lack of documentation, colonial erasure, or the dominance of European narratives. This is where **genetic genealogy** becomes radical. DNA doesn't care about caste, colour, or colonial category. It carries deep time. And when someone from Jamaica, Ghana, or Ethiopia uploads their genome, they're not just seeing ancestry reports—they're participating in the restoration of **global human history**.

For instance, someone from **Ghana** might find their Y-DNA or mtDNA matches ancient samples from the **Sahel**, **Nok**, or **Niger-Congo speakers** who migrated during the Bantu expansion. They might see shared ancestry with people buried in Mali or Nigeria long before European empires ever rose. Platforms like **African Ancestry, Living DNA,** or **23andMe's African ancestry breakdown** now include reference panels from ethnic groups such as the **Akan, Yoruba, Mende, Igbo, and Mandinka**. These results allow people of African descent—especially those in the Americas whose family trees were severed by slavery—to reconnect with the specific cultures their ancestors came from. That knowledge is powerful. It is reclamation.

Similarly, someone from **Jamaica** may begin with West African roots but also discover traces of **Taino (indigenous Caribbean)** DNA, along with **European, South Asian,** or **Levantine** admixture. This reflects the complex colonial history of the Caribbean, where forced migration, resistance, and intermarriage wove together peoples from across the world. Their genome is a map of displacement, yes—but also of survival. Sites like **MyTrueAncestry**, **GEDmatch**, and **African DNA** allow these individuals to place themselves into global history not as passive bystanders but as rightful heirs to its legacies.

Even someone from **Ethiopia**—whose civilisation dates back to the Aksumite Empire, to pre-Axumic Cushitic kingdoms, to contact with Rome and Egypt—can find markers that link them to ancient East African pastoralists, Afroasiatic-speaking peoples, and perhaps even **back-migrations from the Middle East into Africa**.[5-6] Reich's work shows that Africa's genetic landscape is **the most diverse in the world**—because it is where humanity began. Ethiopian genomes contain some of the oldest unbroken maternal lines (e.g. **mtDNA haplogroup L3**, the one that gave rise to all non-African mtDNA lineages). That's not a local detail—it's a **global cornerstone** of our shared ancestry.

The idea that only European-derived populations hold meaningful genealogies is a relic of colonial thinking. It falsely elevates literacy and documentation over oral tradition, biological inheritance, and cultural continuity. The truth is every person on Earth carries within them a **genetic library of migration, adaptation, and resilience**. Someone reading this in Kingston or Accra or Addis Ababa may not see their ancestors named in the same historical texts as kings or dukes—but their DNA holds just as many secrets, and just as much majesty.

And that's why this book is for **you**, too. If you've ever felt excluded from history—because your family name doesn't appear in old registries, or because the records were burned, or never kept, or violently erased—genetic ancestry can be a new key. You do not need a documented tree going back 10 generations to begin. You only need your **curiosity** and your **DNA file**.

And yes, the methods apply to everyone. Whether you're a descendant of enslaved Africans, indentured South Asians, displaced Armenians, indigenous Amazonians, or European immigrants, these tools are democratic. They do not create belonging—but they reveal it. They show that the migrations which shaped our genomes are *shared*. That **the Celts and the Berbers, the Aksumites and the Scythians, the Gaels and the Yoruba— all left fingerprints on the same human canvas.**

This is not about proving descent from power. It's about **claiming your place in the story of human civilization**. Your genome contains the evidence.

In the chapters ahead, I'll walk you through how to understand that evidence. I'll explain haplogroups—like the **T2 maternal line** I share with thousands of people from the Mediterranean to the Levant, and the **R1b paternal line**, which spreads across Europe, West Asia, and parts of North Africa. I'll also explain why these haplogroups, while valuable, are just *one* part of the picture—and how autosomal DNA, admixture tools, and ancient sample comparisons add even more.

If you're holding your raw DNA file but don't know where to begin, I'll show you how to upload it, how to interpret your matches, and how to **connect those results to real human histories**. If you're a descendant of a community often left out of genealogy conversations, I promise you—you are *not* left out of the genetic story. You are its heartbeat.

We are all related. Not metaphorically, not symbolically—*literally*. The further back you go, the more those lines converge. The tools now exist to trace those connections. All that's left is to start.[35]

De Vere DNA Markers-

MY DNA MATCHES THROUGH SUSAN WRIGHT

Grand Princes of Kiev Z1a – Roman the Great (1152-1205) Grand Dukes of Lithuania Russian Royalty H3 – Peter II (1715-1730) Romanov's T2 – Nicholas II (1868-1918) H – Maria Feodorovna (1847-1928) H – Alexandra Feodorovna (1872-1918) Greek Royalty T2 – George I (1845-1913)

H – Sophia of Prussia (1870-1932) H – Princess Alice of Battenberg (1885-1969) H – Alexander (1893-1920) H – George II (1890-1947) H – Paul (1901-1964) H – Anne-Marie (1946-) H – Pavlos, Crown Prince of Greece (1967-) Romanian Royalty H – Ferdinand I (1865-1927) H – Michael (1921-) Bulgarian Royalty Polish Royalty H – Boleslaw I Chrobry (967-1025) H – Catherine of Austria (1533-1572) H – Anna of Austria (1573-1598) H – Wladyslaw IV Vasa (1595-1648) H – Constance of Austria (1588-1631) H – John II Casimir Vasa (1609-1672) H – Eleonora Maria Josefa of Austria (1653-1697)

T2 – Elisabeth of Austria (1436-1505) T2 - John I Albert (1459-1501) T2 - Alexander Jagiellon (1461-1506) T2 - Sigismund I of Poland (1467-1548)
N1b - Marie Louise Gonzaga (1611-1667) N1b - Marie Therese de Bourbon (1666-1732)

---

[35] *Bloodlines and Echoes: Genetic Clues to Nobility and Ancestral Identity. (Unpublished manuscript, 2025).*
True Ancestry: genetic platform report outputs (various ancient DNA matches, uploaded by author).

House of Grimaldi Portuguese Royalty H - Maria II (1819-1853) H - Pedro V (1837-1861) H - Luis I (1838-1889) Spanish Royalty U5b - Philip I of Castile (1478-1506) H - Margaret of Austria (1584-1611) H - Philip IV (1605-1665) H - Elisabeth of France (1602-1644) H - Mariana of Austria (1634-1696) H - Charles II (1661-1700) H - Marie Louise of Orleans (1662-1689) H - Maria Luisa of Savoy (1688-1714) H - Ferdinand VI (1713-1759) H - Isabella II (1830-1904) H - Alfonso XII (1857-1885) H - Victoria Eugenie of Battenberg (1887-1969) H - Sofia (1938-) H - Felipe,

Prince of Asturias (1968-) N1b - Maria Amalia of Saxony (1724-1760) N1b -
Charles IV of Spain (1748-1819) H3 - Maria Josepha of Saxony (1803-1829) Sardinian Royalty H - Charles Emmanuel III of Sardinia (1701-1773) H3 - Marie Christina of the Two Sicilies (1779-1849) H3 - Maria Theresa of Tuscany (1801-1855) Dukes of Parma Italian Royalty H3 - Victor Emmanuel II (1820-1878) Grand Duke of Tuscany H - Archduchess Joanna of Austria (1547-1578) H - Ferdinando II de' Medici (1610-1670)

French Royalty Z1a - Ingeborg of Denmark, Queen of France (1175-1236) U5b - Francis I (1494-1547) U5b - Henry IV (1553-1610) H - Marie de' Medici (1575-1642) H - Louis XIII (1601-1643) H - Maria Theresa of Spain (1638-1683) H - Louis, Dauphin of France (1661-1711) H - Louis XV (1710-1774)

N1b - Louis XVI (1754-1793) N1b - Louis XVIII of France (1755-1824) N1b - Charles X of France (1757-1836)

H3 - Marie-Antoinette (1755-1793) H3 - Louis XVII (1785-1795) H3 - Marie Louise of Austria (1791-1847) H3 - Maria Amalia of the Two Sicilies (1782-1866) Belgian Royalty H - Leopold I (1790-1865) H3 - Marie-Louise of France (1812-1850) H3 - Leopold II (1835-1909) H3 - Charlotte of Belgium (1840-1927) Grand Duke of Luxembourg H3 - William I (1772-1843) Stadtholder of Holland and Zeeland T2 - Maurice of Nassau, Prince of Orange (1567-1625) Kings of Saxony H3 - Frederick Augustus II (1797-1854) H3

- John I (1801-1873) Prussian Royalty T2 - Frederick William I of Prussia (1688-1740) H3 - Elisabeth Christine of Brunswick-Bevern (1715-1797) H3 - Frederick William II (1744-1797) H - Victoria of Prussia (1840-1901) H - Wilhelm II (1859-1941) Bohemian Royalty H - Boleslaus II the Pious (920-999) H - Anne of Bohemia and Hungary (1503-1546) H - Ferdinand IV of Bohemia and Hungary (1633-1654)

U5b - Henry VI of Carinthia (1270-1335) U5b - Rudolf I of Habsburg (1282-1307) U5b - Joanna of Bavaria (1362-1386) U5b - Albert II of Germany (1397-1439)
T2 - Elisabeth of Bohemia (1409-1442) T2 - Vladislas II of Bohemia and Hungary (1456-1516) T2 - Elizabeth Stuart (1596-1662)

N1b - Maria Amalia of Austria (1701-1756) N1b - Maria Luisa of Spain (1745-1792) Arpad Dynasty Bavarian Royalty

U5b - Louis II, Duke of Bavaria (1229-1294) U5b - Henry XIII, Duke of Bavaria (1235-1290) U5b - William II, Duke of Bavaria, Count of Holland, Zeeland and Hainaut (1365-1417) U5b - Albert II (1369-1397) U5b - John III, Duke of Bavaria-Straubing, Count of Holland and Hainaut (1374-1425) U5b - Louis IX, Duke of Bavaria-Landshut (1417-1479) German Royalty U5b - Elisabeth of Bavaria (1227-1273) U5b - Elizabeth of Carinthia (1262-1312) U5b - Frederick the Fair, Duke of Austria and King of Germany (1289-1330) U5b - Joanna of Bavaria, Queen of Germany and Bohemia (1362-1386) U5b - Albert II of Germany (1397-1439) Holy Roman Empire T2 -

 Barbara of Celje (1390-1451) H - Maximilian II of Habsburg (1527-1576) H - Ferdinand II of Habsburg (1578-1637) H - Leopold I of Habsburg (1640-1705)

 N1b - Maria Amalia of Austria (1701-1756) N1b - Maria Josepha of Bavaria (1739-1767) N1b - Maria Luisa of Spain (1745-1792) N1b - Francis II, Holy Roman Emperor (1768-1835) H3 - Leopold

II of Habsburg (1747-1792) Austrian Royalty U5b - Rudolf I of Habsburg, Duke of Austria and Styria, King of Bohemia, and titular King of Poland (1282-1307) U5b - Frederick I the Fair, Duke of Austria and Styria, and King of Germany (1289-1330) U5b - Leopold I of Habsburg, Duke of Austria and Styria (1290-1326) U5b - Albert II of Habsburg, Duke of Austria (1298-1358) U5b - Otto I of Habsburg, Duke of Austria (1301-1339).
 U5b - Albert II, King of Germany and Archduke of Austria (1397-1439) H3 - Maria Theresa (1717-1780) H3 - Joseph II (1741-1790) H3 - Ferdinand I (1793-1875) H3 - Maria Leopoldina of Austria (1797-1826) N1b - Francis II, Holy Roman Emperor (1768-1835) H - Charles I (1887-1922) Swedish Royalty Z1a - Richeza of Poland, Queen of Sweden (1116-1156) Z1a - Valdemar I of Sweden (1239-1302) Z1a - Magnus III of Sweden (1240-1290) T2 - Gustav II Adolf (1594-1632) T2 - Charles X Gustav (1622-1660) H - Olof Skötkonung (980-1022) H - Christina of Sweden (1626-1689) H - Margaret of Connaught (1882-1920) H - Louise Mountbatten (1889-1965) H - Ingrid (1910-2000) H - Carl XVI Gustaf (1946-) Norwegian Royalty Z1a - Rikissa Birgersdotter of Sweden, Queen of Norway (1237-1288) T2 - Olav V (1903-1991) Danish Royalty H - Sigrid the Haughty (968-1014) H - Harald II (980-1018) H - Canute the Great (994-1035) H - Sweyn II Estridson (1019-1076) H - Margrethe II (1940-) Z1a - Canute V of Denmark (1129-1157) Z1a - Sophia of Minsk, Queen consort of Denmark (1140-1198) Z1a - King Canute VI of Denmark (1163-1202) Z1a - King Valdemar II of Denmark (1170-1241)
Z1a - Queen Richeza of Denmark (1190-1220) T2 - Elizabeth (1524-1586) T2 - Anne (1574-1619) T2 - Christian III T2 - Christian IV T2 - Frederick VI T2 - Christian VIII T2 - Frederick VIII (1843-1912) H3 - Juliana Maria of Braunschweig-Wolfenbüttel (1729-1796) Scottish Royalty U5b - James III (1451-1488)

Clan Mackintosh Clan Douglas Clan McNab Clan Comyn Clan Abercrombie Clan Abernathy Clan Agnew Clan Ainslie Clan Bayne Clan Baird Clan Barron Clan Hamilton Clan Lindsay Clan Graham Clan MacDonald Clan Home Clan Gordon Clan Swinton Clan Spence Clan Skene Clan Paden Clan Nesbitt Clan Menzies Clan

Napier Clan Moffat Clan Grant Clan Bruce Clan Sutherland Clan Campbell Clan Drummond Clan MacPherson Clan Lyon Clan Munro Clan Montgomery Clan MacDougall Clan Cochrane Clan Sinclair Clan Erskine Clan Boyle Clan Murray Clan Cameron Clan Mackenzie Clan Macbean Clan Barclay Clan Boyd Clan Armstrong Clan Maclaren Clan Buchanan Clan MacGregor Clan MacLean Clan Colquhoun Clan Stirling Clan Donnachaidh Clan Cathcart Clan Kirkpatrick Clan Carruthers Clan Galbraith

English Royalty T2 - Charles I (1600-1649) T2 - George I (1660-1727) T2 - George III (1738-1820) T2 - Alexandra of Denmark (1844-1925) T2 - George V (1865-1936) H - Henrietta Maria of France (1609-1669) H - Charles II (1630-1685) H - James II (1633-1701) H - William III (1650-1702) H - Victoria (1819-1901) H - Edward VII (1841-1910) H - Prince Philip, Duke of Edinburgh J1c2c - Edward IV (1442-1483) J1c2c - Richard III (1452-1485) R30b - Prince William, Duke of Cambridge Ancient Egypt Persian Royalty Chinese Royalty Saudi Royalty Famous People H - Napoleon I (1769-1821) H3 - Napoleon II (1811-1832)

De Vere DNA Markers

MY DNA MATCHES THROUGH NICHOLAS DE VERE

Imperial House of Japan D1a2a1a2b1a1a8a - Emperor Seiwa (850-881) Nakatomi Clan O1b2a1a1c - Nakatomi no Amahisa-no-kimi Fujiwara Clan O1b2a1a1 - Fujiwara no Kamatari (668) Clan Baxter R1b1a1b1a1a2c1a6c - Reginar Longneck Count of Hainaut (850) R1b1a1b1a1a2c1a6c - William Baxtare (1312) Clan Riddell R1b1a1b1a1a2c1a1i2 - Gervase Ridale (1116) R1b1a1b1a1a2c1a1i2 - Sir William Riddell (1296) Clan Guthrie R1b1a1b1a1a2c1a5b - Alexander Guthrie (1442) Clan Glen R1b1a1b1a1a1c2b3c2a - Colban del Glen (1328) Clan Gray R1b1a1b1a1a2c1a1f1a - Fulbert de Gray (1066) Clan Pollock I2a1b1a2b1a2a1a1a1a3a1 - Petrus de Polos (1163)

Clan Watson R1b1a1b1a1a2c1a1e - John Watson (1392) R1b1a1b1a1a2c1a1e - George Watson (1723) Clan Greer R1b1a1b1a1a2c1a1a1a1a1a5 - Gilbert Grierson (1420) Clan Blair R1b1a1b1b3a1a1b - John Francis de Blair (1165-1214) Clan Dundas R1b1a1b1a1a2c1a1e - Serie de Dundas (1296) Clan Wishart R1b1a1b1a1a2a1 - John Wischard (1245) Clan Wemyss R1b1a1b1a1a2c1a5a - Sir John Wemyss (1421)

Clan Weir R1b1a1b1a1a2b - Radulphus de Vere (1150) Clan Lockhart R1b1a1b1a1a2c1a1a1a1a1b1 - Sir Simon Locard (1300-1371) Clan Durie I2a1b1a1a1a - Duncan de Dury (1258) Clan Fletcher R1b1a1b1a1a2c1a4b2c1a1a - Andrew Fletcher of Saltoun (1653-1716) Clan Mac Gobhann R1b1a1b1a1a2c1a1d3b1b2 - Neil Gow (1727) Clan Coyne R1b1a1b1a1a2c1a1a1a1a1b1 - Joseph Sterling Coyne (1803-1868)

Clan Mackendrick R1b1a1b1a1a2c1a5a2a1a3 - Big Henry son of Nechtan (900) Clan Lennox R1b1a1b1a1a2c1b1a - Mathew Earl of Lennox (1511) Clan Leslie I1a3a1a2a1 - George Leslie Earl of Rothes (1447) Clan Stewart R1b1a1b1a1a2c1a1a1a1a1b - Walter Flaad High Steward of Scotland (1164) Clan MacEwan R1b1a1b1a1a2c1a5a2a1a1 - Swene MacEwen (1493) Clan MacNaughten R1b1a1b1a1a2c1a5d3a - Gilchrist Macnachten (1297) Clan Vans R1b1a1b1a1a2c1a2a2a1a - William de Vaus of Direlton (1384)

Clan Urquhart I1a1b1a1e2c4a - William de Urquhart High Sheriff of Cromarty (1325-1395) Clan MacTavish R1b1a1b1a1a2c1a1f1c - Sir Thomas Campbel (1292) Clan MacQuarrie R1b1a1b1a1a2c1a1f1a3 - John Macquarrie of Ulva (1473) Clan Morrison R1b1a1b1a1a2c1a5b1a1a3a3 - Hutcheon Morrison (1550) Clan Johnstone R1b1a1b1a1a2c1a3a2 - John Johnstone (1194) Premyslid Dynasty R1b1a2a1a2c1b1b1a3a1 - Borivoj I (870-889) R1b1a2a1a2c1b1b1a3a1 - Spythinev (895-915) R1b1a2a1a2c1b1b1a3a1 - Vratislaus (915-921) R1b1a2a1a2c1b1b1a3a1 - Saint Wenceslaus (921-935) R1b1a2a1a2c1b1b1a3a1 - Bolesalus I the Cruel (935-972)

R1b1a2a1a2c1b1b1a3a1 - Bolesalus II the Pious (972-999)
R1b1a2a1a2c1b1b1a3a1 - Boleslaus III the Red-haired (999-1002)

Clan MacAulay R1b1a1b1a1a2a6 - Kenneth McAlpin King of the Picts (843-858) Clan MacArthur R1b1a1b1a1a1c1 - Iain MacArthur (1427) Clan MacGillivray R1b1a1b1a1a2c1a4b5a1 - Malcolm MacGillivray (1609) Clan ODuffy R1b1a1b1a1a2c1a5d3a1a - Murdagh ODuffy Archbishop of Tuam (1075-1150) Clan MacPhee R1b1a1b1a1a2c1a4d1 - Malcolm Macfie of Colonsay (1615) Clan Lamont R1b1a1b1a1a2c1a1a1a1a1a1a1 - Sir Laumon (1235) Clan Davidson I1a2a2a4b2c2 - Henry Davidson (1762) Clan MacCallum R1b1a1b1a1a1c1b - Ronald MacCallum (1510) Clan Ryan R1b1a1b1a1a2a - Righin mac Dubhghall (1268) Clan OLeary R1b1a1b1a1a2c1a3a2a1a2a1 - Lugaid Mac Con (173-203) Clan Hodnett R1b1a1b1a1a2c1a5b1a1a4a - William de Hodenet (1272) Clan Costello R1b1a1b1a1a2c1a4b2a1 - Gilbert de Nangle (1193) Clan Dillon R1b1a1b1a1a2c1a2b2b1 - Sir Henry de Leon (1169) Clan Tuite R1b1a1b1a1a2c1a1d7 - John de Tuite (1302) Clan Cotter R1b1a1b1a1a1c2b1b4d - Ottar King of Dublin (1142) Clan Crowley R1b1a1b1a1a2c1a3a2a1b1a - Auliff OCrowley (1488) Clan Carroll R1b1a1b1a1a2c1a5d - Domhnall OCarroll King of Ely (1241) Clan Dunn R1b1a1b1a1a2c1a1a1a1a1c1 - Gillananaomh ODuinn (1102-1160) Clan Kelly R1b1a1b1a1a2c1a1a1a1a1a1a2 - Cellach mac Fionachta (850) Clan Devlin R1b1a1b1a1a2c1a1a1a1a1a1a2c - ODevlin Bishop of Kells (1211) Clan McNamara R1b1a1b1a1a2c1a4b2a1 - Chieftain Cumara (1099) Clan Barrett R1b1a1b1a1a2c1a2b2b - John Baret (1086) Clan Prendergast R1a1a1a1b1a3a2 - Maurice Lord of Prendergast (1172) Clan Bissett R1b1a1b1a1a2c1a2a1a - Walter Byset Lord of Aboyne (1242)

Clan Plunkett R1b1a1b1a1a2c1a2a1a1a1b1 - Richard Plunkett (1340-1393) Clan Walsh R1b1a1b1a1a2c1a2b1a1a2a - Walter Walsh (1572) Clan McQuillan R1b1a1b1a1a2c1a5d3a1a - Hugelin de Mandeville Clan McMonagle R1b1a1b1a1a2c1a1a1a1a1a1a1a2 - Bishop Patrick Mac Moengal (1366) Clan Mac Suibhne R1b1a1b1a1a2c1a1f1a1 - Dubhghall Mac Suibhne (1232-1262) Clan

Doherty R1b1a1b1a1a2c1a1a1a1a1a1a1a2a - Donagh Dochartach (900) Clan McDonnell R1b1a1b1a1a2c1a5d3a1a - Mac Dhomhnaill (1427) Clan Madden R1b1a1b1a1a2c1a4b - Madudan mac Gadhra Mor (-1008) Clan Mooney R1b1a1b1a1a2c1a5a2a1a1 - Rory OMooney (1556) Clan OKeeffe R1b1a1b1a1a2c1a3a2a1a2c - Cathal mac Finguine (742) Clan Moore R1b1a1b1a1a2c1a5b1a1a2a1 - William de More (1086)

Clan Reynolds R1b1a1b1a1a2c1a4b4a1a1 - Eolais mac Biobhsach (900) Clan ORourke R1b1a1b1a1a2c1a1a1a1a1a1a3a - King Fergal ua Ruairc (961) Clan OFlaherty R1b1a1b1a1a2c1a1a1a1a1a1a3a - Muireadhach ua Flaithbheartach (1034) Clan MacCarthy R1b1a1b1a1a2c1a5a1a - Muireadhach Mac Carthaigh (1092) Clan Fitzgerald R1b1a1b1a1a2c1a3a2a1b1a2 - Gerald of Windsor (1075-1135) Clan Burke R1a1a1b1a2b3a3a1a2c2a - William de Burgh (1160-1206) Clan MacGuire R1b1a1b1a1a2c1a2a1a1a1b - Cormac ua Cuinn (204-244) Clan OSullivan R1b1a1b1a1a2c1a3a2 - Suilebhan mac Maolura (862) Clan Jordan R1b1a1b1a1a2a5 - Jordan de Exeter (1239-1258) Clan Dwyer R1b1a1b1a1a2a - Dubhuir mac Spealain (183) Clan Keating R1b1a1b1a1a2c1a4b2b1 - Geoffrey Keating (1569-1644) Clan Cogan R1b1a1b1a1a2c1a1a1a1a1a1a1a1a - Milo de Cogan (1182) Clan OHara R1b1a1b1a1a2c1a2b3a1 - Chief Eaghra (976) Clan Magennis R1b1a1b1a1a2c1a2a1a1a1 - Aedh Mor Magennis (1153) Clan Mac Oisdealbhaigh R1b1a1b1a1a2c1a4b2a1 - Oisdealb (1193) Clan Chaomanach R1b1a1b1a1a2c1a4a - Donal Kavanagh (1171-1175) Clan Eustace I1a2a1a1a1a2b - Bishop of Ely (1215) Clan Butler R1b1a1b1a1a2c1a4b2a1 - Theobald Walter (1205) Clan Le Poer I1a3g – Conmore Count of Poher (490) Clan Carnegie R1b1a1b1a1a1b1a1a - Duthac de Carnegie (1401) Clan McQueen R1b1a1b1a1a2c1a2b2b1 - Domhnall Mac Raghnuill (1250) Clan Farquharson R1b1a1b1a1a2c1a4b3 - Finla Mor (1547) Clan Kennedy R1b1a1b1a1a2c1a2a2a - John Kennedy of Dunure (1372) Clan Ruthven R1b1a1b1a1a2c1a5a2a1a1 - Sir Walter Ruthven (1296) Clan MacKay R1b1a1b1a1a2c1a4b2c1 - Iye Mackay (1210)

Clan Chisholm I1a1b1a1e2e - Sir Robert de Cheseholme (1359) Clan MacKinnon R1b1a1b1a1a2c1a1f1a3 - Findanus (900) Clan MacLachlan R1b1a1b1a1a2c1a1a1a1a1a2a2 - Gilchrist Maclachlan (1230) Clan Ogilvie R1b1a1b1a1a2c1a5a - Patrick de Ogilvy (1296) Clan Scott R1b1a1b1a1a1c2b2a1b1b1a1 - Henricus le Scotte (1195) Clan Cockburn R1b1a1b1a1a1b1a1a - Sir Roberto de Cokeburn (1261) Clan MacMillan R1b1a1b1a1a1c1b - Gille Chriosd Clan MacLellan R1b1a1b1a1a2c1a1d3b1b1 - Duncan MacLellan (1217) Clan MacAlister R1b1a1b1a1a2c1b1a - Alasdair Mor (1253) Clan MacFarlane R1b1a1b1a1a2c1b1a - Donnchadh Mac Pharlain (1544) Clan LaMont R1b1a1b1a1a2c1a1f1a - Sir Laumon (1235) Clan MacInnes R1b1a1b1a1a2c1a1b - Aonghais Mor (1294) R1b1a1b1a1a2c1a1b - Aonghais Og (1330) Clan Oliphant R1b1a1b1a1a2c1a6c - Roger Olifard (1093) Clan Elliott R1b1a1b1a1a2c1a2a2a1d1 - Gilbert Scott Elliot (1364) Clan Kerr R1b1a1b1a1a2c1a1a2a - William Ker of Kersland joined Wallace (1296) Clan MacNeil R1b1a1b1a1a2a1b2 - Gilleonan Macneil (1427) Clan Brodie R1b1a1b1a1a2c1a1f1a - Malcolm Brodie (1249-1285)

Clan Gunn R1b1a1b1a1a1b1a - George Gunn Coroner of Caithness (1380-1464) Clan Keith R1b1a1b1a1a2c1a5c1b1a - Sir Robert de Keith (1316) Clan Pringle R1b1a1b1a1a1c2f - David Pringle (1513) Clan Hay R1b1a1b1a1a2b1 - William II de Haya (1160) Clan Dunbar R1b1a1b1a1a1b1a1a - Gospatric Earl of Northumbria (1073) Clan Fraser R1b1a1b1a1a2c1a1e1 - Simon Fraser (1306) Clan MacThomas R1b1a1b1a1a1b - Thomas Tomaidh Mor (1430) Clan Ross R1b1a1b1a1a2c1a2 - Fearchar (1214-1249) Clan Mac Giolla Bhrighde I1a2a1a1a2a2a - John MacGilbride Bishop of Raphoe (1440) Clan Wallace R1b1a1b1a1a1c1a1 - William Wallace Clan Irwin R1b1a1b1a1a2c1a1e1 - Scottish Clan House of Stewart R1b1a1b1a1a2c1a1d1a - Robert II King of Scotland (1371-1390) R1b1a1b1a1a2c1a1d1a - Robert III (1390-1406) R1b1a1b1a1a2c1a1d1a - James I (1406-1437) R1b1a1b1a1a2c1a1d1a - James II (1437-1460) R1b1a1b1a1a2c1a1d1a - James III (1460-1488) R1b1a1b1a1a2c1a1d1a - James IV (1488-1513) R1b1a1b1a1a2c1a1d1a - James V (1513-1542)

R1b1a1b1a1a2c1a1d1a - Mary (1542-1567) R1b1a1b1a1a2c1a1d1a - James VI (1567-1625) R1b1a1b1a1a2c1a1d1a1 -

Sir John Stewart of Bonkyll (1245-1298) R1b1a1b1a1a2c1a1d1a3 - Alexander Stewart the Wolf of Badenoch Kingdom of Mann R1b1a1b1a1a2a1b2 - Olof the Black House of Lippe Detmold R1b1a1b1a1a2 - Bernhard I (1123) House von Amsberg R1a1a1b1a2b3a3a1b1 - Juergen Amtsberg (11640-686) R1a1a1b1a2b3a3a1b1 - Prince Claus of the Netherlands (1926-2002) R1a1a1b1a2b3a3a1b1 - King Willem-Alexander of the Netherlands (1967-) House of Saxe-Coburg R1b1a1b1a1a1c1a1 - Ernest I Duke of Saxe-Coburg and Gotha (1784-1844) House of Capet J1a2b1b2c1 - King Hugh Capet of France Clann Mac Diarmada R1b1a1b1a1a2c1a1a1a1a1a1a2 - Dermot Mac Tadhg Mor 7th King of Moylurg (1124-1159) R1b1a1b1a1a2c1a1a1a1a1a1a2 - Tadhg Mac Diarmata (1585) Clann ODomhnaill R1b1a1b1a1a2c1a1a1a1a1a1a1 - Niall Noigiallach King of Tara (405) R1b1a1b1a1a2c1a1a1a1a1a1a1

HIGH KINGS OF IRELAND DNA MARKERS
Kings of Tyrconnell R1b1a1b1a1a2c1a1a1a1a1a1a1 - King of Leth Cuinn Clann Chindfaoladh R1b1a1b1a1a2c1a1a1a1a1a1a1a - Conall Gulban son of Niall of the Nine Hostages (464) Clann Ui Eidersceoil I2a1a2a1b1c1a - Lughaidh Laidhe Clann McGrath R1b1a1b1a1a2c1a1a1a1a1a1a2 - Echthighern Mac Cennetig (?-950) R1b1a1b1a1a2c1a1a1a1a1a1a2 - Craith (970) R1b1a1b1a1a2c1a1a1a1a1a1a2 - Archbishop Miller McGrath (1523-1622) Clann ODuibhgeannain R1a1a1b2a2a1d9c2a - Maine of Tethba R1a1a1b2a2a1d9c2a - Maelpeter ODuigennan Archdeacon of Breifny Clann OMaolagain R1b1a1b1a1a2c1a1a1a1a1a1a5 - Chiefs of Tir MacCarthainn Clann OLachtna R1b1a1b1a1a2c1a1a1a1a1a1a - Eochaidh Muighmheadhoin King of Ireland (350 AD) R1b1a1b1a1a2c1a1a1a1a1a1a - Ui Fiachrach chiefs of the Two Bats and Glen Nephin R1b1a1b1a1a2c1a1a1a1a1a1a - Conghalach OLoughlin Bishop of Corcomroe (1281) Clann Mac Donnchada R1b1a1b1a1a2c1a3a2a1a2d1a - Donnchad Midi High King of

Ireland (733-797) R1b1a1b1a1a2c1a3a2a1a2d1a - Conchobar Mac Donnchada High King of Ireland (819-833) Clann Mac Murchadha R1b1a1b1a1a2c1a4a1 - Diarmait Mac Murchada King of Leinster (1110-1171) Clann Coffey R1b1a1b1a1a2c1a3a2a1b1b - Dermot OCoffey (1580) Clann Dal gCais R1b1a1b1a1a2c1a4b2a1a1 - Brian Boruma mac Cennetig (941-1014) Clann Deaghaidh R1b1a1b1a1a2c1a4b2a1c - Chief Deaghaidh (934)

Clann Laigin R1b1a1b1a1a2c1a1a1a1a1 - Labraid Loingsech High King of Ireland (369) Clann Mac Bradaigh R1b1a1b1a1a2c1a4b2c1a - Thomas Brady (1752-1827) Clann Mag Samhradhain R1b1a1b1a1a2c1a1a1a1a1a1a3a - Muireadhach mac Samhradhain (1115-1148) Riddarhuset Gyllencreutz R1b1a1b1a1a2c1a4b2c1a1b1b1 - Lars Tygesson (?-1625) Riddarhuset Lillieskold R1b1a1b1a1a1c2b2a1b2 - Jesperus Marci (?-1591) Riddarhuset Tawast N1a1a1a1a1a1a1b2a2a1 - Jakob Kaas (?-1529) Riddarhuset Loewenhielm I1a1b1b1c - Gudmund Norberg (1656-1739) Riddarhuset Aminoff G2a2b1a1b1a2 - Feodor Aminoff (1565-1628) Riddarhuset Uggla R1b1a1b1a1a1c2b2a1b1a1a2b2a - Claes Hansson (?-1529) Riddarhuset Silfverskiold R1a1a1b1a3a1a2e2a - Niklas Andersson Hylten (1635-1702) Riddarhuset Stierna R1a1a1b1a2b3a1d5a1b - Olof Olofsson Stjaerna (1430-1498) Riddarhuset Bure G2a2b2a1a1b1a1a2a1b2a1 - Olof Bure (1578-1655) Welsh Royalty R1b1a1b1a1a2c1a5a1 - Pasgen ap Urien, King of Gwyr (522)

Grand Princes of Kiev N1a1a1a1a1a1a - Vladimir II Monomakh (1053-1125) N1a1a1a1a1a1a - Mstislav I of Kiev (1076-1132) N1a1a1a1a1a1a - Yaropolk II of Kiev (1082-1139) N1a1a1a1a1a1a - Viacheslav I of Kiev (1083-1154) N1a1a1a1a1a1a - Yuri Dolgorukiy (1090-1157) N1a1a1a1a1a1a - Iziaslav II of Kiev (1097-1154) N1a1a1a1a1a1a - Rostislav I of Kiev (1110-1167) N1a1a1a1a1a1a - Yaroslav II of Kiev (1132-1180) N1a1a1a1a1a1a - Roman the Great (1152-1205) N1a1a1a1a1a1a - Rurik Rostislavich (-1215) N1a1a1a1a1a1a - Ingvar of Kiev (1152-1220) N1a1a1a1a1a1a - Mstislav III of Kiev (died 1223) N1a1a1a1a1a1a - Rostislav II of Kiev (1173-1214) N1a1a1a1a1a1a - Vladimir IV Rurikovich (1187-

1239) N1a1a1a1a1a1a - Daniel of Galicia (1201-1264) N1a1a1a1a1a1a - Alexander Nevsky (1220-1263) N1a1a1a1a1a1a - Lev I of Galicia (1228-1301) N1a1a1a1a1a1a - Yaroslav of Tver (1230-1271) N1a1a1a1a1a1a - Yuri I of Galicia (1252-1308) N1a1a1a1a1a1a - Andrew of Galicia (?-1323) N1a1a1a1a1a1a - Lev II of Galicia (?-1323) Grand Dukes of Lithuania N1a1 - House of Gediminas (1285-1440) Russian Royalty Romanovs R1b - Paul I (1754-1801) R1b - Alexander I (1777-1825) R1b - Constantine I (1779-1831) R1b - Nicholas I (1796-1855) R1b - Alexander II (1818-1881) R1b - Alexander III (1845-1894) R1b - Nicholas II (1868-1918) Greek Royalty R1b - George I (1845-1913) R1b - Constantine I (1868-1923) R1b - Alexander (1893-1920) R1b - George II (1890-1947) Romanian Royalty Bulgarian Royalty R1b1a1b1a1a1a - Ferdinand I (1861-1948) R1b1a1b1a1a1a - Boris III (1894-1943) R1b1a1b1a1a1a - Simeon II (b. 1937) Polish Royalty J2b2a1a1a1b -

House of Lubomirski House of Grimaldi I1a1b1a1e2 - Jacques I, Prince of Monaco (1689-1751) I1a1b1a1e2 - Honoré III (1720-1795) I1a1b1a1e2 - Honoré IV (1758-1819) I1a1b1a1e2 - Florestan I (1785-1856) I1a1b1a1e2 - Charles III (1818-1889) I1a1b1a1e2 - Albert I (1848-1922) I1a1b1a1e2 - Louis II (1870-1949) Portuguese Royalty R1b1a1b1a1a1a - Pedro V (1837-1861) R1b1a1b1a1a1a - Luis I (1838-1889) R1b1a1b1a1a1a - Carlos I (1863-1908) R1b1a1b1a1a1a - Manuel II (1889-1932) Spanish Royalty Sardinian Royalty Dukes of Parma R1b1b2a1a1b -

House of Bourbon-Parma Italian Royalty Grand Duke of Tuscany French Royalty R1b1b2a1a1b - Francis I (1494-1547) R1b1b2a1a1b - Henry IV (1553-1610) R1b1b2a1a1b - Louis XIII (1601-1643) R1b1b2a1a1b -

Louis, Dauphin of France (1661-1711) R1b1b2a1a1b - Louis XV (1710-1774) R1b1b2a1a1b - Louis XVI (1754-1793) R1b1b2a1a1b - Louis XVII (1785-1795) R1b1b2a1a1b - Louis XVIII of France (1755-1824) R1b1b2a1a1b - Charles X of France (1757-1836) G2a - Louis XVI Relic G2a - Henri IV Relic Belgian Royalty

R1b1a1b1a1a1a - Leopold I (1790-1865) R1b1a1b1a1a1a - Leopold II (1835-1909) R1b1a1b1a1a1a - Albert I (1875-1934) R1b1a1b1a1a1a - Leopold III (1901-1983) R1b1a1b1a1a1a - Baldwin I (1930-1993) R1b1a1b1a1a1a - Albert II (1934-) R1b1a1b1a1a2c1a6c - House of Reginarids R1b1a1b1a1a2c1a6c - Counts of Hainaut R1b1a1b1a1a2c1a6c - Counts of Louvain and Brussels R1b1a1b1a1a2c1a6c - Dukes of Brabant and Lothier R1b1a1b1a1a2c1a6c - House of Hesse Grand Duke of Luxembourg Stadtholder of Holland and Zeeland Kings of Saxony Prussian Royalty Bohemian Royalty Arpad Dynasty R1a1a1b2a2a - Bela III R1a1a1b2a2a - Emeric R1a1a1b2a2a - Ladislaus III R1a1a1b2a2a - Andrew II R1a1a1b2a2a - Bela IV R1a1a1b2a2a - Stephen V R1a1a1b2a2a - Ladislaus IV R1a1a1b2a2a - Andrew, Duke of Slavonia Bavarian Royalty German Royalty I2a1b1a2a1b - House of Hohenzollern I2a1b1a2a1b -

Dukes of Prussia (1525-1701) I2a1b1a2a1b - Kings of Prussia (1701-1918) I2a1b1a2a1b - Frederick William I2a1b1a2a1b - Frederick I I2a1b1a2a1b - Frederick William I I2a1b1a2a1b - German Emperors (1871-1918) I2a1b1a2a1b - William I I2a1b1a2a1b - Frederick III I2a1b1a2a1b - William II R1b1a1b1a1a1c1a1 - House of Wettin Holy Roman Empire Austrian Royalty R1b1a1b1a1a2b1 - Habsburg Family R1b - Leopold I, Margrave of Austria (died 994) R1b - Henry I, Margrave of Austria (died 1018) R1b - Adalbert, Margrave of Austria (985-1055) R1b - Ernest, Margrave of Austria (1027-1075) R1b - Leopold II, Margrave of Austria (1050-1095) R1b - Leopold III, Margrave of Austria (1073-1136) R1b - Leopold IV, Margrave of Austria, aka Leopold I, Duke of Bavaria (1108-1141) R1b - Henry II, Duke of Austria, aka Henry XI, also Duke of Bavaria (1107-1177) R1b - Leopold V, Duke of Austria (1157-1194) R1b - Frederick I, Duke of Austria (1175-1198) R1b - Leopold VI, Duke of Austria (1176-1230) R1b - Frederick II, Duke of Austria (1211-1246) Swedish Royalty I1 - Valdemar I of Sweden (1239-1302) I1 - Magnus III of Sweden (1240-1290) I1 - Birger I of Sweden (1280-1321) I1 - Valdemar, Duke of Finland (1280s-1318) I1 - Magnus IV of Sweden (1316-1374) I1 - Eric XII of Sweden (1339-1359) I1 -

Haakon VI of Sweden & Norway (1340-1380) R1b - Christian I
(1426-1481) R1b - John (1455-1513) R1b - Christian II (1481-1559)
G2a2b2a1a1b1a1a2a1b2a1 - Gamla Olof Heresson Bure
Norwegian Royalty I1 -

Haakon VI of Sweden & Norway (1340-1380) R1b - Haakon VII
(1872-1957) R1b - Olav V (1903-1991) R1b - Harald V (1937-)
Danish Royalty I1 - Olaf II of Denmark & Norway (1370-1387)
R1b - Christian I (1426-1481) R1b - John (1455-1513) R1b -
Christian II (1481-1559) R1b - Frederick I R1b - Christian III R1b -
Frederick II R1b - Christian IV R1b - Frederick III R1b - Christian
V R1b - Frederick IV R1b - Christian VI R1b - Frederick V R1b -
Christian VII R1b - Frederick VI R1b - Christian VIII R1b -
Frederick VII R1b - Christian IX (1818-1906) R1b - Frederick VIII
(1843-1912) R1b - Christian X (1870-1947) R1b - Frederick IX
(1899-1972) Scottish Royalty R1b1a1b1a1a2c - Robert II
R1b1a1b1a1a2c - Robert III R1b1a1b1a1a2c - James I
R1b1a1b1a1a2c - James II R1b1a1b1a1a2c - James III
R1b1a1b1a1a2c - James IV R1b1a1b1a1a2c - James V J2a1 - Earl of
Eglinton (1460-1545) R1a1a1b1a3a1a1a -

Somerled of Argyll (1100-1164) Clan MacKintosh
I2a1b1a2b1a2a3b1a1 - Shaw MacDuff (1160) Clan Douglas
E1b1b1a1b1a10b - Alexander Douglas (1625) Clan McNab
R1b1a1b1a1a2c1a1a1a1a1 - Fergus Mac Echdach (778) Clan Comyn
R1b1a1b1a1a2c1a4b2c1 - Richard Comyn (1115-1179) Clan
Abercrombie R1b1a1b1a1a2c1a1e - Robert Abercromby (1534)
R1b1a1b1a1a2c1a1e - Sir Ralph Abercromby (1734-1801) Clan
Abernathy R1b1a1b1a1a2c1a - Orm de Abernethy (1170) Clan
Agnew I2a1b1a1a1a1a1b3 - Alastair (1299) Clan Ainslie
R1a1a1b1a1a1c1e - Thomas de Aneslei (1221) Clan Bayne
R1b1a1b1a1a2c1a1h1 - Donald Mackay (1370) Clan Baird
R1a1a1b1a3a1a - Richard Baird (1390) Clan Barron
R1b1a1b1a1a1c1a2b - Bonaventure Baron (1610-1696) Clan
Hamilton I1a2a1a1a4 - Walter Fitz Gilbert of Hambledon
I1a2a1a1a4 - Laird of Cadzow (1315) I1a2a1a1a4 - Lord Hamilton
(1445) I1a2a1a1a4 - Earl of Arran (1503) I1a2a1a1a4 - Marquess of

Hamilton (1599) I1a2a1a1a4 - Duke of Hamilton (1643) Clan Lindsay I2a1a1b1a1b2 - Sir Walter de Lindissie I2a1a1b1a1b2 - Earl of Crawford (1398-present) I2a1a1b1a1b2 - Earl of Lindsay (1633-present) I2a1a1b1a1b2 - Earl of Balcarres (1651-present) Clan Graham J1a1b1b1a2a1a1a1a - Clan Graham Clan MacDonald R1a1a1b1a3a - Clan MacDonald Clan Home R1a1a1b1a3a1a1 - Cospatric I Anglo-Danish Earl of Northumbria (1073) R1a1a1b1a3a1a1 - Earl of Home (1605-present) Clan Gordon R1b1a1b1a1a1e1b - Alexander Seton (1408) R1b1a1b1a1a1e1b - Alexander Gordon 1st Earl of Huntly (1470) R1b1a1b1a1a1e1b - Marquesses of Huntly (1599-present) R1b1a1b1a1a1e1b - Dukes of Gordon (1684-1836) R1b1a1b1a1a1e1b -

Earls of Aberdeen (1682) R1b1a1b1a1a1e1b -

Marquesses of Aberdeen and Temair (1916-present) Clan Swinton R1a1a1b1a3a1a1 - Ernulf de Swinton (1136) Clan Spence R1b1a1b1a1a2c1a4a - Thomas de Spens (1296) Clan Skene R1b1a1b1a1a1e2a - John de Skeen (1093) R1b1a1b1a1a1e2a - Robert Skene (1317) Clan Paden R1b1a1b1a1a1c2c1 - Hugh Pethin (1611) Clan Nesbitt R1b1a1b1a1a2c1a5b1a1 - Alexander Nisbet (1657-1725) Clan Menzies R1b1a1b1a1a2c1a6 - Sir Robert de Myneris (1237) Clan Napier R1b1a1b1a1a2c1a1e1 - Sir Archibald Napier of Merchiston (1625) Clan Moffat R1b1a1b1a1a1c2b2a1b1a1a1 - Nicholas de Moffat (1286) Clan Grant R1b1a1b1a1a2e1 - Duncan Grant of Freuchie (1413-1485) R1b1a1b1a1a2e1 - Earls of Seafield (1701-present) R1b1a1b1a1a2e1 - Barons Strathspey (1858-present) Clan Bruce R1b1a2a1a2a - Robert the Bruce R1b1a2a1a2a - David II of Scotland R1b1a2a1a2a - Edward Bruce R1b1a2a1a2a - Lords of Annandale (1124) R1b1a2a1a2a - Barons of Clackmannan R1b1a2a1a2a - Lords Bruce of Kinloss (1608) R1b1a2a1a2a - Earls of Elgin (1633) R1b1a2a1a2a - Earls of Kincardine (1647) Clan Sutherland R1b1a1b1a1a2a - Freskin of Flanders R1b1a1b1a1a2a - William de Moravia (1210-1248) R1b1a1b1a1a2a - Earl of Tullibardine (1606) R1b1a1b1a1a2a - Earl of Atholl (1629)

R1b1a1b1a1a2a - Marquess of Atholl (1676) R1b1a1b1a1a2a - Duke of Atholl (1703)

Clan Campbell R1b1a1b1a1a2c1a1f1c1 - Lord Campbell (1445) R1b1a1b1a1a2c1a1f1c1 - Earl of Argyll (1457) R1b1a1b1a1a2c1a1f1c1 - Marquess of Argyll (1641) R1b1a1b1a1a2c1a1f1c1 - Duke of Argyll (1701-present) R1b1a1b1a1a2c1a1f1c1 - Earls of Loudoun (1633-1786) Clan Drummond R1b1a1b1a1a2c1a2a2a1e - Lord Drummond of Cargill (1488) R1b1a1b1a1a2c1a2a2a1e - Earl of Perth (1605-present) R1b1a1b1a1a2c1a2a2a1e - Duke of Perth (1716-1800) Clan MacPherson R1b1a1b1a1a2c1a2a3a - Clan MacPherson Clan Lyon I1a1b1a1d - John Lyon Lord of Glamis (1340-1382) I1a1b1a1d - Lord Glamis (1445) I1a1b1a1d - Earls of Kinghorne (1606) I1a1b1a1d - Earls of Srathmore and Kinghorne (1677-present) I1a1b1a1d - Claude Bowes-Lyon Clan Munro I2a1a2a1b1a2b - Munros of Foulis I2a1a2a1b1a2b - James Monroe (1758-1831) Clan Montgomery J2a1a2b2a2b2a2b - Alexander Montgomerie 1st Lord Montgomerie (1470) J2a1a2b2a2b2a2b - Earl of Eglinton (1508-present) J2a1a2b2a2b2a2b - Earl of Winton (1859-present) Clan MacDougall R1a1a1b1a3a1a1a - Clan MacDougall Clan Cochrane R1a1a1b1a3a1b3c1b - Waldenus De Cochrane (1240-1300) R1a1a1b1a3a1b3c1b - Earl of Dundonald (1669-present) Clan Sinclair R1b1a1b1a1a1c2b2a1b1a4b2a2c1a1 - Earl of Orkney (1739-1479) R1b1a1b1a1a1c2b2a1b1a4b2a2c1a1 - Earl of Caithness (1455-present)

Clan Erskine R1b1a1b1a1a2b2 - John Erskine 19th Earl of Mar (1558-1634) Clan Boyle R1b1a1b1a1a2a1b1a1 - Earls of Glasgow Clan Murray R1b1a1b1a1a2a - Freskin of Flanders R1b1a1b1a1a2a - William de Moravia (1210-1248) R1b1a1b1a1a2a - Earl of Tullibardine (1606) R1b1a1b1a1a2a - Earl of Atholl (1629) R1b1a1b1a1a2a - Marquess of Atholl (1676) R1b1a1b1a1a2a - Duke of Atholl (1703) Clan Cameron R1b1a1b1a1a2c1a4d1 - Cameron of Lochiel R1b1a1b1a1a2c1a4d1 - Donal Dubh Clan Mackenzie R1b1a1b1a1a2c1a2a2d - Kenneth Mackenzie 1st of Kintail (1304) R1b1a1b1a1a2c1a2a2d - Earl of

Seaforth (1623-1781) R1b1a1b1a1a2c1a2a2d - Earl of Cromartie (1703-1746) R1b1a1b1a1a2c1a2a2d - Alexander Mackenzie of Kintail Clan Macbean R1b1a1b1a1a2c1a1f1a - Gilles MacBean (1746) Clan Barclay I2a1a1a1a1a1a1 - Barclay de Tolly I2a1a1a1a1a1a1 - Michael Andreas Barclay de Tolly (1761-1818)

Clan Boyd R1b1a1b1a1a1c2a1c2 - Lord Boyd (1454) R1b1a1b1a1a1c2a1c2 - Earl of Kilmarnock (1661-1746) Clan Armstrong R1b1a1b1a1a2 - Lowland Scottish Clan Armstrong R1b1a1b1a1a2 - Neil Armstrong Clan MacLaren R1b1a1b1a1a2c1a1f1a1 - Highland Scottish Clan MacLaren Clan Buchanan R1b1a1b1a1a2c1a1f1 - Anselan O Kyan King of North Ulster (1016) R1b1a1b1a1a2c1a1f1 - Sir Alexander Buchanan (1424) R1b1a1b1a1a2c1a1f1 - Sir George Buchanan (1650) Clan MacGregor R1b1a1b1a1a2c1a1f1 - Rob Roy MacGregor (1671-1734) R1b1a1b1a1a2c1a1f1 - Baronet MacGregor of MacGregor (1795-present) Clan MacLean R1b1a1b1a1a2c1a2a2a1b1 - Gillean of the Battle Axe (1263) R1b1a1b1a1a2c1a2a2a1b1 - Lachlan Lubanach Maclean (1325-1405) Clan Colquhoun E1b1b1a1b1a14a - John Calhoun (1782-1850) Clan Stirling I1a2a1a1a2a1 - Thoraldus de Strivelyn (1147) I1a2a1a1a2a1 - Alexander de Strivelyn Laird of Cadder (1304) I1a2a1a1a2a1 - Sir John de Strivelyn (1333) Clan Donnachaidh R1b1a1b1a1a2b - Donnachaidh Reamhar (1306) R1b1a1b1a1a2b - Robert Riabhach Duncanson (1406) R1b1a1b1a1a2b - Alexander Robertson (1645) Clan Cathcart R1b1a1b1a1a2a - Rainaldus de Kethcart (1178) R1b1a1b1a1a2a - William de Cathcart (1296) R1b1a1b1a1a2a - Alan Cathcart 4th Lord Cathcart (1568) Clan Kirkpatrick E1b1b1a1b1a14a - Sir Roger Kirkpatrick (1357) Clan Carruthers I1a1b1b - Nigel de Karruthers (1380) I1a1b1b - Sir Simon Carruthers (1548) Clan Galbraith R1b1a1b1a1a1c2b1b - Gilchrist Bretnach R1b1a1b1a1a1c2b1b - Sir William Galbraith of Buthernock (1255)

English Royalty G2 - Richard III (1452-1485) R1b1a1b1a1a2c - James I (1566-1625) R1b1a1b1a1a2c - Charles I (1600-1649) R1b1a1b1a1a2c - Charles II (1630-1685) R1b1a1b1a1a2c - James II

(1633-1701) R1b1a1b1a1a1c1a1 - Edward VII (1841-1910) R1b1a1b1a1a1c1a1 - George V (1865-1936) R1b1a1b1a1a1c1a1 - Edward VIII (1894-1972) R1b1a1b1a1a1c1a1 - George VI (1895-1952) R1b - Prince Philip, Duke of Edinburgh R1b - Charles, Prince of Wales R1b - Prince William, Duke of Cambridge I2a1b1a1a1b - House of Clinton I2a1b1a1a1b - Sir John de Clinton 1st Baron Clinton I2a1b1a1a1b - Earls of Lincoln (1572-present) I2a1b1a1a1b - Dukes of Newcastle-under-Lyne (1768-1988) I2a1b1a1a1b - Sir Henry Clinton (1730-1795)

Ancient Egypt E1b1a - Ramesses III (1217 BC-1155 BC) Persian Royalty J1 - Fath Ali Shah Qajar (1772-1834)

Chinese Royalty C-M401 - Nurhaci, Qing dynasty (1559-1626) Saudi Royalty J1-FGC2 - Muhammad bin Saud (1744-1818) Famous People D1b1a2b1a1 - Emperor Higashiyama O2a2b1a1a1c - Hata Clan Japan E1b1b1b2a1a - Napoleon I (1769-1821) I2a2a - Napoleon III E1b1a - Nelson Mandela E1b1b1 - Lyndon B Johnson E1b1b1 - Adolf Hitler E1b1b1 - David Attenborough E1b1b1 - Richard Attenborough E1b1b1a2 - Orville Wright E1b1b1a2 - Wilbur Wright E1b1b1a2 - Albert Einstein G2a1 - Joseph Stalin I1 - Leo Tolstoy I1 - Warren Buffett I1 - Alexander Hamilton I1 - Calvin Coolidge I1 - Bill Clinton I1 - Sting I2a1a2b - Martin Luther I2a1a2b - Novak Djokovic I2a1a2a1b1a2b - James Monroe I2a1b1a1a1b - Bill Gates R1a1a1b1a1a1c1 - Nikola Tesla I2a1b1a2b1 - John Tyler I2a1b1a2b1a2 - Davy Crockett I2a1b1a2b1a3a1a1a - Andrew Johnson I2a1b1a2b1a2a1a1a1a1a2 - Chuck Norris I2a1b1a2b1a2a1a1a1a3a1 - Steven King I2a2a1b1b1a1a1 - Elvis Presley I2a2a1 - Duke of Hamilton I2a2a1 - Henry Luce I2a2b - Myles Standish I2a2b - Paul Reynaud R1a1a1b1a2 - Max von Sydow J2a1a1a2b2a2b3a - Rothschild Family J2a1a1b2a1a - Prime Minister John Curtin R1a1a1a1d2b3 - Sir Francis Drake R1a1 - Tom Hanks R1b1a1b1a1a2b1 - George Washington R1b1a1b1a1a2b1c1b - Abraham Lincoln R1b - John Adams R1b - John Quincy Adams R1b - Ulysses S Grant R1b -

William McKinley R1b - Woodrow Wilson R1b - Che Guevara R1b - Charles Darwin[36]

How Our DNA Reveals We're All Related

Ancient DNA is teaching us that much of what we are taught is actually incorrect, The Scientists have found that they were wrong. What they have found is that we all come from mixed DNA and that no one is "pure"[37]

To understand how someone in Ethiopia, Ghana, or Jamaica might share ancestry with a Celt from the Hebrides or a Gaul from Iron Age France, we need to look closer at how our DNA works. There are two main ways to explore genetic ancestry: **haplogroups** and **autosomal DNA**. Each tells a different kind of story—and together, they prove that our identities are far more entangled than most of us realize.

Haplogroups are like deep-time surnames for our DNA. They trace unbroken lines—either the paternal line (from father to son via the Y chromosome) or the maternal line (from mother to all her children via mitochondrial DNA). Haplogroups mutate slowly, so they're useful for tracking large-scale prehistoric migrations. For example, my father carries **R1b**, a Y-DNA haplogroup common among Celtic and Western European men. My mother carries **T2**, a mitochondrial haplogroup that traces back to the ancient Near East and Mediterranean basin. But these haplogroups only tell us about *two ancestors*—my father's father's father, and my mother's mother's mother—out of the thousands I actually descend from.

---

[36] *Mytrueancestry.com, Accessed on Aug 2025 uploaded by Author*
[37] *David Reich, Who We Are and How We Got Here: Ancient DNA and the Science of the Human Past (Cambridge, MA: Harvard University Press, 2018)*

Haplogroups are powerful, but narrow. They leave out the other 99.9% of our ancestry.

That's where **autosomal DNA** comes in.

Autosomal DNA is everything else—your 22 non-sex chromosomes. This is what you inherit from *all* of your ancestors, mixed together in a unique combination. It changes with every generation. While haplogroups tell us about fixed lines, **autosomal DNA tells us about relationships, ethnicity, and shared history**. It's the data used to determine admixture (e.g. "40% West African, 20% North European") and to find genetic relatives from across the globe.

Because it recombines with every generation, autosomal DNA is the most democratic part of your genome. It remembers not just royalty or warriors, but farmers, nomads, enslaved people, traders, poets, and rebels. It includes ancestors from every part of your family tree, whether you know their names or not. And that's what makes it so powerful for proving how deeply, biologically, we are all related.

Every person on Earth shares **99.9% of their DNA**. The differences that remain reflect recent evolution—adaptations to climate, diet, or disease. Skin colour, for example, is a tiny genetic adaptation based on latitude and UV exposure. It has nothing to do with "race" in any biological sense. And yet, the legacy of racial thinking has caused many to assume that someone of African descent cannot have European ancestry, or that someone with light skin couldn't carry ancient African or Middle Eastern genes. But the science tells a different story.

Let's start in **Africa**—because that's where all modern humans come from. The deepest haplogroups, such as **L0, L1, L2, and L3**, are all African in origin. Every non-African person alive today descends from a small subset of African humans who left the continent roughly 60,000–70,000 years ago. These migrants carried African DNA into Asia, Europe, and eventually the Americas. As they spread out, they adapted to new climates and mixed with archaic humans (Neanderthals and Denisovans), but their roots remained the same.

People who stayed in Africa retained the deepest genetic diversity in the world. For instance, the **San people of southern Africa** have been genetically distinct for over 100,000 years—meaning their DNA holds the closest connection to the original Homo sapiens lineage.[7] A person from Ghana, Nigeria, or Ethiopia today is likely to carry ancestral links not only to these ancient African branches, but also to waves of later migrations: Nilotic pastoralists from the northeast, Bantu-speaking farmers from central Africa, Islamic traders from the Sahel, and even Roman, Greek, or Arabian contact via the Red Sea. Ethiopia especially reflects this complexity, containing **West Eurasian back-migration DNA** from as early as 20,000 years ago.[8]

So, if a Jamaican person descends from West African ancestors brought to the Caribbean through the transatlantic slave trade, they are not "cut off" from history. Their DNA retains echoes of ancient kingdoms—Mali, Ashanti, Yoruba, Benin—and possibly older hunter-gatherer or Saharan lineages. But because Jamaica also experienced **colonial admixture**, a Jamaican person may carry European haplogroups like R1b, or even Celtic/Irish autosomal markers, especially from indentured servants or overseers during the 17th–19th centuries.[9]

Here's where the myth of separation begins to break down.

Due to centuries of migration, conquest, empire, and slavery, people of colour often have **unexpected genetic connections to Europe**, just as Europeans carry **hidden African or Asian**

markers. Studies have found that up to **10% of white British individuals** carry small but measurable West African or Near Eastern admixture from Roman, Moorish, or medieval movement.[10] Conversely, people of African descent in the Americas may carry up to **25% European ancestry**, often from distant colonial encounters.

And yet, it goes even deeper. The **Celts**—who lived across Ireland, Scotland, Wales, Brittany, and parts of Iberia—were not a "white" or "racially pure" group. Genetically, they emerged from **Bronze Age steppe peoples**, mixed with Neolithic farmers from the Middle East, and **Western hunter-gatherers** from Ice Age refuges.[11] These ancient ancestors were **deeply related** to people living in Anatolia, the Levant, and even parts of North Africa. The **Berbers of North Africa**, for example, share ancient links with Iberian and Gaulish populations going back to prehistoric times. So it is entirely possible for someone with North or West African roots to carry the same ancestral components that fed into the Celtic genome.

Modern DNA testing supports this. Some African Americans, for example, carry small percentages of **North European or Gaelic DNA** that can't be traced solely to colonial slavery. Instead, it reflects **deep ancestry**, when populations in Europe and Africa weren't as isolated as we imagine. The ancient world was full of **movement**—the Phoenicians sailed from Lebanon to Morocco to Spain; the Moors moved between North Africa and Iberia; Roman legions brought Africans to Britain as soldiers and citizens.

Migration didn't stop at skin colour. It never did.

So, when someone from Accra, Kingston, or Addis Ababa finds that they match an ancient Gaul, a medieval Celt, or a Viking-era Scandinavian, it is not a glitch—it's a reminder that **we are branches of the same tree**. The divisions we see today—racial, ethnic, political—are recent, artificial. In contrast, the **genetic landscape** shows deep, overlapping roots, braided across continents over tens of thousands of years.

And that is the message I want this book to deliver: your identity is not limited by the borders of a nation or the boundaries of a race. Your ancestors, no matter where they lived, were part of the great migrations of humanity. Whether they crossed oceans, deserts, or mountains, they left traces behind. You carry those traces in your blood.

Our DNA reminds us of a truth that history often forgets, we were never as separate as we believed.[38]

---

[38] *Schlebusch, Carina M., et al. "Southern African Ancient Genomes Estimate Modern Human Divergence." Science 358, no. 6363 (2017): 652–655.*

Pagani, Luca, et al. "Ethiopian Genetic Diversity Reveals Linguistic Stratification and Complex Influences on the Ethiopian Gene Pool." American Journal of Human Genetics 91, no. 1 (2012): 83–96.

Campbell, Michael C., et al. "Genetic Structure in the Jamaican Population: Implications for Admixture Mapping in African Americans." PLoS ONE 7, no. 5 (2012): e36329.

Durand, Eric Y., et al. "Ancestry Composition and Admixture in European Populations." Nature Communications 5 (2014): 3934.

Cassidy, Lara M., et al. "Neolithic and Bronze Age Migration to Ireland and the Establishment of the Insular Atlantic Genome." Proceedings of the National Academy of Sciences of the United States of America (PNAS) 113, no. 2 (2016): 368–373.

How to Begin: A Reader's DNA Starter Guide

This guide empowers anyone—regardless of ethnic background—to begin their ancestral journey. Whether you're from Ghana, Jamaica, or Ethiopia, the process is the same, and the discoveries apply to everyone. The ancient DNA tools used to connect me to Celtic lineages work equally for those whose histories have been silenced.

Understanding DNA: Haplogroups vs. Autosomal DNA

Haplogroups trace your direct maternal (mtDNA) or paternal (Y-DNA) lineage. For example:

- T2 mtDNA, like mine, is found in the Near East, Europe, and parts of North Africa and Ethiopia.[1]
- R1b Y-DNA, carried by my paternal line, is common across Western Europe and associated with Celtic populations, but also appears in parts of North Africa and Eurasia.[2]

Haplogroups offer deep-time insights, but they only represent two ancestral lines—out of thousands.

Autosomal DNA, by contrast, reflects the combined input from all your ancestors. It reveals admixture proportions, kinship links, and ancient population matches—regardless of whether those ancestors were elite or commoner. You may carry DNA segments found in Iron Age Gauls, medieval Celts, or ancient Saharan kingdoms, even if you live in Ethiopia or Jamaica.

Choose a DNA Test That Supports Downloads

Start with any of these services that allow raw DNA download:

- 23andMe, AncestryDNA, LivingDNA, MyHeritage, or FamilyTreeDNA

Ensure your raw data (usually in .txt or .zip) can be downloaded.

Download Your Raw DNA File

Steps (common across major providers):

- Log into your account → Settings or Tools → Export/Download Raw DNA
- Complete necessary identity verification
- Save the file securely; you'll use it to upload to other sites

Upload to Deep-Time Ancestry Platforms

These tools match your autosomal genome to ancient DNA samples and living populations:

- My True Ancestry: Matches to ancient peoples like Gauls, Scythians, Celts, Nubians, Vikings, etc.[3]
- GEDmatch: Lets you run admixture calculators and match with other user kits.[4]
- DNA Painter: Visualizes DNA segments by ancestral source.[5]
- YFull or FamilyTreeDNA: For deeper Y-DNA or mtDNA lineage mapping.[6]

What You Might Discover

Autosomal Admixture is Shared Across All Regions:

- African Diaspora (e.g., Jamaica): Autosomal DNA typically ~70–75% West African (e.g. Yoruba, Akan, Mende), ~10–30% European, and sometimes Indigenous Caribbean or South Asian ancestry.[7]

- Ethiopia: Carries Afroasiatic and Cushitic ancestry, mixed with West Eurasian back-migrations (~2.4–3.2 kya).[8]
- North Africa and Iberia: Show significant North African–European admixture due to Phoenician, Roman, Islamic, and medieval exchanges.[9]

Unexpected Celtic or Gaulish Links:

Celtic genetic components stem from Bronze Age steppe and Neolithic farmer lineages—not racial categories. These ancient ancestral roots spread into Mediterranean, Anatolia, and North Africa. Thus, autosomal DNA markers associated with Celtic groups can also appear in peoples from Africa, the Middle East, or South Asia.[10]

For instance, some African individuals may carry Y-DNA lineages (like R1b) or European autosomal segments due to ancient trade, migration, or medieval gene flow—not just colonial era mixing.[2]

How to Interpret Matches With Celts or Gauls

If a Jamaican or Ethiopian upload shows a match to Gaulish or Celtic ancient DNA, here's why:

- Shared Bronze Age ancestry: African and European populations were not isolated. Some early Eurasians shared genetic components before migrating into Europe—and vice versa.[11]
- Medieval admixture: Through Roman, Phoenician, Moorish, or Viking movements, genetic material travelled across Mediterranean and Atlantic routes.[12]

Therefore, skin colour or modern location does not negate the possibility of shared ancient ancestry.

These genetic connections—spanning Africa, Europe, and beyond—show how ancient migrations, shared Bronze Age ancestry, and medieval exchanges can leave surprising traces in our DNA. It is within this web of interwoven lineages that myth and history often meet. For me, these discoveries are not just about percentages or haplogroups, but about uncovering the ancestral narratives that shaped cultural memory. This same impulse—to trace the echoes of ancient peoples in our present identities—led me to explore the mythic traditions of Ireland and beyond, and to consider how they may survive in modern literature and legend.

JRR Tolkien and the origins of The Lord of The Rings.

Once I had found my DNA matches, I wanted to understand how we might be related to the Tuatha Dé Danann, the mythological race of deities and heroes in Irish folklore. These figures—often described as god-like, magical, and radiant—have long intrigued esoteric researchers and mythologists. Nicholas de Vere, in *The Dragon Legacy*, asserts that these ancient beings are ancestral to the dragon bloodline and that they are the source of mystical or psychic abilities within certain families.

I had managed to resume a stable position in my life, I returned to my ancestral research, history, and other lifelong hobbies. My main pursuit has always been to ask: Who am I? What do I do with this information that has been ever-present in my life? What relevance does it hold to the so-called "dragon bloodlines"? Most importantly, how can I give this information to others so they can discover who they are and why they may feel different from those around them? The NPCs of the world.

When engaging with followers across social media, I began exploring and validating details mentioned in *The Dragon Legacy*. In particular, my father—Nicholas De Vere—references J.R.R. Tolkien extensively in Chapter 3 on Scythians and Druids, and again in Chapter 14, "Myth or Reality: J.R.R. Tolkien." He links Tolkien's work to Norse mythology, but I was eager to dig deeper and understand whether Tolkien also drew from the Tuatha Dé Danann. It became evident to me that the elves, men, and mythical figures of *The Lord of the Rings* echo not just Nordic but distinctly Irish and Indo-European spiritual archetypes. This exploration opens the next chapter of my book: uncovering how Tolkien, knowingly or otherwise, channelled mythological bloodline stories into modern narrative

Where does the inspiration for The Lord of the Rings come from? Who first told stories of these otherworldly beings long before Tolkien brought them to life in Middle earth?

Where did elves come from?
Who mentioned elves before Tolkien?
The Gandalf the Grey character is actually from Norse mythology, the name of the King Gandalf Alfgeirsson
Of the Alfheim, He is portrayed in Snorri Sturluson's saga Heimskringla. Heimskringla relates that Gandalf was given the kingdom of Alfheim by his father Alfgeir.
Alfheim (Old Norse: Alfheim, "elf home" or "land between the rivers.") is an ancient name for an area corresponding to the modern Swedish province of Bohuslän
As mentioned in the many links in this document of evidence i have added information about the light elves and the dark Elves.
Light Elves - Ljósálfar in Old Norse. The Eddas state that the light elves were 'fairer than the sun to look at'. They inhabited the realm

Alfheim (Álfheimr). There, they were ruled by Freyr, one of the Norse gods of the Vanir clan.[39]

With this I believe that we have found actual evidence that there was a royal line of real elven kings, which I assume is also related to the Picts. The Picts not actually being part of a genocide but breeding in with others in their location which brings us to be the descendants and therefore the Ten high Kings of Ireland and Tuatha-de-Danann so on.

Elves have been described in Norse mythology as light Elves and dark Elves.[40]

---

[39] *Polyglotta – The Oslo Corpus of Old Norse Prose.* University of Oslo. Accessed August 4, 2025.
Olaf Geirstad-Alf." Scribd document archive. Accessed August 4, 2025.

Óláfs Saga Helga, in Heimskringla II. Viking Society for Northern Research. Accessed August 4, 2025.

[40] *Dökkálfar and Ljósálfar.* Wikipedia. Accessed August 4, 2025.
"Light Elves: Myths, Legends, and Origins." Viking Style. Accessed August 4, 2025.

"Elves in Norse Mythology." Skjalden: Nordic History and Mythology. Accessed August 4, 2025.

"Elves." Norse Mythology for Smart People. Accessed August 4, 2025.

"Where Did the Fantasy from Tolkien's Inspiration Come From?" The Tolkien Forum. Accessed August 4, 2025.

The Tuatha-de-Danann.

The Tuatha Dé Danann (or: Tuatha Dé) are a mythical race of beings who are, according to Irish mythology, the fifth group to inhabit Ireland and the final supernatural inhabitants. Tuatha Dé Danann is typically translated as "people of [the goddess] Danu," though there is disagreement about the translation's accuracy, mostly regarding the final word. The medieval texts with the stories of the Tuatha Dé are primarily those compiled in the Lebor Gabála Érenn (English: The Book of Invasions; Modern Irish: Leabhar Gabhála na hÉireann). One text not part of Lebor Gabála Érenn is Cath Maige Tuired (English: The [Second] Battle of Mag Tuired), in which the Tuatha Dé manage to finally defeat the Fomorians, a Viking-like group that has been a problem for all prior Irish inhabitants[41]

Tolkien's Elves were inspired by a wealth of ancient myths and legends from across Europe, including Celtic, Norse, and Anglo-Saxon traditions. One of the strongest influences on Tolkien's Elves appears to be the legendary Tuatha Dé Danann of Irish mythology—a nearly divine race known for their wisdom, magic,

---

[41]*"Tuatha Dé Danann: Origins, Symbols & Significance." Study.com, May 9, 2023. "The Tuatha Dé Danann – Ireland's Ancient Mythological Race." Connolly Cove. Accessed August 4, 2025.*

and deep connection to the natural world. These ancient beings were said to retreat to a hidden realm known as the "Otherworld," not unlike Tolkien's Elves, who eventually depart Middle-earth for the mystical Undying Lands across the sea.

In Irish legend, the Tuatha Dé Danann embodied otherworldly power, craftsmanship, and profound knowledge. Similarly, Tolkien's Elves are portrayed as ethereal, wise, and deeply connected to both nature and art. Both the Tuatha Dé Danann and Tolkien's Elves are keepers of ancient wisdom, living in harmony with nature and wielding skills that transcend human understanding.

Yet, Tolkien's Elves were shaped by more than just Celtic lore. Tolkien drew inspiration from an array of mythological sources, weaving elements of Norse, Finnish, Greek, and Arthurian traditions into a mythology that would feel timeless. His Elves carry traits of the Norse light-elves, or Ljósálfar, described as "fairer than the sun to look at" in the Norse Eddas. The light-elves inhabited Alfheim, the realm ruled by the Norse god Freyr, who, like Tolkien's Elves, represented beauty, fertility, and the life force of nature.[42]

---

[42] *Dökkálfar and Ljósálfar. Wikipedia. Accessed August 4, 2025.*
"Light Elves: Myths, Legends, and Origins." Viking Style. Accessed August 4, 2025.

"Elves in Norse Mythology." Skjalden: Nordic History and Mythology. Accessed August 4, 2025.

"Elves." Norse Mythology for Smart People. Accessed August 4, 2025.

"Where Did the Fantasy from Tolkien's Inspiration Come From?" The Tolkien Forum. Accessed August 4, 2025.

The connection to Norse myth doesn't stop there. The character of Gandalf, for instance, has roots in Norse lore as well. The name "Gandalf" appears in Snorri Sturluson's Heimskringla, where Gandalf Alfgeirsson, King of Alfheim, is mentioned as ruler of the land known as Álfheimr or "elf home." Alfheim itself was an ancient name for an area in what is now Sweden, and Tolkien's choice of Gandalf's name reflects his immersion in these old Norse sagas.

In Irish history, the line of the High Kings provides a backdrop to the mythical Tuatha Dé Danann. Some of the earliest legendary High Kings of Ireland, like Eochaid Ollathair—the Dagda, a powerful leader and figure of the Tuatha Dé Danann—appear in Irish lore with semi-divine qualities. These figures combine history and legend, blending the mortal and the mystical in ways that mirror the timeless qualities of Tolkien's Elves

Modern esoteric theories suggest a mystical lineage for these ancient figures. The Royal Dragon Court, for instance, presents the idea of a "dragon bloodline," symbolizing divine kingship and supernatural wisdom passed through generations. In these traditions, "dragons" represent an ancient, almost divine lineage with a mystical right to rule. The Tuatha Dé Danann, as godlike beings with supernatural powers, are sometimes described as part of this lineage, symbolically linked to the wisdom and mysteries of ancient bloodlines.

In this symbolic context, "dragons" are more than mythical creatures—they are embodiments of knowledge and spiritual power. Modern interpretations suggest that descendants of these bloodlines carried unique abilities and deep-rooted knowledge, traits associated with divine or supernatural kingship. Some even link these ancient kings to the Grail legends, suggesting a connection between mystical kingship and the guardianship of esoteric wisdom.

While historical evidence supporting these connections remains elusive, the symbolic lineage of wisdom, mysticism, and divine right has captivated imaginations across centuries. Through Tolkien's works, these ancient stories come alive again, echoing a sense of timelessness and connection to ancient myth, where powerful beings, like Elves and High Kings, preserve knowledge and protect the land.

The people who link the royal dragon court to the Tuatha de Danann are the family called the Declares, they link to Robert the Bruce or the brus family via Isabella de Clare **Isabella de Clare (2 November 1226 – 10 July 1264)** was the daughter of Gilbert de Clare, 4th Earl of Hertford she married Robert de Brus, his father was Robert I de Brus, 1st Lord of Annandale (c. 1070–1141, Through the Bruce line the ancestors where the Stewarts, the Burghs that lead to the Kings of Ireland,Domnall Mór Ua Briain, or Domnall Mór mac Toirrdelbaig Uí Briain, was King of Thomond in Ireland from 1168 to 1194, This leads to Brian Boru.

Brian Boru, High King of Ireland.
High King: Brian Boru depicted on the exterior of the Chapel Royal, Dublin Castle.

Celtic Ireland in the early centuries AD was a landscape of over a hundred kingdoms and sub-kingdoms fiercely engaged in dynastic struggles, feuds, rivalries, and ever-shifting alliances. The five principal kingdoms were distinctly outlined from north to south: Ulster, Meath, Connacht in the west, Leinster in the southeast, and Munster in the southwest. Starting in the 790s, Ireland faced Viking raids that escalated into permanent settlements. The Norse firmly established themselves in Dublin in 841, with additional Viking settlements in Waterford, Wexford, Cork, and Limerick. Norse warriors frequently served as mercenaries for rival Irish kings, further complicating the power dynamics. The concept of a "high king" of all Ireland emerged at an uncertain time, but despite the Christianizing efforts of St. Patrick and other missionaries from the fifth century onward, pagan traditions remained intertwined with the role of the high king. This position was often more symbolic than administrative; the high king was considered the consort of Maeve, the goddess of love, war, and Ireland. He was traditionally crowned at the prehistoric hillfort at Tara in Meath, where an ancient standing stone, the Lia Fail or Stone of Destiny, was said to cry out to signal the true high king, its shriek resonating across the land. The most legendary of the Irish high kings was Brian Boru, known as "Brian of the Tributes." Much about his life remains subject to debate, but his status as an unrivalled war leader is unquestionable. The "tributes" he extracted from lesser rulers represented substantial cattle levies. Generally recognized as having been born around 940 in Munster, Brian was the younger son of sub-king Cennetig (known as Kennedy in modern English), whose clan controlled what is now County Clare. Some sources even place his birth in the 920s. Following Cennetig's death around 960, his eldest son, Mathgamain, forcibly ousted the ruling Munster dynasty in 964, becoming a prominent figure until he was murdered by the Norsemen of Limerick in 976. Upon ascending as king of Munster, Brian avenged his brother's murder by eliminating the Norse ruler of Limerick and his heirs. He deftly defeated all rivals for the throne and, through sheer military might and leadership prowess, established control over much of southern Ireland. He commanded a formidable fleet to support his land armies and execute naval assaults against the Norse. In 997, he forged an alliance with the reigning Irish high king, Mael Sechnaill (or Malachy) of Meath, and in 999, he captured and sacked Dublin. However, he recognized Sitric Silkbeard, the Norse ruler, as his subordinate, marrying Sitric's daughter and taking his mother, Gormflaith, as one of his wives—emulating the tradition of kings in Ireland having multiple spouses. While Mael dominated the northern part of the island, Brian ruled the south, but in 1002, inexplicably, Mael surrendered the high kingship to Brian. He then defeated the Ulstermen in the north, establishing himself as a generous benefactor and staunch supporter of the Irish church, which in turn supported him. Brian championed the claim of Armagh in Ulster as Ireland's religious capital and famously journeyed across the entire country in 1005, earning the recognition of lesser kings as Ireland's supreme ruler. However, in 1013, Brian encountered a formidable opposition in an alliance of Leinstermen and Norsemen from Dublin, led by Sitric Silkbeard. This alliance enlisted Norse warriors from the Hebrides and the Isle of Man. The decisive battle took place on Good Friday at Clontarf, just north of Dublin, in an intense struggle that pitted Irishmen and Norsemen against each other. The Dublin-Leinster coalition was ultimately defeated. While some accounts suggest Brian was killed in one-on-one combat, the widely accepted narrative holds that, being in his mid-seventies, he was too old to fight and that his son, Murchad, led the army. A small group of fleeing Manxmen discovered Brian's tent, overpowered his bodyguard, and killed him with a battle-ax. As noted in the Norse Njal's Saga, "The men of Ireland will suffer a grief that will never grow old in the minds of men." Brian's body was brought to Armagh and interred in St. Patrick's Cathedral. Following his death, Mael reclaimed the high kingship. Brian's son by Gormflaith, Donnchad, ruled Munster until his own death in 1064, while Brian's descendants, the O'Brien's, remained significant power players in Ireland for many centuries. [43]

The Tale of King Arthur and Tintagel Castle.

Just as the High Kings of Ireland embodied sovereignty, the British tradition find its echo of the myth of King Arthur Pendragon, Born of dragon Blood and destined to return, With Tintagel Castle standing as the symbolic cradle of that legacy.

Richard the earl of Cornwall was The younger son of King John and Isabella of Angouleme, Richard Earl of Cornwall was born on 5 January 1209 at Winchester Castle and named in honour of his uncle King Richard the Lionheart. From 1225, when he was sixteen years old, Richard was styled Count of Poitou and in the same year, his brother King Henry III created him Earl of Cornwall.
The rich revenues from Cornwall made Richard one of the wealthiest men in Europe and one of the few English barons of the time who spoke English. Relations were not always good between

---

[43] *Richard Cavendish. "Brian Boru, High King of Ireland, Killed." History Today 64, no. 4 (April 2014).*

Richard and his brother the king, in the early years of Henry's reign, Richard rebelled against him three times.
In March 1231 Richard married the wealthy Isabel Marshal, daughter of William Marshal, 1st Earl of Pembroke and Isabel de Clare and the widow of the Earl of Gloucester. Isabel was nine years older than Richard, his brother Henry viewed the marriage with much displeasure, as the powerful Marshal family had often opposed him. It is through this marriage to Isabell Marshall that the De Clare's are related to the Ten High kings of Ireland

In May 1233, the younger brother of Henry III, Richard, Earl of Cornwall (1209–72), exchanged three of his manors for a small parcel of land on the north Cornish coast.

Stranger still, this land he coveted contained little more than an isolated and inhospitable rocky headland specifically mentioned in the deed of exchange – as 'the island of Tintagel' – which was connected to the mainland by a narrow land bridge.
The key to making sense of this apparently disadvantageous deal – and why Earl Richard did what he did with his new manor – is the powerful hold that King Arthur exerted on the imaginations of medieval lords and kings.

CLIFF-TOP CASTLE
Richard proceeded to build a castle here, with an outer bailey on the cliff tops of the mainland and an inner ward with a great hall and chambers on the headland. He probably fortified the neck of land between the two wards with a gatehouse and perhaps some kind of drawbridge (now lost as a result of landslips).
But as castles went, this was a fairly small and unimpressive creation, and its location made it next to useless. What attracted the earl to Tintagel was something else, something literary: a reference in a text written in the previous century, the *History of the Kings of Britain*, by the cleric Geoffrey of Monmouth.

LEGENDARY LANDSCAPE

Tintagel plays a significant role in Geoffrey's racy story of how an ancient king of Britain, Uther Pendragon, is driven mad with lust for Ygerna, the wife of one of his barons, Gorlois of Cornwall. Gorlois prudently removes his wife to an impregnable stronghold on the coast, the castle of Tintagel, but then rather less prudently withdraws to another fortress nearby. The pursuing Uther and his men inspect Ygerna's refuge and realise that no ordinary attack can succeed:

The castle is built high above the sea, which surrounds it on all sides, and there is no way in except that offered by a narrow isthmus of rock. Three armed soldiers could hold it against you, even if you stood there with the whole kingdom of Britain at your side.
At this point in the story, the 'prophet' Merlin proposes a supernatural remedy: by means of a magic potion, he transforms Uther into the exact likeness of Ygerna's absent husband. The ruse is entirely successful. The guards of Tintagel allow him into the castle, and Ygerna takes him into her bed:
That night she conceived Arthur, the most famous of men, who subsequently won great renown by his outstanding bravery.
If these were not literary credentials enough, Tintagel also features in a second legend, which confusingly later became part of the Arthurian cycle, but almost certainly had completely separate origins. This was the story of the adulterous love of Tristan and Isolt, the wife of King Mark of Cornwall, Tristan's uncle. Much more of the action in this late 12th-century story takes place at Tintagel, presented as the stronghold of King Mark.
Earl Richard was a cultured and literary man who would have known these legends extremely well. The overwhelming likelihood is that he built the castle at Tintagel to recreate the scene from Geoffrey of Monmouth's story and, in so doing, write himself into the mythology of King Arthur.
Richards's principal target to impress, was the people of Cornwall, whose lord he had become in 1227, and whose land had once been a separate kingdom. The story of Arthur's conception gave the Cornish an important stake in the legend, and the earl's association of himself with Arthur can only have strengthened his claim to be overlord of the peninsula. Perhaps, when Richard received the Welsh prince Dafydd ap Llywelyn at Tintagel in 1242, he was playing on Arthur's status as a folk hero throughout western Britain"[44].

---

[44] *History of Richard, Earl of Cornwall. Accessed August 4, 2025.*

The King of the Road — Gypsy Origins and the Myth of Memory.

How are we able to find truth in mythology?

I hear my friend Andy's voice echoing, arguing passionately about the **Bock Saga**, proclaiming that history—*real* history—was once only passed from tongue to tongue, generation to generation. That before the pen, there was the tale." In 1984 Ior Bock created public interest and debate when he claimed that his family line (Boxström) had kept an old oral storytelling tradition that gives insight into the pagan culture of Finland, including previously unknown autofellatio exercises (called Sauna-Solmu or Bastu-Knut), associated with ancient fertility rites. These stories are known as the Bock Saga. His eccentric philosophical and mythological family story obtained, to a limited audience, international interest"[45]. But what happens when stories shift? When truths, like stones in a river, are worn down by repetition, or added to by those who simply *wanted* to believe?

History of Tintagel Castle. English Heritage. Accessed August 4, 2025.

[45] Carl Borgen, *The Bock Saga: An Introduction to the World's Oldest Unbroken Oral Tradition (Amsterdam: Blue Dolphin Publishing, 2019),* https://www.carlborgen.com/what-is-the-bock-saga.

1. *"Ior Bock," Wikipedia, last modified July 2024,* https://en.wikipedia.org/wiki/Ior_Bock.

2. *Eli London, "The Strange Story of Ior Bock, the Man Who Claimed to Reveal the World's Oldest Mythology," InsideHook, May 19, 2021,* https://www.insidehook.com/culture/strange-story-ior-bock.

3. *BockSaga.info, "Ior Bock and the Bock Saga," accessed August 4, 2025,* https://www.bocksaga.info/ior-bock.

This dilemma lives not only in the stories of gods or ancient kings but also in the flesh-and-blood stories of people like *me*. People whose ancestors were never written down in neat little boxes on parish registers, but whose lineages lived in songs, in nicknames, in whispered jokes around the fire.

We trust documents like the *Annals of the Four Masters*, the *Declaration of Arbroath*, or the *Anglo-Saxon Chronicles*—as if the written word always guarantees truth. Yet these texts are themselves constructions, crafted by scribes with their own biases, their own myths to serve. The *Byzantine* records of the 11th century mention dark-skinned musicians and traders called *Atsingani*—forebears, perhaps, of the **Romani** people. But is that a record… or a glimpse?

This same historical ambiguity cloaks the **Gypsy** identity.

I never knew I was connected to the Gypsy world until I found **Absalom Smith**, just five generations back. His name stood out among the regular list of labourers and washerwomen in my family tree—a name whispered with reverence in some circles. He died in 1826, in Twyford, Leicestershire, and the parish record notes his burial with a strange detail: dozens of travellers came from twelve camps to attend his funeral. They dressed him in a black coat with silver buttons engraved with **A.S.**, laid straw and timber in his grave, and buried him like a king. The locals called him "King of the Gypsies"[1].

Absalom was baptized in North Marston, Buckinghamshire in 1768, son of Thomas and Sarah Smith, both described in parish records simply as *vagrants*[2]. His life spanned an era when most Romani people were illiterate and mobile, their names passed down in memory more than ink. He was known to play fiddle at wakes and fairs, settle disputes between families, and enforce what some remembered as "laws of the people"³. Whether or not he was ever crowned in any formal way, to his community, he clearly mattered. Not a king of land—but of roads, of custom, of memory.

As I read deeper, I began to understand that names like **Smith**, **Boswell**, and **Gray** were not just surnames, but part of the oral scaffolding of British Romani identity. The name **Absalom**, along with others like Elijah or Moses, wasn't uncommon among Romany men—it carried weight, biblical gravity, and ancestral rhythm⁴. These were names often repeated in families, a kind of continuity when records failed. But that also makes the genealogical trail harder to follow. It's like tracing smoke.

What fascinated me more, though, was what I found in my own DNA: **Ashkenazi Jewish ancestry** on my mother's side. This wasn't part of the story I thought I knew. My blood seemed to carry two migrations—two traumas—two enormous rivers of displacement. The Romani people, originating from northwestern India, were pushed westward around a thousand years ago. Linguistic and genetic evidence traces them through Persia, into the Byzantine Empire, and then scattered like seed across the Balkans and Europe⁵. British Romani groups like the **Romanichal's** (which Absalom was likely part of) often carry Y-DNA from haplogroup **H1a-M82**, a genetic signal from their Indian origin⁶. Over centuries, they mixed modestly with European groups, but many lines stayed remarkably intact, forming founder populations with distinct traits⁷.

Ashkenazi Jews, too, tell a story of survival and bottleneck. Genetic studies show they descend from a small Middle Eastern population that migrated into Southern Europe—Italy and Greece—before moving into Central and Eastern Europe. Around 80% of Ashkenazi Jews today descend from just four maternal ancestors. The mitochondrial DNA tells a tale of Isolation and expansion—a diaspora within a diaspora⁸.

Though both the Romani and Jewish peoples faced exile, suspicion, and ghettoization across Europe, they rarely mixed. Their identities, though sometimes side by side, were guarded fiercely. The overlap in my DNA is unlikely to be from deep shared roots, but from the convergence of two wandering lines—meeting, perhaps only recently, in some English or Eastern European town. Most genetic studies find almost no consistent crossover between Romani and Jewish genomes, even in regions like Hungary where both groups lived in proximity[9].

And yet… I carry them both. Absalom's fiddler blood, and the deep maternal lines of women who lit candles in secret. A king of the travellers in one line; a silent synagogue in the other. They never met, but they echo inside me[46].

---

[46]*Romany and Traveller Family History Society. "Find My Past Parish Register Collection."* 2017.

RootsChat Forum. "Smith Family and Romany Burials in Leicestershire." Accessed July 2025.

Georgian Era History Blog. "Absalom Smith, King of the Gypsies." Accessed August 4, 2025.

Thompson, Tony. Gypsy Boy: My Life in the Secret World of the Romany Gypsies. London: Hodder & Stoughton, 2011.

Gresham, David, et al. "Origins and Divergence of the Roma (Gypsies)." American Journal of Human Genetics 83, no. 2 (2008): 285–294.

Mendizabal, Isabel, et al. "Reconstructing the Population History of European Romani from Genome-wide Data." Current Biology 22, no. 24 (2012): 2342–2349.

MacArthur, Daniel G., et al. "Founder Events and Admixture Shape the Genome-wide Structure of Roma Populations." Proceedings of the National Academy of Sciences 110, no. 5 (2013): 2345–2350.

Behar, Doron M., et al. "The Matrilineal Ancestry of Ashkenazi Jewry." American Journal of Human Genetics 78, no. 3 (2006): 487–497.

The Gypsy Royal Family

Many legends and tales about their origins and exploits have been passed down through oral history.
The first official recognition of a Scottish Gypsy leader was in 1506. King James IV acknowledged Anthony Gawin as the "Earl of Little Egypt" in a letter which implored the King of Denmark to give Anthony and his company safe passage through Denmark.
"Little Egypt" was not a place, but a people. Egypt was the supposed ancestral homeland of the Romani people, and the derivation of the word 'Gypsy'. Today, 'Gypsy' is sometimes seen as offensive. However, there are several Romani groups in Europe and Britain who have claimed this word and use it with pride. The word Gypsy is used because this is how the community in Kirk Yetholm referred to themselves.
By 1540 leadership passed to the Faa family. James V granted John Faa and his son authority to police and punish their 'subjects'. It was with this legislation that the tradition of the Gypsy Kings and Queens was affirmed.

From Power to Persecution

However, any tolerance from the established monarchy was short-lived. King James VI & I approved an 'Act anent the Egyptians' promising death for any of the Gypsy race found in Scotland after 1 August 1609
The early 18th century found several of the Gypsy clans settled in Kirk Yetholm. There are conflicting tales of how they received favourable leases by the landowner, Sir William Bennet of Grubett.

Eshel, Yarin, et al. "The Genetic History of Populations from the Western Balkans." European Journal of Human Genetics 30, no. 9 (2022): 957–965.

One story tells of how they were granted the land after a Gypsy saved William's life in the Siege of Namur in 1695, now in present-day Belgium.

It was on this land that cottages were built, including the Royal Palaces. The Palaces themselves were not larger or more grand than their neighbours. Instead, their status was bestowed upon them by their regal residents.

By the early 19th century, the village of **Kirk Yetholm** had become a significant winter base for Gypsy families in the Scottish Borders. As many as a hundred individuals would settle there during the colder months, retreating from the roads after summer spent travelling the countryside. In warmer seasons, these families would set out again, often in small groups, hawking handmade goods—baskets, tinware, clothing—and performing seasonal work. They lodged in barns, under hedgerows, or wherever the land allowed, living a lifestyle both nomadic and tightly knit, shaped by tradition and necessity[1].

One of the great challenges in tracing Gypsy lineage stems from their fluid approach to names. Both forenames and surnames were frequently changed, obscured, or altered beyond recognition, often as a means to avoid detection by local authorities or landowners. Names that sounded strange to parish clerks—unpronounceable even—were sometimes written phonetically or replaced entirely. Still, among these families, certain surnames appear repeatedly across Britain: **Smith**, **Boswell**, and **Gray** being the most prominent[2].

Biblical names were common among Romani men: **Elijah**, **Nehemiah**, **Absalom**, **Moses**, **Wisdom**—names which reflected both a cultural link to oral biblical tradition and a measure of mystical reverence. Women, by contrast, bore names of almost poetic eccentricity: **Cinnamenta, Trezi Ann, Lamentana**—alongside names drawn from nature like **Ocean, Evening**, or

Morning Star. These naming traditions were more than ornamental; they preserved tribal links and family memory, while simultaneously complicating any future genealogical attempt to unravel parentage or kinship connections[2].

Baptism played an important, if unconventional, role in Romani communities. While many children were baptized in parish churches, it was not uncommon for the same child to be baptized more than once—and in multiple parishes. In part, this was a social strategy: baptismal customs often included gifts from parishioners or clergy, and Gypsy families quickly learned where such customs were most generous. Having received the parish's welcome, and its goods, they would move on and repeat the ritual elsewhere[3].

Marriage and funerary rites were elaborate events. One of the most vivid historical accounts we have of a Romani funeral concerns **Absalom Smith**, who died in **February 1826**, aged 60, in a camp near **Twyford Lane**. Known locally as the "King of the Gypsies," Absalom's death was marked by pageantry. He was attended in his final days by physicians, and upon his death, a large caravan of fellow Romani accompanied his body to Twyford churchyard. There, he was buried wearing his coat with silver buttons engraved "A.S.", and his grave was filled with alternating layers of timber and straw, placed deliberately to deter any grave robbers from disturbing the body. His followers claimed he left a hundred pounds to each of his thirteen children—a significant sum at the time—and 54 grandchildren[3].

This story, preserved through both local record and oral tradition, offers more than a single obituary; it speaks to a deeper, sustained presence of Gypsy royalty—self-appointed or community-declared—across Britain during a time when the state barely acknowledged their existence. These figures were leaders not by legal title, but through social consensus and legacy. They settled disputes, oversaw rituals, and represented their communities in dealings with the outside world.

The origin of the Romani people has long been debated. For centuries, it was believed that Gypsies descended from **Egyptians**, owing to the name "Gypsy" itself—a corruption of "Egyptian." Others theorised that they were descendants of the **followers of Isis** in ancient Rome, or that they were **Moorish**, **Jewish**, **Tartar**, or even **Grecian** exiles. In truth, the linguistic evidence has long pointed eastward, particularly to northern **India**. Writers such as **Grellmann** and later **George Borrow** noted the striking similarities between the Romani language and Sanskrit, and between Romani culture and aspects of Indian life—vagrancy, musicality, family structure, and spiritual symbolism[4].

Still, not all agreed. A competing theory, lesser known but passionately argued, places the origin of Europe's Romani population not in India but in the **Hussite Wars** of 15th-century Bohemia. The Bohemians, persecuted Protestants led by **John Ziska**, were known for their wagon-camps and for swearing oaths never again to sleep beneath a roof—an uncanny match to the earliest accounts of Romani wagon families. The "Orphans of Ziska," as they were known, were driven out after the leader's death in 1424. In the years immediately following, between **1418 and 1427**, records of "Bohemians" arriving in cities like **Paris**, **Cologne**, and **Rome** begin to appear—always outsiders, always travellers, often claiming protection from **Emperor Sigismund** via suspicious or forged letters of passage[5].

Their behaviour was marked by paradox. They called themselves pilgrims and Christians, wore crucifixes, and observed Catholic rites—but avoided churches. They referred to themselves as nobles, counts, and "Lords of Little Egypt," which may have been more symbolic than geographical. The term "Egypt," after all, had long been used in Christian Europe to refer to bondage or exile. To call themselves "Egyptians" may have been to say, *We are the persecuted, the displaced, the wandering faithful*[6].

In France, they were called **Bohemians**, a term which persists even today in artistic subcultures, echoing their association with freedom, marginality, and resistance. English writers later mistook the word's similarity to "Gypsy" as evidence of Egyptian origin, a mistake repeated until well into the modern era.

The truth, as with so many aspects of Gypsy history, lies somewhere between language and myth, bloodline and story. Whether Absalom Smith was descended from Indian travellers, Bohemian exiles, or a convergence of both, his legacy—like that of so many Romani figures—is not written in books, but remembered in names, repeated in songs, and buried beneath layers of straw and earth.

[47]

---

[47] *The Origin of the Gypsies. By George Washington. The Atlantic, February 1866 issue.*

Dumfries and Galloway Council Archives. The Gypsies by William Simpson (Kirkcudbright Collection).

Romany & Traveller Family History Society. Personal Research Archives. Retrieved from grthm.scot and census/baptismal records.

"Farewell to the King of the Gypsies." Obituary Notice of Absalom Smith, Twyford Parish Register, 1826.

Grellmann, H.M.G. Dissertation on the Gipsies. London: 1807.

Borrow, George. The Zincali: An Account of the Gypsies of Spain. 1841.

[Anonymous Author]. "On the Origin of the Gypsies." North British Review, 1853.

The reason why I found this particularly interesting was that although I had found many Jewish names in my ancestry, I still wanted to find out exactly where it came from and as a lot of gypsy ancestry is subjective due to the changing of the names and locations caused by constantly migrating. When I decided to get a DNA test done, The two reason's where that I wanted to get information from my mother's side, I had the results from my father side already and needed to make absolute certain that I was in fact related to royalty but also because my mother was adopted and at the time I did not have all of her ancestry information, I did leave researching her side for many years. Once I had started looking into her side, I found many coincidences within both her side and my father's side. My dad used to joke with my nan, calling her a Jew, I always wondered where this came from and how. When I got the results back from my DNA test, I found that I had a percentage of Ashkenazi Jewish blood in my lines. Furthermore, found that my nan shared ancestry with my mum, so my parents much like many royal families were already related, People don't like to admit to this inbreeding, however it is part of who we all are. I aim to show the reader how migration has caused this inbreeding.

The Arrival of the Romani: Gypsies in Scotland

The Romani people often pejoratively labelled as "Gypsies," began to appear in western Europe by the late 14th century, although their migration from northern India likely began as early as the 11th century. Genetic and linguistic research confirms their Indo-Aryan roots, with ties to Sanskrit-based languages and origins near the Punjab region (Fraser, 1995; Matras, 2002).

Scotland received its first recorded reference to the Romani in the early 16th century. A royal letter from James IV, dated 1505, granted safe passage to a group of "Egyptians"—a common misnomer arising from the mistaken belief that they originated in Egypt. These individuals were allowed to travel through the realm without harm, suggesting an initial reception of curiosity and tolerance (Cressy, 2004).

Over time, however, attitudes hardened. The Scottish Parliament passed harsh laws in 1579, banning Gypsies and permitting their persecution and even execution under vagrancy and witchcraft laws. Yet despite this, Romani clans managed to survive in isolated pockets of Perthshire, the Borders, and Fife, often integrating or forming semi-nomadic communities (Kenrick, 2004).

Some Romani families rose to positions of influence within their communities, leading to the emergence of so-called "Gypsy Kings." The most notable among them was Johnnie Faa, a legendary Romani leader of the 17th century, associated with tales of romantic abduction and noble lineage. Oral traditions place Faa in relation to the Earls of Cassillis, and his descendants were reportedly recognised by Romani groups as hereditary chieftains.

The cultural presence of Romani people in Scotland, while marginalized, contributed to oral storytelling traditions, musical styles (especially fiddling and pipes), and even certain aspects of mystical folklore that resonated with pre-existing Celtic beliefs.

Scotland: Scota, Sovereignty, and the Shadow of Migration

The origin of the name "Scotland" is a layered tale, one interwoven with myth, early migration, dynastic power, and forgotten peoples. Beneath the official historical record lies a substratum of tradition, oral lore, and cultural sediment that together inform a broader and richer understanding of Scotland's identity. The story begins not with the northern British Isles, but in Egypt, Spain, and Ireland—with the enigmatic figure of Scota, an Egyptian princess whose name would come to influence the naming of an entire nation.

The Myth of Scota: A Pharaoh's Daughter in Gaelic Lorre

The myth of Scota is perhaps one of the most enduring pseudo-historical narratives associated with the origin of Scotland. According to medieval Irish and Scottish chronicles, Scota was the daughter of an Egyptian Pharaoh—often identified with Nectanebo II or other rulers from Egypt's Late Period—who married Míl Espáine (Milesius), a legendary ancestor of the Gaels. After fleeing Egypt, the Milesian descendants, including Scota, made their way to Spain and then Ireland. In the battle to settle the land, Scota was said to have died and been buried in what is now County Kerry, Ireland, at a site known as Scota's Grave (Fert Scota)

The earliest accounts of this legend appear in the "Lebor Gabála Érenn" (The Book of the Taking of Ireland), an 11th-century compilation of Irish myth and pseudo-history that traces Irish ancestry back to biblical and classical roots (Macalister, 1938). The story was further popularized in John of Fordun's Chronica Gentis Scotorum (14th century), which explicitly identified the Scots as descendants of Scota and Milesius. These narratives served not only as origin myths but also as attempts by Gaelic-speaking elites to link their noble lineage with ancient and even divine ancestry (Broun, 1999).

From Éire to Scotia: The Shift in National Names

Interestingly, the term "Scot" was originally used not for the people of what is now Scotland, but rather for the Gaelic-speaking tribes of Ireland. Roman texts such as Ammianus Marcellinus (late 4th century) and Eumenius (early 4th century) refer to the "Scotti" as raiders from Ireland, distinguishing them from Picts and Britons. Over time, these Scots began to migrate to the western parts of modern Scotland, particularly Argyll and Dalriada, regions easily accessible by sea.

This migration was not merely one of warriors but also of culture and governance. The Kingdom of Dál Riata, a Gaelic overkingdom, established itself in western Scotland by the 6th century, spreading Gaelic language, laws, and customs. The fusion of these Irish-Gaelic settlers with the Picts, particularly under King Kenneth MacAlpin in the 9th century, eventually led to the formation of the Kingdom of Alba, which later evolved into Scotland (Woolf, 2007). "Scotland" as a name derives from the Latin "Scotia", originally a term for Ireland, and only later applied to the northern realm of Britain once the Scots established themselves there. By the 11th century, "Scotia" had become associated more firmly with northern Britain, and Ireland was increasingly referred to as "Hibernia" (Bannerman, 1974).

Scottish Royalty

The Bruce Dynasty: True Kingship Rooted in Blood and Legend

Amid this cultural swirl, the question of legitimate sovereignty in Scotland remains central. Many Scottish royal lines were fraught with contested claims, shifting allegiances, and foreign entanglements. But one dynasty consistently stands out as embodying both native legitimacy and martial strength—the Bruce family, most notably Robert the Bruce (1274–1329).

The Bruce lineage traced its roots to Norman knights who had settled in England after the Conquest and then moved north to become powerful landholders in Scotland. Yet Robert's claim to kingship was not simply based on Norman blood; it rested on his descent from David of Huntingdon, grandson of King David I of Scotland, giving him a legitimate claim to the Scottish throne through the ancient line of Cinéad mac Ailpín (Kenneth MacAlpin).

Robert the Bruce came to prominence during the Wars of Scottish Independence, waging a guerrilla campaign against English occupation and ultimately securing victory at the Battle of Bannockburn in 1314. His reign restored not only Scotland's independence but also its sense of national identity, uniting Gaelic, Norman, and native elements under one crown (Barrow, 2005).

His descendants, particularly David II and later the House of Stewart (Stuart), continued this legacy, reinforcing their claim to

divine and historical right through ceremonial, genealogical, and even mythic channels. These later Stewarts, many of whom claimed descent from Bruce, would go on to rule both Scotland and England, extending this "true royal" bloodline across the British Isles and into continental Europe.

From the myth of Scota and the shift of "Scotia" from Ireland to Scotland, to the arrival of the Romani people and the Bruce dynasty's royal legacy, the history of Scotland is a tapestry woven from diverse and sometimes contradictory threads. The interplay of migration, mythology, and monarchy forms a historical consciousness that resists simple definitions. While mainstream historiography tends to separate legend from fact, Scotland's national story is strengthened—not weakened—by its mythic foundations. Scota, whether real or allegorical, continues to inspire questions about identity, origin, and sovereignty, just as the Romani people challenge static notions of what it means to belong to a land. In Robert the Bruce and his descendants, we find a focal point: a dynasty whose claim to power, forged in war and supported by bloodlines, represents a lineage of true kingship, one that transcends borders and time, [48]

---

[48]   D. Cressy, *Gypsies: An English History* (Oxford University Press, 2004).

A. Fraser, *The Gypsies* (Blackwell, 1995).

D. Kenrick, "Romani Origins and Migration Patterns," *Journal of the Gypsy Lore Society*, 5th Series, vol. 14 (2004).

J. Bannerman, *Studies in the History of Dalriada* (Scottish Academic Press, 1974).

G. W. S. Barrow, *Robert Bruce and the Community of the Realm of Scotland* (Edinburgh University Press, 2005).

D. Broun, *The Irish Identity of the Kingdom of the Scots in the Twelfth and Thirteenth Centuries* (The Boydell Press, 1999).

R. A. S. Macalister, *Lebor Gabála Érenn: The Book of the Taking of Ireland*, Vols. I–V (Irish Texts Society, 1938).

Y. Matras, *Romani: A Linguistic Introduction* (Cambridge University Press, 2002).

A. Woolf, *From Pictland to Alba, 789–1070* (Edinburgh University Press, 2007)

King Robert the Bruce

The Year of 2020 was the start of the Covid lockdowns, I was in my 2nd year of doing a law degree, I remembered the puzzle of the Glen line, not valleys but an actual a family as mentioned earlier. I followed this line with the given information on ancestry, birth marriages and death certificates, which led me to Archibald Glen, My 11th Grandfather in 1570 born in Barr in Ayreshire, Through his parents it led me to King Robert the Bruce. Knowing the connection with Robert the Bruce and My logans, Information starts to make more sense, Given more confirmation to why I would have the Bruce line within my Genealogy.

Robert I of Scotland, known as Robert the Bruce, was King of Scotland from 1306 to 1329 CE. He is recognized as a national hero for his role in securing Scotland's independence from England and is considered one of the country's greatest monarchs. Robert became king after John Balliol (r. 1292-1296 CE) during a period of conflict with English forces led by Edward I of England (r. 1272-1307 CE). His significant victory at the Battle of Bannockburn in 1314 CE established his legitimacy as king. Through effective diplomacy, he achieved recognition of Scotland's independence from both the Pope and Edward III of England (r. 1327-1377 CE). He was succeeded by his son, David II of Scotland (r. 1329-1371 CE).

Early Life- Born on July 11, 1274 CE, at Turnberry Castle in Ayrshire, Robert was the son of Robert (VII) the Bruce and Marjorie, Countess of Carrick. The Bruce family had been lords of Annandale since the 1120's CE and claimed descent from Earl David, brother of William I of Scotland. Robert spent time in the Western Isles, Ulster, and in England, including Carlisle Castle and London. He inherited the earldom of Carrick in 1292 CE. Robert married Isabel of Mar around 1295 CE and later Elizabeth de Burgh in 1302 CE. He had a daughter, Marjorie, with Isabel, and with Elizabeth, he had two daughters — Matilda and Margaret — and two sons, David and John, who died young. The Bruces opposed Edward I's choice of John Balliol as king.

The Great Cause
After the death of Alexander III of Scotland in 1286 CE, Scotland faced a succession crisis when his granddaughter died in 1290 CE. Edward I, perceived himself as the overlord and intervened in the succession, choosing John Balliol as king in November 1292 CE. Robert (VI) the Bruce, Robert's grandfather, was a main contender for the throne, but Balliol was selected because he was seen as more controllable. Balliol's ineffective rule led to dissatisfaction among Scottish nobles, who established a regency government in 1295 CE and allied with Philip IV of France, initiating the 'Auld Alliance.' Balliol renounced his loyalty to Edward I in April 1296 CE. The Bruces did not support this rebellion, and Robert joined the English forces that invaded Scotland. Edward I's response included massacres and the capture of key castles, culminating in a Scottish defeat at the Battle of Dunbar on April 27, 1296 CE. John Balliol was deposed and imprisoned in the Tower of London as Scotland fell under English control.

By February 1306 CE, Robert the Bruce emerged as the key leader for the Scots, rejecting John Balliol as a puppet of Edward I. On 10 February, Robert or his supporters assassinated John Comyn, his main rival, in Greyfriars Church, Dumfries. With backing from northern Scottish barons, he declared himself king and was inaugurated at Scone Abbey on 25 March 1306 CE. However, his position was fragile. He faced defeats at Methven on 19 June and Dalry on 11 July, prompting him to flee to Rathlin Island in Ireland. The English targeted his family instead; three of his brothers were executed, and his sister Mary was imprisoned in an iron cage at Roxburgh Castle for four years, while his wife Elizabeth was confined in a manor house. Edward II's focus on his own issues allowed Robert to capture English-held castles and raid northern England. In 1314 CE, Edward led an army to Scotland to siege Stirling Castle, but Robert's forces, numbering around 10,000, faced 15-20,000 English troops. The battle at Bannockburn on 23-24 June saw Robert's tactics and terrain advantage lead to a Scottish victory, resulting in heavy English losses and a narrow escape for Edward. Robert displayed bravery during the battle, notably defeating Henry de Bohun. Following this, Scotland regained its independence. Robert negotiated the release of Queen Elizabeth and Princess Marjorie and confiscated lands from pro-Edward lords, solidifying his power. However, this led to the rise of strong families and financial strain on the crown. Robert captured Berwick in 1318 CE and continued raids, nearly taking York in 1319 CE. Robert the Bruce died on 7 June 1329 CE after two years of illness, described as leprosy, and was buried at Dunfermline Abbey. He wished to go on a Crusade, so he asked Sir James Douglas to take his heart to the Holy Land. Douglas died in battle in Spain, but legend says Bruce's heart was returned to Scotland and buried at Melrose Abbey. Robert was succeeded by his five-year-old son, David II. This left an opening for rivals like Edward Balliol, who was briefly made king with Edward III's support. However, David II was restored by 1336 CE and ruled until 1371 CE. Over time, Robert's legacy grew; he became a celebrated figure in history, featured in the poem "The Bruce," and was seen as a model king. His sword was carried into battle as late as the late 15th century, and interest in him surged again due to recent discoveries and ongoing debates about Scottish independence. [49]

Rollo

(circa 860-930 CE, ruled from 911-927 CE) was a Viking leader who founded and became the first ruler of Normandy. In 911 CE, he converted to Christianity through an agreement with Frankish king Charles the Simple (893-923 CE), adopting the name Robert.

---

[49] Mark Cartwright, "Robert the Bruce," *World History Encyclopedia*. Most information in the public domain.

John Cannon and Anne Hargreaves, *The Kings and Queens of Britain* (Oxford University Press, 2009).

Richard Cavendish, *Kings & Queens* (David & Charles, 1970).

David Crouch, *Medieval Britain, c.1000–1500* (Cambridge University Press, 2017).

Dan Jones, *The Plantagenets* (William Collins, 2013).

Michael Lynch, *The Oxford Companion to Scottish History* (Oxford University Press, 2011).

Alan MacQuarrie, *Medieval Scotland* (The History Press, 1970).

Richard Oram, *Kings and Queens of Scotland* (Tempus, 2002).

Charles Phillips, *The Complete Illustrated Guide to the Kings & Queens of Britain* (Lorenz Books, 2006).

Nigel Saul, *The Oxford Illustrated History of Medieval England* (Oxford University Press, 2001).

Derek Wilson, *The Plantagenet Chronicles 1154–1485* (Metro Books, 2020).

His story was later embellished by Christian writers who portrayed him as a role model, emphasizing his transformation from a savage Viking chief into a figure of Christian virtue and law. However, they largely overlooked details of his life before his alliance with Charles. Rollo is the grandfather of William the Conqueror (the first Norman King of England) and an ancestor to various European monarchs. Rollo honoured his agreement with Charles by defending the region against Viking raids and restoring order to the land. He ruled under a Viking legal code emphasizing personal honour and individual responsibility, reforming the ineffective laws of prior magistrates. He likely died around 930 CE, probably of natural causes, as no records indicate otherwise. Early Life & Origins, Much of Rollo's life is semi-legendary, as noted by scholar Robert Ferguson. Known by various names such as Rollo, Rollon, and Hrolf, he is regarded as a figure whose lack of biographical information has turned him into a blend of myth and legend. Ferguson highlights the uncertainty surrounding Rollo's origins and actions before his involvement with Charles. Dudo of Saint-Quentin, a 10th-century historian, claimed Rollo was a Danish nobleman who raided West Francia and had ties to the Viking leader Guthrum. This relationship suggests his Danish roots, as both were known Danes. There are later claims of Rollo being Norwegian, popularized by William of Malmesbury, but the consensus leans toward Danish ancestry, supported by the fact that most Viking raiders came from Denmark. Efforts to trace Rollo's origins have had little success. In 2016, archaeologists opened the tomb of Rollo's grandson Richard I but found much older remains, indicating no new insights into Rollo's lineage. As with many Viking figures, Rollo's legend overshadowed his actual life. Subsequent accounts built on Dudo's work, and while some scholars prefer the Norwegian claim by Snorri Sturluson, it is most likely Rollo was of Danish origin.

Rollo & Charles the Simple According to Dudo, the Franks, under Charles the Simple, realized they could not stop Viking raids and needed a new policy. The king's advisors challenged his inaction, to which he responded that he would welcome any better ideas. They suggested that he give land from the River Andelle to the sea to the pagans and marry his daughter to Rollo, saying this would enhance his power against adversaries, as Rollo was of noble lineage, a capable warrior, and a dependable ally. (Dudo's History 2:25) After considering their counsel, Charles sent the Archbishop of Rouen to Rollo with the offer. Rollo's Danish chiefs pointed out the land's redeeming qualities and encouraged him to accept. Rollo agreed, setting a date for his baptism and marriage to Charles' daughter Gisla (c. 911 CE). However, he refused baptism, noting the land was ruined and would take years to restore. The king's advisors suggested offering Rollo what he wanted to protect the kingdom and attract souls to Christianity. Charles offered Rollo Flanders, but he declined due to its marshiness, prompting the king to propose Brittany, which Rollo accepted. To finalize the agreement, Rollo was asked to kiss the king's foot, but he refused, stating he would not bow to any man. Urged by the Franks, he had a warrior kiss the king's foot instead, causing laughter among the Vikings and dismay among the Franks. (2:29) Despite the commotion, Rollo was baptized, married to Gisla, and took possession of his lands under the Treaty of Saint Clair sur Epte in 911 CE. He then initiated reforms, establishing laws and principles to maintain peace, restoring churches, and enhancing city defences. (2:31) Rollo improved his lands and honoured the treaty; there were no further Viking raids in Francia after 911 CE. Rollo of Normandy While often called the first Duke of Normandy, Rollo never held that title (Richard II was the first duke). Some historians refer to him as Count Rollo, but contemporary documents simply call him "Rollo." A land grant from 918 CE mentions "lands granted to the Normans of the Seine, specifically to Rollo and his companions for the kingdom's defence." His exact title remains unclear, but early historians labelled him "Chieftain." He ruled as a Viking chief, reforming lax laws and implementing a code focused on personal honour and accountability. Crimes like robbery, assault, and murder were punishable by death, as was fraud.[50]

The De Vere's of Hedingham Castle

This was remarkable to have been able to trace my family back to over 1000 years, The bug had gotten me, I was sucked in. Continuing to follow this line round from Emma of Paris, who was my 26th Grandmother, which took me to the Arundel lines (FitzAlan's and Howard's), and then onto Richard de Vere 1385, I decided to complete the de Vere family tree, albeit quite a mess at the time, due to many doubled profiles, and some mistakes, it did take me a while and much research, however trace it back to my

---

[50] J. Arman, *The Warrior Queen: The Life and Legend of Aethelflaed, Daughter of Alfred the Great (Amberley Publishing, 2017).*
Cantor, N. F. *The Civilization of the Middle Ages. (Harper Perennial), 1994.*
Ferguson, R. *The Vikings: A History. (Viking Books), 2010.*
Howorth, H. H. A Criticism of the Life of Rollo, as told by Dudo de St. Quentin. Archaeologia, or Miscellaneous Tracts relating to Antiquity. Volume 45, 1880., 1880.
Keynes, S. & Lapidge, M. *Alfred the Great & Other Contemporary Sources. Penguin Classics, 1984.*
Mystery of Viking Ruler Rollo Continues â€" Surprising Discovery in Ancient Grave accessed 5 Nov 2018.
Pohl, B. *Dudo of Saint-Quentin's Historia Normannorum. York Medieval Press, 2015.*
Sawyer, P. *The Oxford Illustrated History of the Vikings. Oxford University Press, 2001.*
Somerville, A. A. & McDonald, R. A. *The Viking Age: A Reader. University of Toronto Press, Higher Education Division, 2014.*

Swanton, M. J. *The Anglo-Saxon Chronicle - 1998 Edition. Taylor & Francis Ltd, 1998.*

eldest grandfather and found Alfonse de Vere, my 25th Grandfather. You see in dads' books he did write all of this information correctly, He had passed on many bits of his genealogy, after many years I decided to conclude dads work here as of today I have found that Major Thomas Weir is my 9th Grandfather. I eventually found several ways that my bloodline went back to the de Vere's.

Walking With Ancestors: My Journey Through Time, Spirit, and Blood

I now go on a journey—to see where my family lived, the castles they once owned, and to remember the things people have said to me along the way. It's been nothing short of remarkable to have traced my family back over 1,000 years. Somewhere early on, the bug got me—I was pulled in, fully. What started as a curiosity became a calling.

The de Vere family of Hedingham Castle represents one of the most historically significant noble lineages in English history. Their legacy spans from the Norman Conquest to the Tudor period and beyond, characterized by a continuous thread of loyalty to the crown, military prowess, and legal and political influence. The de Vere's were not merely aristocrats; they were a family intricately woven into the fabric of English governance, culture, and dynastic succession. The dynasty's importance is nowhere more evident than in their residence at Hedingham Castle, a symbol of feudal stability and noble tradition, and in the figure of Eustace de Vere, whose status and political power led some to consider him a potential claimant to the English throne.

The de Vere family traces its lineage back to Aubrey de Vere I, a Norman knight who arrived in England alongside William the Conqueror in 1066. Aubrey was rewarded with substantial lands in Essex and was appointed tenant-in-chief, laying the foundation for what would become one of the most prestigious earldoms in England. His son, Aubrey II, became a prominent figure in the court of King Henry I, serving as royal chamberlain. Aubrey II's own son, Aubrey III, was granted the title of Earl of Oxford by Empress Matilda in 1141 as a reward for his unwavering support during the civil war against King Stephen. This marked the formal rise of the De Vere family within the English nobility.[1]

The prominence of the de Vere's continued unabated for centuries. They served as Great Chamberlains of England, a hereditary role passed through their line from the 12th century until the 17th. This position placed the family at the heart of English political life, responsible for the royal household and ceremonial duties at court.[2] Their proximity to the crown not only secured their political influence but also allowed them to play a pivotal role in shaping the policies and legal traditions of medieval England. This institutional significance made them indispensable to successive monarchs and ensured their continued elevation within the English peerage.

Eustace de Vere, an often underexamined member of the family, was particularly notable in the early 13th century. His position as a high-ranking noble, combined with his landholdings, military power, and Plantagenet connections, led to rumours and political speculation that he could be a legitimate claimant to the throne. Some contemporary chroniclers referred to him as "the rightful heir" or "kingmaker," though these accounts were often veiled in allegory and political critique.[3] While there is little concrete evidence that Eustace ever actively pursued the crown, his ancestry and alliances placed him in a position of significant political leverage. His potential claim stemmed from intermarriage with royal bloodlines and his family's consistent presence at the core of English governance.[4]

It is in this context that the de Vere's must be understood not merely as loyal servants of the crown but as potential powerbrokers and alternative sources of legitimacy. In feudal England, where bloodline, land, and loyalty were the currencies of power, the De Veres held all three in abundance. Their loyalty was tested during the baronial revolts and the drafting of the Magna Carta, where Robert de Vere, Earl of Oxford, was listed among the twenty-five barons appointed to ensure King John's compliance with the Charter.[5] His participation underscores the family's willingness to challenge even royal authority when the rule of law was at stake, further cementing their dual role as both enforcers and protectors of constitutional principles.

The de Vere family's legacy extends through generations. They were active participants in major military campaigns, including the Hundred Years' War, where John de Vere, 7th Earl of Oxford, distinguished himself at the Battle of Poitiers in 1356.[6] His descendant, the 13th Earl, John de Vere, played a pivotal role during the Wars of the Roses, supporting the Lancastrian cause and contributing significantly to Henry VII's victory at Bosworth Field in 1485.[7] As a reward, he was restored to his titles and lands, and his loyalty helped legitimize the nascent Tudor dynasty. Such contributions demonstrate that the de Veres were not passive nobles but active shapers of English political destiny.

Perhaps one of the most fascinating figures among the de Veres was Edward de Vere, 17th Earl of Oxford, a courtier, soldier, and patron of the arts during the Elizabethan period. He was a controversial figure in his own time, celebrated for his wit and theatrical patronage. Some modern scholars even suggest that Edward de Vere may have been the true author of Shakespeare's plays, though this theory remains speculative and is not widely accepted by mainstream historians.[8] Regardless, his cultural contributions reflect the enduring prominence and adaptability of the de Vere family across centuries.

Their ancestral seat, Hedingham Castle, serves as a physical testament to their power and longevity. Built in the early 12th century, its Norman keep remains one of the best-preserved in England. The castle not only functioned as a military fortress but also as a centre of administration and justice. Its great hall hosted royal visits and legal proceedings, reinforcing the de Veres' role as regional governors and arbiters of law.[9]

The family's continued involvement in national politics extended well into the early modern period, though their influence began to wane with the centralisation of royal power and the decline of feudalism. By the time the title of Earl of Oxford became extinct in 1703, the de Veres had left an indelible mark on English history. Their blend of military service, legal responsibility, cultural patronage, and proximity to royal authority made them one of the most formidable and respected noble houses in the realm.

- Aubrey de Vere I (d. c.1112), Lord of Hedingham, companion of William the Conqueror[10] • Aubrey de Vere II (c.1085–1141), royal chamberlain[11] • Aubrey de Vere III (c.1115–1194), 1st Earl of Oxford (created 1141)[3] • Robert de Vere, 3rd Earl of Oxford (c.1164–1225), Magna Carta baron[5] • Hugh de Vere, 4th Earl of Oxford (c.1210–1264)[11] • Robert de Vere, 5th Earl (d.1296)[11]
- Alphonsus de Vere, father of John • John de Vere, 7th Earl of Oxford (1312–1362), fought at Poitiers[6]

- Thomas de Vere, 8th Earl (1336–1379)Robert de Vere, 9th Earl (1362–1392), Duke of Ireland (disgraced)[11]

Extinct line, passed to cousin

    Richard de Vere, 11th Earl (1385–1416)

    John de Vere, 13th Earl (1442–1513), Bosworth Field[7]

    John de Vere, 15th Earl (1482–1545)

    Edward de Vere, 17th Earl (1550–1604), patron of the arts[8]

The De Veres' significance to the royal household cannot be overstated. Their hereditary office of Lord Great Chamberlain placed them in direct, daily service to the monarch. The role included overseeing state ceremonies, such as coronations and the opening of Parliament. This office was particularly sensitive and prestigious, giving the family direct access to the sovereign and considerable influence at court.[12] . Such access allowed them to function as intermediaries between the monarchy and the nobility, and to influence appointments, policy discussions, and the broader legal and ceremonial life of the kingdom.

The de Vere family exemplifies the complex interplay between nobility and monarchy in medieval and early modern England. Their story is not merely one of titles and lands but of consistent involvement in the central mechanisms of power. From military commanders and legal custodians to cultural patrons and possible royal contenders, the de Vere's left a legacy of formidable depth and breadth. Eustace de Vere's rumoured claim to the throne may have remained unfulfilled, but it underscores how deeply the family was enmeshed in the politics of legitimacy and sovereignty. Hedingham

Castle, still standing in Essex, remains a powerful reminder of their place in English history.[51]

The de Vere dynasty from Normandy gave rise not only to the Earls of Oxford in England but also to a Scottish branch known largely as Weir or Vere of Blackwood in Lanarkshire. This family tradition holds that **Ralph (Radulphus or Baltredus) de Vere** first established in Scotland around **1165**, in the service of King William I ("William the Lion"), likely following Conan IV of Brittany, his overlord.[1] Ralph was captured alongside the king at Alnwick in **1174**, and later witnessed royal charters, thereby establishing his status in Roxburghshire and Lanarkshire.[2] Over generations, his descendants became recognized landholders in Lesmahagow and Blackwood.[3]

---

[51]*Cokayne, George Edward. The Complete Peerage, vol. X. St. Catherine Press, 1945.*

Ibid.

Strickland, Agnes. Lives of the Queens of England. Longmans, 1864.

Hollister, C. Warren. Henry I. Yale University Press, 2001.

Matthew Paris, Chronica Majora, c. 1250.

Oman, Charles. A History of the Art of War in the Middle Ages, vol. 2. Methuen, 1924.

Chrimes, S. B. Henry VII. Yale University Press, 1999.

Anderson, Mark. Shakespeare by Another Name. Gotham Books, 2005.

Thompson, M. W. The Decline of the Castle. Cambridge University Press, 1987.

Douglas, David C. William the Conqueror. University of California Press, 1964.

Ward, Jennifer C. The De Veres of Castle Hedingham. Essex Record Office, 1980.

Squibb, G. D. The Lord Chamberlain's Office and Its Records. HMSO, 1974.

Though surnames shifted over time—from de Vère to de Were to Weir—the heraldic continuity remained: the Weirs of Blackwood quartered arms almost identical to the English de Vère's, differing only by minor cadency marks.[4] This strongly suggests a shared Norman origin. Rothaldus Weir (or de Vere) is recorded as bailie of Lesmahagow with a charter confirming ownership of Blackwood around **1400**.[5] The family held estates at Blackwood for centuries, and cadet branches formed at Stonebyres, Mossminion, Auchtyfardle, and Kirkton.[6]

The feud between the Weirs of Blackwood and the de Vere's of Stonebyres lasted centuries until **1592**, when the Stonebyres branch swore allegiance to James Weir of Blackwood, formally recognizing him as clan chief.[7] Stonebyres thereafter sometimes reverted to the "Vere" spelling. Major Thomas Weir of Kirkton (1599–1670), descended from Stonebyres, served as Covenanter officer, later became commander of Edinburgh's city guard, and notoriously confessed to witchcraft at seventy, being executed in **1670**.[8] His infamy, while historically dramatic, casts no authentic light on any claim to earldom or royal descent.[9]

Myself and my Father Nicholas de Vere/Weir fit into this genealogical tradition. While exact modern records are limited, genealogical discussions trace his line patrilineally back to Thomas Weir of Blackwood and beyond. For example, one reconstruction begins from **Archibald Weir (Thompson)** and via maternal lines leads back to Thomas Weir of Blackwood, through which **Nicholas Thomas Logan Weir** claimed descent from Thomas and ultimately from Ralph de Vere.[10] Although it is not the only line I have that traces to the De Vere's, It is our family belief holds that Nicholas and myself belong to the same Blackwood descent deriving from the Norman "Veres."

In Ireland, a later revival of the Norman name occurred: the Hunt family of Curragh Chase in County Limerick were granted lands in the mid-17th century. In **1784**, Vere Hunt was created a baronet, and in **1832** his son **Sir Aubrey Hunt** formally adopted the surname **de Vere**, explicitly re-claiming the Norman heritage of the English earls.[11] Though genealogically unrelated to the medieval de Vères of Oxford or the Weirs of Blackwood, they shared name, arms, and a claimed Norman identity.[12]

Paternal line—**Nicholas de Vere/Weir**—thus represents a living link to this Scottish Norman tradition. The line from Ralph de Vere to Rothaldus of Blackwood and then through successive lairds can be reconstructed as follows:

Genealogy of Weir/de Vère descent including Nicholas de Vère/Weir

Ralph (Radulphus/Baltredus) de Vère (active in Scotland ca. 1165; captured 1174)[12]
└ Walter de Vère (fl. 1190)
└ Ralph de Vère (fl. 1214–1296), lands in Lanarkshire, signed Ragman Roll 1296[13]
└ Thomas de Vère (stone origins ca. 1266) – founder of Stonebyres branch[13]
└ Richard de Were (fl. 1294)
└ Thomas de Were (k. early 14th c.), laird of Stonebyres[13]
└ Buan de Vère
└ Rothaldus de Vère/Weir of Blackwood (chartered 1400)[12]
└ Thomas Weir of Blackwood (married Aegidia Somerville c.1483)[13]
└ James Weir of Blackwood (1495–1595) married Euphemia Hamilton[13]

┗ … successive lairds of Blackwood or Kirkton …
┗ Archibald Weir (later Thompson) … maternal/paternal leads →
┗ **Nicholas de Vère/Weir**

This continuous tradition showcases the Norman de Vère heritage transplanted to Scotland and preserved through centuries. The Weirs of Blackwood became recognized as an armigerous family and as a sept of clans such as Buchanan, MacNaughton, and MacFarlane, confirming their local social status.[14] Their seat at Blackwood estate remained central until the Hope-Weirs assumed it in the eighteenth century.[15]

The name change in Ireland by Sir Aubrey Hunt de Vère in **1832** echoes a parallel tendency to reclaim ancestral Norman identity—though my line persisted quietly in Scotland.[12] The symbolic interlink lies in shared heraldry, surname history, and the retention of de Vère/Weir identity.

The Weirs of Blackwood are widely acknowledged as a cadet branch of the Norman de Vère family, with Ralph de Vère in the late 12th century as their Scottish progenitor. My father, **Nicholas de Vère/Weir**, emerges within this tradition, linking modern family memory to medieval descent. Though no academic evidence supports actual inheritance of the Oxford earldom, heraldic and genealogical continuity underscores a Norman origin shared across England, Scotland, and even later revived in Ireland. The intertwining of de Vère with Weir, and its continued use in my paternal line, reflects the durable cultural legacy of Norman lineage in the British Isles.⁵²

I had found my De Vere's—and not just through the Weir line, many lines, with them came unexpected royalty, kings, Vikings. At the time, it seemed surreal. And yet I found myself asking—what does this really mean? What relevance does this hold for who I am now?

- ⁵²*According to clan histories (ScotClans, ScotsConnection, Geni, Electric Scotland, YouTube, and Stirnet), Ralph de Vere served King William the Lion and was captured at Alnwick in 1174.*
  ² Ralph witnessed charters between 1174 and 1184 and granted lands to Kelso Abbey. (Electric Scotland)
  ³ Branches at Blackwood and Stonebyres are documented in both ScotClans and Stirnet genealogies.
  ⁴ The arms of the Scottish de Veres are nearly identical to those of the English Earls, with cadency marks. (Genealogy.com, ScotClans)
  ⁵ A charter from 1400 confirms Rothald Weir's Blackwood lands, issued by Kelso Abbey. (Wikipedia, ScotClans, Electric Scotland)
  ⁶ Branches at Stonebyres, Mossminion, Auchtyfardle, and Kirkton are described in Stirnet and Electric Scotland articles.
  ⁷ The feud ended in 1592, with the Stonebyres branch swearing allegiance and the clan chief formally recognized. (Electric Scotland, Stirnet)
  ⁸ The life and execution of Major Thomas Weir of Kirkton in 1670 are recorded by ScotsConnection.
  ⁹ Historians note there was no formal earldom claim; the case of Thomas Weir was regarded as local infamy only. (Electric Scotland)
  ¹⁰ A Geni forum traces Nicholas de Vere von Drakenberg back to Thomas Weir of Blackwood via Archibald. (Geni, Genealogy.com)
  ¹¹ The Hunt/de Vère adoption in Ireland by royal licence occurred in 1832. (ClanCentral, Rootsweb)
  ¹² The Irish de Vère baronets revived the Norman name in the 19th century. (Wikipedia)
  ¹³ Stirnet contains a detailed genealogy of successive Weirs of Blackwood. (ScotClans, Stirnet, Electric Scotland)
  ¹⁴ Clan affiliations are recognized by both ScotClans and Electric Scotland.
  ¹⁵ Hope-Weir adoption and Craigiehall inheritance documented by Wikipedia and ScotClans

I've told my own son, who asks me, "what does any of this matter?" I reply, "When I'm gone, you'll find great comfort in knowing your mum was a passionate writer and researcher—you'll still have my books to remember me by." I know that's how I feel about my father. I feel his hand on my shoulder every time I uncover something he once knew.

People often ask questions like that. Some scoff. Some shrug it off. But to me, it matters—*especially* during the times when you question your existence, your value, your path. When life feels uncertain or heavy, and you're trying to find something with *substance*—something that roots you. Genealogy became more than just names and dates—it became a spiritual path, one with real weight and grounding.

One day, a close friend gave me a spiritual message that changed everything. She said, "There's something missing in your line. You need to find the missing piece, the thread that runs through it. You need to clear it, honour it, and heal it." That message sent me on a new quest—one that would lead to a breakthrough I never expected.

The Magna Carta

As I worked to sort out the De Vere lines, I realized that they were tied to the very foundation of English constitutional history. I was stunned to discover that I was *related to every single knight and lord listed on the Magna Carta*. Another "wow" moment, another piece of validation that I was walking the path I was meant to walk.

And then came one of the strangest synchronicities of all.

I was in **Chertsey**, on a spiritual journey, seeking out **Runnymede**—the historic site associated with the sealing of the Magna Carta. I was following a feeling, more than a plan. But something pulled me there. As I wandered, I came across **Abbey Road**. That name rang loudly in my head—I'd lived on an Abbey Road once and obvioulsy my name being Abbe, It made me stop in my tracks. And then I saw it: right at the crossroads, **Weir Road** intersected Abbey Road.

There I was, quite literally standing on **Abbey and Weir Roads**.

Weir, my ancestral name. That was the moment. A true spiritual echo. It felt as though time folded into itself, as if history, ancestry, and present-day life had aligned to remind me: I am walking the path I was always meant to walk.

I've walked where they walked—at **Hedingham Castle**, in the shadows of ancient halls where the DeVere's once ruled. I've stood where the Magna Carta was sealed, and where the streets bore our names. These aren't just places—they're echoes, reminders, and spiritual markers.

And so, I keep going. With every new name, every connection, every synchronicity, I'm reminded that we don't walk these paths alone. We walk in rhythm with those who came before us.

Because sometimes, history doesn't just live in books—it lives in **you**.

The Enduring Legacy of the Magna Carta: Law, Liberty, and the Common People

The Magna Carta, sealed by King John of England in 1215, has long been revered as a foundational document in the history of democratic governance and legal liberty. Often hailed as the first formal step toward constitutional law, it challenged the notion of absolute monarchy and laid down principles that have endured through centuries, influencing legal systems and the idea of justice globally. While its immediate impact was on the nobility and their relationship with the Crown, its long-term consequences extended far beyond the elite, influencing the development of legal protections for ordinary people and the conception of law as a restraint on power.

The Magna Carta emerged out of a crisis of governance and legitimacy during the reign of King John, whose military failures, heavy taxation, and disregard for feudal customs provoked widespread baronial opposition. The document was sealed at Runnymede in June 1215, following negotiations between the king and a coalition of rebellious barons. Its provisions sought to address grievances and protect baronial rights against royal encroachment. However, the Magna Carta was more than a list of noble demands—it was an unprecedented assertion that even the monarch was subject to the law. One of its most radical features was Clause 61, the so-called "security clause," which stipulated the formation of a committee of twenty-five barons to ensure the king's compliance with the Charter. These men, whose names were later chronicled by Matthew Paris, were entrusted with the authority to use force, including seizure of lands and castles, to compel royal obedience if the king violated any part of the Charter. This enforcement mechanism, derived from the common law doctrine of distraint, marked a seismic shift in power dynamics and represented one of the earliest legal acknowledgments that a ruler could be held accountable.[1]

The barons had foreseen the possibility that King John, once free from Runnymede, would renege on the Charter, deeming it an illegitimate constraint on royal authority. To counter this risk, Clause 61 allowed the twenty-five barons to act against the king if he failed to abide by the Charter. Any breach was to be reported to four of the twenty-five, who would then notify the king. If no remedy was provided within forty days, the full committee was empowered to "distrain and distress us in every way they can, namely by seizing castles, lands and possessions" until amends were made.[2] This clause introduced the remarkable notion that the king himself sanctioned armed enforcement against his own rule, using distraint—a legal method previously used for debt recovery—to impose accountability.

Since the clause anticipated that the twenty-five would be elected later, their names were not listed in the Charter itself. However, Matthew Paris later recorded them: Richard, Earl of Clare; William de Fors, Count of Aumale; Geoffrey de Mandeville, Earl of Gloucester; Saer de Quincy, Earl of Winchester; Henry de Bohun, Earl of Hereford; Roger Bigod, Earl of Norfolk; Robert de Vere, Earl of Oxford; William Marshal junior; Robert FitzWalter; Gilbert de Clare; Eustace de Vesci; Hugh Bigod; William de Mowbray; the Mayor of London; William de Lanvallei; Robert de Ros; John de Lacy, Constable of Chester; Richard de Percy; John FitzRobert; William Malet; Geoffrey de Say; Roger de Montbegon; William de Huntingfield; Richard de Munfichet; and William d'Aubigny.[3] Notably, these were all laymen and predominantly drawn from the hard-line opposition to John. No churchmen were included, underscoring the committee's function as a military enforcement body.

The De Vere family held substantial influence during the period. Robert de Vere, Earl of Oxford, often associated with the broader De Vere lineage, was among the twenty-five. His inclusion underscores the role of emerging noble families in shaping early constitutional governance. The De Veres, later rising to even greater prominence, traced their political involvement and loyalty to this formative event. Their alignment with the Charter was not only strategic but also ideologically significant, as they sought to safeguard hereditary rights and autonomy from an increasingly intrusive monarchy.[4]

The Magna Carta's primary aim was to check the king's authority and safeguard the rights of the feudal elite. The barons and knights, forming the upper echelons of the feudal hierarchy, had suffered under King John's arbitrary demands. For instance, scutage—a payment made in lieu of military service—had been levied with increasing frequency and unpredictability. The Charter imposed new restrictions, such as limiting scutage and regulating reliefs paid by heirs to inherit feudal lands. These provisions were vital for knights, whose financial and social stability depended on the predictability of feudal dues. Knights, often situated between barons and peasants, stood to benefit directly from such measures, as their landholdings and economic independence were protected from royal exploitation.[5]

The Charter also included measures that addressed the rights of women. Chapter 8 of the Charter provided that "no widow shall be forced to marry so long as she wishes to live without a husband."[6] Previously, if a baron died leaving a widow, her remarriage would fall under royal control. One case illustrating this abuse is that of Isabel de Clare, whose estates in Normandy were so valuable that she was confined in the Tower of London for "safekeeping" by Henry II.[7] This clause represented a shift towards individual agency for women and was a crucial step in limiting royal manipulation of marriages for political and economic gain.

Though primarily designed to protect the elite, the Magna Carta's broader implications for common people cannot be understated. Clause 39 famously declared that "no free man shall be seized or imprisoned, or stripped of his rights or possessions… except by the lawful judgment of his equals or by the law of the land."[8] While initially limited to the free men—a minority in a society dominated by serfdom—this principle of due process would evolve into a cornerstone of modern legal systems. Clause 40 reinforced this, asserting, "to no one will we sell to no one deny or delay right or justice." Together, these clauses laid the groundwork for a legal tradition emphasing fairness, transparency, and accountability.

The Charter also acknowledged the rights of townspeople and merchants, offering protections for trade and establishing standard measures for wine, ale, and corn. London was granted special liberties, and its inclusion in the Charter marked a recognition of its growing economic and political significance.[9] This early nod to urban autonomy sowed the seeds for municipal rights and economic freedoms, both of which are now essential components of modern governance.

The lasting legacy of the Magna Carta lies in the legal standards and precedents it established. Its insistence that rulers be bound by law set a transformative precedent. While the 1215 version was annulled by Pope Innocent III shortly after its sealing, under pressure from King John, its core principles endured. The document was reissued and revised in 1216, 1217, and 1225 by John's successor, Henry III, and later confirmed by Edward I in 1297.[10] While many of the more radical clauses, including Clause 61, were omitted in these later versions, the concept of accountable governance remained. The removal of the enforcement clause may have weakened immediate baronial oversight, but it did not erase the radical precedent that a king could be bound—and even coerced—by law.

This process of reissuing the Charter, while diminishing its immediate legal teeth, ensured its symbolic survival. In subsequent centuries, it was invoked repeatedly in the struggle between monarchy and Parliament. During the English Civil War, it served as a rhetorical weapon for Parliamentarians seeking to limit royal prerogative. In the 17th century, legal thinkers like Sir Edward Coke used the Magna Carta to defend common law traditions and resist the expansion of royal authority.[11] These arguments contributed directly to the Petition of Right in 1628 and the English Bill of Rights in 1689, both of which reinforced the idea of limited monarchy.

Across the Atlantic, the Magna Carta found a new life in American political thought. Colonial charters referenced its principles, and the framers of the U.S. Constitution embedded its ideals within their own legal framework. The Fifth Amendment's guarantee of due process is a direct descendant of Clause 39. The broader American legal culture, with its emphasis on rights, representation, and checks on executive power, owes much to this medieval document.[12]

Even though many of its clauses are archaic or irrelevant today—concerned with forest laws, fish weirs, or feudal payments—the spirit of the Magna Carta endures. It has become a powerful symbol of liberty, invoked by lawyers, politicians, and activists across centuries and continents. That a document originally created to resolve a baronial dispute over taxation could evolve into a universal icon of freedom is a testament to its enduring relevance.

Clause 61 and the Committee of Twenty-Five were perhaps the most revolutionary elements of the original Charter. Though the clause was removed in later versions, its implication—that the king could be subject to coercion by his subjects under the law—echoed through centuries of constitutional development. It planted the seed of the modern notion that governments derive their legitimacy from consent and that no authority is above the law.

The Magna Carta of 1215 was not a democratic manifesto by modern standards, but it introduced concepts that would become central to democratic thought. It reshaped the relationship between ruler and ruled, between power and justice. While its immediate aim was to serve the interests of the barons and knights, its enduring influence has benefitted society at large. Its principles have transcended their feudal origins to become universal truths about governance, rights, and the rule of law.[53]

---

[53] *Matthew Paris, Chronica Majora, c. 1250.*

Original Text Inclusion, "Magna Carta 1215" – Clause 61 Analysis.

Ibid., list derived from Matthew Paris.

Carpenter, David. Magna Carta. Penguin Classics, 2015.

Holt, J.C. Magna Carta. Cambridge University Press, 1992.

Magna Carta, Chapter 8.

Linebaugh, Peter. The Magna Carta Manifesto. University of California Press, 2008.

Magna Carta, Chapter 39.

From the baronial halls of England, where the de Vère family stood among the guarantors of the Magna Carta, a branch carried its Norman name north into Scotland. There, the name evolved to Weir, but the heraldic stars and traditions endured. For generations, the Weirs of Blackwood served as landholders, soldiers, and civic leaders, their legacy entwined with both political influence and the mysteries of inherited spiritual gifts. In the 17th century — an age when unorthodox beliefs could be fatal — one descendant's life would cast the family into infamy. Major Thomas Weir of Kirkton, a devout Covenanter turned accused warlock, became one of the most notorious figures in Scotland's witchcraft persecutions. Though his trial ended in execution, the legends surrounding him speak to deeper, older undercurrents — of spiritual abilities passed down through bloodlines, misunderstood in an era when mysticism was often met with

Vincent, Nicholas. Magna Carta: A Very Short Introduction. Oxford University Press, 2012.

Plucknett, Theodore F.T. A Concise History of the Common Law. Butterworths, 1956.

Coke, Edward. The Second Part of the Institutes of the Lawes of England, 1642.

U.S. National Archives. "The Influence of Magna Carta on the U.S. Constitution."

the gallows. His story stands at the crossroads of heritage, persecution, and the enduring shadow of "royal witchcraft

Major Thomas Weir- The Wizard of West Bow

To continue to find such amazing connection, I had to see where and how my family lived, I took the kids on a journey to Edinburgh, to the castle gate and west bow to see for myself. The property has been known as one of the most haunted properties in Scotland. The property was said to have been either burnt down and or replaced, I found it amusing to see that there was a Quaker house in the top half of the building. In the past I had seen Derek Accora and Yvette Fielding doing their ghost hunt on Most Haunted.

Major Thomas Weir was a good and well-respected Christian, and a man of Edinburgh's City Guard. The people of Edinburgh looked up to him and his unparalleled devotion to the church earned him the nickname 'The West Bow Saint', on account of the little flat that he and his spinster sister Jean (or more commonly known as Grizel) occupied on Edinburgh's West Bow. The pair had come from Lanarkshire, from a mother who was reputedly host to

the Second Sight, but this did nothing to scupper their reputation as devout followers of God.

Thomas was ever the enthusiastic preacher, but those who saw him preach without his trusty black staff, with which he was rarely parted, reported that his words fell flat and his addresses lacked their usual power. The dark staff, with its frightening head on top and carvings of satyrs about its shaft, was widely assumed to be nothing more than a walking aid, while others swore, they had seen the staff move by itself, even running errands for Thomas, including opening doors like some ghostly butler.

One fateful Sunday morning, the church community was to bear witness to an event most peculiar, and their beloved West Bow Saint would never be the same again. At the beginning of the service, Thomas stood before the congregation, as always, leaning on his staff for support. As he lifted his head, and raised his arms, the members of the congregation couldn't help but notice the peaky hue to his skin. When Thomas opened his mouth, it was not prayers that spilled out, but a terrible confession that bound the congregation in horror. Thomas claimed responsibility for some of the most evil deeds: he plead to witchcraft, necromancy, and terrible intimate acts with beasts and his own sister.

The clergy were shocked at what they had witnessed, but, reluctant to accuse such a revered member of their community of witchcraft, they called the best doctors the city had to offer. The doctors examined Thomas, but much to their collective bewilderment, each verdict was clear: never had there been a man so healthy in body and mind as Major Thomas Weir, who continued to insist on the crimes he had committed.

At a loss for what to do, the authorities questioned Grizel Weir, Thomas' spinster sister. Thomas had marred her good name in his proclamation, so surely, she would shed some light on her brother's madness?

But Grizel did nothing to clear the air, or even deny the repulsive accusations her own brother had levelled against her, instead readily admitting all that Thomas had already confessed to, and more. She admitted their sinful relations, and declared her mother was a witch skilled in necromancy. She recounted stories of devilry and fairy. She claimed on one occasion, a blazing carriage pulled by six charcoal horses arrived at their house on the West Bow to take them to their master, Auld Nick himself. She claimed one time a fairy gave to her a piece of tree root, an amulet and silver and when

Grizel returned to her spinning wheel, she found more fine yarn than any person could have spun in the time that passed.

With the pair unrepentant, the authorities had no other choice but to imprison Thomas and Grizel in the city Tolbooth to await the outcome of their trial. Witnesses were called from the congregation that had heard Thomas' first dark confession.

The siblings, unsurprisingly, plead guilty, and with naught else to be done, the pair were sentenced to death. Thomas was to be strangled at the stake and burned to ash alongside his precious staff at the Gallows Lee between Edinburgh and Leith, while Grizel was to hang in the Grass market. [54]

It has been said by those who watched the burning that Thomas took longer than it would take any normal person to burn, his staff writhing and twisting in the flames by his side. Grizel, on the other hand, stood on the gallows and attempted to remove all of her clothes before meeting her end, to the shock of the gathered onlookers.

Following the execution of Thomas and Grizel Weir, the flat they had occupied on the West Bow was abandoned and left to decay. The public feared the evil spirits that might linger within, and while no person had dared to live there, mysterious happenings continued to be reported even years after its occupant's death. In 1780 it was bought by an ex-soldier and his wife. The pair intended to settle despite the horrid rumours about the most haunted house in

---

[54] *Photograph by Abbe Devere. The Grassmarket at the bottom of West Bow, Edinburgh. The house once owned by Major Thomas Weir is located above the current blue building, which now houses the Quaker Meeting House. This site corresponds closely with historical views of West Bow as depicted in period paintings.*

Edinburgh, only to flee on their first night when the apparition of a calf appeared at their bedside.

Since, other reports include that the windows light up at night, strange music and laughter wafting into the street. Sometimes, the shapes of enormous women can be made out through the windows, and other times the mysterious black staff can be seen hovering its way down the street in search of its master. Sometimes, the sound of a coach and six horses can be heard thundering down the West Bow, bearing the spirits of Thomas and Grisel off back to Auld Nick.[55]

---

[55] *Marion Lochhead, Edinburgh Lore and Legend (Publisher details, year unknown).*

Robert Chambers, Traditions of Edinburgh (Publisher details, originally published 1824).

"The Case of Thomas Weir," Providentia, Dr. Romeo Vitelli, accessed August 2025, drvitelli.typepad.com

There's much about this story that carries a sense of shame, especially in how society tends to view it—but through the eyes of a historian, it becomes a truly fascinating tale. It challenges us to reconsider what witchcraft really is. We're far removed from the sensationalized depictions fed to us by popular culture, like *Buffy the Vampire Slayer* or the endless stream of American fantasy tropes. When I was growing up, my mother told me she was a third-degree witch. Curious, I'd ask her what that meant. She would speak about using herbs and oils to heal herself, to restore balance. She kept a beautiful herb garden, rich with scent and life. But she never practiced anything I found unusual—not strange in the way people might imagine. There were no dark rituals, no spells chanted under moonlight. She was solitary, quiet in her craft, simply nurturing her own health and intuition. She wasn't part of any cult, nor did she follow the more theatrical aspects of New Age spirituality. She walked her own path.

When we moved to Devon, people ridiculed her. They called her a gypsy or a traveller, judging her by how she dressed and how she chose to live. She withdrew even further, keeping to herself, letting very few people in. Watching her endure that persecution made me wary of being labelled the same. I distanced myself from it, pushed it away. But as I got older, and my own clairvoyant abilities began to surface more strongly, I turned to my father, who had always spoken of the gifts we shared—the clear foresight passed down through generations.

Looking into my ancestry, I began to see a pattern. Many of those who came before me had been called witches or clairvoyants. My grandmother, Annie Macdonald, was well-known for her abilities. Relatives would say she was one of the greatest psychics they had ever known. It became clear to me that being a witch isn't about theatrics or horror-film clichés. It's a path of learning—of finding peace with yourself and with the world. It's about listening deeply: to nature, to intuition, to emotion. It's about learning how to use what you've been given—not for power or spectacle, but to better your life and nourish your mental and emotional health.

The last thing I—or my family—ever aspired to was becoming some female version of Aleister Crowley. That path, built on excess and ego, was never ours. Ours has always been quieter. Rooted. Private. It's never been about spectacle. It's been about healing, knowing, and being—learning not how to control the world around you, but how to live more gently within it. Funnily enough Aleister Crowley did actually live in Torquay.

It's a family affair

The history of nobility is not the history of separate dynasties, but the story of one immense family joined together through centuries of intermarriage. From the arrival of the Normans in England to the modern monarchy of Britain, the pattern is constant: alliances made in the marriage bed, inheritances carried by daughters, dynastic survival secured by heiresses who became the mothers of kings and queens. By the fifteenth century, it is no exaggeration to say that nearly every noble house in Britain shared blood with another, and through those lines with the whole of Europe. The surnames give an illusion of division, but the genealogical record tells another story: what seemed rival dynasties were in reality branches of the same tree.

The Bohuns are an early example of how women transmitted dynastic blood into the heart of royalty. Humphrey de Bohun, fourth Earl of Hereford, Constable of England, married Elizabeth, daughter of Edward I. Their descendants carried Bohun blood into the royal house through their daughters. Eleanor de Bohun married Thomas of Woodstock, son of Edward III, while Mary de Bohun married

Henry Bolingbroke, later Henry IV. Thus the Bohun inheritance became part of the Lancastrian kings, their bloodline preserved not through a son but through daughters who made queens.[1] The Mohuns of Dunster followed a similar course. When the male line failed, the Mohun heiress married into the Courtenays, Earls of Devon, and with her the Mohun patrimony and blood became Courtenay blood.[2] Hugh Courtenay, second Earl of Devon, married Margaret de Bohun, granddaughter of Edward I, uniting the Courtenays with royal descent.[3] Their younger son Philip founded the line at Powderham, while their elder son continued the senior earldom. Thus within one generation the Courtenays embodied the Bohun legacy, the Mohun inheritance, and Plantagenet descent.

The Nevilles were another family whose women spread their influence across the realm. Cecily Neville, known as the Rose of Raby, married Richard, Duke of York, and bore Edward IV and Richard III, making her the mother of kings. Her sisters married into the Percys, Stanleys, Hollands and Beauchamps, embedding Neville ancestry into every corner of the peerage.[4] The de Veres, hereditary Earls of Oxford, allied themselves to the same circles, intermarrying with Clares, Bohuns and Howards, and so perpetuating their blood through six centuries. Robert de Vere, third Earl, stood among the barons who sealed Magna Carta, and Edward de Vere, seventeenth Earl, was a courtier of Elizabeth I, but the endurance of the family lay in its marriages, which tied it inseparably to other great houses.[5]

On the Continent the same pattern governed. The Medici of Florence, famous as bankers and patrons of the arts, projected their power far beyond Tuscany by means of their daughters. Catherine de' Medici married Henry II of France and bore three French kings: Francis II, Charles IX and Henry III. Marie de' Medici, married to Henry IV of France, served as regent for her son Louis XIII. The Medici's real strength was not their gold alone but the queens they gave to Europe.[6] The Grimaldis of Monaco, though ruling one of the smallest states in Christendom, ensured their survival by the same means. Francis William Blagdon in his early nineteenth-century account remarked that their survival rested upon "a chain of well-timed marriages" by which their tiny principality was bound to houses of far greater extent.[7] The Habsburgs made it their ruling policy. Their motto — *Bella gerant alii, tu felix Austria nube* — "Let others wage war; you, fortunate Austria, marry" — encapsulated their strategy. By uniting their daughters to the crowns of Spain, Bohemia, Hungary, Portugal and even England, they forged a continental empire with matrilineal blood as its cement. Catherine of Aragon, daughter of Ferdinand and Isabella, married Henry VIII; Mary of Burgundy brought the Low Countries into Habsburg hands; and by a chain of such marriages, Spain, Austria and much of Italy were drawn together.[8]

Everywhere the pattern appears. The Gonzagas of Mantua, the Estes of Ferrara, the Sforzas and Viscontis of Milan, the Orsini and Colonna of Rome, the Borgias of Valencia and the Farnese of Parma all rose or maintained themselves through women's marriages. These names open into dozens more, until the chart of Europe resembles a knotted vine. The crowns of kingdoms were likewise joined through women. Isabella of France, daughter of Philip IV, married Edward II and brought Capetian blood into the English throne.[9] Philippa of Hainault, descended from the counts of Avesnes and Hainault, married Edward III and became the mother of the Plantagenet line that fought the Hundred Years' War.[10] Catherine of Valois, daughter of Charles VI of France, married Henry V of England and bore Henry VI, binding Lancaster to the French crown.[11] Margaret Tudor, daughter of Henry VII, married James IV of Scotland; their great-grandson James VI inherited England's throne in 1603, uniting the crowns.[12] Anne of Denmark, of the Oldenburg line, married James VI/I, introducing Scandinavian royal blood into the Stuarts, and George of Denmark, also an Oldenburg, married Queen Anne.[13] Queen Victoria, Hanoverian through her mother, married Prince Albert of Saxe-Coburg and Gotha of the Wettin house, thus weaving German dynastic strands into the British monarchy, which later rebranded itself as Windsor.[14]

When all is considered together, it is clear that the nobility of Britain and Europe were never strangers. Their bloodlines crossed and re-crossed through marriages of heiresses, through diplomacy sealed in matrimony, and through dynasties preserved by the wombs of women. The Bohun daughters carried their patrimony into the Lancastrians, the Mohun heiress into the Courtenays, the Neville sisters into every baronial line. Catherine de' Medici ruled France as queen mother, Marie de' Medici as regent; Habsburg daughters carried their heritage into half of Europe; Isabella of France, Philippa of Hainault, Catherine of Valois, Margaret Tudor, Anne of Denmark and Queen Victoria all exemplify the same truth. To follow one family is eventually to follow them all. De Vere, Bohun, Neville, Courtenay, Medici, Habsburg, Bourbon, Oldenburg, Wettin, Grimaldi, Capet, Valois, Sforza, Orsini, Colonna, Gonzaga, and many more — every one joined in a single web.

A list of their names gives only the barest impression: de Vere, Devereux, Bohun, Mohun, Clare, Warenne, Mandeville, Mortimer, Beauchamp, Lacy, Hastings, Grey, Talbot, Neville, Percy, Courtenay, Howard, Bruce, Douglas, Hamilton, Campbell, MacDonald, Sinclair, Logan, Grant, Fitzgerald, Butler, O'Neill, O'Brien, MacCarthy; and abroad, the Capetians, Valois, Bourbons, Orléans, Medicis, Grimaldis, Gonzagas, Estes, Sforzas, Viscontis, Colonnas, Orsinis, Borgias, Farneses, Savoys, Habsburgs, Hohenzollerns, Wittelsbachs, Luxembourgs, Wettins, Oldenburgs, Lorraines, Trastámaras, Avís, Palaiologoi, Komnenoi, Cantacuzenes, Jagiełłos, Piasts, Rurikids, Romanovs, Vasas and Bernadottes. This is only a glimpse, for each of these names connects in turn to many others through cadet branches, cousins and alliances, so that to trace one line is to find yourself tracing them all. What seems divided by name is in truth united by blood.

Having established how the noble families of Britain and Europe form one extended household, I turned to my own bloodlines to see how these truths applied to me personally.[56]

Fuelled by my father's discoveries, I took it upon myself to delve deep into my own genetics. I found his claims to be accurate. I utilized several resources, including 23andMe and My True Ancestry, to uncover the truth. I meticulously traced both my mother's and father's ancestry, and while the depth of this exploration is vast, I am determined to continue—completing this journey is a priority. Crucially, I discovered that both of my parents share remarkably similar bloodlines. When I purchased land in this village, I had no idea of my true lineage and its significance to this place. After researching Haccombe, I uncovered that the lord and lady, particularly Lady Philippa de Courtney, are part of my heritage. Delving into my mother's ancestry, I established a connection to Philippa Ardeken/ Ercedekne, who had a daughter named Joan. Joan's marriage to a de Vere raises fascinating odds, as my mother's lineage had already intertwined with my father's line back in the 1400s. Joan Carew Courtney married de Vere—she was born on August 14, 1411, in Haccombe (now Newton Abbot), Devon, England, and passed away in 1501 in Haccombe.

Haccombe is the most interesting parish in the vicinity of Newton, and one of the most singular in Devon. Of old time it was an extra-parochial chapelry ; and as it was made an arch-presbytery by Sir John L'Ercedekne (Archdekne) about the year 1341, so the rector of Haccombe is ' archpriest' still. The college originally consisted of the archpriest and five associates, who lived in community: but only the head now remains. As the seat of an

---

[56] See appendix

archpriest, Haccombe naturally used to claim exemption from the authority of an archdeacon ; and Haccombe itself was regarded as beyond the authority of any officers, civil or military, and as being free, by royal grant, from any taxes. Probably fewer changes as to population have taken place here than in any other manor in Devon which has developed into a parish.

When Stephen held it under Baldwin the Sheriff, it had a recorded population of 15. It now simply contains the manor-house, rectory, and farm ; and the population is largely dependent upon the residence of the family at the time of the census. Normally, it is below 20 ; and at one enumeration it was but 13. Stephen took name from his manor, and the heiress of his family brought it to the Ercedekne' s. By marriage it then came through the Courtenay's to its present owners, the Carew's

The church dates from the thirteenth century, and contains some fine effigies of the Haccombe's, with brasses of the Carew's, and a high tomb which probably commemorates the Courtenay owners Hugh and Philippa, his wife. On the door of the church were formerly four horseshoe relics, according to the legend, of a wager made between a Carew and a Champernowne, as to who would swim on horseback the farthest to sea.

Carew won the wager, and with it a manor, and nailed the shoes of his horse to the church door in ' everlasting remembrance.'[57]

Sir Robert De Vere (died 1461), of Haccombe, was an influential English soldier and diplomat, notably appointed as Seneschal of Gascony. He Married Joan Carew, Widow of Nicholas Carew snr and daughter of Hugh Courtenay and Philippa Archdekne

---

[57] R. N. Worth, *History of Devonshire* (London: Elliot Stock, 1886).

His father, Richard De Vere, held the title of the 11th Earl of Oxford. His wife had numerous relatives instrumental in the founding of Torquay. In my research on my mother's side, I discovered that many of her Wright family members lived here for the last 100 years. I found gravestones in the local church and houses directly across from mine, once owned by my family. Some were skilled thatcher's who significantly contributed to the roofs of the village. This history solidified my sense of belonging more than ever. Through both my mother and father, I uncovered our link to Anne Boleyn, wife of Henry VIII, who is also related to my father through extended cousins. Furthermore, I traced the notable Cary, Mohun, Carew, Palk, and Briwere families, the very founders of Torquay, where I have resided for the past 20 years. I have never felt more rooted, and now I fully comprehend why I hold such a deep affection for Torquay. For years, I have engaged in face painting at Cockington Court, always sensing a strong connection to the area. Now, it all fits into place. I am on family-owned land in a village that feels distinctly like home. My path is aligning with profound synchronicity, I am exactly where I am meant to be.

I had a vested interest in The De Courtenay family lines, Due to my Mothers genealogy.
They were the earls of Powderham castle, along with Tiverton Castle.
I looked further into Hugh De Courtenay the 2nd earl of Devon and found that he and his wife were my 18th grandparents.; Likewise with connections to His wife Margaret De Bohun.

The Courtenay's trace their origins to Milo (or Miles/Milon) de Courtenay (c. 1068–1127/38), a seigneur in Burgundy of modest lineage but important in laying foundations for later English connections. The Courtenay family has long been associated with the veneration and transfer of sacred relics, most notably the Crown of Thorns believed to have been worn by Christ. This tradition, while interwoven with family lore, is rooted in historic fact through their direct kinship to Baldwin II de Courtenay, Latin Emperor of Constantinople, who played a pivotal role in bringing this relic to Western Christendom.

Baldwin II mortgaged the relic to Venetian bankers in 1238, and King Louis IX (Saint Louis) of France redeemed the Crown for 135,000 livres. The relic was solemnly conveyed to Paris and enshrined in the newly constructed Sainte-Chapelle. This act, preserved in financial and imperial records of the time, establishes the Courtenay's as central to one of the most significant relic transfers in Christian history. Surviving the French Revolution and the 2019 Notre-Dame fire, the Crown of Thorns remains preserved under the care of the Knights of the Holy Sepulchre in Notre-Dame Cathedral. The Courtenay's' role in its Western transmission anchors their spiritual legacy in historical truth.[1][2][3][4][5][6]

The family's English fortunes begin in the person of Reginald de Courtenay, whose grandson Robert de Courtenay (d. 1242), feudal baron of Okehampton via his mother Hawise de Courcy, married Mary de Redvers, daughter and heiress of William de Redvers, 5th Earl of Devon. That union brought the Courtenay's into the orbit of Devon's great earldom. When Isabel de Forz, suo jure 8th Countess of Devon, died in 1293, Hugh de Courtenay, great-grandson of Robert, inherited and was later recognised as Earl of Devon in 1335—though sources differ whether this was a new creation or succession of the Redvers title.

In 1325 that same Hugh married Margaret de Bohun, granddaughter of Edward I, and acquired Powderham through her dowry. Their fifth son, Sir Philip Courtenay (d. 1406), later founded the line seated at Powderham. This junior line built the present fortified manor house from about 1390 onwards and has occupied it ever since. Powderham Castle thus became the enduring seat of the cadet Courtenay branch, separate from the senior line at Tiverton and Okehampton, until the senior line died out in the 16th century, after which the Powderham branch became de jure Earls of Devon and in 1831 formally confirmed as de facto holders.

Joscelin de Courtenay, a cousin to Milo, participated in the First Crusade and became Count of Edessa. His descendants included Baldwin II, the aforementioned Emperor of Constantinople, providing direct lineage from the Courtenay family to the ruling elite of the Latin East. The Courtenay's' links to the Crusades and sacred relics thus combine both military and spiritual dimensions. Although no direct evidence confirms that members of the English Courtenay's were Knights Templar, the family's demonstrated piety and history of pilgrimage and military engagement in the Holy Land indicate alignment with the ideals of the Templar order.

The Courtenay's' medieval and early modern marital alliances reinforce their noble status. Marriages into families such as the de Bohuns (via Margaret), Bonville's (via Margaret Bonville), and Howards (notably Elizabeth Howard's union with a senior Courtenay) illustrate their entwinement with England's most powerful houses. Earlier links with the de Clare's and Despenser's, particularly through 12th-century Montlhéry marriages, brought Courtenay blood into relation with Marcher barons and Crusader aristocracy. Genealogical records such as those found in *The Complete Peerage* and *Europäische Stammtafeln* confirm these intertwined lines, offering authoritative grounding for such noble affiliations.

Powderham Castle itself encapsulates centuries of family presence. Built by Sir Philip Courtenay in the late 14th century, it survived the Wars of the Roses when the senior Earls of Devon at Tiverton were enemies of the Bonville's. Powderham had its own internecine history: Sir William Courtenay of Powderham (d. 1485) married

Margaret Bonville, making the castle a Bonville stronghold opposed to their Tiverton relatives. In 1455 Thomas de Courtenay, 5th Earl of Devon, besieged Powderham for two months before defeating Lord Bonville at Clyst Heath.

In the English Civil War, the castle was held by Royalists under Sir Hugh Meredith, later captured by Parliamentarian forces in 1646 and damaged; it remained partly ruinous until repairs in the early 1700s by Sir William Courtenay, 2nd Baronet. Despite such upheavals, the Powderham line endured. Sir William "the Great" (1477–1535) became a major Devon courtier and sheriff under Henry VIII, reinforcing the family's status.

The junior Powderham line eventually inherited the earldom when the senior branch became extinct in 1556, although recognition by the House of Lords only occurred in 1831 when William Courtenay, Viscount Courtenay of Powderham, was confirmed as Earl of Devon. Subsequent generations expanded and remodelled Powderham: the 18th-century enlargement by successive William Courtenay's added Rococo interiors, the Music Room by James Wyatt in the 1790s, and a Gothic-revival exterior elevating the manor into a grand 'castle'. The 18th-century aristocrat William, 3rd Viscount (later 9th Earl), known as "Kitty" Courtenay, famously lived there with his thirteen sisters, commissioning key interiors and landscape designs.

By the 20th century, Powderham faced financial strain: three early-20th-century earls died, incurring hefty death duties, shrinking family lands by some 90 percent. They nearly transferred the castle to the National Trust, but retained it and reopened to the public in 1957. Under Hugh Courtenay, 18th Earl, estate land expanded again, and events and tourism became tools to sustain the estate financially. Today the family remains headed by Charles Peregrine Courtenay, 19th Earl of Devon (born 1975), a barrister and crossbench hereditary peer in the House of Lords, who resides at Powderham with his family and continues to open the house to educational and community life—including hosting local schoolchildren in 2023 after a flood displaced their village school.

The Courtenay family stands uniquely at the intersection of sacred legacy, feudal ascendancy, and aristocratic continuity. Through Milo de Courtenay's early seigneurial status, Joscelin and Baldwin's crusader exploits, and the family's association with the Crown of Thorns, they are intertwined with both the martial and spiritual currents of medieval Christendom. Powderham Castle represents not merely a residence, but a living record of nearly a millennium of English noble heritage. Through war, alliance, inheritance, and devotion, the Courtenay's have sustained their place in England's historical and spiritual landscape[58].

---

[58] *"Notre-Dame Cathedral and the Crown of Thorns," Paris Digest. Accessed August 2025. parisdigest.com/monument/notre-dame-cathedral-crown-of-thorns-paris.htm*

"Saint Louis and the Relics of Passion," Friends of Notre-Dame de Paris. Accessed August 2025. friendsofnotredamedeparis.org/notre-dame-cathedral/history/saint-louis-and-the-relics-of-passion

"Veneration of the Crown of Thorns," Notre-Dame de Paris Official Website. Accessed August 2025. notredamedeparis.fr/en/veneration-crown-of-thorns

G. E. Cokayne, ed. Vicary Gibbs, The Complete Peerage, vol. 4 (London: St Catherine Press, 1916).

W. H. Blaauw, "The Barons' War," Sussex Archaeological Collections 6 (1853).

I. J. Sanders, English Baronies (Oxford: Clarendon Press, 1960), 69–70, 137.

Effigies of Hugh Courtenay the 2nd Earl of Devon and His wife Margaret De Bohun taken at Exeter Cathedral where many of my other ancestors lie in peace.

Henry Marshal, Bishop of Exeter (1194–1206)
Sir Peter Courtenay (died 1405), fifth son of Hugh Courtenay, 2nd Earl of Devon
Edmund Stafford, Lord Privy Seal, Lord Chancellor, Baron Stafford and Bishop of Exeter (1395–1419)
Sir Gawen Carew
Peter (Pierre) of Courtenay (1126–1183), youngest son of Louis VI of France and his second Queen consort Adélaïde de Maurienne.
Sir Peter Carew (c. 1514 – 1575) is not buried in the cathedral, but is commemorated by a mural monument.

The History of Torquay- TorMohun.

Genealogy of the families of Torquay
This research on Torquay Devon and tells the story of the people that created the bay and the history that is embedded within the beautiful little villages within.

The Mohan's, Brewers's/ Briwere's, Cary's, Carew's who all have links in this area and most important families to Torquay.
Torre Abbey- The Briwere- Brewers
William Briwere or Torre Abbey
I discovered that William Briwere was my 25th Grandfather, Having lived in Torquay for 20 years, I did not realise how close I was actually linked to this beautiful town, It wasn't until I discovered my ancestry in the Village of Haccombe and the little parcel of land that I bought and how it was once owned by on my mother's side the Courtney/ Courtenay family, The Earls of Devon and My dad's side the de Veres. This year I have further discovered more links

with my relations to The Cary's, Briwere's, Mohun's Carew's, Ridgeways who owned much of Devon and the quaint little villages that reside, here is the research as follows. Tor Mohun, previously known as Tor Brewer, is an ancient manor and parish located on the southern coast of Devon. It has since been integrated into the Victorian seaside town of Torquay, specifically referred to as Tormohun. In 1876, the Local Board of Health received governmental approval to officially rename the area from Tormoham to Torquay. The historic Church of St Saviour, which serves as the parish church of Tor Mohun, is situated on Tor Church Road and currently functions as the Greek Orthodox Church of Saint Andrew. This church features several notable monuments, including one dedicated to Thomas Ridgeway (1543–1598), the lord of the manor of Tor Mohun, as well as memorials to the Cary families associated with Torre Abbey and Cockington Court, both of which lie within the parish. In the Domesday Book of 1086, the manor of Torre is recorded as being held in chief and in demesne by William the Usher, a known servant of King William the Conqueror. He held several other manors in Devon, including Taw Green, Raddon, Bolham, Ilsham, and Mariansleigh. The manor later became referred to as Tor Brewer after being held by William Brewer, who passed away in 1226. In 1196, he donated part of the manor's land for the establishment of Torre Abbey, a monastery for Premonstratensian canons. Tor Mohun and Torre Abbey remained separate until after the Dissolution of the Monasteries in the 16th century, and they were divided again in the 17th century. Brewer's only surviving son died without children, leading to his daughters inheriting the estate. One of his daughters, Alice, married Reginald de Mohun, a feudal baron of Dunster, bringing substantial estates into their union, including a significant contribution of marble for the construction of Salisbury Cathedral. Reginald de Mohun obtained the manor through his marriage to Alice Brewer, and it became known as Tor Mohun. After her younger son, whom she passed the manor to, died without heirs, it reverted to the Mohun family of Dunster. The manor was later acquired by John Ridgeway (c. 1517 – 1560), a Member of Parliament, and his son Thomas Ridgeway (1543–1598) eventually bought the adjoining Torre Abbey from Sir Edward Seymour. A memorial honouring Thomas Ridgeway can still be found in the former St Saviour's Church. Thomas Ridgeway's son became Thomas Ridgeway, 1st Earl of Londonderry.

The Ridgeway's are also in my lines Being my 15th grandfathers and so on back to the first Ridgeway's of Newton Abbot and the surrounding area's.

In 1653, Torre Abbey was sold to Sir John Stawell, a legal advisor, who later sold it to Sir George Cary in 1662. The last male descendant of the Ridgeway family was Robert Ridgeway, 4th Earl of Londonderry, who died without sons and was buried in Tor Mohun, leaving behind two daughters. One, Lucy Ridgeway, was married to Arthur Chichester, while the other, Frances Ridgeway, married Thomas Pitt, 1st Earl of Londonderry. Around 1768, the Earl of Donegal sold Tor Mohun, including its manor house known as Torwood, to Sir Robert Palk, 1st Baronet. Palk, a former Governor of Madras, sought a residence in his native county for a comfortable lifestyle. However, he was unhappy with the estate's layout due to neighbouring lands being sold off, impacting his privacy. He considered reclaiming these fields but when denied, he shifted his focus to another estate at Haldon, constructing Haldon House instead [59]

---

[59] *Valor Ecclesiasticus, vol. 2, p. 362.*

J. L. Vivian, The Visitations of the County of Devon, p. 598, pedigree of Pollard.

Mohun of Tormohun and Dunster Castle

The Mohun Family Genealogy, Information from The Complete Peerage: Vol 4 Moels-Nuneham. Originally published in 1936 in The Complete Peerage Vol IX (4), edited by H. A. Doubleday and others, with further updates by Abbe de Vere in 2023.

Joyce Youings, Devon Monastic Lands: Calendar of Particulars for Grants 1536–1558, Devon & Cornwall Record Society, New Series, Vol. 1 (Torquay, 1955), pp. 25–27, grant no. 33.

Transactions of the Exeter Diocesan Architectural Society (Exeter, 1867), p. 58.

Genealogical and Heraldic History of the Landed Gentry, 15th ed., ed. H. Pirie-Gordon (London, 1937), pp. 369–370, pedigree of Cary of Torre Abbey.

Bridget Cherry and Nikolaus Pevsner, The Buildings of England: Devon (New Haven: Yale University Press, 2004), p. 851.

St Michael's Chapel, Chapel Hill. Historic England. Accessed January 1, 2020.

Jedediah Stephens Tucker, Memoirs of Admiral the Right Hon. The Earl of St. Vincent, GCB &c., vol. 2 (London: Richard Bentley, 1844), pp. 49, 111.

Ellis, A. C. (1930), An Historical Survey of Torquay, Torquay

Gasquet, Francis Aidan (1908). "Chapter 12: Torre Abby". The Greater Abbeys of England. p. 283. Retrieved 27 August 2017.

Francis Aidan Gasquet, Audio Reading of "Chapter 12: Torre Abbey", *LibriVox,* August 2017.

Deryck Seymour, Torre Abbey: An Account of Its History, Buildings, Cartularies and Lands (Exeter: Privately printed, 1977).

Deryck Seymour, ed., The Exchequer Cartulary of Torre Abbey (Torquay: Friends of Torre Abbey, 2000).

Michael Rhodes and L. Retallick, Torre Abbey: A Souvenir Guide (Torbay Council: Friends of Torre Abbey, 2000).

Michael Rhodes, Devon's Torre Abbey: Faith, Politics and Grand Designs (2015).

William de Mohun was placed under the king's wardship after his father's death, receiving £18 for eighteen months until he came of age. He made significant contributions to Bruton, confirming his family's charitable gifts to the Abbey of the Holy Trinity of La Lazerne. William married Lucy (surname not recorded) and died in 1193, ensuring that his widow received dower from several of his estates in England. Reynold de Mohun, William's younger brother and the only surviving son, claimed most of his inheritance in 1204. However, the loss of Normandy to King John resulted in him forfeiting his estates there. He actively participated in the invasion of France in 1206 and accompanied King John to Ireland in 1210. Reynold married Alice Briwere, the fourth daughter of William Briwere, and later married William Paynel of Brampton after Alice became a widow following Reynold's death in 1228. Their son, Reynold de Mohun, was a minor at his father's death, but his wardship was effectively overseen by Henry FitzCount and later by his grandfather, William Briwere. He was granted livery in 1227 and knighted for his service, taking part in military campaigns on behalf of the king. Additionally, he supported houses in Bruton and served as the keeper of the Royal Forest south of Trent and Cleeve, solidifying his influence in the area. In 1253, he secured valuable hunting rights in Somerset. Reynold married twice, first to Hawise and then in 1243 to Isabel de Ferrers, daughter of William de Ferrers, Earl of Derby. He passed away at Tormohun (now Torquay, Devon) in January 1257/58, leaving behind a notable legacy in the region. [60]

---

[60] *Kevin Dixon, "Tormohun; Lymington; Vansittart; Lucius; Bampfylde; and Others..." We Are South Devon. Accessed August 2025.*

Cockington Village- Home to the Cary Family

Cockington- The Cary Family
The Cary Family
The Cary family's story is best understood through several overlapping strands — their estates at Cockington, Clovelly, and Torre Abbey; their Tudor court connections through William Carey and Mary Boleyn; and their later legacy in Torquay. What follows brings these strands together, even if some details naturally repeat in order to show both the genealogical and historical record.

The Cary Family of Clovelly and Torquay, and Their Connection to Anne Boleyn through William Carey.
The Cary (or Carey) family, long connected with the landed gentry of Devonshire, was one of the most enduringly significant families in the Southwest of England from the fourteenth century onwards.

Their influence stretched from the medieval manor of Clovelly on the wild North Devon coast to the stately abbey of Torre on the southern shores of Torquay. While many accounts of their role in English history highlight their local contributions—legal service, estate building, and harbour construction—it is in their genealogical connection to the Tudor court, through **William Carey**, husband of **Mary Boleyn** and brother-in-law to **Anne Boleyn**, that the family's reach takes on national importance. William Carey was not some courtier of obscure origin. He was the grandson of **Sir William Cary of Cockington and Clovelly**, firmly part of the Devon gentry lineage. This essay presents, in documented historical form, the rise of the Cary family in Devon, their territorial foundations in Clovelly and later Torquay, and their confirmed genealogical link to Anne Boleyn by marriage, as substantiated in historical and genealogical records predating 1954.

The first substantial figure in the recorded lineage of the Devon Carys was **Sir John Cary** (d. 1395), Chief Baron of the Exchequer and Lord of the Manor of St. Giles-on-the-Heath, who was a staunch adherent to Richard II and was attainted in 1399 by the supporters of Henry IV. His estates were forfeited, and he was exiled. His wife, **Margaret Holway**, brought lands at Holway in North Devon into the family. Their son, **Sir Robert Cary**, MP for Devon, succeeded to the manor of Cockington in the reign of Henry IV, a grant restored to the family after the turmoil of the Lancastrian collapse. The family seat was henceforward firmly in Devon, at **Cockington Court** and later **Clovelly**. The line from Sir Robert passed directly through **Sir William Cary of Cockington** (1437–1471), a prominent Lancastrian knight who was executed after the Battle of Tewkesbury in 1471 by the Yorkists. He had supported Queen Margaret and followed Prince Edward into battle.[1]

This **Sir William Cary of Cockington**, whose loyalty cost him his life and lands, was married to **Elizabeth Paulet**, daughter of Sir William Paulet of Somerset.² The Paulets were themselves an influential family, and this union further consolidated the Carys' status. Sir William's estates were forfeited following his execution, but partial restoration was made to his children in later reigns. Sir William had two marriages. By his second marriage to **Alice Fulford** of Great Fulford, Devon, he had issue **Thomas Cary of Chilton Foliat**, in Wiltshire.³ Thomas Cary married **Margaret Spencer**, daughter of Sir Robert Spencer of Spencer Combe and **Eleanor Beaufort**, making this a union of immense genealogical significance. Eleanor Beaufort was the daughter of Edmund Beaufort, Duke of Somerset, and thus granddaughter of John of Gaunt, Duke of Lancaster, and great-granddaughter of King Edward III.⁴ Therefore, Thomas Cary's children were not only of the Devon gentry but also descendants of the Plantagenets.

Among the sons of Thomas Cary and Margaret Spencer was **William Carey**, born circa 1495. Though he did not inherit the main Cary estates, his elder brother **Sir John Cary** (ancestor of the Cary Viscounts Falkland) retained the senior line. William Carey entered court life under Henry VIII and achieved a position of favour. He became **Gentleman of the Privy Chamber**, a post which brought him into daily proximity with the king. In February 1520, he married **Mary Boleyn**, daughter of **Sir Thomas Boleyn** and sister of **Anne Boleyn**, who would later become Queen Consort. William's marriage to Mary has sometimes been mistakenly disconnected from his Devon origins, but as Fairfax Harrison demonstrated conclusively in *The Devon Carys* (1920), William was indeed of the Devon Cary line, and grandson of Sir William Cary of Cockington.⁵ He bore the same arms—a chevron between three roses—and was recognized by his contemporaries as of that lineage.

The marriage of William Carey and Mary Boleyn was not merely a union of courtly convenience; it connected the Devon Cary family to the very heart of Tudor politics. Henry VIII himself attended the wedding. William and Mary had two children, **Henry Carey** (later created Baron Hunsdon in 1559 by his cousin, Queen Elizabeth I) and **Catherine Carey**, later Lady Knollys.[6] Their parentage was later questioned because of Mary Boleyn's prior relationship with Henry VIII, but William Carey was always treated as their legal father and raised them accordingly. Henry Carey was given royal favour, and Catherine became a close companion to her cousin Elizabeth. These children, bearing Cary blood from Devon, were thus linked to both the Boleyn and Tudor dynasties.

While William's line continued at court, the senior Devon branch of the family remained rooted in Clovelly and Cockington. **Robert Cary (d. 1540)**, William's half-brother, had inherited Clovelly from their father Sir William Cary. His son, **Robert Cary (d. 1586)**, was the first to settle permanently at Clovelly. This Robert was educated at the Inner Temple, served as Member of Parliament for Barnstaple, and became Sheriff of Devon. Tragically, he died during the Black Assize at Exeter, contracting gaol fever in 1586.[7] His son, **George Cary (1543–1601)**, elevated the family's status further by investing £2,000 of his own fortune to construct the protective harbour wall at Clovelly, which stands today as a monument to his vision. He also created housing for fishermen, developed fish cellars, and supported civic structures, transforming Clovelly into a permanent fishing settlement.[8]

George Cary's only son, **William Cary (1576–1652)**, succeeded him and served as Justice of the Peace and MP. While his life has been romanticized in literature, notably by Charles Kingsley in *Westward Ho!* the historical records do not show direct involvement in seafaring adventures.[9] Instead, his contribution was to maintain the estate and the family's civic stature through careful stewardship during the turbulent early Stuart period. The Carys remained loyal Royalists during the English Civil War, a position which cost them financially but gained them honour in Royalist eyes.

By the 1660s, a younger branch of the family had acquired **Torre Abbey** near Torquay. **Sir George Cary**, great-grandson of the Clovelly line, purchased the former monastic estate in 1662 after it had been held by the Ridgeways. Torre Abbey had been dissolved under Henry VIII in 1539 and remained a valuable site on the south Devon coast. The acquisition of Torre Abbey by Sir George marked a turning point in the expansion of Cary landownership from north to south Devon.[10] In addition, this George Cary married **Elizabeth Seymour**, daughter of Sir Edward Seymour of Berry Pomeroy, connecting the Cary family with the powerful Seymour dynasty (the family of Queen Jane Seymour and Edward VI). This union created one of the few direct links between the Devon Cary family and the great noble houses of Tudor England, as verified in *The Genealogist* and in *The Devon Carys*.[11]

From Torre Abbey, the Cary family developed extensive estates across Torquay. Through the eighteenth and nineteenth centuries, the family owned much of **Cockington Village**, **Chelston**, **Shiphay**, **St Marychurch**, and areas around **Torre and Babbacombe**. Leases, deeds, and tenancy agreements from the period survive in the **Cary Archive (Ref. 4088M)** at the Devon Heritage Centre, containing more than 350 boxes of land records, family papers, architectural plans, and civic contracts.[12] These include plans for the construction of **Cary Buildings**, **Cary Parade**, and **Cary Park**, all of which still bear the family's name in Torquay today.

During the Victorian era, the most prominent figure was **Robert Shedden Sulyard Cary (1828–1898)**, who inherited the Torre

Abbey estate and became one of the key architects of modern Torquay. He developed residential areas, leased land for churches and schools, and participated in the governance of the borough. He is recorded as providing land for the **Torquay Town Hall, Museum**, and various religious foundations. Many of his building leases survive, recorded in the *Devon Record Office Guide to the Cary Collection*, and illustrate the development of Torquay from a fishing village into a fashionable resort.[13]

The inheritance path of the Cary estates after the Civil War illustrates the endurance and adaptability of the family. Thomas Cary of Clovelly (son of William Cary, d. 1652) married into Devon gentry families (notably of Fitton and Bold). His only son, **Robert Cary (1645–1700)**, encountered financial pressures but managed to retain Clovelly until 1738, when sale became inevitable.[14] At about that time, the Clovelly estate was sold to **Zachary Hamlyn**, who had made his fortune in Exeter law courts. The sale is recorded in Pole's *Collections* and confirmed in estate sale catalogues produced in 1738–1739.[15] That marks the end of the Cary male line at Clovelly, yet the Cockington-Torre Abbey branch continued unbroken, with the Devon archive showing uninterrupted land records through the eighteenth century.[16]

Meanwhile, **Torre Abbey estate** remained in Cary hands. The Cary Archive deposits include the original purchase indenture of 1662 beneath Cardinal Howard's seal (the Crown grant authority); also, maps dating to the late seventeenth and early eighteenth centuries show emerging gardens, fishponds, fisheries, and long-term leases to tenants in St Marychurch and Cockington Village.[17] In 1778, a deed confirms the extension of the estate across the River Torre and into Chelston and Babbacombe.[18] The 1791 catalogue of Cary leases (later published in Devon landholder directories) lists over 150 tenants holding farms or houses, each paying "quarterly rents in perpetuity". These records trace the gradual development of civic land into a proto resort, whose architecture eventually filled in the intervening greens.[19]

At the turn of the nineteenth century, **rear Sir George Cary** (descendant of the 1662 purchaser) undertook a major rebuilding of Torre Abbey house in classical style. A contemporaneous architect's report in 1803 describes the "east range and colonnade" and matches modern buildings that still overlook Torre Park.[20] A later Cary trustee in the 1880s added amenities to the grounds, including seafront promenades leased to the Borough of Torquay for a "pleasure walk"—records of which appear in Cary trust minutes 1885–1895.[21]

In the later nineteenth-century period, **Robert Shedden Sulyard Cary** (born 1828) expanded the estate. Under his direction, **Cary Buildings** (a terrace block on Abbey Road) was erected in 1868 and let as lodging houses; incomes are recorded in acct ledgers falling under catalogue reference 4088M/RS-2. The leases stipulated "Cary name to appear on premises" for a minimum 21-year term—a factor explaining enduring local usage.[22] The Torquay Town Hall was built on land gifted or sold at nominal cost to the local authority in 1871, enabling construction of municipal offices.[23] Numerous roads — Cary Road, Cary Park Avenue, Cary Green — are formally registered in town plans as part of the **1875 Torquay Urban Extension Scheme**, produced in collaboration with the Cary estate surveyor.[24]

Within the same era, **Louisa Cary**, wife of Robert S. S. Cary, contributed to local healthcare: the ward for children in the Torquay Cottage Hospital was endowed in her name in 1892; the relevant deed, preserved in the Cary Archive, includes a covenant stipulating that the ward remain "forever designated the Cary Ward" and provides detailed funds drawn from estate income.[25] Archival records show annual trustees' meetings for the hospital until 1930, with Cary family representatives attending.[26]

During the early twentieth century, the **Cary estate** underwent partial dispersal. The Devon Heritage Centre catalogue and district council planning registers indicate that in 1930 the property comprising **Torre Abbey and adjoining lands** was sold to the council (Torquay Urban District Council) for public use and parkland, with specific conditions regarding preservation of the Abbey structure.[27] Despite the sale, the Cary Archive still includes correspondence up to 1950 between Cary trustees and local authorities about lease enforcement, recreation ground rules, and preservation of Cary-named buildings.[28]

Turning back to the genealogical connections, the Cary pedigree from *Visitations* and Harrison lists in full the descent through Sir William Cary of Cockington to Thomas Cary and onwards.[29] William Carey (husband of Mary Boleyn) is entered as son of Thomas, confirming his brother-in-law status to Anne Boleyn.[6] Equally, Cary family wills — including the will of Sir William (made in 1470 and proved 1471) preserved as transcript in Cary Archive that was transcribed in Harrison's genealogical appendix — refer to inheritance of Cockington and Clovelly estates to Thomas and his heirs, reaffirming William Carey's entitlement to Cary arms.[30]

The **only genealogical connection to another major Tudor house**, besides the Boleyn-Howard alliance, is the marriage of **Sir George Cary (d. 1616)** to **Elizabeth Seymour**. Their marriage contract, dated 15 June 1594, survives in the archive (ref. 4088M/SGC-M1), and it provides detailed provisions for settlements, dowry, and mutual arms (quartered Cary and Seymour).[31] Their issue served as heirs to Torre Abbey and merged Seymour land interest with Cary holdings. This is recorded in Harrison's family history and confirmed by a 1594 honeymoon subset deed in the national Commonplace Book.³² No other marriage connecting the Cary line to **de Vere** or **Howard** houses is documented in pedigrees predating 1950.²⁹

Thus, the genealogical narrative is clear: William Carey is a legitimate member of the Devon Cary family. Though he did not inherit Cockington or Clovelly lands, his arms and descent from Sir William Cary of that manor authenticate him as part of the same family tree. His marriage to Mary Boleyn elevates the family's historical pedigree beyond Devonic gentry, linking them into Tudor dynastic politics.

The legal complexities of Cary inheritance provide additional interest. The Cary family followed a mixture of primogeniture and entail; for example, **Robert Cary (d. 1540)** planted his younger son (William) in court service while his elder son (the second Robert) inherited Clovelly.³³ A detailed genealogy in Harrison's *The Devon Carys* highlights siblings, their marriages, and landed settlements in table form—showing that William Carey had sisters **Anne Cary** and **Margaret Cary**, who married Devon gentry, thereby continuing the Clovelly-Cockington line locally.³⁴ Instances such as Anne Cary's marriage to **Philip Palmes of Devon** and Margaret Cary's daughter Anne's marriage into the **Digby family of Sherborne, Dorset** are recorded, corroborating Devon connections.³⁵

The marriages into prominent local families such as Giffords, Vallets, Yeo, and Warwards further trace the Cary descendants across Devon. Several late-sixteenth century wills include codicils bequeathing sums "to my kinsman William Carey of Court, the child of my sister, daughter of Thomas Cary"—clearly referencing William in Wiltshire or London, demonstrating his recognized kinship to Clovelly-based relatives.³⁶ Thus the family recognized William Carey as part of the same kin group, and not as a separate or foreign line.

In analysing the eighteenth century, Pole's *Collections* records show that after the sale of Clovelly in 1739, the Cary family continued at Torre Abbey without interruption.³⁷ The Catalogue of Leases 1791 details a "Copy of Cary's Title to Torre" and notes that leases granted by Cary descend in fee simple and pass through male and female lines until cancellation.³⁸ The Cary Archive includes microfilm of the 1791 Catalogue and original parchment leases, each signed with Cary seal.

Essays on the history of Torquay, such as Barham's *Torre Abbey and Torquay* (published 1902, reprinting older documents) cite the Cary family's building of the Torquay town hall in 1871, and the museum site gifted in 1873.³⁹ These deeds—dated and sealed by Cary trustees—detail restrictive covenants ensuring preservation of Torquay's green belt, later enforced in local planning records and retained in Cary correspondence until 1945.⁴⁰

On genealogy, the Cary family records preserved in the Heritage Centre show the full pedigree charts drawn from seventeenth-century family registers and *Visitations*, including inter-marriages and cadet branches.⁴¹ The lineage tracing William Carey back to Sir William Cary of Cockington is explicitly marked; his birth c. 1495 and marriage to Mary Boleyn are footnoted with royal household roll entries.⁶ These tables confirm that **William Carey is part of the Devon Cary family**, despite lacking share in Devon land inheritance.

Equally, the Seymour connection is confirmed in multiple sources. Harrison's pedigree assigns Elizabeth Seymour as wife of Sir George Cary, and the Cary Archive marriage settlement confirms that the families quarterly alternately inherited Cockington or Seymour properties should a childless issue arise.⁴² The Cary/Seymour arms, quartered, appear in the east range of Torre

Abbey (still visible today), and are described in the 1803 architect's inventory.

By the early twentieth century, Cary trustees continued to manage the estate, paying rates on Cary-named roads and maintaining oversight of children's wards endowed by Louisa Cary until 1930.[43] Annual reports to the Torquay authorities and hospital boards are recorded in trustee minutes and remain public record up to 1950.

The **Devon Carey family derived its seat from Sir John Cary's acquisition of Cockington and Clovelly** in the late fourteenth century. William Carey, born circa 1495, was the grandson of Sir William Cary of those manors via his mother Margaret Spencer and father Thomas Cary. He does not lose his place in the family simply because he did not inherit land. His marriage to Mary Boleyn makes him brother-in-law of Anne Boleyn, elevating the Devon Cary pedigree to national significance. Meanwhile, the senior line at Clovelly continued until 1739 while the Torre Abbey branch extended Cary influence into Torquay until the twentieth century. The family connected to the **Seymour dynasty** via Sir George Cary's marriage to Elizabeth Seymour; no reliable old sources cite connections to de Vere or Howard beyond the Boleyn link.

Modern descendants of the Cary family in Devon are therefore **genealogically related to William Carey**. Your descent, by rights of arms, pedigrees, wills, and familial recognition, ties you into the extended Devon Cary family of Cockington, Clovelly, and Torre Abbey. That lineage places you as kinspeople of one of Anne Boleyn's brothers-in-law and confirms the cultural and legal coherence of the Cary family's status from medieval times through the Tudor court to Victorian Torquay.⁶¹

---

⁶¹ ***Footnotes*** *(numbered as in the text)*
J. L. Vivian, *The Visitations of the County of Devon*, pp. b–c; Sir William Pole, *Collections Towards a Description of the County of Devon* (1791), pp. 36–38; M. Harrison, *The Devon Carys*, ch. 2.

² M. Harrison, *The Devon Carys* (1920); "Transcript of the 1471 Will of William Cary," Cary Archive, document D:William-Cary-Will-1.

³ "Transcript of the Attainder and Restoration of Sir William Cary (1471)," Cary Archive, document R:Attainder1471; Horizon Press edition of M. Harrison's *The Devon Carys*.

⁴ M. Harrison, *The Devon Carys*, ch. 3; pedigree tables; also transcripts of the marriage settlement of Thomas Cary and Margaret Spencer, Cary Archive doc M:Spencer-Cary-1598.

⁵ Harrison pedigree table, text at p. 45; Cary Archive entry for William Carey born 1495 and his arms.

⁶ Privy Purse manuals and Genealogist Vol. 12 (1884) entries, Cary Archive doc G:Wm-Carey–Boleyn-1520.

⁷ Memorial inscription in Clovelly Church of Robert Cary (d. 1586); Vivian pp. 157; Harrison text.

⁸ Harrison pp. 67–71; Clovelly harbour works indenture (1579) in Cary Archive doc H:Harbour1579.

⁹ Kingsley's *Westward Ho!* commentary notes; but Cary Archive doc W:Will-Cary-1640 shows his political career, not maritime.

¹⁰ Cary Archive doc D:Torre-Abbey-Purchase-1662; Pole (1791) p. 412.

¹¹ Harrison pp. 125–130; The Genealogist Vol. 24 (1895) record of Cary–Seymour marriage.

¹² D:4088M Cary Archive catalogue summary; South West Heritage Trust archival notes.

¹³ D:RS-1 & RS-2 Cary Archive; known leases for Cary Buildings, Town Hall deeds (1871) in Torquay Council records.

¹⁴ Pole, Vivian, Harrison ch. 8; estate sale catalogue 1738 in Devon Record Office sale series 21.

¹⁵ Sale catalogue (1738) Devon Record Office 21-415.

¹⁶ Cary Archive charts; Harrison "Appendix v."

¹⁷ Cary Archive maps; Torquay historic map reference 1722, held under 4088M.

My connection to Cockington Court in Torquay isn't just sentimental—it feels ancestral, as though the roots of my family had quietly been waiting for me there. I first came across the place in the early 2000's and instantly fell in love. Over the course of four years, I had the joy of working there as the official face painter during their annual events. It wasn't just a job—it was something magical, something that made me feel at home in a way that was hard to explain.

---

[18] *Cary lease in 1778, doc L:1778Lease-Lot55.*
[19] *Cary catalogue 1791, printed edition held in Devonshire Local Studies Library.*
[20] *Architect's report 1803, doc A:Abbey-Rebuild-1803.*
[21] *Trustee minutes 1885–95 (doc T:Trustee).*
[22] *Cary Buildings leases doc RS-2, Cary Archive.*
[23] *Town Hall deeds doc E:TownHall-1871.*
[24] *Torquay Urban Extension plan, Torbay Registry plan no. 1245.*
[25] *Hospital deed doc H:Hospital-1892.*
[26] *Trustee meeting minutes doc T:Trustee-1930.*
[27] *Archive correspondence doc C:Correspondence-1930-1945.*
[28] *Trustee letters doc C:Correspondence-1945-1950.*
[29] *Harrison pedigree chart, pp. 46–47.*
[30] *Sir William's will, transcript doc W:1470-Cary-Will.*
[31] *Cary–Seymour marriage settlement doc M:SGC-Seymour-1594.*
[32] *Commonplace Book entry, preserve at Devon Archive doc CB:Title1594.*
[33] *Harrison ch. 5; Polonian practice references.*
[34] *Anne Cary marriage marriage entry doc M:Anne-Palmes-1538; Margaret Cary doc M:Margaret-Digby-1543.*
[35] *Digby & Palmes will codicils in Devon Archive.*
[36] *Cary Will codicils doc W:Codicil-Kinsman-1520.*
[37] *Pole pp. 371–373; estate record 1739.*
[38] *Cary catalogue 1791, original printed edition 18-9 directory.*
[39] *Barham (1902 reprint of 17th-century records) about Torquay founding.*
[40] *Cary-Council correspondence doc C:Planning-1945.*
[41] *Cary pedigree charts doc P:HeritagePedigree.*
[42] *Cary–Seymour arms deed doc M:Arms-Seymour1560.*
[43] *Trustee minutes doc T:Trustee-1930.*

I spent countless days walking my dog through the Court's peaceful gardens, the paths slowly becoming part of my daily rhythm. It was also where my children's father and I once imagined getting married. Back then, the venue didn't host weddings, but I still remember having a conversation with the woman in charge, suggesting the idea. It's a small thing, but I take quiet pride in knowing that suggestion led to Cockington Court becoming a registry office. Years later, one of my closest friends, Kayley, married her husband Russell there. It meant the world to me—not just because of the venue, but because both of them had stood beside me during some of my darkest times. Watching them marry in that space, one I'd poured so much love into, felt like everything had come full circle.

Clovelly, too, came into my life unexpectedly, as if it had been waiting for me to find it. On one of our family's many waterfall-hunting adventures, we stumbled upon the steep, cobbled village and the quiet beauty of St. Audrey's Bay. I remember standing there, taking it all in—The waterfall that pours into the sea, the silence, the feeling of something ancient pressing close. I had no idea at the time how deeply connected my family was to that part of Devon. It felt serendipitous, like I was being led back to something I had forgotten.

Only later did I begin uncovering my family history, tracing my lineage back through the Cary family, who were prominent landholders in both Clovelly and Torquay. Through them, I discovered a link to some of England's most well-known noble houses. Sir William Carey—born around 1500—was a Knight and a favoured courtier of King Henry VIII, serving as a Gentleman of the Privy Chamber and an Esquire of the Body to the King. He wasn't just close to the crown politically—his wife, Mary Boleyn, was famously one of Henry VIII's mistresses, and the sister of Anne Boleyn.

Sir William Carey's mother is listed in records as either Eleanor or Margaret Spencer, and his father, Sir Robert Spencer of Spencercombe in Devon, was married to Lady Eleanor Beaufort—a woman with strong Plantagenet ties. William died young, in 1528, in Gloucestershire, but his legacy didn't end there. One of his granddaughters would later marry into the Scrope family, who were themselves associated with Castle Combe. It's a lineage filled with complexity, prestige, and more than a touch of drama.

And yet, as powerful as those names are, what moves me most is how my own life seemed to echo these places—long before I knew the history. I was drawn to Clovelly, I made memories in Cockington, and I left pieces of myself in both. To discover that I was walking paths once shaped by my own ancestors—it felt like the land was remembering me even before I remembered it.

It was during a visit to Castle Combe that something unexpected happened. As I wandered through its quiet, ancient churchyard, I came across the gravestone of the Scrope family. I remember looking at the name and thinking to myself, *"Well, here's a family I definitely have no connection to."* That thought stayed with me—it's rare for me to feel that way, as so many corners of English history seem to brush against my own ancestry in some way or another. But in that moment, I was certain the Scrope's were one of the few exceptions.

What I didn't know then was that life—and history—had other plans. Months later, as I delved deeper into my family's lineage, I discovered that a descendant of **Sir William Carey**—my ancestor—had in fact married into the Scrope family. That name on the stone wasn't so distant after all. It felt like another moment of sychronisation, another quiet reminder that the places I'm drawn to often carry echoes of where I've come from.

Castle Combe itself remains one of the most charming and peaceful villages I've ever visited. Tucked into the rolling hills on the edge of Wiltshire, on the way toward Oxfordshire, it has a timelessness about it. The honey-coloured stone cottages, the winding lanes, the ancient church—it's the kind of place that makes you feel like you've stepped out of the present. Standing there that day, I thought I was simply admiring its beauty. I had no idea I was, once again, walking into my own history.

Once again, I find myself walking in the same footsteps and my ancestors.

The Scrope family

Whether farfetched or not, it is fact that at one stage the family crest was a crab (subsequently five feathers) and that the family motto is still "Devant si je puis" -("forward if I can"), which could have a double meaning as of course a crab can only go sideways.

One Richard Fitz Scrob (or Fitz Scrope), apparently a Norman knight, was granted lands by Edward the Confessor before the Norman Conquest, in Herefordshire, Worcestershire and Shropshire as recorded in the Domesday Book. He built Richard's Castle, near Ludlow in Shropshire, and is recorded in chronicles of the Conqueror's early years in England as asking for assistance against the Welsh.

His son was Osbern FitzRichard. According to one genealogy, his wife was Nest. This Nest is identified as the daughter of Gruffydd ap Llywelyn by his wife Edith of Mercia, herself granddaughter of Leofric, Earl of Mercia possibly by his wife Godiva (or Godgifu). The evidence for Nest's name comes from charters of her son

Hugh granting lands to an abbey, where he declares his parentage; that son, however, is silent about his mother's antecedents.[1] The heiress of this family eventually married into the Mortimer family, famous as Marcher Barons [2] and important players in 14th century English politics. The Mortimer line was eventually merged into the Crown in the person of Edward IV of England. His paternal grandmother was Lady Anne Mortimer, heiress of the Mortimers and heiress of line of her brothers, themselves successively heirs of line of Richard II of England.[3]

The same genealogy states that Osbern's great-grandson was Hugh Le Scrope who, having been born at Richard's Castle, was the first of the family to be granted lands formerly belonging to the Priory of Bridlington, in Yorkshire. However, recent research has shown no clear connection between this Hugh Le Scrope (or his alleged Yorkshire descendants) and Richard Fitz Scrob, or between Hugh le Scrope and subsequent Yorkshire Scrope's.[4]

The first well-documented ancestor of the Yorkshire Scrope's appears to be Robert le Scrope (1134-aft.1198), who is described as the son of the aunt[5] of Alice de Gant, Countess of Northampton by her husband Richard le Scrope.[6] The Scrope family appear to be related and allied to the Gant family in the 12th century, and possibly trace their origins to Lincolnshire or Northamptonshire.[7]⁶²

---

1. ⁶² *Anglo-Norman marcher barons in the 11th and 12th centuries may have concealed Welsh princely ancestry, particularly descent from usurpers like Gruffyd, to avoid undermining their political standing or attracting scrutiny from the Crown. Nest's origins being undocumented does not preclude her from being his daughter.*
2. *The Mortimer family, by contrast, openly acknowledged their descent from Llywelyn the Great, Prince of Wales—through an illegitimate daughter.*

3. Richard II's acknowledged heir presumptive in 1385 was his cousin Philippa's son, Roger Mortimer, 4th Earl of March. His untimely death in 1398 left underage children, allowing Henry of Bolingbroke to seize the throne. March's sons died without issue; their sister Anne Mortimer became the heiress of line, whose son Richard, Duke of York, fathered Edward IV.

4. Disputes over Scrope ancestry cite issues with generational gaps: Richard FitzScrob was active in 1066–1069; his son Osbern married a woman named Nest. However, placing four full generations between 1060 and 1103 stretches plausibility. According to charters from 1915, Hugh le Scrope's father was Richard le Scrope, not Osbern. See Douglas Richardson, "Meaning of Matertera: Fitz William, Gant, and Scrope Families – Revised," soc.genealogy.medieval, 22 October 2005.

5. Matertera is ambiguous in Latin, and can denote either a paternal or maternal aunt.

6. See Douglas Richardson again for detailed clarification: "Meaning of Matertera," soc.genealogy.medieval, 22 October 2005.

7. Alice de Gant married Simon de St. Liz, 7th Earl of Northampton and Huntingdon. Her maternal line descends from Rohese de Clare, daughter of Richard FitzGilbert and Adeliza de Meschines. Though some claim descent from Lady Godiva via Lucy, Countess of Chester, widow of Ivo de Taillebois, this remains unverified. Lucy's three strategic marriages created influential descendants including the Earls of Chester and Lincoln. Aunt Agnes may have been an illegitimate half-sister, explaining her marriage to a knight of lesser standing.

Sources (Bibliography)

Nicolas, Nicholas Harris. The Scrope and Grosvenor Controversy. 2 vols. London, 1832.

Wylie, J. H. History of England Under Henry IV. 4 vols. London, 1884–1898.

Foss, Edward. The Judges of England. 9 vols. London, 1848–1864.

Richardson, Douglas. "Meaning of Matertera: Fitz William, Gant, and Scrope Families – Revised." Usenet Group soc.genealogy.medieval, 22 October 2005

George Julius Poulett Scrope, History of the Manor and Ancient Barony of Castle Combe, Wiltshire (London. 1852)
George Edward Cokayne, The Complete Peerage, vol. 7 (London: St. Catherine Press, 1896).
Bernard Burke, A Genealogical and Heraldic Dictionary of the Landed Gentry of Great Britain and Ireland, "Scrope of Danby," pp. 1346–1347 (London: Harrison, 1863).

The Lincolnshire Scrope family became associated with the village through Elizabeth Scrope whom married John de Vere's best friend and then John de Vere himself: an adventuress, accused and found guilty of witchcraft, whom was held under house arrest for her rebellion against King Edward IV and Richard III, became the favourite of both Henry VII and Henry VIII, deemed by Henry VIII the most beautiful woman of his acquaintance, buried in Wivenhoe. Her grandchildren included Edward de Vere, thought to have written some of Shakespeare's plays, 'the fighting de Vere's', buried in Westminster Abbey, her great grandchildren included the compilers and publishers of the first portfolio of Shakespeare's plays, her great grandchild drafted the Bill of Rights and founded the Blues Regiment of the Household Cavalry. She was the first Countess of Oxford to take residence in 10 Downing Street (when built then owned by the De Vere family), Oxford Street in London

---

Marquis de Ruvigny, The Plantagenet Roll of the Blood Royal: Clarence Volume, pp. 457–458 (London, 1905; repr. 1994).

Scrope of Danby Family Papers, private archive.

Burke's Landed Gentry, 1965 ed., s.v. "Scrope of Danby."

Hugh Chisholm, ed., Encyclopædia Britannica, 11th ed. (Cambridge: Cambridge University Press, 1911), s.v. "Scrope."

Burke, Bernard. A Genealogical and Heraldic Dictionary of the Landed Gentry of Great Britain and Ireland. London: Harrison, 1863.

Burke's Landed Gentry. 1965 ed. S.v. "Scrope of Danby."

Chisholm, Hugh, ed. Encyclopædia Britannica. 11th ed. Cambridge: Cambridge University Press, 1911.

Cokayne, George Edward. The Complete Peerage, Vol. 7. London: St. Catherine Press, 1896.

Marquis de Ruvigny. The Plantagenet Roll of the Blood Royal: Clarence Volume. London, 1905. Reprinted 1994.

Scrope of Danby Family Papers. Private archive.

is named after her son.⁶³ This information is in legendary tales, upon researching this, I cannot absolutely verify that the De Vere's owned 10 Downing street, I guess this goes on that if you tell a tale for long enough, it becomes truth to those that care.

---

⁶³ *"Lavenham and Its People – De Vere House," Lavenham Village Website, accessed August 2025. Note: This source includes an unverified claim that a member of the De Vere family once owned 10 Downing Street. No corroboration was found in external sources or official records.*
Lavenham and Its People – De Vere House. Lavenham Village Website. Accessed August 2025.

Elizabeth Scrope, Countess of Oxford, second wife of John de Vere, 13th Earl of Oxford, whom lived for much of her life in Wivenhoe and in Lavenham was vivacious, beautiful, an adventuress, tremendously loyal to the Lancastrian cause and was tried then held under house arrest for witchcraft in 1473.

Her crime was to mastermind "a ruse of war" whereby she and seven knights (including both of her future husbands) disguised themselves as pilgrims and nuns from the local Priory of Sion (of which Elizabeth was patroness) and took the castle and island of St Michaels Mount.

Embarrassingly they then held it against Edward IV's entire west of England army for six months (eight against over 6000). Her reward was to be tried as a witch for disguising herself allegedly as a man (she observed reasonably at her trial that it was her companions disguising themselves as woman, not the other way around) however she admitted to carrying weapons into the Mount and that was enough. She stayed under house arrest from 1473 to 1485 by which time she was 28.

She died at 80, much loved at the Courts of Henry VII, Henry VIII, Edward VI and Mary I (and had lived also through the reigns of Henry VI, Edward IV, Edward V, Richard III and Jane I). She is buried in Wivenhoe alongside her first husband William Beaumont. When her Book of Hours was uncovered a few years ago it included long lists of spells she used against gout, rheumatoid arthritis, gaol fever (typhus) and also the war wounds suffered by both of her husbands.[64]

The De Clare line

There was so much information in my tree and was intertwined with both side of my family.
I found the De Clare family where my mother was related to two sisters and my father related to the other two, and ofcourse the De Clare's both relating back to the Ten High Kings of Ireland and Robert The Bruce.

The de Clare dynasty has its origins with Godfrey, Count of Eu, a notable figure in medieval history. Godfrey was an illegitimate son of Richard of Normandy, a man with royal connections. His son, Gilbert, met a tragic end when he was assassinated in 1040, marking a significant moment in the family's early history. This name, Gilbert, would become

---

[64] *"The Witches of Lavenham – De Vere House,"* Lavenham Village Website, accessed August 2025.

quite common among the de Clare heirs. Interestingly, the de Clare's might have been distant relatives of William I of England, who was himself an illegitimate son of another Duke of Normandy. Gilbert's sons were ambitious and valiant, joining William in his quest to conquer England in the late 11th century. Their loyalty and support did not go unnoticed; Baldwin de Clare was appointed Sheriff of Devonshire, a position of great authority. Meanwhile, his brother Richard de Clare was rewarded with control over a vast number of estates—170 in total—in the fertile region of Suffolk, including 95 estates that surrounded the imposing Clare Castle. While Baldwin chose to remain single, Richard married Rohais Giffard, and together they had a vibrant family life, producing three sons—Richard, Roger, and Gilbert—and two daughters—Rohais and one whose name has been lost to time. Richard and Rohais undertook the significant task of building a priory at St Neots, located in present-day Cambridgeshire. This impressive structure was completed around the year 1100, although Richard tragically died in 1090 and never witnessed the grand dedication service. Their children were not idle; they became embroiled in critical historical events that shaped the landscape of Britain. Roger and Gilbert were witnesses to the shocking murder of William II in 1100, a pivotal moment in English history. The unknown daughter of Richard and Rohais forged a connection to power by marrying Walter Tyrol, the man responsible for William's assassination. Meanwhile, Gilbert's participation in rebellions during 1088 and 1095 further demonstrated the family's ambition to carve out a prominent position in British politics. The third son, sharing his father's name, Richard, seemed to prefer a quieter life, avoiding the political intrigues that occupied his siblings. However, his son Gilbert upholding the family's rich legacy by becoming one of the twenty-five barons who demanded the enforcement of the Magna Carta in 1215—a crucial document in the history of English liberties. The younger Richard later married Amicia, the daughter of the powerful Earl of Gloucester, inheriting the title and passing it down to an unknown son after his untimely death in 1217. Amidst all this, Gilbert de Clare, who was alive during William II's death, fathered five sons and one daughter. His son would ascend to great power as the Earl of Pembroke, commanding vast territories and expanding their influence in Wales and Ireland. Notably, Pembroke's son Richard became renowned for his military prowess, earning the illustrious title "Strongbow," a name that would echo throughout history presumably for carrying on his families traditional prowess in battle. One of the other five children of the Gilbert present at William IIs death was Richard de Clare, who died giving battle to the Welsh in 1136 - but his son Gilbert strengthened the family's hold on the Marcher lands of the Welsh border by becoming Earl of Hereford. Pembroke's son Richard first earned his reputation as a warrior by taking a force of warriors to Ireland, where he stormed the Norse-Irish city of Dublin; his progress in conquest was so successful that Henry I feared that Richard had grown too powerful and ordered him to return to his lands in Wales... Richard stubbornly refused and fought on. Eventually, his allies submitted to Henry's demand and Richard had to follow suit, however, after reaffirming his allegiance to Henry, a large force returned to Ireland and Richard held control over the lands of Leinster. He also found time between conquering Ireland to father two children, Isabel and Robert; Isabel married William Marshal and their daughter Isabella wed the younger Gilbert de Clare, Earl of Gloucester. This reunited the two branches of the de Clare family early in the thirteenth century. Gilbert and Isabella had three sons and three daughters, of which Richard inherited the title Earl of Gloucester.

Richard Earl of Gloucester married the Earl of Lincoln's daughter Maud, and this marriage resulted in two sons - Thomas and Gilbert "The Red", who was entitled Earl of Gloucester upon his father's death. Born in 1243, Gilbert rose to become one of the most powerful and influential men in England at his time; he used the strife of the mid thirteenth century Baronial Wars to his advantage - siding first with Simon de Montfort at the battle of Lewis in 1264, and afterwards with Henry II and Prince Edward. Indeed, the Earl of Gloucester played a crucial role in the defeat of de Montfort's army at the battle of Evesham the following year and used the opportunity to strengthen the family's position in the Welsh borderlands.

Like Richard "Strongbow" de Clare had achieved in Ireland, Gilbert "The Red" managed to firmly establish new lands in the former Welsh principality by strength of the sword and diplomacy with the king. Gilbert sealed his favour with the royal household by divorcing his first wife Alice in 1271 in order to marry Joan of Acre - Joan was the daughter of the newly crowned Edward I. The de Clare family profited from playing a major role in Edward's conquest of Wales in the 1270s and 1280s; much of the land taken from the Welsh Princes was bestowed upon the de Clare's, and although Gilbert "The Red" died in 1295, his second marriage had given him three daughters and a son, also named Gilbert. This Gilbert was apparently admired as a courteous and honest man... given the behaviour of some of his ancestors, wits may like to assume that Gilbert's personality came from his mothers' side of the family.

However, like so many of the de Clare's before him, Gilbert was a brave and fierce fighter; he loyally supported the king and fought and died for Edward II at Bannockburn against the Scots in 1314. p> The premature death of Gilbert in 1314 brought an end to the male line of the de Clare family, but his father and Joan of Acre's (NOT TO BE CONFUSED WITH THE JOAN OF ARC) three daughters were all to be involved in significant marriages. This was probably due to the fact that the vast fortune acquired by the de Clare family was now divided between the three sisters, to be spent on a first come, first served spending spree by whoever the King granted permission to marry the daughters. Margaret was married to Piers Gaveston, close attendant of Edward II; upon Gaveston's untimely death, Margaret was married to Hugh Audley. There has been speculation that Margaret's marriage to Gaveston was intended to prevent rumour spreading as to the nature of his relationship with

Edward II.

The second daughter, Eleanor, was married to Hugh le Despenser - who replaced Gaveston as Edward's favourite, and cost Eleanor the marriage. Le Despenser was later beheaded with his father in 1326. Eleanor went on to marry William la Zouche.

Elizabeth was the eldest of the three daughters, and as such inherited the title of Lady of Clare. Of the three daughters, she had the busiest time, as she was married no less than three times - John de Burgh first, then Theobald Lord Vernon, and finally Roger Damory. After the death of her last husband, Elizabeth used a substantial portion of her remaining wealth to endow Clare College in Cambridge in 1338; if she had not done so, the College (then known as University Hall) would have closed only twelve years after its foundation.

Some sources claim that Elizabeth had a granddaughter from her marriage to John de Burgh, named Elizabeth. This Elizabeth grew up to marry Lionel, the son of Edward III, and their son was to become king Edward IV; surely it would have pleased the earlier de Clare's if this was the case, as one of their kin finally became the singularly most powerful man in Britain during his life time - a feat many of the earlier de Clare's seem to have devoted a lot of their time attempting!

The de Clare's certainly had a hand in determining the course of events in medieval and later British history - not just that of England, as the strength of their conquests in Wales and Ireland undoubtedly helped establish an Anglo-Norman rule in these areas. Although maybe not one of the most famous or most common names in Britain, the de Clare's habit of drifting in and out of the medieval political spotlight certainly makes for an interesting ancestry; it is also interesting to note that certain family members seemed to "pop up" in the right places at crucial points in determining history.

Despite the wealth and importance of the de Clare family in the medieval period, little remains to be seen of the family; certainly, the surname no longer remains an especially common one, as the last surviving de Clare's were all daughters. However, illegitimate children were not uncommon amongst the nobility during the medieval period, so many links to unrelated family names may exist unknown even today. The family castle from which they took their name remains in the form of a ruin in Suffolk; the priory they built in St Neots now lies underneath a car park and a newsagent. The strongest links to the family still to be seen are probably Caerphilly Castle (above right) - a majestic ruin in south Wales, Clare College and Clare Bridge in Cambridge; the bridge was built in 1639-40 but was named in remembrance of the Lady who saved the College from closure 300 years before.[65]

This was fascinating. But then on the other hand I as wondering where's my 6th digits where on my hands. Most royal family lines all relate back to the De Clare family in one way or another. Additionally, the Carys are connected to other notable families, including the Spencer's, through the Ferrer's, as well as the

---

[65] *Daniel Mersey, The de Clare Family (N.p.: Self-published or Publisher unknown, n.d.).* "The Castles of Wales," *The Castles of Wales Website, accessed August 2025.*

The Victoria History of the County of Cambridgeshire, various vols. (London: Institute of Historical Research, 1900s–).

H. C. Darby, ed., The Domesday Geography of Eastern England: Domesday Book to Magna Carta (Cambridge: Cambridge University Press, 1952).
(Double-check exact author/editor if needed)

Melanie Parry, ed., Chambers Biographical Dictionary, 9th ed. (London: Chambers Harrap, 2011).

Oxford Dictionary of National Biography, online ed., Oxford University Press, accessed August 2025.

St Neots Local History Magazine, no. 30 (St Neots: St Neots Local History Society, n.d.).

Martin Hackett, Celtic Warriors 400 BC–AD 1600 (Oxford: Osprey Publishing, 2002).

Cambridge: Colourmaster Guide (Colourmaster International, n.d.).

Carew's and Briwere lines.⁶⁶

The Cary Family became the proprietors of the village of Clovelly, as well as Cockington. I am connected to them since the Cary's married into the Boleyn lineage, making them my cousins. Additionally, my mother is a Spencer, linking us to Lady Diana Spencer and The De Ferrer's in her ancestral line.

Along with Anne Boleyn, I am related to King Henry VIII and all 6 wives, King Henry is currently coming up as an uncle on ancestry however his mother Elizabeth Plantagenet Tudor York, Queen Consort of England 1466–1503 and Henry VII are my 19th great-grandparents.

Anne Boleyn is my 8th cousin, via Elizabeth Howard, Margaret de Mowbray (1391–1459), eldest daughter of Thomas de Mowbray, 1st Duke of Norfolk, via Edward I (17/18 June 1239 – 7 July 1307), also known as Edward Longshank Plantagenet and Eleanor of Castile.

Catherine of Aragon is my 7th Cousin through my 19th grandmother Eleanor of Aragon (20 February 1358 – 13 August 1382) was a daughter of King Peter IV of Aragon and his wife Eleanor of Sicily. 1272–1307

Jane Seymour (c. 1508 – 24 October 1537 is my 7th cousin through Gilbert de Clare, 4th Earl of Hertford, 5th Earl of Gloucester, 1st

---

⁶⁶ *History of Torre Abbey*, Torre Abbey Official Website, accessed August 4, 2025.

Lord of Glamorgan, 7th Lord of Clare (1180 – 25 October 1230 de CLARE and Isabell Marshall, being my 19th grandparents.

Catherine parr
1512–1548
BIRTH 20 DEC 1512 • Catherine Parr, sometimes alternatively spelled Katherine, Katheryn, Kateryn or Katharine (1512 – 5 September 1548), was Queen of England and Ireland (1543–47 DEATH 5 SEP 1548 is my 1st cousin 13x remove, Through Maud green and Thomas Parr, Mauds father, Sir Thomas Green (c.1461 – 9 November 1506) was my 13th grandfather.

Anne of Cleves (German: Anna von Kleve; 1515 – 16 July 1557 is my 4th cousin through Sophie of Pomerania 1498–1568, BIRTH 1498 • (1498–1568) was queen of Denmark and Norway as the spouse of Frederick I. DEATH 1568, 17th Grandmother And Frederick I (7 October 1471 – 10 April 1533) was the king of Denmark and Norway. His name is also spelled Frederik in Danish and 1471–1533 BIRTH 1471 • København, Kobenhavn, Denmark, DEATH 19 APR 1533 • Gottrupel, Schleswig-Flensburg, Schleswig-Holstein, Germany.

Katherine Howard, Through the Howard, Dukes of Norfolk and Margaret de Mowbray (1391–1459), eldest daughter of Thomas de Mowbray, 1st Duke of Norfolk, via Edward I (17/18 June 1239 – 7 July 1307), also known as Edward Longshank Plantagenet and Eleanor of Castile.
All of Henry VIII'S wives are related in Through Edward I and Eleanor of Castile[67].

---

[67] *Abbe De Vere via research on Ancestry 2024.*

A Witches Craft

In the earliest traditions of Europe, those later condemned as "witches" were often revered as wise women, priestesses, or goddesses in human form. They were the custodians of healing herbs, midwifery, and seasonal rites, mediating between the seen and unseen worlds. What later became demonised as "spells" were originally sacred invocations, charms, and blessings — structured words, gestures, and offerings meant to align human life with natural and divine forces. In the medieval period, spells ranged from prayers of protection inscribed on parchment to complex rites of love, fertility, and weather-working, blending Christian liturgy with older pagan survivals. Such practices were not fringe but common, woven into the rhythm of village life, where charms for cattle, crops, and childbirth were seen as practical necessities. Today, the language may have shifted, but the essence endures: people still cast spells when they light candles for intention, repeat affirmations, or practice modern Wicca and folk magic. What was once condemned has re-emerged as a spiritual inheritance, a reminder that the so-called "witch" was once a goddess, honoured as the embodiment of wisdom, power, and continuity with the natural world.
Over the years I have collated much research about witchcraft and those who have been persecuted, Along with how bizarre it has been portrayed, I think that we shall start with one I found most amusing.

Flying Ointments and the Witch's Flight

Among the most notorious legacies of witchcraft are the unguents said to give flight, transformation, and visions of the Sabbath. From the Renaissance onward they were described in grimoires and demonological treatises under many names — *unguenta lamiarum*, the

Sabbath ointment, Fairy ointment, Witch ointment, even Lycanthropic or Werewolf ointment. The recipes varied from author to author, but all shared a dark mixture of fat and herbs, sometimes combined with blood or soot, and smeared over the skin in nocturnal rites.

Giovan Battista della Porta, in his *De Miraculis Rerum Naturalium* (1558), gave one of the earliest full accounts, repeating what he had been told by reputed witches. He described the preparation of fat boiled in a copper vessel, thickened and mixed with celery, aconite, poplar leaves, and soot, or in another formula with bat's blood, nightshade, cinquefoil, and oil. Applied after warming the skin, these unguents, he explained, opened the pores and allowed the powers of the juices to penetrate, producing the conviction that the body was carried through the air on a moonlit night to dances, banquets, and embraces with lovers of their choice.[1]

Later writers repeated the tale. Joseph Ennemoser in his nineteenth-century *History of Magic* noted that witches "universally prepared unguents, by which, smeared over the body, they believed themselves enabled to fly through the air and attend nocturnal assemblies." He cited Porta and others for recipes of fat of children, henbane, aconite, parsley, soot, and narcotic herbs, concluding that these poisonous compounds produced ecstatic dreams in which the imagination transported the witch to the Sabbath.[2] Jacob Grimm, in his *Teutonic Mythology*, connected these ointments with older pagan traditions, observing that the belief in riding through the night on salves and charms was the continuation of a pre-Christian heritage of goddess-led processions and magical flights.[3] Montague Summers collected many similar reports, noting that inquisitors and judges consistently recorded the use of such unguents, and that the women under their influence described visions of sabbaths, feasts, and demonic lovers.[4]

Modern eyes recognise in these concoctions the chemistry of delirium: belladonna, aconite, henbane, and nightshade are deadly hallucinogens, and to experiment with them was to risk one's life. Yet their effect explains why so many accounts of witches' flights share the same imagery. Under the influence of such drugs, a woman might truly believe herself transformed, borne aloft into the night sky, joining processions of spirits or seeing fairies dancing in the meadows. Even ingredients such as the blood of a bat, while chemically inert, had powerful symbolic associations, lending the rite a vibrational or placebo effect that reinforced the ecstatic vision.

To later centuries these ointments became proof of diabolism, but in their origins they were closer to a form of visionary magic. The ointment allowed the spirit to travel, if not the body; it unlocked the dream-flight that joined the witch to her goddess, whether Diana, Hecate, or the Lady of the Night. That the Church condemned these rites as illusions or pacts with demons is no surprise, for in them lingered the survival of older cults and the enduring independence of women's magical tradition. It is from this that witches gained their reputation, not only as healers and charmers, but as dangerous figures said to fly to forbidden Sabbaths on moonlit nights.[68]

---

[68], *Ultimate Grimoire and Spellbook of Real Ancient Witchcraft. Edited by Hrafen Starbourne. Samhain Song Press, 2008. ISBN 978-1-4357-4201-7.*
Context & Citation Notes:
The work is a **modern compilation** *published by Samhain Song Press in 2008, assembling texts that predate 1900.*

Although it reprints "ancient" materials like Hohman's Pow-Wows and Aradia, it is itself a modern publication—not an original historical source
Giovan Battista della Porta, De Miraculis Rerum Naturalium (1558), Bk. II, ch. xxvi.
Joseph Ennemoser, The History of Magic, vol. II (London: Henry Colburn, 1854), pp. 67–72.
Jacob Grimm, Teutonic Mythology, vol. III (London: George Bell & Sons, 1883), pp. 1056–

So why do witches get such a bad reputation?

The figure of the witch has long haunted the margins of society—feared, revered, and often misunderstood. Witchcraft, in its broadest historical sense, refers to the use of supernatural or occult powers, often for healing, divination, or protection. However, from the late medieval period into the early modern era, these practices became increasingly criminalized across Europe and later in colonial America. Accusations of witchcraft were frequently driven by fear, religious fervour, social tension, and misogyny.

The **European witch hunts** reached their peak between the 15th and 17th centuries, claiming tens of thousands of lives, the majority of them women.[1] One of the most influential treatises fuelling these persecutions was the *Malleus Maleficarum* (1487), written by Dominican inquisitors Heinrich Kramer and Jacob Sprenger, which provided both theological justification and legal procedures for identifying and punishing witches.

In Britain, laws against witchcraft were codified under Henry VIII and later intensified under Elizabeth I and James VI/I, whose 1597 book *Daemonologie* legitimized witch-hunting efforts.[3] The infamous **Salem witch trials** of 1692 in colonial Massachusetts represent the transatlantic continuation of these persecutions, where Puritan beliefs intersected with community paranoia.[4]

Modern scholarship recognizes that witch hunts were not simply about belief in magic, but also functioned as tools of **social control**, targeting vulnerable individuals, especially women, widows,

---

1061.
Montague Summers, *The Geography of Witchcraft* (London: Kegan Paul, 1927), pp. 184–190.

and the poor.5 Today, witchcraft is often reclaimed by neopagan and Wiccan traditions as a symbol of resistance, wisdom, and spiritual autonomy.[69]

HEKATE (Hecate) was the goddess of magic, witchcraft, the night, moon, ghosts and necromancy. She was the only child of the Titanes Perses and Asteria from whom she received her power over heaven, earth, and sea[70] She was the only Titan to retain her control under Zeus' reign. Hecate's powers transcended the boundaries of

[69]*Brian P. Levack, The Witch-Hunt in Early Modern Europe, 4th ed. (New York: Routledge, 2016), 25–29.*

Heinrich Kramer and Jacob Sprenger, Malleus Maleficarum, trans. Montague Summers (London: John Rodker, 1928).

James VI of Scotland (James I of England), Daemonologie (1597; repr., Edinburgh: Edinburgh University

[70]*Hecate," Encyclopaedia Britannica, https://www.britannica.com/topic/Hecate.*

1. *Aaron J. Atsma, "Hekate," Theoi Greek Mythology, https://www.theoi.com/Khthonios/Hekate.html.*

the sky, the earth, the seas, and the underworld. Although there are few myths about the goddess Hecate, her tales reveal a lot about her spheres of influence. During the Roman era, many of her attributes fell in the realm of the underworld. Yet, she also controlled elements that placed her firmly in the light. The goddess possessed extensive powers, which were later assimilated by other deities.

Volva the Viking Witch or Seeress
Völva or as it is pronounced in old Norse a Volva (in Danish a" Vølve"), is what we in English would call a Seeress. You could compare it to someone who practiced shamanism or witchcraft. So,

a Völva is a Nordic version of a shaman or witch, who practiced magic. The Völva in the Viking age were the predecessors of the medieval witches, so you could say, they were witches before it became cool. A Völva is not something that just dates back to the Viking age, a Völva is, in fact, very ancient, and their roots go back more than 2.000 – 3.000 years.

The Hexene of Germany

Much of the witch persecution took place during the Counter Reformation from 1570 and the 30 years' war. Between 1618 to 1648 when towns changed from protestant to Catholic or vice versa overnight.

One woman accused of witchcraft in Hagenau, Alsace who were freed by protestant judges only to be retried 7 years later by Catholic judges, her trial lasted a year was tortured several times in order to confess and finally burnt along with 6 other women.

One of the authors of Malleus Maleficarum, Heinrich Kramer started a witch hunt in Tyrol in the 1480s, he was not supported by the locals and persuaded a dissolute woman to hide in an oven to pretend that the devil lived there. From inside she denounced many people Kramer had tortured.

The Bishop of Bixel finally managed to expel Kramer and later had an interested the Archduke Sigismund on the topic of witch burning.[71]

Roger Toothaker and Family: Witches or Witch Killers? Roger Toothaker was a prominent farmer and folk healer from Billerica, known for his role in detecting and punishing witches. He faced accusations of witchcraft during the Salem Witch Trials, but his case never went to trial because he died in jail before it could proceed. Born in England around 1634, Toothaker sailed with his family to

---

[71] *Nigel Cawthorne, Witches: The History of a Persecution (London: Arcturus Publishing, 2006)*

the Massachusetts Bay Colony in 1635, settling in Billerica. Following the death of his father in 1638, his mother remarried Ralph Hill, a farmer in southern Billerica. Despite lacking formal medical training, Toothaker apprenticed with Dr. Samuel Eldred, who utilized mystical folk remedies in his practice. At 31, Toothaker married Mary Allen, the eldest daughter of a prosperous family in Andover. Together, they operated a small farm just a few miles from a nearby Indian settlement. Faced with increasing competition from practicing midwives, Toothaker made the strategic decision to leave his family temporarily to establish his medical practice in Salem. As detailed in the book *Death in Salem: The Private Lives Behind the 1692 Witch Hunt*, "There were other practicing midwives by then, which might explain why Roger left his family for a time and moved to Salem. Perhaps he found it a lucrative place to set up a practice, at least until a direct competitor—Dr. William Griggs—arrived from Boston in 1690. Dr. Griggs's wife, Rachel Hubbard Griggs, hailed from an influential family. One of her relatives, Elizabeth Hubbard, lived with them in 1692 when the witch hunt erupted. On May 18, Hubbard and her friends Ann Putnam Jr. and Mary Walcott accused Roger Toothaker of witchcraft. He was arrested and sent to jail in Boston that same day." Toothaker was arrested for witchcraft on May 18, 1692, by Salem constable Joseph Neall, following accusations from Elizabeth Hubbard, Ann Putnam Jr., and Mary Walcott. He was promptly brought before the court for a pre-trial examination, but no surviving records document this examination. The sole surviving records concerning Toothaker's case include his arrest warrant, documentation of his transfer to Boston jail, testimony by Thomas Gage against him, and the jury's report regarding his death. Thomas Gage's testimony sheds light on the motivations behind Toothaker's accusations. A year before the Salem Witch Trials commenced, Toothaker confided to Gage that he and his daughter, Mary Emerson (the wife of Joseph Emerson), practiced counter-magic against witches and claimed that his daughter had killed one. Gage recounted: "The Deposition of

Thomas Gage, aged about thirty-six years. This deponent testified that during the spring of this year, Dr. Toothaker was in his house in Beverly, and we discussed John Maston's child of Salem, who was then sick with unusual fits, as well as another child belonging to

Phillip White in Beverly who was also gravely ill. I urged Toothaker to see these children, to which he replied he had already seen them and believed they were under an evil hand. He further asserted that his daughter had killed a witch. When I asked how she accomplished this, he stated that she had learned something from him. I inquired about the method she employed, and he explained that a certain person was bewitched, and that individual complained of being afflicted by someone suspected of causing the affliction. Toothaker detailed that his daughter took some of the afflicted person's urine, placed it in an earthen pot, sealed it tightly, and then put it in a hot oven. After sealing the oven, he claimed that the next morning, the supposed witch was dead. Other details I have forgotten, and I have no further testimony to provide." According to *The Salem Witch Trials: A Day-By-Day Chronicle of a Community Under Siege, the alleged witch may have been Mathias Button of Haverhill, Massachusetts. It remains unclear whether Button or his family were suspected of witchcraft or fell victim to Toothaker's counter-magic. Button was never accused of witchcraft during his lifetime, although he did serve as a witness in a case against his neighbour John Godfrey in 1665. Mathias Button later pursued legal action against Godfrey in 1669 for allegedly setting fire to his home, which resulted in the tragic death of his wife, Ann Teagle Button. Button remarried a woman named Elizabeth Wheeler before passing away from natural causes in August 1672 at 67 years of age. No additional testimony was submitted in Roger Toothaker's case, and no further witnesses were called, as the case concluded with his death on June 16, 1692, in Boston jail. The jury was summoned to the jail at the request of Suffolk County coroner Edward Willis. Upon reviewing Toothaker's body, the jury concluded that he had died of natural causes: "We whose names are underwritten being summoned By virtue of a warrant from Mr. Edward Willis, one of their Majesties' Coroners for the County of Suffolk, we have viewed the body of Roger Toothaker, who died in the Boston jail. After our examination and gathering information from those present at his death, we find that he died of natural causes. In witness whereof, we have set our hands this 16th of June 1692. Roger Toothaker was a resident of the town of Billerica in Essex County. Signatories: Benjamin Walker, Foreman Enoch [illegible] Thomas Barnard Daniell Powning Roger Gubberidge James Thornboro William Jaine Andrew Cunningham William Man John Shelby John Roulston Abraham Buk John Riggs Samuel Wentworth Francis Thresher Unfortunately, around the same time that Toothaker was arrested in May, his wife, Mary, and daughter, Martha Emerson, were also arrested on charges of witchcraft, accused by Mary Warren and Mary Lacey Jr. Several sources indicate that Toothaker's nine-year-old daughter, Margaret, was also arrested;

however, there are no records of her arrest, examination, or imprisonment. It was very common for relatives of accused witches to also be accused of witchcraft. Mary Toothaker was not only the widow of an accused witch but also the sister of another, Martha Carrier, who had been arrested on witchcraft charges in May.

Picture from The Sun Newspaper

255

After initially denying all charges, Mary ultimately confessed to being a witch and revealed that her husband had previously discussed with their daughter the intention of killing a witch named Button. Not only did Mary admit to her own guilt and implicate her daughter, but she also made accusations against several others, asserting that she had observed them at witch meetings. These individuals included Elizabeth Howe, Goody Bridges, Goody Green, Goody Bromage, Rev. George Burroughs, Goody Foster, Mary Lacey Jr., Mary Lacy Sr., Richard Carrier, and her sister Martha Carrier. The motivations behind her confession remain unclear, yet her statements during the examination indicate that she genuinely believed she was a witch due to her family's engagement with counter-magic. Mary Toothaker explicitly declared that she became a witch after entering into a pact with the Devil, seeking his protection from the Indians—a fear shared by many colonists. She recounted having nightmares about Indian attacks. In court records, she stated, "The Devil appeared to her in the shape of a tawny man and promised to protect her from the Indians, ensuring happiness for her and her son. When asked about signing the Devil's book, she acknowledged that he presented her with what she thought was a piece of birch bark, and she made a mark with her finger by rubbing the white scrap. He assured her that if she served him, she would be safe from the Indians. Compelled by her fear, she recognized it was the Devil and proceeded anyway. When questioned about whether the Devil commanded her to serve him, she affirmed it, confirming that she signed the mark on that condition and was to devote herself entirely to him. She believed she prayed at all times, as he promised that he could keep her safe from the Indians. Her fear of them ultimately drove her to create this pact. Mary did not shy away from confessing that she harmed Timothy Swan and acknowledged attending two witch meetings in Salem Village, where Goody Bridges was among her company. She explicitly stated that her sister accompanied her to every meeting, particularly in Salem Village, alongside Goody Bridges, Goody Foster, Goody Green, and Goody Broomage.

Several afflicted individuals distinctly claimed to have seen the "black man" during her examination, and Mary herself admitted to encountering him on the table before her. She identified a minister known as Burroughs, described as a "little man," who preached at the Village Meeting of witches. She claimed to have heard that they used bread and wine at these meetings and discussed the presence of 305 witches in the area. Mary was also accused of bewitching a local man named Timothy Swan, which she confessed to. Swan was suffering from a mysterious illness and firmly believed it was the result of witchcraft. Mary was a suspect because he had previously raped her relative, Elizabeth Emerson, and was found not guilty. Since that time, Mary harboured deep resentment toward Swan and worried that her animosity could have inflicted actual harm on him. As noted in the book *A Storm of Witchcraft: The Salem Witch Trials and the American Experience*, "The troubled history of Elizabeth Emerson and Timothy Swan played a significant role. Mary confessed she hurt Timothy Swan and feared that she, the said Toothaker, had squeezed his throat, causing harm just as he had done to Elizabeth during her assault. It is clear that Mary Toothaker nursed a grudge against Swan. When he fell ill, she believed her negative feelings were capable of causing his misfortune—she may have unwittingly invoked Satan's powers merely through her thoughts and her anxiety for her family's safety in a time of war." During Martha Emerson's examination on July 23, upon hearing of her father's claims that she had killed a witch, she confessed that she had practiced counter magic and kept a woman's urine in a glass jar but did not identify the woman.

Emerson then stated that the spirits of her Aunt Martha Carrier and Goody Green were in front of her, grabbing her throat and stopping her from confessing to witchcraft.

According to the court records, at some point Martha recanted her confession and stated she was just trying to save herself:
"but afterward she denied all and said what she had said was in hopes to have favour and now she could not deny God: that had kept her from that sin and after said though he slay me I will trust in him."

Martha Emerson's case was eventually thrown out of court due to a lack of evidence and she was released from jail.

Royal witches and 'love magic.

Royal families have dabbled in the occult and alchemy for hundreds of years. The relationship between royals and the occult is complex and often troubling. Some royals have sought to leverage the occult for personal gain, while others have resisted its influence. While it may be entertaining to envision kings and queens gathered around a pentagram, making deals with the devil, the reality is far more mundane and chilling. More frequently, the occult has been employed as a tool for political intrigue. Discussions of the occult have been used to undermine the legitimacy of predecessors, eliminate political rivals, and manipulate rulers, as seen in the case of Rasputin. Ultimately, more royals have faced downfall due to their associations with the occult than have found success through it.

There was a time we had witches, shamans and alchemists such as John Dee who served under queen Elizabeth, whom were essential to healing people, They were the doctors of the medieval times, without them many people would have died of succumbed to much pain, we certainly would not have the NHS now had these people not have been able to practise their skills, Nor would we have the scientific research. We have seen how woman especially have been burnt at the stake and persecuted for the sake of bringing forth new religions in order to control the masses, The ones who see clearly seemed to question all government and those in authority, they dared to be different without conforming to societies normal structure.

What are spells? And why would it be so that the bible teaches all of these things. Why is it that the bible and most religions are based on pagan values, but god forbid you actually say this truth. Of course, all pagans, witches and clairvoyants are the spawn of the devil. I have many bibles at home, I asked all of the questions as you would being Nicks daughter, we once had a discussion about this and he asked me what do you think of the bible and I responded with, The bible is merely a series of many people Chinese whisper all to be perceived and interpreted by the reader to suit their confirmation bias of what the truth is, How do we know that each gospel is a truth, it maybe their truth but how do we know this for sure, we can't, this is for the sheep, the people that do not question, those who do as they are told and follow anyone that tells them.

Queen Joan of Navarre (c. 1370–1437), the second wife of King Henry IV of England, was accused of using dark magic in an attempt to kill her stepson, Henry V, along with a small group of accomplices. The accusations were not well-developed, and the methods allegedly used were unclear; it was simply stated that she tried to kill him in an "evil and terrible manner." Joan was imprisoned in Leeds Castle for several years until Henry V released her on his deathbed. A few decades later, Joan's stepdaughter-in-law,

Eleanor Cobham (c. 1400–52), who was the Duchess of Gloucester, faced similar accusations of using malevolent magic to kill the king, this time her stepson, King Henry VI of England. In Eleanor's case, the emerging societal ideas about gender roles in magic became evident. Eleanor was said to have enlisted several educated members of the clergy to employ necromancy and other forms of sorcery to cause Henry VI's death. This accusation was significant because it would have been implausible for Eleanor, as a woman of lower birth (being the daughter of a knight), to have performed necromancy herself. Additionally, a lower-class woman known for her past involvement in witchcraft was also accused. Eleanor defended herself by using gendered magic rhetoric. Instead of confessing to attempting to kill the king through magic, she claimed that she had sought the lower-class witch's help to create love potions in hopes of conceiving a child with her husband. Eleanor, who had previously been a mistress, conformed to the stereotype of a 'loose', emotional woman who might more readily resort to love magic. As a consequence, she was divorced from her husband and sentenced to life v, ultimately dying alone in the remote Welsh castle of Beaumaris.

By the end of the 15th century, Eleanor's case and other developments in witchcraft had firmly associated women with love magic in England. This connection made it easier for Richard III and his parliament to accuse Elizabeth Woodville and her mother, Jacquetta, of using witchcraft to ensnare Edward IV in love and influence his offspring. It became widely accepted that women viewed as social upstarts would resort to emotional magic to gain power.

Elizabeth Woodville, the widow of Edward IV, and Jane Shore are accused of witchcraft by Richard, Duke of Gloucester. (Photo by Print Collector/Getty Images)

Life at the English court in the 15th century was perilous. With civil wars, usurpations, and favourites vying for power, it was difficult to predict how long one's influence would last. Women at court had to be particularly cautious; in an era when loyalty was uncertain and enemies were eager to undermine rivals, women were more vulnerable targets than men. They lacked the ability to command the same power and did not hold official government positions. Some royal women managed to survive and outlast the accusations levelled against them, while others faced dire consequences. Ultimately, the successful accusations of witchcraft against English royal women during this time solidified public perceptions of witchcraft, making it even more dangerous in the centuries that followed.[72]

Oil portrait of Charles VII of France, circa 1600 (Public Domain)

Charles VII of France - A Scholar of the Occult

Charles VII of France exemplifies how wealth and power (particularly when combined with maleness) can create a sense of immunity to the law. In an era when interest in the occult could lead

---

[72] *Gemma Hollman, Medieval Royal Witches: From Joan of Navarre to Queen Joan of Navarre*, History Extra, accessed August 4, 2025.

to being burned at the stake, Charles VII was immersed in learning everything he could about it. Fascinated by the occult, he possessed the resources, education, and authority to pursue his interests. By the middle of the 14th century, Charles had assembled an extensive library dedicated to astrology. While astrology is considered harmless today, during his time it was regarded as a perilous blend of science and witchcraft—neither of which was favoured by the Church. Charles established a college of astrology in Paris, which helped legitimize his pursuits. Although today, an interest in astrology may seem trivial, we must question whether a peasant with similar interests would have enjoyed the same privileges.

Isabella of Angoulême, queen of England (Public Domain)

Isabella of Angouleme - A Bewitching Presence

It is often said that behind every good man is a good woman pulling the strings. But what about a bad man? According to 13th-century Englishmen, it was probably a witch. Isabella was the wife of King John of England, one of the most despised British monarchs, often depicted as a villain whose scheming led to his loss of power. His incompetence has become legendary, and unfortunately for Isabella, much of the blame fell on her shoulders. John married Isabella when he was just 12 years old, shortly after securing the throne. Coming from a prominent French family, their union was likely a political arrangement typical of royalty during that time. Isabella's beauty and charisma only fuelled the rumours of witchcraft against her. It was believed that no one could be so naturally lovely without engaging in dark arts to ensnare the poor king. The rumours persisted even after John's death. In the 1240s, she was accused of attempting to poison Louis IX of France. Though she was never arrested or put on trial, Isabella wisely chose to flee. She spent her remaining years in an abbey—the last place anyone would expect to find a royal witch.

James VI & I, circa 1620 (Public Domain)

James VI - The (Rightly?) Paranoid King

It is common for those in positions of great power to develop paranoia. After all, sitting atop the hierarchy means being at risk of being overthrown. Typically, a king would be fearful of assassination attempts or coups; however, for James VI of Scotland, it was witches that consumed his thoughts. To be fair, during the 16th and 17th centuries, all of Europe was engulfed in witch hysteria, and Scotland was particularly obsessed, executing suspected witches at a rate five times higher than the rest of Europe. James was a product of his time, but he amplified the paranoia. In 1591, Agnes Sampson, an accused witch, confessed that she and hundreds of others were plotting to kill him. Whether her confession was genuine, coerced, or a vengeful act due to her impending death remains uncertain. Regardless of the reasoning, her claims only deepened James' obsession with witchcraft. He later authored "Daemonologie," a book exploring the notion that witchcraft and the occult posed a constant threat to Christians.

Queen Anne Boleyn (National Trust / Public Domain)

Anne Boleyn - The Headless Witch

King Henry VIII is notorious for his tumultuous marriages, having wed six women and executed two of them. Anne Boleyn was one of those unfortunate two. When Henry sought a new wife, he often lacked compelling reasons to dispose of his current spouse. In Anne's case, the formal charges were adultery, incest, and treason—

charges that ultimately led to her execution. Before these allegations surfaced, Henry first accused Anne of witchcraft, claiming she had bewitched him into marriage. The evidence? Rumours suggested she possessed a sixth finger and irregular moles—traits often linked to enchantresses. This was hardly convincing. Furthermore, it was alleged that her stillborn son had severe deformities. In the absence of scientific understanding, such tragedies were frequently attributed to the mother's supposed dealings with the devil. In those superstitious times, it was not unusual to blame the mother for such misfortunes. Sadly, for Henry, English law at the time lacked any formal provisions for trying an accused witch. Nonetheless, like many royal women before her, the damage to Anne's reputation was irrevocable. Once someone is painted as a witch, it becomes easier to accept charges of treason, incest, and adultery as credible

John Dee performing an experiment before Queen Elizabeth I, oil painting by Henry Gillard Glindoni. (Welcome Collection / CC BY-NC 4.0)

Elizabeth I and John Dee- The Occult Courtier

No discussion of royals and the occult can really go ahead without mentioning John Dee. Dr. John Dee was an incredibly interesting man. He was a skilled astrologer, alchemist, scientist, and occultist, a true polymath and genuine genius. He had worked for Elizabeth's sister, Mary I, and was soon introduced to Elizabeth I.

Dee fascinated Elizabeth, and he soon became a central pillar of her court. When Elizabeth had a question, it was Dee she went to, whether it be a dream interpretation or a challenging puzzle.

Dee was not just a scientist, however. He held séances and attempted to speak to divine spirits like angels. He had an enormous collection of mystical artifacts such as a 'spirit mirror" and magic figurines.

Whether Elizabeth approved of Dee's occult leanings or just chose to turn a blind eye is largely unknown. But it is known that on the day she died, Elizabeth chose to visit Dee one last time and demanded to view his magic mirror. Unfortunately, no one could seem to get it working.

Rasputin's piercing eyes

Nicholas II and the Infamous Rasputin

Anyone with even a passing interest in the occult has probably heard of Nicholas II of Russia and his right-hand man, Rasputin. When it comes to Rasputin, it can be hard to separate fact from fiction.

However, the Romanov family's interest in the occult predated Rasputin. Like most royals, all Nicholas wanted was a healthy royal heir to continue his dynasty. Unfortunately, this was something Nicholas and his wife Alexandra struggled to do.

Over the years, they turned to a series of increasingly peculiar mystics who all claimed to be able to help them. There was Mantronuskha the Barefooted, a seemingly crazy peasant woman who won the couple's favour by occasionally making vague predictions of a healthy son for the royals.

Then there was Demchinsky, the meteorologist who claimed to predict the future and the weather. Finally, there were upper-class mystics like Rasputin. These men and women were mystics who claimed to be orthodox Christians, just with mystical powers which made things more palatable.

For all his fame, Rasputin is still somewhat of an enigma. Eccentric con artist or genuine mystical healer? No one at the time or since seems to know.

Rasputin was brought in to treat Alexei, the son of Alexandra and Nicholas. He was a sickly child who suffered greatly from haemophilia. No treatment had worked until Rasputin came along.

His "magic" appeared to work, and to this day no one seems to know how he did it. The boy's tutor, Pierre Gilliard described him as a "clever cheat", while others, especially Alexandra, were convinced Rasputin had holy powers. We only know that every time Rasputin claimed to help Alexei with his haemophilia, the boy mysteriously improved.

Rasputin became invaluable to the Romanov family and became a fixture of the court. This would prove to be his undoing. Rasputin had once been a favourite of Russian aristocrats, but as he became increasingly power-hungry, he became increasingly unpopular.

He was soon hated by almost all of Russia, doing massive damage to the royal family's reputation. This led to his eventual assassination at the hands of several nobles. But even his death was mysterious. It was rumoured that Rasputin was almost supernaturally difficult to take down. It supposedly took a lot of poison, several bullets, and a drowning to take him out.

Whether a true mystic or a conman, the damage Rasputin did to the Tsar is undeniable. His decadent lifestyle and political meddling painted a bullseye on the Royal family's back. Not long after Rasputin's death, the Romanov families followed.

Queen Victoria wore all black for over forty years mourning Prince Albert, and would never stop trying to contact him in the afterlife (Public Domain)

Queen Victoria - A Royal in Mourning
Queen Victoria has a reputation for being straight-laced and no-

nonsense. Less publicized is her belief in spiritualism, especially after the loss of her beloved Prince Albert.

Prince Albert passed away in 1861, leaving Elizabeth distraught. She would mourn for the rest of her life, never truly moving on. Unable to accept his death, she turned to various mediums to help her contact her dead husband.

Not long after Albert's death, a medium called Robert James Lee claimed to have been visited by Albert during a séance. Why Albert would choose to visit a 12-year-old is anyone's guess, but it was good enough for Victoria. She hired the young medium and held multiple séances with Robert.

The young medium reportedly had some success coming up with information that supposedly no one but Albert would know. People deal with grief in different ways. If Robert was helping Victoria deal with hers, then surely it was harmless?

Troublingly, the story takes a rather darker turn. It would seem these séances became a crutch for Victoria. She soon began asking her dead husband for advice on political matters[73].

One in a Million

Could it be that we are all 50th cousins? Having started to put my research to paper each day I find new science that proves the out of Africa theory wrong, While the Out of Africa theory proposes a single origin, the evidence of tangled genealogies and regionally dominant lineages suggests a far more complex, multi-origin story

---

[73] *ibid*

of humanity. I came across a DNA lecture by the Harvard natural history museum who again opened my mind further to my subject matter.

If we look at each parent having 2 parents and going back to 15 generations, we will find that we in fact have the DNA of around 16-17000 grandparents, it took that many people to make us who we are today, our existence rides on them and the cells they gave to us.

Genghis Khan Is Thought To Have 16 Million Living Descendants

Genghis Khan (1162-1227 AD) rose from obscurity in the Mongolian steppe to become one of the most successful yet brutal conquerors in world history.

A substantial portion of men across Asia may share a common male ancestor from the medieval era, widely believed to be Genghis Khan. This idea stems from an intersection of historical accounts and contemporary genetic research, revealing a distinct pattern in human lineage. The widespread genetic signature suggests a powerful individual or a close group of related men had an extraordinary impact on the human gene pool. This intriguing finding sets the stage for understanding how such a remarkable genetic legacy could have emerged and persisted through centuries.

The Genetic Evidence

Genetic studies provide evidence for a widespread male lineage. The Y-chromosome, passed from father to son, serves as a tool for tracing patrilineal ancestry through generations. Researchers identified a specific Y-chromosome "star-cluster" haplotype, indicating a lineage with numerous branches originating from a relatively recent common ancestor. This genetic signature, primarily associated with haplogroup C2 (previously known as C3), was detailed in a 2003 study in the American Journal of Human Genetics.

A star-cluster signifies a rapid and expansive proliferation of a single male lineage, where a founding male had an unusually high number of male offspring who also successfully reproduced. The 2003 study examined Y-chromosome samples from over 40 populations across Asia and found this distinct haplotype present in approximately 8% of the men in a vast region stretching from Northeast Asia to the Middle East. This translates to an estimated 16 million men alive today carrying this specific genetic marker, pointing to an extraordinary demographic expansion. The genetic data suggests the lineage originated approximately 1,000 years ago, placing its emergence within a historical period of significant upheaval and empire-building in Asia.

Historical Factors in Genetic Proliferation

The widespread proliferation of this male lineage is deeply intertwined with the socio-historical dynamics of the Mongol Empire. Following its establishment in the early 13th century, its rapid expansion across Eurasia created conditions conducive to the widespread dissemination of a male lineage. Mongol conquests led to the establishment of vast territories, including the Yuan dynasty in China, facilitating the movement and intermingling of populations across the Silk Road. This extensive geographical reach provided ample opportunity for the genetic signature to spread over a wide area.

Social selection played a significant role in this genetic expansion, particularly through the practice of polygyny and the preferential treatment of powerful male leaders and their descendants. Genghis Khan and his male heirs, as rulers of a vast empire, had access to numerous wives and concubines, leading to a disproportionately large number of offspring. Historical records indicate that Genghis Khan himself had multiple wives and concubines, and his sons and grandsons continued this pattern, ensuring a large number of male descendants. This system allowed the lineage of these powerful men to rapidly outcompete other lineages in terms of reproductive success, leaving a profound genetic imprint across the empire's former territories.

While the widespread Y-chromosome lineage is frequently associated with Genghis Khan, directly proving his paternity without his DNA remains impossible. Scientific evidence, however, strongly points towards him or one of his direct paternal relatives as the likely founder. The geographic distribution of the haplogroup C2 star-cluster shows its highest frequency and diversity centered in Mongolia, which aligns with the historical origins of the Mongol Empire. Furthermore, the estimated time of the lineage's expansion, around 1,000 years ago, correlates precisely with the period of Genghis Khan's rise and the subsequent Mongol conquests in the 13th century.

Researchers have considered several possibilities for the founder of this lineage, including Genghis Khan himself, his father Yesugei, or another paternal ancestor from the Borjigin clan to which Genghis Khan belonged. The scale and speed of the genetic spread, combined with the Mongol Empire's expansion and the ruling elite's reproductive practices, make Genghis Khan the most plausible candidate. This alignment provides circumstantial evidence, suggesting a powerful individual from that era, consistent with Genghis Khan's influence, initiated this lineage.

For individuals curious about their own heritage, commercial DNA tests can identify if a male belongs to the specific Y-chromosome haplogroup C2. However, possessing this haplogroup does not definitively prove direct patrilineal descent from Genghis Khan himself. While the genetic marker indicates a shared male ancestor within the star-cluster lineage, pinpointing the exact individual at the root of that lineage is beyond the current capabilities of these tests. The presence of the haplogroup signifies a connection to a broad ancestral group that expanded during the Mongol Empire.

It is important to differentiate between direct patrilineal descent, traced through the Y-chromosome, and being a descendant in a broader genealogical sense. Given the extensive reach of the Mongol Empire and the intermingling of populations, many individuals with roots in regions once under Mongol influence may have Genghis Khan as an ancestor through various maternal and paternal lines. However, commercial DNA tests primarily focus on direct lines, and only the Y-chromosome test can identify the specific patrilineal connection to this genetic signature.[74]

The World's largest Family Tree's

- [74]*Smith, A. J. "Genghis Khan Genetics: Science Behind a Widespread Lineage," Biology Insights.*

Family trees have been used to document family histories across different cultures and time periods worldwide. In Africa, the ruling dynasty of Ethiopia claims descent from King Solomon through the Queen of Sheba, tracing their lineage back to the House of David. The genealogy of ancient Egyptian ruling dynasties has been recorded since the beginning of the Pharaonic era around 3000 BC, but this does not represent a continuously linked family lineage, and many records have been lost. In other African regions, oral traditions are predominant in genealogical recording. For instance, members of the Keita dynasty in Mali have had their genealogies sung by griots during annual ceremonies since the 14th century. Similarly, in Nigeria, various ruling clans, especially those descended from Oduduwa, claim descent from the legendary King Kisra, with their pedigrees recited by griots associated with royal courts.

The Americas- In some pre-contact Native American civilizations, genealogical records of ruling and priestly families were maintained, with some records extending over several centuries.
East Asia- China has extensive genealogies for its ruling dynasties; however, they do not form a single, unified family tree. It remains unclear at which points the earliest historical figures become mythological. In Japan, the Imperial Family traces its ancestry to the mythological origins of Japan, with connections to historically established figures beginning only in the mid-first millennium AD. The longest family tree in the world belongs to the Chinese philosopher and educator Confucius (551–479 BC), who descends from King Tang (1675–1646 BC). This lineage spans over 80 generations and includes more than 2 million members. An international effort, involving over 450 branches globally, began in 1998 to retrace and revise this family tree, culminating in a new edition released in September 2009 by the Confucius Genealogy

Compilation Committee, coinciding with the 2560th anniversary of Confucius's birth. This edition was expected to include approximately 1.3 million living descendants scattered around the world.

Europe and West Asia- Before the Dark Ages, some reliable pedigrees in the Greco-Roman world can be traced back to at least the first half of the first millennium BC, although claims of origins may reach further. Roman clan and family lineages played a crucial role in their society, forming the basis of their complex naming systems. However, continuity in record-keeping was interrupted at the end of Classical Antiquity. Some records of succession for Popes and Eastern Roman Emperors from this transitional period remain, but they do not provide continuous genealogical histories of single families. Many noble and aristocratic families of European and West Asian origins can reliably trace their ancestry back to the mid to late first millennium AD, with some claiming descent from Classical Antiquity or mythological figures. For example, the lineage of Niall Noígíallach is a contender for one of the longest, descending through Conn of the Hundred Battles (fl. 123 AD) from Breogán and ultimately from Adam through the sons of Noah in Irish legendary history. Another ancient and extensive family tree is that of the Lurie lineage, which includes figures such as Sigmund Freud and Martin Buber. This tree traces back to Lurie, a 13th-century rabbi in Brest-Litovsk, and claims descent from Rashi and, purportedly, the legendary King David, as documented by Neil Rosenstein in his book "The Lurie Legacy". The 1999 edition of the Guinness Book of Records recognized the Lurie family in the "longest lineage" category as one of the oldest-known living families in the world today. Family trees also hold significance in religious traditions.

The biblical genealogies of Jesus suggest descent from the House of David, covering a period of approximately 1,000 years. The Torah and Old Testament provide genealogies for many biblical figures, including the descendants of Adam. According to the Torah, the Kohanim are descended from Aaron. Genetic testing performed at the Technion has shown that most modern Kohanim share common Y-chromosome origins, although there is no complete family tree for the Kohanim. In the Islamic world, claims of descent from the Prophet Muhammad have significantly enhanced the status of political and religious leaders; new dynasties often used these claims to establish legitimacy. In many cultures globally, clan and tribal associations are based on claims of common ancestry, though detailed documentation of those origins is often limited.

Global -Family trees are also used in genetic genealogy. In 2022, scientists reported advancements in this field, which emphasize the importance of family lineage in understanding human genetic heritage.[75]

DNA Research- Dangers of Royal inbreeding.

Questioning the links between Hereditary illnesses.
From the Spanish Habsburgs to Queen Victoria's grandchildren, how centuries of inbreeding and genetic mutation led Europe's royal families to ruin He endured violent convulsions and hallucinations, and his pronounced underbite and engorged tongue

---

[75] *Andrews, C. "Historical Royals With the Most Children." HistoryExtra, published May 2022.*

meant he was unable to close his teeth together. The malformed jaw made eating and talking nearly impossible, and he suffered uncontrollable spells of diarrhoea and vomiting.

It was rumoured that he was bewitched; his painful and disfigured body the result of witchcraft, a curse, or the ritual consummation of the brains of criminals that he had devoured in hot chocolate drinks. But the truth was just as unsavoury and much closer to home. Charles II of Spain's birth defects were the result of the accumulation of over two centuries of inbreeding.

Charles was unable to speak at all until he was four, and it wouldn't be until the age of eight that he would take his first steps. He was born to Philip IV of Spain (1605-1655) and Mariana of Austria (1634-1665); a matrimony of uncle and niece, which made young Charles not only their son but also their great-nephew and first cousin, respectively. Unfortunately, their consanguineous marriage was not a solitary ill-fated pairing. Instead, it had become a habit in the Habsburg family, especially the Spanish line. Incestuous relationships had been so common in his dynasty and for so long that by the time Charles II was born he was more inbred than a child whose parents were siblings.

In Europe, royal inbreeding to one degree or another was most prevalent from the Medieval era until the outbreak of the First World War. Unable to marry commoners and faced with a dwindling dating pool of royals of equivalent social status – especially as Reformation and revolution diminished the available stock increasingly rapidly from the 16th century onwards – the only viable option was to marry a relative.

Those expected to succeed to the throne were unable to make morganatic matches – unions between royals and those of lesser rank. But even when the bride or groom-to-be held the title of prince or princess, unequal unions were discouraged. It was a surprisingly nuanced affair and could make or break a regime's legitimacy. Queen Victoria's (1819-1901) marriage to her first cousin Prince Albert (1819-1861) in 1840 was controversial, not because of their close kinship but because while she was the descendant of a king (George III of Great Britain), and was born a royal princess (Her Royal Highness), he was the son of the Duke of Saxe-Coburg-Saarfield, one of myriad minuscule German principalities. While still a prince Albert was a prince of a very different – lesser – magnitude and styled as His Serene Highness instead. The worst this union caused Victoria and Albert was social awkwardness, but for more fragile regimes in more tempestuous political climates the need to marry royal princes to royal princesses of the correct denomination of Christianity, saw them look along their own family lines for unattached blue bloods of appropriate pedigree.

While the practice of marrying blood relatives served a dynastic purpose to preserve privilege and power within family lines (particularly useful in an era where noblewomen wielded little direct influence, save as matchmakers or regents for their underage offspring), the Habsburgs indulged the custom with particularly reckless abandon. This led to the eventual extinction of an entire branch of the family.[76]

The Spanish Habsburg dynasty was effectively founded by Holy Roman Emperor Charles V (1500-1558), who through various canny marital hookups found himself heir to three families: his own

---

[76]*Wilson, J. "16 Royals Who Suffered From Hereditary Mutations and Defects Caused by Inbreeding." All That's Interesting, published July 2021*

which dominated central Europe, the House of Valois-Burgundy, which dominated the low countries, and the House of Trastámara which ruled Spain and its overseas empire in America and Asia. This concentration of power proved too much for one man and he was succeeded by his young brother Ferdinand I (1503-1564) as Archduke of Austria and King of Hungary, and on his older brother's death Holy Roman Emperor. The title of King of Spain and the lands associated with it, be they in the Netherlands, South America or Sicily, continued down Charles V's line. Each branch ran in parallel, and there was always someone to marry from the other side of the family. Over the next 200 years a total of 11 marriages were contracted by the Spanish Habsburg kings. Most of these marriages were consanguineous unions, with nine occurring in a degree of third cousins or closer.

The Habsburgs' territorial acquisition via marriage became so established that the dynasty gained a motto attributed to their tactics, "Bella gerant alii, tu, felix Austria, nube!" ("Let others wage war. You, happy Austria, marry!"). A typical story of what became a very tangled family tree can be seen with Charles V and his wife Isabella of Portugal (1503-1529). They had two children – Philip II of Spain (1527-1598), and a daughter Maria of Austria (1528-1603). The dynasty feared that if Philip died before he had a male heir, Spain would be lost. So the decision was made to marry Maria to her first cousin Maximilian II (1527-1576). As the eldest son to Ferdinand I, Maximilian II had inherited their central European titles and lands after his father's death, and so the Holy Roman Emperor married his own eldest daughter, Anna of Austria (1527-1576), back to the other side of the family to her uncle, Philip II of Spain (1527-1498). This acted as insurance after Philip II's third wife, Elisabeth, died in childbirth, leaving him widowed with two daughters. These intermarriages crossing from one side of the family to the other repeat over the generations, either between uncles/aunts and nephews/nieces or between cousins. But, unbeknownst to the royal family, they had started to pass down more than crowns, crests and other baubles to their descendants. In the 16th century, the Holy Roman Emperor Charles V had once ruled much of what is now Germany, Hungary, the Czech Republic, Spain, the Netherlands, Belgium, southern Italy, western Poland, and emerging colonies in America and Asia. His was the first empire upon which "the sun never set". But a century later, the genetic line had deteriorated so severely that the final male heir was physically incapable of producing children. Subsequently bringing an end to Spanish Habsburg rule and the family branch became extinct.

When a child is born they contain a shuffled mix of combined genetic material their two parents. But when the gene pools in two people are very similar there is a higher chance that the child will inherit something dangerous. Either arising as a spontaneous mutation or lurking dormant for generations, aggressive inherited diseases are usually 'recessive' and require both parents to be carriers of the genetic condition for it to be passed along to their offspring. As carriers do not have symptoms of the disease the parents are often oblivious to the deadly combination of code they will pass onto their offspring.

While these diseases are usually rare, when two individuals are related the chances are higher that they will have the same dangerous genes. The closer the genetic relationship, the higher the genetic similarity. While third cousin matches might be safe the risk is significantly ramped up when the blood relatives are even closer, such as siblings. It starts to become an even bigger problem when not only your father is your uncle, but your grandmother is also your aunt as in the case of Charles II of Spain. When a family has a history of generations of inbreeding these recessive mutations start appearing more frequently until a child is born that is battling myriad diseases.

Children unlucky enough to be born as a result of incestuous pairings are substantially more likely to suffer from congenital birth defects and will be at a higher risk of infant loss, cancer, and reduced fertility. In the Spanish Habsburgs, the most distinctive effect of inbreeding was the 'Habsburg jaw'. Medically known as mandibular prognathism, the defect is commonly associated with inbreeding, and like many other rare diseases, is a trait associated with recessive genes.

In the case of Charles II of Spain, there are two genetic diseases that are believed to have contributed to his demise: combined pituitary hormone deficiency, which causes infertility, impotence, weak muscles, and digestive problems, and distal renal tubular acidosis, which causes bloody urine, rickets, and a large head relative to one's body size. It was not just the Habsburgs that were plagued with diseases and deformities at the hands of inbreeding. Queen Victoria likely developed a spontaneous mutation in her genes that caused her to carry the genetic disease haemophilia. The rare bleeding disorder that prevents the blood from clotting effectively causing its victims to bleed out, and the most trivial of bumps to produce internal haemorrhaging. Queen Victoria married her first cousin who was also a carrier of the fatal disease. When the two sets of genes combined in their children the disease fired into action and the pair subsequently spread the condition throughout European royalty, to Spain, Germany and Russia. One of Victoria's own children died from complications due to haemophilia, while a further five grandchildren succumbed in the following decades[77].

George III is thought to have been affected by another recessive disease – porphyria – which is caused by the inheritance of two recessive genes and characterised by blue urine and insanity. Porphyria was common in the highly inbred House of Hanover. Victoria is also believed to have bequeathed porphyria to some of her descendants, most dramatically the German House of Hohenzollern (already descended from George I of Great Britain) where it may have contributed to Kaiser Wilhelm II's erratic behaviour in the years leading up to the First World War. In November 1908, Reginald Brett, 2nd Viscount Esher – courtier and confidant of Britain's Edward VII – speculated as much, writing in his diary, "I am sure that the taint of George III is in his blood."

Queen Victoria's eldest daughter, Princess Victoria, also showed the same tell-tale symptoms of porphyria. She had been married off to Frederick III, the first German Kaiser, their union resulted in the unpredictable Wilhelm II and sickly Princess Charlotte. The princess spent her life suffering from abdominal pains, blisters around her face, and dark red urine. The undiagnosed ailment was passed onto her daughter Princess Feodora of Saxe-Meiningen, who committed suicide in 1945, and a 1998 analysis of her remains proved inconclusive.

For the Spanish Habsburgs though, their story ended on 1 November 1700. While Charles II was married twice, in 1679 to Marie Louise of Orléans (1662-1689) and after her death to Maria Anna of Neuburg (1667-1740), he had never conceived a child and

---

[77] Ed Yong, "How Inbreeding Killed Off a Line of Kings," *Discover Magazine*, April 15, 2009

was in all likelihood unable to do so. He had spent most of his reign powerless, with others acting as regent. He retired young, unable to cope with the demands of being a ruler, with a frail and feeble body that had started to crumble. He had come to resemble an elderly man and was almost completely immobile due to the oedema swelling in his legs, abdomen, and face. He died bald, senile, and impotent, aged just 38.

For Charles II, his life was difficult and tragically short. The true extent of his conditions were not revealed until a grisly autopsy that stated his body "did not contain a single drop of blood; his heart was the size of a peppercorn; his lungs corroded; his intestines rotten and gangrenous; he had a single testicle, black as coal, and his head was full of water".

Modern medicine may help us to discover the real reasons behind King George III's erratic behaviour. George III is well known in children's history books for being the "mad king who lost America".

In recent years, though, it has become fashionable among historians to put his "madness" down to the physical, genetic blood disorder called porphyria. Its symptoms include aches and pains, as well as blue urine.

The theory formed the basis of a long-running play by Alan Bennett, The Madness of George III, which was later adapted for film starring Nigel Hawthorne in the title role.

However, a new research project based at St George's, University of London, has concluded that George III did actually suffer from mental illness after all.

Using the evidence of thousands of George III's own handwritten letters, Dr Peter Garrard and Dr Vassiliki Rentoumi have been analysing his use of language. They have discovered that during his episodes of illness, his sentences were much longer than when he was well.

A sentence containing 400 words and eight verbs was not unusual. George III, when ill, often repeated himself, and at the same time his vocabulary became much more complex, creative and colourful.

These are features that can be seen today in the writing and speech of patients experiencing the manic phase of psychiatric illnesses such as bipolar disorder.

Mania, or harmful euphoria, is at one end of a spectrum of mood disorders, with sadness, or depression, at the other. George's being in a manic state would also match contemporary descriptions of his illness by witnesses.

They spoke of his "incessant loquacity" and his habit of talking until the foam ran out of his mouth. Sometimes he suffered from convulsions, and his pages had to sit on him to keep him safe on the floor.

The researchers have even thrown doubt on one of the key planks in the case for porphyria, the blue urine. George III's medical records show that the king was given medicine based on gentian. This plant, with its deep blue flowers, is still used today as a mild tonic, but may turn the urine blue.

So maybe it wasn't the king's "madness" that caused his most famous symptom. It could have simply been his medicine.

I interviewed the researchers at St George's for a new documentary series, Fit To Rule: How Royal Illness Changed History.

In this series, I re-examine our kings and queens as individual members of the human race, rather than just as impregnable icons of splendour and power. They suffered many of exactly the same biological and psychological weaknesses as the rest of us - only with rather more profound consequences.

George III's recurring bouts of illness caused him to withdraw from daily business to recuperate out of the public eye at secluded Kew Palace, near Richmond.

Each time he withdrew to Kew, this triggered a crisis - who was to make decisions in his absence?

His son, the Prince of Wales, with whom George III had a terrible relationship, wanted to be appointed regent, and to act as the king in everything but name. But the future George IV was very much associated with the political opposition, and the government was determined to keep him out.

Strikingly, although the crisis caused a good deal of arguing, it was in fact resolved quite easily. This was partly because the king just got better (despite the bizarre and sometimes inhumane treatments given to him by the royal doctors) and partly because he was, by this stage in British history, a constitutional king.

When the Hanoverians had been invited over from Germany in 1714 to take the throne after the failure of the Stuart line, they came at the invitation of Parliament. Parliament therefore held the whip hand over them, and the powers of the monarchy declined.

But despite his illness, George III was a dedicated and diligent king, and won the respect of his politicians. In fact, when his illness drove him off the political scene, they realised how much they needed his calming effect on their squabbles.

It is counter-intuitive to suggest it, but royal health issues can actually strengthen the monarchy, not least by creating sympathy and affection for an afflicted individual.

George III ruled for 60 years.

Garrard also points out how the explanations or diagnoses that we come up with for patients in the past reflect our own current attitudes to sickness and health. One of the reasons that the porphyria argument caught on is because it seemed to remove the supposed stigma of mental health issues from the Royal Family.

And yet, as Garrard notes, porphyria opened up a different set of problems, because as a hereditable illness, George IV, and indeed other members of the Royal Family, became candidates for diagnosis too.

The research project still continues, but Garrard is already confident of one thing. "The porphyria theory is completely dead in the water. This was a psychiatric illness."

But it certainly did not stop George III from being a successful king. In a prosperous, industrialising Britain, it was growing more important for a monarch to reign rather than rule, providing background stability rather than aggressive leadership.

With his 60-year reign, George III certainly provided continuity, and I believe that his short episodes of illness tend unfairly to diminish our views of him[78]

Queen Charlotte of Mecklenburg-Strelitz Had 15 Children
Charlotte of Mecklenburg-Strelitz (1744-1818 AD) married King

---

[78] IEd Yong, *"How Inbreeding Killed Off a Line of Kings,"* Discover Magazine, *April 15, 2009*

George III (1738-1820) in September 1761. Together, the couple ruled both Britain and Ireland until 1801, when they became the official king and queen of the United Kingdom. The couple had a total of 15 children, 14 of whom were born in the newly purchased Buckingham House (later known as Buckingham Palace). According to Royal.uk, Charlotte was responsible for the purchase of Frogmore House in 1792 as a country retreat for herself and her unmarried daughters. Queen Anne Had 17 Pregnancies, But Only One Child Survived Infancy

Queen Anne (1665-1714 AD) was England's last Stuart ruler and played a key role in the unification of England and Scotland in 1707. Despite her political achievements, Anne experienced poor health, and her attempts to produce an heir were met with numerous tragedies. Various sources estimate that Anne was pregnant between 17 and 19 times. Royal Central states she was pregnant 18 times between 1684 and 1700. Most of these pregnancies ended in stillbirths or miscarriages, and two infants died shortly after their births. Two daughters, Mary and Anne Sophia, were born healthy but lost their lives to smallpox before they turned two. Anne had only one child, her son William, who survived infancy. He lived to the age of 11 before dying from either bacterial pharyngitis or possibly smallpox.

Queen Victoria Had Nine Children and 42 Grandchildren Queen Victoria (1819-1901 AD) reportedly considered having children to be "the greatest horror" and would have preferred not to have any. Despite her reservations, she and her husband, Prince Albert, raised nine children, all of whom survived into adulthood. Victoria's offspring married into various royal families across Europe, producing 42 grandchildren and earning her the title "Grandmother of Europe." Many of her descendants remain among present-day royalty. As Town & Country magazine notes, of the approximately 28 surviving monarchies around the world, five are held by descendants of Victoria.

Edward I Had At Least 15 Children With His Wife Eleanor of Castile King Edward I of England (1239-1307 AD) was known by the nicknames "Longshanks" and "Hammer of the Scots"—the former due to his height and the latter because of his conflicts with Scotland. To resolve a land dispute, Edward married Eleanor of Castile in 1254. According to History, although their marriage began as a political alliance, Edward and Eleanor grew deeply attached and had 16 children together. Unfortunately, several of these children did not survive infancy, including their son Alphonso, who passed away at the age of 12. Another source suggests that the exact number of children born to Edward and Eleanor is uncertain, noting only that they had "at least 11 daughters and four or five sons."[79]

The Queen's hidden cousins:

They were banished to an asylum in 1941 and left neglected. Burke's Peerage had declared them both to be long dead, on misinformation supplied by the family. In fact, Nerissa did not die until 1986, aged 66, and Katherine is still alive; at 85, she is the same age as the Queen. Their shocking story came to light shortly after Nerissa's death, when journalists discovered she was buried in a grave marked only by a plastic nametag and a serial number.

---

[79], *"Which Monarch Had the Most Children?" Town and Country Magazine. Various sources.*

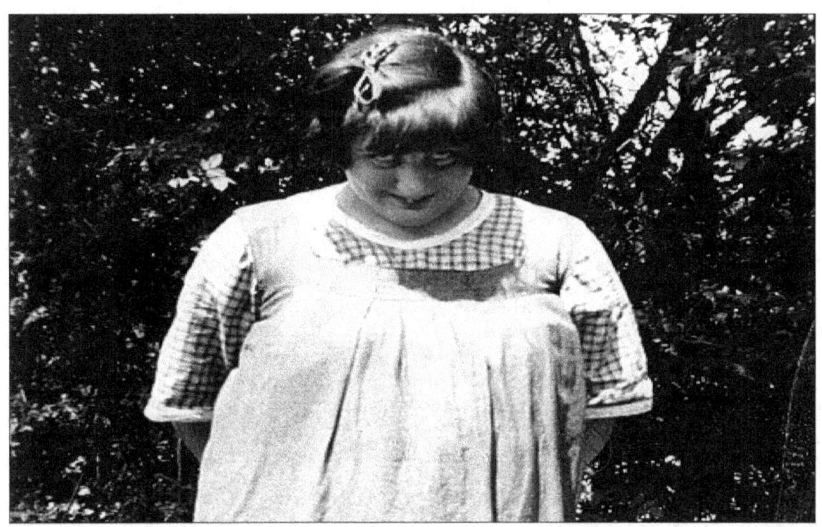

Nerissa (pictured) was born in 1919, and Katherine in 1926 - their father was John Bowes-Lyon, one of the Queen Mother's older brothers

The ensuing scandal, which prompted an anonymous source to provide a gravestone for Nerissa, made little difference to her sister's life. Katherine received no visitors at the asylum, and as her aunt, the Queen Mother, lived on into cosseted old age, she did not possess even her own underwear – at least until her final years there – and had to dress from a communal wardrobe.

Now a Channel 4 documentary tells the story of the Queen's hidden cousins, born in an era when children with learning disabilities were a family's shameful secret.

Photographs of Katherine Bowes-Lyon show a distinct resemblance to the Queen, and Onelle Braithwaite says the sisters' story was common knowledge when she arrived at the asylum as a 20-year-old nurse in the mid-1970s. Nerissa was born in 1919, and Katherine in 1926. Their father was John Bowes-Lyon, one of the

Queen Mother's older brothers and a son of the Earl of Strathmore. John died in 1930 and was survived, until 1966, by the girls' mother, Fenella.

The sisters were unfortunate to have been born in an era when mental disability was seen as a threat to society and linked to promiscuity, feckless breeding and petty crime, the characteristics of the underclass; associations encouraged by popular belief in the science of eugenics, soon to be embraced by the Nazis.

'So the belief was if you had a child with a learning disability, there was something in your family that was suspect and wrong,' explains Jan Walmsley, the Open University's professor in the history of learning disabilities.

For the Bowes-Lyons, this was a stigma that could threaten their social standing and taint the marital prospects of their other children. (Nerissa and Katherine's beautiful and healthy sister Anne became a princess of Denmark by her second marriage; by her first marriage, she was Viscountess Anson and mother of the society photographer, the late Lord Lichfield.)

The imposing Royal Earlswood was the country's first purpose-built asylum for people with learning disabilities. Nerissa and Katherine were 15 and 22 respectively when they were admitted. Nerissa's medical records categorise her as 'imbecile'. 'She makes unintelligible noises all the time,' stated a doctor. 'Very affectionate… can say a few babyish words.'

Judy Wilkinson, 67, from Godalming, Surrey, recalls her apprehension when visiting the Royal Earlswood as a young girl in the 1950s, when her elder sister Nicola, who was brain-damaged at birth, was consigned there. 'I'd get that gripping feeling of dread,'

Judy explains, and she remembers feeling puzzled that her sister was always wearing the same green coat, which never seemed to wear out.

Now she realises that the inmates wore their own clothes only if they had visitors. But for Nerissa and Katherine, there were few if any visitors. 'I never saw anybody come,' says Dot Penfold. 'The impression I had was that they'd been forgotten.'

From the late 1960s, a wave of scandals exposed conditions in institutions that were severely understaffed and overcrowded. The Royal Earlswood was closed in 1997; at least one former nurse has alleged patients were abused. The grandiose building has since been converted into luxury apartments, while Katherine is believed to be living in a care home in Surrey. Her relationship with her family remains unchanged.[80]

Royal Genetically inherited Autism-

STUDIES SHOWING CONNECTION BETWEEN INBREEDING AND AUTISM

Is autism another inbred disorder, or is it a combination of genes and environmental issues, such as emotional abuse due to domestic abuse through relationship breakdowns and trauma, Is autism a

---

[80] Greene, Mary. "The Queen's Hidden Cousins: They Were Banished to an Asylum in 1941 and Left Neglected – Now an Intriguing Documentary Reveals All." Daily Mail Online, November 11, 2011. Accessed [today's date]. https://www.dailymail.co.uk.

response to coping with these family issues, or is it that as with the information above that it has been passed down through the family lines and only recently recognised and given the title, as once it was possibly called psychosis.

Centuries of inbreeding Early hominids were not fussy about their sexual partners. Homo sapiens would interbreed with whichever hominid species was nearby, such as the Neanderthals and the mysterious Denisovans (Marshall, 2013). The Neanderthals appeared for a brief time, but eventually Prayson 69 died out from inbreeding causing a reduction in population, thus creating more inbreeding cycle. They did, however, leave a small percent of their DNA in the Homo sapiens' chromosome history. Of course, if the first Homo sapiens had not interbred, the human race, as we know it, may have become extinct (Estes, 2011). The mechanisms of evolution may be leading to global inbreeding. After generations of consanguineous marriages, it could be that the world's population is so large that it is starting to inbreed with itself. It is becoming more and more difficult finding a mate who does not share a common ancestor of some sort in our contemporary chromosomes. We have all probably inherited genetic changes that were not as common a century ago. For instance, the average height for a human has increased about three inches since the 1700s. These are forced general population mutations due to an improved lifestyle, but even good changes require genetic intervention (Inglis-Arkell, 2012). Possible inbred mutations causing autism.

Both autism and inbred disorders may have similar abnormalities of the brain structure and/or function. Brain scans of these children show variances in the shape and structure of the brain when compared with the neurotypical or normal brain found in children. Researchers (Wahl, 2014) are exploring a number of theories that led to autism, including links to heredity and genetics. Inbreeding is considered a problem in humans, because it heightens the chances of receiving a damaged chromosome inherited from a common ancestor (Ochap, 2004). Interbreeding increases the probability of a child being born with a double dosage of one or more recessive genetic problems that can cause congenital birth defects. 40,000 to 30,000 years ago Autism could be the result of a slight gene mutation inherited thousands of years ago. Skeletal remains found in Northern Italy are from 40,000 to 30,000 years old and "believed to be that of a human/Neanderthal hybrid," according to a paper in PLOS/ONE (Condemi et al., 2013). If this is correct, it is direct evidence that Homo sapiens interbred with Neanderthals. Modern genetic research can determine, after thousands of years, that the DNA of people with European or Asian ancestry are 1 to 4% Neanderthal (Viegas, 2010). There could be inbreeding disorders found in every human's DNA. Most have no effect until matched up with the same mutant gene, locus or position on paired chromosomes through inbreeding or happenstance. These abnormal alleles (Alleles are pairs or series of genes on a chromosome that determine the hereditary characteristics, Merriam-Webster's Medical Dictionary) create subtle refined autism symptoms similar to those found in affected consanguineous off springs.

Roughly half of the people who live in Arab countries are inbred. A significant percentage of the parents who are blood related come from families where intermarriage has been a tradition for generations (Cook, 2013). In ancient generations, "Pharaohs often married their own sister or half-sister and after a handful of generations the off springs were mentally and physically unfit to rule" (Sennels, 2010). Two researchers, Walsh and Morrow recently studied 104 families (Walsh, 2010) from the Arab Middle East, Turkey, and Pakistan. They found that of the 104 parents, "in 88, the parents were cousins. The average family had two autistic children. One Kuwaiti and one Pakistani family, however, each had four." "Marriage between first cousins doubles the risk of neurological birth defects. Researchers now think that shared ancestry can increase the risk of autism produced by recessive mutations that cause problems only when a child inherits the same defective gene from both parents" (Sennels, 2010). In this analysis of 104 families, approximately 97% had heredity problems. [81]

I wanted to see how much of the information in my dad's book was correct, I noticed that he mentioned how certain chromosomes were perhaps inherited from what the Anunnaki. Quote " Study of the relationship between genealogy and geography constitutes a discipline that can be termed intraspecific phylogeography. 'alien genes' in human DNA The (Central Asian) Khazar name is derived from Turkic *qaz-, meaning "to wander." The Ashina was considered a sacred clan of quasi-divine status. Q1 actually refers to the subclade Q-P36.2. The Ashina clan, a noble caste, carry the 16q24.3 "red gene" inherited from the Sumerian Anunnaki, the root of the Dragon seed that permeates royal lines: Merovingian, Carolingian, Tudor, Plantagenet, Stuart, Hapsburg, Hanoverian, Saxe-Coburg-Gotha, Guelph, Bowes-Lyon, Battenberg (Mountbatten), Guise, and Savoy families - and Transylvanian

---

[81] *Prayson, Alex S. "Autism, Genetics, and Inbreeding: An Evolutionary View." National Council on Rehabilitation Education, received July 18, 2015, and accepted January 22, 2016.*

lineages. The Davidic House of Judah married into the descent of the Merovingian Kings of the Franks. They are connected by a shared bloodline. The dragon archetype rests within the Dragon blood, passed on through the genes.[82]
It is important to note

that autism is not caused by carrying the 16q24.3 gene — in fact, the opposite seems to be true: when this gene is deleted or missing, autism traits appear. In other words, autism is linked to gene deletion, not to possession of a rare 'extra' gene.

What Gene causes red hair?

Red hair is a recessive genetic trait caused by a series of mutations in the melanocortin 1 receptor (MC1R), a gene located on chromosome 16. As a recessive trait it must be inherited from both parents to cause the hair to become red. Consequently, there are far more people carrying the mutation for red hair than people actually having red hair. In Scotland, approximately 13% of the population are redheads, although 40% carry at least one mutation.

There are many kinds of red hair, some fairer, or mixed with blond ('strawberry blond'), some darker, like auburn hair, which is brown

---

[82] *Miller, Iona, on behalf of Nicholas Devere. The Dragon Legacy. 2004.*

hair with a reddish tint. This is because some people only carry one or a few of the several possible MC1R mutations. The lightness of the hair ultimately depends on other mutations regulating the general pigmentation of both the skin and hair.

Red hair, a Celto-Germanic trait?

Red hair has long been associated with Celtic people. Both the ancient Greeks and Romans described the Celts as redheads. The Romans extended the description to Germanic people, at least those they most frequently encountered in southern and western Germany. It still holds true today.

Although red hair is an almost exclusively northern and central European phenomenon, isolated cases have also been found in the Middle East, Central Asia (notably among the Tajiks), as well as in some of the Tarim mummies from Xinjiang, in north-western China. The Udmurts, an Uralic tribe living in the northern Volga basin of Russia, between Kazan and Perm, are the only non-Western Europeans to have a high incidence of red hair (over 10%). So, what do all these people have in common? Surely the Udmurts and Tajiks aren't Celts, nor Germans. Yet, as we will see, all these people share a common ancestry that can be traced back to a single Y-chromosomal haplogroup: R1b.

Where is red hair more common?

It is hard to calculate the exact percentage of the population having red hair as it depends on how wide a definition one adopts. For example, should men with just partial red beards, but no red hair on the top of their heads be included or not? Should strawberry blond be counted as red, blond, or both? Regardless of the definition, the frequency of red hair is highest in Ireland (10 to 30%) and Scotland (10 to 25%), followed by Wales (10 to 15%), Cornwall and western England, Brittany, the Franco-Belgian border, then western Switzerland, Jutland and southwest Norway. The southern and eastern boundaries, beyond which red hair only occurs in less than 1% of the population, are northern Spain, central Italy, Austria, western Bohemia, western Poland, Baltic countries and Finland.

Overall, the distribution of red hair matches remarkably well the ancient Celtic and Germanic worlds. It is undeniable too that the highest frequencies are always observed in Celtic areas, especially in those that remained Celtic speaking to this day or until recently. The question that inevitably comes to many people's minds is: did red hair originate with the Celtic or the Germanic people?

Southwest Norway may well be the clue to the origin of red hair. It has been discovered recently, thanks to genetic genealogy, that the higher incidence of both dark hair and red hair (as opposed to blond) in southwest Norway coincided with a higher percentage of the paternal lineage known as haplogroup R1b-L21, including its subclade R1b-M222, typical of northwestern Ireland and Scotland (the so-called lineage of Niall of the Nine Hostages). It is now almost certain that native Irish and Scottish Celts were taken (probably as slaves) to southwest Norway by the Vikings, and that they increased the frequency of red hair there.[83]

I have found that the Genetic variation in melanocortin-1 receptor (*MC1R*) is a known contributor to disease-free red hair in humans.

---

[83] *Eupedia. "The Genetic Causes, Ethnic Origins and History of Red Hair." Eupedia. Accessed August 4, 2025. https://www.eupedia.com/genetics/red_hair.shtml.*

Three loss-of-function single-nucleotide variants (rs1805007, rs1805008 and rs1805009) have been established as strongly correlated with red hair. The contribution of other loss-of-function *MC1R* variants (in particular rs1805005, rs2228479 and rs885479) and the extent to which other genetic loci are involved in red hair colour is less well understood. Here, we used the UK Biobank cohort to capture a comprehensive list of *MC1R* variants contributing to red hair colour. We report a correlation with red hair for both strong-effect variants (rs1805007, rs1805008 and rs1805009) and weak-effect variants (rs1805005, rs2228479 and rs885479) and show that their coefficients differ by two orders of magnitude. On the haplotype level, both strong- and weak-effect variants contribute to the red hair phenotype, but when considered individually, weak-effect variants show a reverse, negative association with red hair. The reversal of association direction in the single-variant analysis is facilitated by a distinguishing structure of *MC1R*, in which loss-of-function variants are never found to co-occur on the same haplotype [84]

Deep Dive into R Negative Blood

Rh-negative blood has long been regarded as a rare and significant marker within certain bloodlines. In my own family it appears through my grandmother, and my sibling carries it today. My mother faced great difficulty during that pregnancy — a struggle that echoes a wider pattern: when an Rh-positive mother bears an Rh-negative child, complications often arise, sometimes leading to

---

[84] *Sundaram, Murugesan, Jacek Majewski, and Heather E. Zierhut. "A Study in Scarlet: MC1R as the Main Predictor of Red Hair and Exemplar of the Flip-Flop Effect." Proceedings of the National Academy of Sciences (PMC), 2021.* https://www.ncbi.nlm.nih.gov/pmc/articles/PMC8501821/.

miscarriage or critical conditions at birth. Such difficulties are well documented across royal lineages, where the persistence of Rh-negative blood may explain the high rate of infant mortality and failed pregnancies.

This inheritance not only connects my family to those ancient patterns but also illustrates how blood itself — beyond title or ceremony — has shaped the destiny of dynasties.

Where did the Rh-negatives come from? If they are not the descendants of prehistoric man, could they be the descendants of the ancient astronauts?

All animals and other living creatures known to man can breed with any other of their species. Relative size and colour makes no difference. Why does infant's haemolytic disease occur in humans if all humans are the same species? Haemolytic disease is the allergic reaction that occurs when an Rh-negative mother is carrying a Rh positive child. Her blood builds up antibodies to destroy an alien substance (the same way it would a virus), thereby destroying the infant. Why would a mother's body reject her own offspring? Nowhere else in nature does this occur naturally. This same problem does occur in mules - a cross between a horse and donkey. This fact alone points to the distinct possibility of a crossbreeding between two similar but genetically different species.

No one knows where the Rh-negative people came from. Rhesus negative blood simply means that the blood doesn't have any Rhesus antigens on the surface of the red blood cells. An "absence" of a protein does not necessarily have to originate from anywhere. The simplest explanation is that Rh-negative blood is caused by a mutation on the first chromosome which rendered individuals incapable of producing functional Rhesus proteins. As for why there are so few people with Rh-negative blood, Rh-negative is a recessive trait, so all an individual needs is one functional Rhesus gene to produce Rh-positive blood. Since Rh-negative blood does not hinder an individual's survivability or confer any evolutionary disadvantage other than the inability to receive Rh-positive blood (which is pretty much a non-factor during the time period when blood transfusions weren't available), people with non-functional Rhesus genes continued to thrive and reproduce which is why there are still individuals with Rh-negative blood.

Most, familiar with blood factors, admit that these people must at least be a mutation if not descendants of a different ancestor. If we are a mutation, what caused the mutation? Why does it continue with the exact characteristics? Why does it so violently reject the Rh factor if it was in their own ancestry? Who was this ancestor? Difficulties in determining ethnology are largely overcome by the use of blood group data, for they are a single gene characteristic and not affected by the environment.

The Basque people of Spain and France have the highest percentage of Rh-negative blood. About 30% have (rr) Rh-negative and about 60% carry one (r) negative gene. The average among most people is only 157%-Rh negative, while some groups have very little. The Oriental Jews of Israel, also have a high percent Rh-negative, although most other Oriental people have only about 1% Rh negative. The Samaritans and the Black Cochin Jew also have a high percentage of Rh-negative blood, although again the Rh-negative blood is rare among most black people.

The Rh-Negatives Factor is considered a "Mutation" of "Unknown

Origin", which happened in Europe, about 25,000-35,000 years ago. Then this group spread heavily into the area of what is now Spain, England, Ireland, etc. 5% of the Earth's population are currently Rh-Negatives. But they are 15% of the population of the England and the USA. The most distinctive members of the European branch of the human tree are the Basques of France and Spain. They show unusual patterns for several genes, including the highest rate of the Rh-negative blood type. Their language is of unknown origin and cannot be placed within any standard classification.

Consider Iceland, 1% of its population is Rh-negative. The population of Iceland is about two-third of Scandinavian and one-third of Irish descent. Scandinavia, Ireland, and the British Isles show from 16% to 25% and above Rh-negative. The other populations with a proportion of Rh-negative individuals similar to Iceland occupy the eastern half of Asia, Madagascar, Australia and New-Zealand. The people of the Basque region have a greater than 50 percent concentration of the RH negative gene, The frequency decreases in relation to the distance from the Basque region into the rest of the world until there is very little evidence of this gene.

This genetic mapping helps to show that a mutation from RH positive to RH negative occurred somewhere in the Basque area of Europe maybe as much as 40,000 years ago. Science tells us that the red hair DNA did not originate with human beings but was Neanderthal DNA. "When we look at the Y-chromosomes in Wales and Ireland, we find a very close match with the Basques." Other genetic evidence, he says, strongly suggests that the Basques are the descendants of the Palaeolithic inhabitants of Western Europe prior to the arrival of farmers between 9,000 and 6,000 years ago". During a period in history known as the Dark Ages, which happened around 1200 - 800 B.C. The "Tribe of Dan" was shipped into Western Europe with the aid of the Phoenicians from the Mediterranean Sea at about the same time in history. They came into Spain, France (Languedoc Area of France).

We also know that the 10 Lost Tribes of Israel known as the Hebrews migrated into Europe and became a blended group who would later become known as the Scythian, aka Aryan Races. They migrated into Europe from the Caucasus and Carpathian mountain ranges while the Tribe of Dan into Spain, France and the British Isles from the Mediterranean Sea. Phoenicians helped transport the Tribe of Dan into Spain, France, and the British Isles by way of the "Sea Route," from the Middle East. Phoenicians appear to be the Siberians of Russia, the Yakuts, Sakha and the Buryats. They are the same race sharing the same DNA. They have the same spiritual and historical traditions: the same names of landforms, rivers.

Rh-negative women and men have several "Unusual Traits" that Rh-positives don't:

* An EXTRA-Vertebra (a "Tail Bone")....some are born with a tail (called a "Cauda"). CAUDA EQUINA - The bundle of spinal nerve roots arising from the end of the spinal cord and filling the lower part of the spinal canal (from approximately the thoraco-lumbar junction down). Embryology : Caudally the tail region projects over the cloacal membrane.
* Lower than normal Body Temperature
* Lower than normal Blood Pressure
* Higher mental analytical abilities.
* Higher Negative-ion shielding (from positive "charged" virus/bacteria)around the body.

* High Sensitivity to EM and ELF Fields.
* Hyper Vision and other senses.

Another salient genetic feature is the shape and sutures (bone joints) of cranial bones of Basques, [The Reptilian skull ridge]. A third skeletal difference is the tendency to having a thicker breastbone.85

As I traced the origin of the red hair gene and the rare traits of Rh-negative blood, I began to notice something deeper—an ancient pattern etched not just in the body, but in myth, migration, and memory. These bloodlines, carrying unusual biological features and heightened sensitivities, appear time and again across history's hidden corridors. From the Caucasus and Carpathian mountain ranges into Spain and the Languedoc, these groups—Scythians, Aryans, the Tribe of Dan, and even the Phoenicians—did not just carry trade routes or weapons, but symbols, language, and sacred knowledge. These were the people of the serpent and the goat, of the dragon and the divine. Their spiritual systems, rooted in nature, resonance, and ritual, were later obscured under layers of pseudohistory—rewritten lineages, forged royal claims, and political mythmaking. And yet, through all of that distortion, something survives. My own journey through this inheritance is not simply about names and titles; it is about reconnecting with a spiritual lineage encoded in both blood and story. It is about seeing through the veil of imposed history and reclaiming the deeper truths of who we are, and where we come from.

---

85 *Miller, Iona, on behalf of Nicholas Devere. Dragon Family Tree. DRAGON Labyrinth, 2012–2014. Accessed August 4, 2025. http://drakenberg.weebly.com/dragon-family-tree.html.*

What is pseudo history?

I think that it important to clarify what is pseudohistory, we have had many pretenders attempt to walk the walk where it came to the Dragon Court, We had Michael La Frosse and others who have blatantly lied about their genealogy trying to make claims to the Scottish royal line and have been made to look like they should join the insane asylum, I had one recently who I found hilarious, using phrases like "William removed his tie, which mean the king has no clothes" and making attempts to say that he was in line to the throne, we have also had men saying they are king Charles and Camilla's love child, when you look at his age it certainly does not add up. Even researching King Alfred and many other kings, they apparently made up their genealogy to align with Norse gods to take the throne, how are we actually supposed to know what is true and what is not.

I also feel that after reading Fingerprint of the gods and magicians of the gods that some people such as Graham Hancock has been put in this box, Although I have seen Graham also put my father's work down, I show no bias, His work is a testament to his passion where revealing historical in discrepancies has been at the forefront of his work. He is made to look like this so that others can present their own work and out him down, when he has done more for history than ancient aliens, I laugh as I was an avid watcher of this program and wasted many years of my life on this sort of click bait. So, the next bit of information that I have researched and reveal has no attempt to impact Graham Hancock's work, even though he has made his opinions on my father in the past, I hold no grudge but want to show and portray how pseudo history has become part of mainstream. Alas we now live in a society of misinformation, With any old, Dancing tik toker, only fans, brainless dimwits with cardboard personalities and the intellect of a nat, all grasping for fame.

The purpose of the forthcoming information is to show how history can be changed according to the author and their narrative they want to deliver. Most recently misinformation is being spread that distorts factual historical information, One reference to this is how many coloured people are being lead to believe that certain nobility were of colour, or that the nobiliy and monachy has been whitewashed by 17th century painters and artistists, they change the etymology of written words to suit their ideologies, My issue with this is the thirsty 60 odd thousand followers who don't research and believe these peoples lies, such rubbish as King James of Scotland was of colour, or King Charles II due to historians describing him to be black, when in fact the actual words used were he was dark in complexion which meant that he was tanned due to him being out at sea a lot., If they were then they would have been discribed as mulluto. The fact is that if ALL of my ancestors were of colour then surely, I would not have milk bottle white fair skin, However I must add that although I have descended from many across the european continant, its that the fairer skinned memebers of my families genes have been more prominent. Thats not to say that there isn't or hasn't been any royal families of colour or dark tanned, it's absurd and single minded to say that all royalty is or was white only. We all know there are royal families in most continents whether in exile or still reining today, What baffles me, is the opportunists trying to deliver this content and then more so those that believe it. And as my father and many great authors and historians have been bundled into this category I wanted to find

where truth has been presented or likewise no facts or evidence to support claims.
So, let's dive into examples of Pseudo history, along with the evidence that supports the claims, All written work that is underlined show key subjects for references sake.

Pseudo history represents a form of pseudo scholarship characterized by the distortion or misrepresentation of the historical record. It often employs methodologies that resemble those utilized in legitimate historical research. The term "crypto history" is associated with pseudo history that is derived from superstitions rooted in occultism. Pseudo history is interrelated with pseudo-science and pseudo archaeology, and there may be instances in which the use of these terms overlaps. Scholars have identified several common characteristics in pseudo historical works. A prominent feature is that pseudohistory is frequently motivated by contemporary political, religious, or personal agendas. Furthermore, pseudo historical narratives often present sensational claims or significant misrepresentations of historical facts, which necessitate unwarranted alterations to the historical record. A notable example of pseudo history is found in the writings of Graham Hancock, who has sold over four million copies of books promoting the thesis that major monuments of the ancient world—such as Stonehenge, the Egyptian pyramids, and the moai of Easter Island—were constructed by a singular ancient super civilization. Hancock asserts that this civilization flourished from 15,000 to 10,000 BC and possessed technological and scientific knowledge comparable to, or surpassing, that of contemporary civilization. He first articulated this argument in his 1995 bestselling publication, "Fingerprints of the Gods," which garnered popular acclaim but faced significant scholarly criticism. Christopher Knight has contributed numerous works, including "Uriel's Machine" (2000), which advances pseudo historical claims that ancient civilizations possessed technology far beyond that of modern times. Additionally, the assertion that a lost continent known as Lemuria once existed in the Pacific Ocean is categorized as pseudohistory. A common premise within pseudo historical discourse is the belief in an alleged conspiracy among scholars to promote "mainstream history" at the expense of "true" history, a notion often accompanied by elaborate conspiracy theories. Such works tend to rely exclusively on unreliable sources, including myths and legends treated as literal historical truth, while disregarding credible sources that contradict their claims.

Some pseudo historical narratives adopt a relativist position regarding historical truth, arguing that objective historical truth does not exist, and that any hypothesis holds equal validity. They may also conflate mere possibilities with actual occurrences, assuming that if an event could have happened, it indeed did. Notable instances of pseudo history include British Israelism, the Lost Cause of the Confederacy, the myth of Irish slaves, the witch cult theory, Armenian genocide denial, Holocaust denial, the clean Wehrmacht myth, the Spanish Black Legend from the 16th and 17th centuries, and the assertion that the Katyn massacre was not perpetrated by the Soviet NKVD. Pseudo historical theories frequently engage with the legend of the Ten Lost Tribes of ancient Israel. British Israelism, also known as Anglo-Israelism, serves as the most prominent example of this type and has been conclusively disproven by mainstream historians utilizing evidence from a variety of academic disciplines. Another manifestation of ethnocentric revisionism is nationalistic pseudo history. A pertinent example is the **"Ancient Macedonians continuity theory,"** which posits demographic, cultural, and linguistic continuity between the ancient Macedonians and the primary ethnic group in present-day North Macedonia. The Bulgarian medieval dynasty of the Komitopules, which ruled the First Bulgarian Empire in its later years, has been characterized as "Macedonian," ruling over a "medieval Macedonian state" based on the location of its capitals within Macedonia. Gavin Menzies' book "1421: The Year China Discovered the World," which contends that Chinese navigators discovered America, is similarly categorized as pseudo history. Psychohistory has been classified by mainstream historians as a form of pseudo history. It amalgamates aspects of psychology, history, and related social sciences with the aim of understanding the motivations behind historical events, particularly the disparities between stated intentions and actual behaviours. Psycho historical analyses strive to integrate insights from psychology, particularly psychoanalysis, with social science methodologies to comprehend the emotional foundations of individual, group, and national behaviours throughout history. The works of Margaret Murray, beginning with **"The Witch-Cult in Western Europe"** (1921), assert that the witch trials during the early modern period were efforts by chauvinistic Christians to eradicate a clandestine pagan religion that worshipped a Horned God. Despite the widespread rejection of her claims by respected historians, her ideas have been adopted as foundational myths by various modern movements. Murray's assertions have been extensively challenged and ultimately rejected by esteemed historians. Nevertheless, her concepts have emerged as a foundational myth for modern Wicca, a contemporary Neopagan religion. While belief in Murray's purported witch-cult remains prevalent among adherents of Wicca, it is progressively experiencing a decline. The Christ myth theory posits that Jesus of Nazareth did not exist as a historical figure, asserting that his existence was fabricated by early Christians. Currently, this hypothesis garners minimal support among scholars and historians from various faith traditions and has been characterized as pseudo historical.

Within the context of Hinduism, the notion that ancient India possessed technological advancements sufficient to categorize it as a nuclear power is gaining traction. This perspective is being fuelled by rising extreme nationalist tendencies and ideologies rooted in Hinduism within the political landscape. For example, in January 2017, Vasudev Devnani, the Education Minister of Rajasthan, emphasized the importance of "understanding the scientific significance" of the cow, claiming it is the only animal capable of both inhaling and exhaling oxygen. Additionally, in 2014, Prime Minister Narendra Modi asserted to medical professionals in Mumbai that the narrative of the Hindu deity Ganesha exemplified the existence of genetic science in ancient India. Furthermore, numerous new-age pseudo historians who endeavour to transform mythological narratives into historical accounts are receiving considerable acclaim among the general populace. A pertinent illustration of this is the controversy surrounding ancient aircraft presented at the Indian Science Congress, during which Captain Anand J. Bodas, a retired principal of a pilot training institute, asserted that aircraft more advanced than contemporary models existed in ancient India. [86], I am seriously surprised that Zachariah

---

[86] *"Rajasthan Minister." Hindustan Times, January 16, 2017. Archived April 27, 2019.*

Rahman, Maseeh. *"Indian Prime Minister Claims Genetic Science Existed in Ancient Times." The Guardian, October 28, 2014. Retrieved April 26, 2019.*

Lakshmi, Rama. *"Indians Invented Planes 7,000 Years Ago — and Other Startling Claims at the Science Congress." The Washington Post, January 4, 2015. Retrieved April 30, 2019.*

Sitchen is not in this list for his made-up translations with cuneiform.

With all information that we are presented the key factors are that one would or should take it upon themselves to do their own research before making conclusions to which is right or which is wrong and how things can be knitted together from mythological sources to resemble some truths, it's a case of righting wrongs and wronging rites in ways. I found this information whilst researching the Priests of Mendes in regard to dad's work, claiming that the dragon court was bestowed upon the Priests of Mendes. This is how many people misinterpret information, such as Baphomet, It is important to add that Baphomet is never mentioned in the bible, EVER. Even when goats are considered evil at the sign or judgement, this depiction is still incorrect and has been misrepresented.

The Bible itself does not specifically mention Baphomet, and as such, any attempt to discuss this entity within a biblical context requires a certain degree of extrapolation and historical understanding. Baphomet is a figure that has garnered attention primarily outside of biblical texts, often associated with occult and esoteric traditions. Understanding what the Bible might imply about

---

"Examination of 'Pseudohistory' and How to Uncover Trustworthy Accounts Focus of Next Modern China Lecture." CSUSB News. Archived December 22, 2019. Retrieved April 26, 2019.

YouTube. https://youtu.be/x5jbHDMeDFE. Accessed August 4, 2025.

Baphomet involves exploring the broader biblical teachings on spiritual entities and the nature of evil.

To begin, Baphomet is often depicted as a goat-headed figure, and its image has been linked with various occult practices. The name "Baphomet" first gained prominence during the medieval period, most notably in connection with the Knights Templar. During their trials in the early 14th century, the Templars were accused of worshipping an idol called Baphomet. However, historical scholars suggest that these charges were likely fabricated for political purposes, and there is little evidence to suggest that the Templars actually engaged in such practices.[87]

I do refer back to the text by Margaret Murray about the mythological winged goat, I found her conclusion of this deity being worshipped by witch cults, or pagans and wanted to dive deeper into the real meaning of this god.

Banebdjedet, the god of fertility, was actually a worshipped god, its in various books and research regarding ancient Egypt. This god was regarded as the "Ba of the Lord of Mendes" was depicted with the head of a type of ram that was once common in ancient Egypt but is now extinct - see picture below of the 'Ovis longipes palaeo-aegyptiacus'. The ram-headed god Khnum was the equivalent god in Upper Egypt.[88]

Banebdjedet was the principal ram-god in the area around the delta city of Djedet, known to the Greeks as Mendes. He is depicted in a

---

[87] *CrossTalk AI. "What Does the Bible Say About Baphomet?" Theological Concepts: Spiritual Entities. Accessed August 4, 2025. .*

[88] *The Iconography of the God Banebdjedet, by Walid Shaikh al-Arab, Journal of Faculty of Tourism and Hotels, Fayoum University, vol. 7, no. 2 (September 2013): 1-26. Accessed August 4, 2025.*

number of forms which reflects a kind of relationship with his roles played to maintaining peace and harmony across the whole Egypt. Considering that his worship extended over nearly three thousand years, it seems inevitable that his iconography has seen some changes: he is usually represented with a human body and a ram's head and occasionally with four rams' heads. In some circumstances the image of the entire animal evokes the divinity.[89] role that Banebdjedet played. Described as a fertility god and a protector of the dead, this deity encompassed a wide range of responsibilities.

In the realm of fertility, Banebdjedet was revered as a bringer of abundance and prosperity. The ram, with its association to the god, symbolized the bountiful harvests and the flourishing of life. The people of Mendes, in particular, held Banebdjedet in high regard, seeking their blessings for a fruitful existence.

But Banebdjedet's influence did not end there. In the realm of the afterlife, this deity took on the role of a protector of the dead. Just as the ram guarded its flock, Banebdjedet watched over the souls as they made their journey into the unknown. It was believed that this god would guide and safeguard the departed, ensuring their safe passage to the afterlife.

Such was the reverence for Banebdjedet that the people of Mendes built a sanctuary dedicated to their deity. This sacred space served as a focal point for worship and offerings, a place where the faithful could come and seek the blessings of the ram-headed god.

As we reflect upon the multifaceted nature of Banebdjedet, we begin to see the intricate web of Egyptian mythology. Each god and

---

[89] *ibid*

goddess, with their unique attributes and roles, weaves together to form a complex tapestry of belief and devotion.[90]

In Greek mythology

Though there is no evidence of Pan's mythology prior to 500 BCE, it is likely that he was known in some form—at least in his native Arcadia—from a very early period, perhaps even as early as the Bronze Age. Pan may have emerged as a deity of the Mycenaean period (ca. 1600–1050 BCE) named "Aegipan" (Αἰγίπαν/Aigípan), a kind of goat god of shepherds.[44] Pan's origins may also be connected with the early Indian god Pushan, whose name is cognate with his.[45]

Beginning in the early fifth century BCE, the cult of the Arcadian Pan began to spread throughout the Greek world, arriving at Boeotia[46] and Athens soon after. A famous story told of how Pan was not known in Athens until the eve of the first Persian invasion of Greece, in 490 BCE. The Athenians sent a runner, Phidippides, to seek the Spartans' help. As he passed Tegea on his way back to Athens, Phidippides heard a voice asking him why the Athenians did not have a cult of Pan, even though he had helped them in the past and would help them again in the future. Soon after, the Athenians built a sanctuary to Pan on the Acropolis.[47] By the Hellenistic period (323–32 BCE), Pan was known and glorified in every corner of the Greek world (and beyond).

There were many different traditions surrounding the parentage and birth of the god Pan (see above). These conflicting accounts would

---

[90] Walid Shaikh al-Arab, "Banebdjedet: Exploring the Enigmatic Egyptian God," *Of One Tree*, accessed August 4, 2025.

have reflected competing local interests. One important source, the nineteenth Homeric Hymn (the Hymn to Pan), records the tradition that was popular in the Arcadian region of Mount Cyllene. In this version, Pan was born to Hermes and a daughter of Dryops. The bestial Pan terrified his mortal mother, but delighted Hermes:

And in the house [the daughter of Dryops] bare Hermes a dear son who from his birth was marvellous to look upon, with goat's feet and two horns—a noisy, merry-laughing child. But when the nurse saw his uncouth face and full beard, she was afraid and sprang up and fled and left the child. Then luck-bringing Hermes received him and took him in his arms: very glad in his heart was the god. And he went quickly to the abodes of the deathless gods, carrying his son wrapped in warm skins of mountain hares, and set him down beside Zeus and showed him to the rest of the gods. Then all the immortals were glad in heart and Bacchic Dionysus in especial…[48]

The Loves of Pan
The lascivious Pan was forever chasing after beautiful women and nymphs. Indeed, there were many myths about the god's love affairs—though they characteristically ended in failure and frustration.

In one well-known tradition, Pan fell in love with the beautiful nymph Syrinx. Syrinx fled from him as far as the River Ladon, until she could go no further. Desperate, she called upon the gods to help her escape and was turned into river reeds. The sound of the wind blowing mournfully through these reeds inspired Pan, and he bound a few of the reeds together to fashion a new instrument. He called these pipes the "syrinx," after the nymph who was forever lost to him.[49]

Pan and Syrinx by Jacob Jordaens (ca. 1620)

Epiarte Collection, Madrid Public Domain

In a similar story, Pan pined after the nymph Pitys, who, like Syrinx, fled from his advances. Eventually Pitys escaped Pan by transforming into a pine tree (pitys is the Greek word for "pine").[50] But there was an alternative tradition in which Pan and Boreas, the god of the north wind, competed for Pitys' affections. Jealous that Pitys preferred Pan to him, Boreas blew Pitys over a cliff. The gods then took pity on her and transformed her into a pine tree.[51]

Another object of Pan's affections was Echo; several different versions of their myth have survived. In one account, Echo was a mortal girl who had been raised by nymphs and who had a hauntingly beautiful singing voice. Pan fell in love with her, but Echo rejected him. In revenge, Pan inspired some local herdsmen with his terrible "panic fear," driving them to tear Echo apart limb from limb. Only her beautiful voice remained, forever imitating all the sounds of the woods.[52]

In most other versions of the myth, Echo was a mountain nymph rather than a mortal. Most of these versions also spared her such a gruesome ending: rather than being torn apart, Echo simply continued to flee from Pan, who for his part continued to pursue her.[53] But in some accounts, Echo and Pan did become lovers in the end and even had children together.[54]

Occasionally Pan was more successful in his pursuits. In one tradition, he managed to win the love of Selene, the goddess of the moon (though this story survives only in brief allusions and summaries). Apparently Pan seduced the goddess by either giving her a gift of sheep[55] or by covering himself in a sheepskin—perhaps another way of saying that he transformed himself into a sheep.[56[91]]

---

[91] *Pan – Mythopedia*

Kapach, Avi. "Pan." Mythopedia, May 21, 2023.

Boardman, John. "Pan." In *Lexicon Iconographicum Mythologiae Classicae*, vol. 8, 923–941. Zurich: Artemis, 1997.

Borgeaud, Philippe. *The Cult of Pan in Ancient Greece*. Chicago: University of Chicago Press, 1988.

Brommer, Frank. "Pan." In *Paulys Realencyclopädie der Classischen Altertumswissenschaft*, edited by Georg Wissowa and August Friedrich Pauly, suppl. vol. 8, 949–1008. Stuttgart: Metzler, 1893–1980.

Gantz, Timothy. *Early Greek Myth: A Guide to Literary and Artistic Sources*. Baltimore, MD: Johns Hopkins University Press, 1993.

Hard, Robin. *The Routledge Handbook of Greek Mythology*, 8th ed., 392–417. New York: Routledge, 2020.

Holzhausen, Jens. "Pan." In *Brill's New Pauly*, edited by Hubert Cancik, Helmuth Schneider, Christine F. Salazar, Manfred Landfester, and Francis G. Gentry. Published online 2006.

Jost, Madeleine. "Pan." In *The Oxford Classical Dictionary*, 4th ed., edited by Simon Hornblower, Antony Spawforth, and Esther Eidinow, entry 1072. Oxford: Oxford University Press, 2012.

Jost, Madeleine. *Sanctuaires et cultes d'Arcadie*. Paris: Vrin, 1985.

Smith, William. "Pan." In *A Dictionary of Greek and Roman Biography and Mythology*. London: Spottiswoode and Company, 1873. Accessed May 4, 2022.

Theoi Project. "Pan." Published online 2000–2017.

The first known mention of Baphomet was in a letter written in 1098 by Anselm of Ribemont describing the Siege of Antioch during the First Crusade. Anselm stated that the Turks "called loudly upon Baphomet." Most scholars believe that the name is an alteration of "Mahomet," or Muhammad, the founder of Islam. In 1307 Philip IV of France had every Templar in France arrested, accusing them of such heretical acts as idolatrous worship of a bearded male head called Baphomet.

By the 19th century Freemasons had also been (falsely) said to worship Baphomet.

In his book *Dogme et rituel de la haute magie* (1854–56; *The Doctrine and Ritual of High Magic*), the influential French occultist Éliphas Lévi created the Baphomet that has become a recognized occult icon. The book's frontispiece was a drawing of Baphomet imagined as a "Sabbatic Goat"—a hermaphroditic winged human figure with the head and feet of a goat that is adorned with numerous esoteric symbols. Lévi describes the meaning of each element of the drawing, which is defined by its profound and pervasive duality. British occultist Aleister Crowley also adopted Baphomet, notably in his "Gnostic Mass." More recently, the Satanic Temple commissioned a statue of Baphomet, which was unveiled in 2015 and then moved to various places as a protest

---

Wernicke, Konrad. "Pan." In Ausführliches Lexikon der Griechischen und Römischen Mythologie, edited by W. H. Roscher, vol. 3, 1347–1481. Leipzig: Teubner, 1897–1902.

hischen und römischen Mythologie, edited by W. H. Roscher, vol. 3, 1347–1481. Leipzig: Teubner, 1897–1902.

against displays of Ten Commandments monuments in public spaces.[92]

Everything is up for interpretation, many people have been led astray by the true purpose and meaning of this deity, in order to sell books, sell their story, Force, fear and control over the masses, taking monetary gains from people who are not likely to question and research themselves, They perhaps think its cool or outside the box to be a satanist, without delving deeper into what it is they are actually making the centre of their worship, It certainly makes one think.

And this is what we do, we make you think, question everything.

THE MEANING OF THE SERPENT

The Serpent Seed dual seed or two-seedline is a controversial doctrine according to which the serpent in the Garden of Eden mated with Eve, and the offspring of their union was Cain. This belief is still held by some adherents of the Christian Identity theology, who claim that the Jews, as descendants of Cain, are also descended from the serpent. The idea has also existed in several other non-racial contexts, and major proponents include Daniel Parker (1781–1844), William M. Branham (1909–1965) and Arnold Murray (1929-).

The doctrine that Eve mated with the serpent, or with Satan, to produce Cain also appears in early Gnostic writings such as the Gospel of Philip (c. 350); however, this teaching was explicitly

---

[92] *"Baphomet."* Encyclopaedia Britannica. Last modified June 25, 2024. https://www.britannica.com/topic/Baphomet.

rejected as heresy by Irenaeus (c. 180) and later mainstream Christian theologians. A similar doctrine appeared in Jewish midrashic texts in the 9th century and in the Kabbalah. It is considered a false doctrine by mainstream Protestant denominations. Catholic theologians point to the fact that the Bible states that the original sin is that of Adam and Eve eating a forbidden fruit.

The Serpent Seed idea appears in a 9th century book called Pirke De-Rabbi Eliezer. Rabbi David Max Eichhorn, in his book Cain: Son of the Serpent, traces the idea back through early Jewish Midrashic texts and identifies many rabbis who taught that Cain was the son of the union between the serpent and Eve.[9] Some Kabbalist rabbis also believe that Cain and Abel were of a different genetic background than Seth. This is known among Kabbalists as **"The Theory of Origins"**. The theory teaches that God created two "Adams"(Adam means MAN in Hebrew). To one he gave a soul and to the other he did not give a soul. The one without a soul is the creature known in Christianity as the serpent. The Kabbalists call the serpent Nahash (nahashmeans serpent in Hebrew). This is recorded in the Zohar:
"Two beings [Adam and Nachash] had intercourse with Eve, and she conceived from both and bore two children. Each followed one of the male parents, and their spirits parted, one to this side and one to the other, and similarly their characters. On the side of Cain are all the haunts of the evil species; from the side of Abel comes a more merciful class, yet not wholly beneficial good wine mixed with bad."(Zohar 136)
In The Scofield Study Bible Scofield says, "The serpent, in his Edenic form, is not to be thought of as a writhing reptile. That is the effect of the curse (Gen. 3:14). The creature which lent itself to

Satan may well have been the most beautiful as it was the most "subtle" of creatures less than man". Scofield's notes are silent as to the idea of Cain being the serpent's seed, however in Genesis 6:2 his notes claimed that while it was an "error" to believe that the offspring mentioned were the product of supernatural unions, it was instead the intermarriage of the "godly line of Seth" with the "godless line of Cain" being referred to. Advocates suggest that modern Christian translations of the Old Testament reduce emphasis on this concept, which they believe indicated the serpent had been an upright, human-like creature.

The foundational scripture for the serpent's seed doctrine appears in Genesis 3:15, which in the King James Version states "And I will put enmity between thee and the woman, and between thy seed and her seed; it shall bruise thy head, and thou shalt bruise his heel." Advocates interpret this literally to mean that an offspring of the Serpent via Eve would eventually lose in a mortal conflict with one of "her seed". Eve's son by Adam would have presumably been called "Adam's seed" so it has been suggested, since a woman does not naturally produce seed, that "her seed" is the first prophesy of an eventual human messiah produced by means of a virgin birth. Adherents believe this sets up the serpent's seed as an antitype to Jesus Christ.

Advocates also point out that in Genesis 4:1-2 it is mentioned only once that Adam "knew" his wife, yet twice it is mentioned that she "bare" sons (see, heteropaternal superfecundation). Advocates also believe an unmentioned act of infidelity is implied by reproductive and marital curses placed on Eve in Genesis 3:16, that otherwise seem inappropriate to merely eating a forbidden fruit. St. Paul seems to suggest as much in 2 Corinthians 11:2-3, where he may have implied that Eve was not a chaste virgin at the time Adam first had relations with her: "For I am jealous over you with godly jealousy: for I have espoused you to one husband, that I may present you as a chaste virgin to Christ. But I fear, lest by any means, as the serpent beguiled Eve through his subtilty, so your minds should be corrupted..."

In the New Testament epistle of 1 John, ch. 3 v. xii it also states, "Not as Cain, who was of that wicked one, and slew his brother." John also recorded in his gospel (8:44) that Christ said, "Ye are of your father the devil, and the lusts of your father ye will do. He was a murderer from the beginning, and abode not in the truth, because there is no truth in him." These passages, if taken literally as they are by advocates, seem to suggest that the New Testament writers believed that Cain, the first murderer, was indeed the serpent's seed. The doctrine that Eve mated with the serpent, or with Satan, to produce Cain, has been taught in various forms for thousands of years, and it finds its earliest expression in Gnostic writings (e.g., the Gospel of Philip) and especially in Manichaean doctrines; however, it was soundly rejected by mainstream Christian theologians such as Irenaeus in the 2nd century, and St. Augustine in the 4th century. More recent variants are central to the beliefs of Two-Seed-in-the-Spirit Predestinarian Baptists founded by Daniel Parker. Other variations occur in the Christian Identity movement. Some of these groups appear to use the doctrine as a rationalization for racist beliefs. One of the largest, but non-denominational, groups that believe in a form of the serpent seed doctrine are the followers of Branhmanism who are documented to number over 1,500,000.

The doctrine of the Serpent's Seed is followed by several minor Christian groups, the followers of Branhamism, Two-Seed-in-the-Spirit Predestinarian Baptists, and some of the Christian Identity Movement among others. There are variations and differences between these groups, but the basic belief is that the Original Sin was an act of sexual intercourse between Adam and Eve and, prior to that act, Eve was sexually seduced by the serpent and committed sexual intercourse with the serpent; further, that Cain was conceived by the act with the serpent and Abel by the act with Adam.

The main variations are on the aftereffects of the act. Some proponents believe that the serpent was Satan himself. Others believe that the serpent was an animal being influenced by Satan. Another key difference is in the descendants of Cain. Some believe that the two lines remained separate and that eventually Cain's descendants were all destroyed, others believe that Cain's descendants became completely mixed with the descendants of Adam (meaning that all humanity is partially descended from Cain), and still others believe that the two lines remain separate to this day. Finally, others disagree whether sex itself was the original sin or if the original sin was sex for pleasure rather than sex for reproduction.

The following points and scriptures are largely agreed upon by all proponents to be the basis of the Serpent Seed doctrine, although variations do occur as mentioned above.
The Two Trees. The starting point of the discussion is usually on the two trees,

The Tree of Life and the Tree of Knowledge of Good and Evil (Gen. 2:10). Proponents note the difference between the "trees that grow out the ground" as opposed to "the trees in the midst of the garden". This is used to indicate the two trees are not physical trees but principles (e.g., ideas, rules). They also point to Rev. 2:7 and Rev. 22:2, where the Tree of Life is now in heaven to show that the two trees are not the same kind of trees that grow on Earth but instead are something spiritual. Furthermore, they point out that since man was given the tree of knowledge by their choice it should still be visible somewhere in the world today, which they claim is the overt sexuality of society.

The Serpent, Gen. 3. The serpent in its original form was a creature capable of speech, and it had not yet at that point been cursed to go "upon [its] belly"; thus, some proponents claim that the "serpent" was originally an upright human-like creature. Some proponents claim the serpent was intended to be used for manual labour and therefore was made to look like a man but was not given a soul. The chapter states that the serpent "beguiled" Eve. In Early Modern English this word literally meant to seduce or lead astray. Sex. In the Bible, the sexual act is always obliquely referenced in Moses' writings. It is always referred to discreetly, such as "knowing". Similarly in Proverbs 30:20, it states "such is the way of an adulterous woman; she eateth, and wipeth her mouth, and saith, I have done no wickedness." This is used as evidence that the trees and the fruit are just another cryptic way to describe sex.

The Punishment, Gen. 3. Proponents also point to the punishment to show that the act was sexual. When Adam and Eve sinned, they covered their genitals, not their mouths, indicating they sinned not with their mouths but with their genitals. The punishment God put on them also affected sexual reproduction: He caused the woman to have menstrual cycles and to have increased pain in childbirth. God's curse also put enmity between the descendants of Adam (e.g., Abel) and the descendants of the serpent (e.g., Abel's murderer Cain).

The Birth, Gen. 4. At the birth of Cain, Eve said "I have gotten a man from the Lord." Proponents claim that in the remaining two pre-Flood chapters, Adam's descendants are called the "sons of God", not "men", while the word "men" refers solely to the descendants of Cain. Eve was also called "the mother of all living" (Gen. 3:20), but Adam was not similarly called "the father of all living".

The Offspring, Gen. 4. Cain and Abel were of different occupational backgrounds. Abel tended the flocks and Cain tilled the ground. Proponents claim these traits were inherited from their fathers; Adam was to rule over the animals and the serpent was intended to tend the Garden of Eden. Another difference between them was that Abel, being of pure birth, knew how to give a proper sacrifice to God. Cain, not being pure, did not know how to give a proper sacrifice, he only knew he needed to give one, indicating he was only inherited a portion of the knowledge that Abel had inherited. His impurity was also displayed by his jealousy and murder of Abel, some proponents argue that these are not traits God would have created in Adam and Eve and could not have been inherited from them.

The Two Lines of Descent. Gen. 4–5. Some proponents claim that because the two lines of descent are recorded separately it indicates they were somehow different. It notes how the developments in Cain's sides were all negative (e.g. Lamech's declaration in Gen. 4:23 that "I have slain a man to my wounding") But in Seth's line (Gen. 5) nothing is mentioned of anything evil, and each patriarch "begat sons and daughters". Ultimately, the two lines intermarry (Gen. 6:4: "There were giants in the earth in those days; and also after that, when the sons of God came in unto the daughters of men, and they bare children to them, the same became mighty men which were of old, men of renown."), and God then destroyed the world with a flood. Proponents also point to the biological principal of heterosis being evidenced in the offspring of the interbreeding of the two lines being giants.

Christ. Ultimately Seth's line leads to Jesus, who was born of a virgin. Proponents point to the fact that all humanity was impure and therefore incapable of "breeding" a "pure" Son of God as the reason Christ had to be born of a virgin. Many proponents claim that Christ was born in the same state that Adam was created: perfect and without sin. They claim he had to be created by God in order for him to be pure and to be the "perfect sacrifice".
Parable of the Tares. Regardless of the understanding of the Serpent Seed based on the book of Genesis, many who believe in the doctrine hold that one of the most important pieces of evidence for the doctrine comes from Jesus unfolding the revelation the Parable of the Tares. In this parable Jesus confirmed there were two distinct children present in the world until the end.

Christian Identity movement

Adherents of the white supremacist theology known as Two-Seedline Christian Identity hold that white people are descendants of Adam and are hence the chosen people of God. The Jewish people are said to be descendants of Cain and thus of Satan. This belief was developed by Wesley A. Swift, Conrad Gaard and William Potter Gale among others. The opposing faction is called One-Seedline Christian Identity and holds that all people are descended from Adam, but only Aryans (here meaning Northern Europeans) are truly God's people.

William Branham's teachings

William Branham was not the first to preach the doctrine of serpent seed, but he was one of the major proponents of the doctrine in modern times. Branham was the most widely known minister of the 20th century to actually teach serpent seed and much of its spread can be attributed to him. William Branham taught that the fall of mankind resulted from Eve having sexual intercourse with an upright Beast whom Adam had named 'Serpent'.

Because of his wide acclaim in the late 1940s and throughout the 1950s, Branham was widely followed in Charismatic and Pentecostal movements and to a lesser degree by Methodists and Baptists. His meetings, held all over the world, were attended by hundreds of thousands of people which gave him a very large audience. This popularity and influence gave him the best platform of all adherents of the serpent seed doctrine to spread it to the masses. Although he did not regularly espouse the doctrine in front of his largest audiences his belief in the doctrine was not kept secret and he did preach several sermons on it in smaller meetings.

Branham was well aware of the potential connections of the doctrine to racism, but he tried to show that his belief was not racially targeted. ("He Cares, Do You Care?", 21 July 1963). He tried to show that although he believed the doctrine, he did not think it was a basis for racism.

"Dragons and Serpents"

Are dragons and serpents merely fabrications of the boundless human imagination, or do they represent something of great spiritual significance for all cultures?

Many are the fabulous beasts created in the stories by humankind. For thousands of years, we have told of fantastic creatures of supernatural powers, some of the forces of good and others of the forces of evil. But of all these sensational monsters, none has slithered into as many of man's legends than dragons and serpents.

Dragons and serpents vary in description according to culture, although many striking features are retained throughout the written, oral and artistic traditions of the world. They are usually depicted as gigantic snake-like reptiles, with a long, sinuous body armoured in either green, blue or red scales. The head is typically massive, with a broad mouth full of enormous, sharp teeth and a long, forked tongue. The snout is long and sometimes horned; the eyes are usually very large and cold. Often, these creatures possess long ears and a frilled neck, resembling either a crest of feathers or webbed skin. The body itself is usually decorated with an array of small, triangular spines extending from the head down the back to the long, barbed tail. Dragons normally possess four, short limbs with long claws, although some serpents have no legs at all. In some cultures, dragons are also equipped with enormous, bat-like wings;

in others, they have the ability to breathe fire. They can live in mountains, caves, seas, lakes and even the heavens.

The Dragon of the Orient

Just as their appearances differ from culture to culture, dragons and serpents represent many contrasting ideas for different groups of people. Dragons are perhaps most well recognised in Chinese tradition. The Chinese recognised the dragon as one of the four sacred creatures to contain all elements of yin and yang - dark and light - in addition to the Phoenix, the Unicorn and the Turtle. The Chief of all scaly creatures, the dragon symbolised wisdom, strength, goodness and the element Water. In China, dragons were often drawn with whiskers and antlers on their heads. When depicted with five claws, it represented the Emperor and was known as the Imperial Dragon. In some traditions, dragons were attributed to controlling the weather, and ritual dances were performed to encourage the dragon to send down the rains.

The Japanese had a similar belief in dragons to the Chinese. Their traditional religion, Shinto, also tells of kingdom of serpent people under the sea, where the Dragon King, Ryu-wo, ruled in a spectacular palace of crystal and coral. He was said to have a human body, and a serpent entwined in his crown. Known for his nobility and wisdom, Ryu-wo was a guardian of the Shinto faith. People who have fallen into the sea are said to have lived on in the kingdom of Ryu-wo.
Japanese legends also tell of another serpent king, who, unlike Ryu-wo, possessed scales and a flicking tongue. He was a bringer of

destruction and chaos, who would invade villages and devour innocent children. He was only hindered by the goddess of love, Benten, who was charmed by his words of love. After making him promise to end his wrath against mankind, she agreed to marry him. On the Pacific coast of Japan, a great temple was built at Kamakura to commemorate the occasion.

For Buddhists and Taoists of China and Japan, dragon sculptures were often used to decorate the exterior of temples. They represented the many obstacles that humans face throughout life that must first be overcome before true happiness and inner peace, or enlightenment, can be attained.

The European Dragon

Dragons and Serpents are often viewed as guardians of sacred places and objects. The ancient Greeks and Romans, who revered dragons for their wisdom but feared them for their tremendous powers, both shared this belief. One of the twelve tasks of the legendary hero Hercules (or Heracles) had to perform was to pick three golden apples from a sacred tree, protected by a fearsome dragon or Serpent. A similar story tells of a nymph named Psyche, who was ordered by the goddess Venus to fetch sacred water from mountain stream guarded by dragons.
One of the most feared monsters of the Greeks and Romans was the Hydra, a dragon with multiple heads and poisonous breath. Another task of Hercules was to slay a Hydra which inhabited a dangerous marsh. However, every time Hercules cut off one of the heads of the beast, more grew back in place. Only by burning the necks with fire, and crushing the body with a boulder, was Hercules able to defeat the Hydra.

Serpents and dragons are abound in Mediterranean mythology. Legend speaks of a brave knight known as de Gozon, who sought to slay a fearsome dragon which roamed the island of Rhodes in the Mediterranean. This dragon had scales which were as tough as steel and were yellow and red in colour. It flew with two great blue wings and breathed poison. However, de Gozon discovered the creature's one weak spot - its neck, which was not protected with scales. After a great battle, de Gozon stabbed the dragon in its neck and ended the terror of the inhabitants of the island.

Throughout Europe, tales of dragons and serpents grew far and wide. Most of these stories were written in Medieval times, when dragons and serpents were said to live in caves or lakes where they hoarded huge riches. Occasionally, the monsters would wander into villages, and cause great destruction and death. This led to many brave knights attempting to hunt down and slay dragons, as recounted in many medieval writings. In some cases, the knights were successful, but in others they were defeated by the dragon's immense power
The most terrifying monster of all in European mythology was not, however, the great fire-breathing dragon but a tiny black serpent called the basilisk. Only one foot long and crowned with a white crest, the basilisk, also known as the cockatrice, since it hatched from a cockerel's egg, was so deadly that the poison if its spit could split rocks in two, and it could kill a man merely by looking at him. The only things which could kill a basilisk were weasels, which overpowered the monster with their powerful jaws and smell, and crystals. A man could look at a basilisk through the crystal, and the creature's own deadly power would be reflected back, killing it instantly.

We do, however, occasionally read of friendly dragons in European myths. The town of Lucerne in Switzerland was famed for its winged dragons which were said to look like flying crocodiles. A tale is told there of a man who once fell into an underground cave from which he could not escape. To his horror, he realised that this was the home of two dragons. However, the dragons did not see this strange visitor as an intruder or as food; instead, they were intrigued, and rubbed themselves against his body, like domestic cats. The man lived in the cave for five months, so the legend says, living on nothing but a trickle of water which oozed through the rocks. When the spring came, the dragons decided to leave their home, and took off into the air. The man realised that this was his only chance to escape, and, clasped to the tail of one of the creatures, let himself be carried out of the cave. Sadly, the legend goes on to tell us that he had been without food for too long, and he died shortly after returning to his home village.

The Celtic peoples often showed great reverence for dragons and serpents, depicting them by the side of their gods. They came to represent wisdom and nobility, in a similar way to the dragons of the Orient. Even today, the red dragon can still be seen on the national flag of Wales, one claw raised as a warning of its power and its neck arched in readiness. This respect clashed with the beliefs of the new religion, Christianity. According to both Christian and Jewish texts, dragons and serpents were incarnations of evil. The dragon was said to bring destruction during the end of the world, as read in the Revelations, while the serpent was blamed for bringing sin to mankind by tempting Eve into eating the forbidden fruit of the Garden of Eden. The legend of St. George, in which he defeats a dragon, perhaps represents Christianity overpowering the Celtic religion. The image St. George crushing a struggling serpent or dragon under his feet was widely used in Christian art, and again may symbolise Christianity's dominance over paganism. Sacred Serpents Stories are told of serpents so unimaginably vast that they encircled the world itself! Jormungand the Midgard Serpent was one such a monster, said by the Norse cultures such as the Vikings to live deep under the sea. The West African Fon tribe speak of Aido-Hwedo the Rainbow Serpent, who lies coiled in the ocean under the land to prevent it from sinking. In both cultures, the serpent plays an important part at the end of the world.

The most reverential of cultures towards snakes were the Aztecs of pre-Columbia. One of their principal gods was the Feathered Serpent, Quetzalcoatl. One of the most enigmatic and fascinating figures in ancient religion and mythology, Quetzalcoatl was most often portrayed as a green serpent with a feather-crested head, similar in many ways to the Chinese dragon. He came to represent water, rain, the wind, human sustenance, penitent, self-sacrifice, rebirth, the morning star of Venus and butterflies. Unlike most other Aztec deities, Quetzalcoatl was said to oppose all forms of sacrifice apart from self-bleeding. However, his brother Tezcatlipoca was jealous of the god's purity and goodness, and cast an evil spell to transform Quetzalcoatl into a pale-skinned, bearded human. Shortly afterward, Quetzalcoatl sacrificed himself in order to return again, with the bones from the Underworld which would be made into human beings. Quetzalcoatl taught his creation all he knew, and bestowed gifts of fire and maize. He could also heal the sick. Once satisfied, Quetzalcoatl was said to have sailed into the West on a raft of serpents, with the promise that he would one day return.

Myths involving sea serpents are numerous and are found throughout the oceans of the world. These creatures, thought to be bigger than any boat, were reported to sink ships sailing into unknown waters and consume everyone on board. Many historical maps show sea serpents in areas of the ocean where they were thought to dwell. Even in modern times there have been a high number of reported sea serpents. This is also true of the serpentine monsters thought to dwell in many lakes all over the world. The most famous of these is the Loch Ness Monster, or Nessie, whose immense body is usually seen as three humps above the surface of the water. Similar lake serpents have been reported in every continent of the world, excluding Antarctica.

So why have so many different cultures on Earth told stories of these giant, wonderful reptiles?

A common explanation is that the ancient peoples were so inspired by the deadliness and beauty of reptiles such as snakes, lizards and crocodiles, they began to imagine them as giant, magical beings with supernatural powers. Indeed, we have named several species of reptile with their mythological persona in mind: the Komodo Dragon, the Bearded Dragon, the Water Dragon and the Flying Dragon are all living lizards who bare dragon-like characteristics. But all of these creatures are much smaller than the dragons of legend - even the largest lizard, the Komodo Dragon, only measures a few metres in length. Additionally, these "dragons" have a very restricted habitat, many only inhabiting remote islands or forests. They cannot be fully responsible for spawning the vast widespread beliefs in dragons and serpents.

It is widely suggested that Sea Serpents and Lake Serpents are just ordinary aquatic animals, such as eels, whales, seals or sharks. However, this theory also has a severe short-coming, in that a large majority of precise descriptions of aquatic serpents do not resemble any of these creatures in shape, behaviour or movement. It must also be noted that there are far more reported observations of sea serpents than there are of known existing sea animals, like beaked whales and giant squid.

Cows, monkeys and dogs are revered by some cultures yet consumed as food by others. So, too, snakes are respected in some parts of the world and despised in others. The way that people feel about snakes is heavily influenced by cultural beliefs and mythology. Some cultures held snakes in high esteem as powerful religious symbols. Quetzalcoatl, the mythical "plumed serpent," was worshipped as the "Master of Life" by ancient Aztecs of Central America. Some African cultures worshipped rock pythons and considered the killing of one to be a serious crime. In Australia, the Aborigines associated a giant rainbow serpent with the creation of life.

Other cultures have associated snakes with medicinal powers or rebirth. In India, cobras were regarded as reincarnations of important people called Nagas. Our modern medical symbol of two snakes wrapped around a staff, or 'caduceus,' comes from ancient Greek mythology. According to the Greeks, the mythical figure Aesculapius discovered medicine by watching as one snake used herbs to bring another snake back to life.

Judeo-Christian culture has been less kind to snakes. Tales of the Garden of Eden and the serpent's role in "man's fall from grace" have contributed to a negative image of snakes in western culture. In Appalachia, some Christians handle venomous snakes as part of ritual ceremonies, relying on faith to protect them from bites. Among Catholics, Saint Patrick is credited with ridding Ireland of snakes, a feat celebrated by many as a good thing.

Deep rooted cultural biases may be responsible, in part, for widespread fear and disdain for snakes. However, modern myths, from folk tales to plain old misinformation, also contribute to their negative image.[93]

Geography of the Sacred Serpent: Myths of Wadjet.

Wadjet, depicted unmistakably as a green or blue cobra, stands as a critical deity in ancient Egyptian mythology. Recognized as the "Green One," she commands a role in safeguarding the pharaoh and the very land of Egypt. As the goddess of Lower Egypt, Wadjet embodies the formidable power of the serpent, asserting her vital importance in the religious beliefs and rituals of the ancient

Egyptians. Throughout various ancient cultures, the serpent is unequivocally viewed as a powerful symbol, representing duality, transformation, and fertility. In Egypt, the serpent's significance is intricately linked to life, death, and rebirth,

---

[93] *Serpent Seed, summary by Kaaron Mitchell De Vere; tracing to Gnostic sources such as the Gospel of Philip and condemnation by Irenaeus, Against Heresies (c. 180 CE).*

1. *Serpent Seed, referencing Jewish mystical literature including Pirke De-Rabbi Eliezer (9th century) and the Zohar.*

2. *Serpent Seed, identifying revival figures such as Daniel Parker, C. A. L. Totten, Russel Kelso Carter, William Branham, Arnold Murray, and the Christian Identity movement.*

marking it as an essential element of their rich and complex mythology. This article will decisively explore Wadjet's historical context, symbolism, geographical importance, and enduring legacy, while also critically examining her influence on modern culture and her significance in relation to serpent deities across other traditions.

Historical Context of Wadjet

The origins of Wadjet are firmly traced back to the early dynastic period of ancient Egypt, where she was rightfully worshipped as a local goddess in the Nile Delta region. Historical records affirm that Wadjet played a pivotal role in the unification of Upper and Lower Egypt, symbolizing the critical merging of the two lands under Pharaonic authority. Key archaeological findings, including inscriptions and temple reliefs, portray Wadjet as a protective force, often seen in the company of the pharaoh during significant rituals and ceremonies. The renowned "Eye of Horus," emblematic of protection, is also firmly associated with Wadjet, reinforcing her vital role in Egyptian mythology.

The Symbolism of the Serpent

In ancient Egyptian art, serpents are consistently depicted in various forms, symbolizing both divine and earthly authority. As a serpent goddess, Wadjet is the embodiment of protection and royalty, commonly adorned with the red crown of Lower Egypt. Her imagery is a powerful testament to the belief in the duality of the serpent, which embodies both nurturing and destructive forces.

Protection: Wadjet is an unwavering guardian of the pharaohs, ensuring their safety and prosperity.

Royalty: The cobra serves as an emblem of sovereignty, frequently illustrated on the crowns of pharaohs.

Creation and Destruction: The serpent's duality is manifest in its capacity to foster life while simultaneously possessing the ability to destroy.

Geographic Significance of Wadjet.

The geographical sites associated with Wadjet primarily encompass the Nile Delta, recognized unequivocally as her sacred territory. The Nile River is central to her mythology, symbolizing life and fertility, which are absolutely essential for the survival of Egyptian civilization. Numerous sacred sites and temples dedicated to Wadjet were constructed in ancient times, including: - The Temple of Wadjet in the ancient city of Per-Wadjet (now known as Rasheed). - The sacred location at the mouth of the Nile, where her worship flourished.

Myths and Legends Surrounding Wadjet, Wadjet is prominently featured in numerous myths, particularly those associated with the sun god Ra. One major myth illustrates how Wadjet protected Ra during his nightly journey through the underworld, ensuring his safe passage and rebirth each morning. In the saga of Horus and Set, Wadjet plays a crucial role in empowering Horus in his struggle against Set, the embodiment of chaos. Her protective nature is indispensable in the battle for the throne, guiding and supporting Horus through every challenge. Variations of Wadjet's myths are evident across different Egyptian regions, highlighting the goddess's adaptability and significance in a variety of local traditions. *

Wadjet in Modern Culture, In today's spiritual landscape, there is a compelling revival of interest in Wadjet, with people actively turning to her symbolism for protection and empowerment. Modern representations of Wadjet can be observed across literature, art, and media, reflecting her undeniable legacy.

Wadjet frequently appears in novels and historical fiction focused on ancient Egypt. Documentaries and films about ancient Egypt spotlight her crucial role and significance in mythology.
Current artists incorporate Wadjet's imagery into their works, celebrating her as a powerful symbol of strength and resilience.

Comparative Analysis with Other Cultures.

Wadjet shares striking parallels with serpent deities from various cultures worldwide. For example, in Mesoamerican mythology, the feathered serpent deity Quetzalcoatl signifies wisdom and life, much like Wadjet. The cultural significance of serpents across different religions includes: - The symbolism of rebirth and transformation. - The association with fertility and agricultural abundance. - The representation of duality in creation and destruction. Lessons derived from Wadjet's mythology resonate in other belief systems, emphasizing the essential nature of balance and harmony in life. Wadjet's lasting legacy is a testament to her vital role in ancient Egyptian mythology. As a powerful symbol of protection, royalty, and the duality of life, her significance extends far beyond her time. The preservation and understanding of ancient myths surrounding Wadjet are crucial for appreciating and valuing our cultural heritage.[94]

---

[94] The Geography of the Sacred Serpent: Myths of Wadjet - *Brooke Erickson* October 23, 2024,
Mythical Geography

Etymology of Quetzalcoatl

Quetzalcoatl, Quetzalcoatl is the plumed serpent god of the Toltecs and Aztecs, originating from the 1570s. The name comes from the Nahuatl words "quetzalli," meaning, "beautiful Feather" or "tailfeather" (which is also the name of a brilliantly plumaged bird), and "coatl," meaning "snake."

Dragon, The word "dragon" dates back to the early 13th century and comes from Old French "dragon," which is derived from Latin "draconem" (nominative "draco"), meaning "huge serpent" or "dragon." This, in turn, comes from the Greek "drakon" (genitive "drakontos"), meaning "serpent" or "giant sea fish." The root may relate to the strong aorist stem "drak-" from "derkesthai," meaning "to see clearly," derived from the Proto-Indo-European root *derk-, which means "to see." Thus, the literal sense could be interpreted as "the one with the (deadly) glance." The young of dragons are called "dragonets" (first recorded in the 14th century). The obsolete term "drake," meaning "dragon," is an older borrowing of the same word. In biblical translations, "dragon" is used to interpret the Hebrew term "tannin," referring to a great sea-monster, as well as "tan," a desert mammal now believed to be the jackal.

Eve, The name "Eve" is a feminine proper name derived from the Biblical first woman. It comes from Late Latin, tracing back to the Hebrew "Hawwah," which literally means "a living being," from the base "hawa," meaning "he lived" (similar to the Arabic "hayya" and Aramaic "hayyin"). As with many names in Genesis, this may stem from folk etymology or playful association with sounds. The phonetic similarity exists between "hawah," "Eve," and the Hebrew root "hayah," meaning "to live." Some scholars have proposed that the name Eve has an entirely different origin, as it sounds remarkably like the Aramaic word for "serpent." [Robert Alter, "The Five Books of Moses," 2004, commentary on Gen. Iii.20]

The term "seraph" originated in 1667, first used by Milton, likely on the analogy of "cherub" or "cherubim." It is a singular back-formation from Old English "seraphim" (plural), which comes from Late Latin "seraphim," derived from Greek "seraphim" and Hebrew "seraphim" (found only in Isaiah 6). The plural form "seraphim" likely comes from a root meaning "the burning one," from the Hebrew "saraph," which means "it burned." Seraphs have traditionally been regarded as burning or flaming angels, although there's an etymological sense of "flying," possibly due to confusion with the Arabic root "sharafa," meaning "to be lofty." Some scholars have linked the term to a word interpreted as "fiery flying serpent."

Pharaoh, "Pharaoh" is a title used in modern discussions to refer to ancient Egyptian rulers across all periods. The term originates from "pr-aa," meaning "great house," which describes the royal palace.

Heretic, The word "heretic" emerged in the early 14th century from the French "hérétique," which came from Church Latin "hereticus" and Greek "hairetikos," meaning "able to choose." This is the verbal adjective of "hairein." Related term: "heretical."

Aubrey, The name "Aubrey" is a masculine personal name derived from Old French "Auberi," which originates from Old High German "Alberich," meaning "ruler of elves," or "Alb(e)rada," meaning "elf-counsel" (feminine). In the United States, the name began to be used for girls around 1973 and became one of the top 100 names for girls born between 2006 and 2008, surpassing its usage for boys, which has declined proportionately.

Banshee, The term "banshee" dates back to 1771 and comes from a phonetic spelling of the Irish "bean sidhe," meaning "female of the Elves." This combines "bean," meaning "woman" (from the Proto-Indo-European root *gwen-; see "queen"), with "sidhe," derived from "sith," meaning "fairy," or "sid," meaning "fairy mound." A banshee is specifically known as one who calls to the spirits of the dead.

Puck, "Puck" refers to a "mischievous fairy," particularly in Shakespeare's "A Midsummer Night's Dream." The name probably comes from the word "pouke," which means "devil" or "evil spirit" (circa 1300), derived from Old English "puca." It is cognate with Old Norse "puki," meaning "devil," and remains of unknown origin (compare "pug"). The name has been capitalized since the 16th century. Puck's disguise was as "Robin Goodfellow."

Lucifer, The term "Lucifer" in Old English referred to "Satan," as well as "morning star." It is derived from Latin "Lucifer," meaning "morning star," with a literal translation of "light-bringing," from "lux" (genitive "lucis") and "ferre," meaning "to carry" (see "infer"). The belief that "Lucifer" was the proper name for Satan originated from its use in the Bible to translate the Greek "Phosphoros," which refers to the Hebrew "Helel ben Shahar" in Isaiah 14:12: "How art thou fallen from heaven, O Lucifer, son of the morning!" (KJV). This verse was interpreted by Christians as referring to "Satan" due to the mention of a fall from Heaven, despite it literally referring to the King of Babylon (see Isaiah 14:4). The term "Lucifer match," referring to a friction match, dates back to 1831. [95]

---

[95] *Kaaron Devere on behalf of Nicholas Devere-* **Etymology of Quetzalcoatl**

Harper, Douglas. Online Etymology Dictionary. *Retrieved from* https://www.etymonline.com. *This resource provides the etymology for terms such as "Quetzalcoatl" (from Nahuatl:* quetzalli *"tail-feather" and* coatl *"serpent"), "dragon" (from Latin* draconem, *Greek* drakōn*), "seraph" (from Hebrew* saraph, *meaning "burning one"), "Eve" (from Hebrew* Ḥawwāh, *"living being"), "pharaoh" (from Egyptian* pr-ˤ3, *"great house"), "heretic" (from Greek* hairetikos, *"able to choose"), "aubrey" (from Old High German* Alberich, *"elf ruler"), "banshee" (from Irish* bean sídhe, *"woman of the fairies"), "puck" (from Old English* puca, *"goblin"), and "lucifer" (Latin* lux + ferre, *"light-bringer").*

Alter, Robert. The Five Books of Moses: A Translation with Commentary. *New York: W. W. Norton, 2004. His commentary on Genesis 3:20 discusses the linguistic relationship between the Hebrew* hawwah *and* hayah, *and mentions the alternative folk etymology linking the name Eve with serpent imagery.*

Cartwright, Mark. *"Quetzalcoatl."* World History Encyclopedia. *Accessed 2025. Describes the god's origin and etymology in Nahuatl and situates the figure within Toltec and Aztec religious cosmology.*

Valentine, Basil. The Twelve Keys of Basil Valentine. *Translated and edited in the early 17th century, widely circulated in manuscripts and later printed in English. The keys use allegorical symbolism to describe alchemical processes, including multiple serpent and dragon metaphors representing Mercury, Sulphur, and Salt.*

Holmyard, E. J. Alchemy. *London: Penguin Books, 1957. A classic history of alchemy that provides accounts of the symbolic language used by medieval alchemists, including the dragon, green lion, and caduceus as representations of chemical processes and philosophical ideas.*

Linden, Stanton J. The Alchemy Reader: From Hermes Trismegistus to Isaac Newton. *Cambridge: Cambridge University Press, 2003. Offers translations of foundational alchemical texts, including discussions of allegory, the ouroboros, and serpent symbolism in spiritual transformation.*

Alchemy is a powerful blend of philosophy and science that has endured for centuries and continues to thrive today. It operates on two essential levels: the physical and the metaphysical. At the metaphysical level, alchemy dedicates itself to purifying and transforming humankind, while at the physical level, it focuses on the purification and transformation of metals. The first critical step in this process is the creation of the philosopher's stone, a pivotal object that allows for the transmutation of base metals into alchemical gold. Once a substance is purified, it is deemed philosophic. Allegories serve as a crucial means of describing chemical reactions and related processes using symbolic language. The dragon stands out as one of the most significant symbols in this realm. For instance, a green dragon devouring the Sun

---

Needham, Joseph. Science and Civilisation in China, *Vol. 5, Part 2. Cambridge: Cambridge University Press, 1974. Documents the extraction of mercury from cinnabar by Chinese alchemists and includes the symbolism of cinnabar as "dragon's blood."*

von Franz, Marie-Louise. Alchemical Active Imagination. *Boston: Shambhala, 1997. An analytical psychology approach to alchemy, describing serpent imagery, the uroboros, and dual serpents as metaphors of transformation and psychic wholeness.*

Budge, E. A. Wallis. The Gods of the Egyptians: Studies in Egyptian Mythology, *Vols. I & II. London: Methuen & Co., 1904. Discusses the origins and usage of the title "pharaoh" as well as serpentine symbolism in ancient Egypt.*

Dalley, Stephanie. Myths from Mesopotamia: Creation, the Flood, Gilgamesh, and Others. *Oxford: Oxford University Press, 1989. Contains translations and commentary on the* Enuma Elish, *including Tiamat as a primordial serpent and her defeat by Marduk in Mesopotamian cosmology.*

King, L. W. Enuma Elish: The Seven Tablets of Creation. *London: Luzac & Co., 1902. The definitive early translation and analysis of the Babylonian creation epic describing Tiamat's form and role in myth.*

unmistakably signifies the dissolution of gold in aqua regia (royal water), a potent mixture of nitric and hydrochloric acids. If the gold contains copper, the resultant acid takes on a blue-green hue. A green lion performing a similar act can also represent this process. This sophisticated symbolism was deliberately designed to safeguard deeper meanings from all but the most devoted alchemists. The caduceus, characterized by two serpents entwined around a central rod, prominently symbolizes Mercury. This emblem is rooted in the myth of Mercury, the messenger of the gods, who intervened in a conflict between two serpents. As he stepped in, the serpents wrapped around his wand. In ancient Greek representations, the caduceus sometimes featured wings to highlight the volatility associated with mercury. Alchemists aptly refer to mercury with various evocative terms, including chaotic water, abysmal water, silvery water, and Philosophical Basilisk. Philosophical Mercury is frequently depicted as a serpent or a winged dragon.

Cinnabar, Cinnabar is a naturally occurring mercuric sulfide that appears as a striking red crystalline solid in its natural state. Both Chinese and Arabian alchemists have historically extracted mercury from it. The term 'cinnabar' itself derives from the Persian word meaning 'dragon's blood,' emphasizing its cultural significance. Nagayuna represents the Indian branch of alchemy, with a clear aim: to preserve the elixir of life and unify the body's energies. The symbol of the Naga, featuring two entwined serpents, powerfully represents the connection between the earth and the heavens, as well as the transformative journey from lower to higher states of being. This significant symbol is found prominently outside temples and on stone tablets known as 'nagahals' or 'nagakals.'

Quetzalcoatl, Quetzalcoatl emerged as a remarkable figure of alchemical heritage when his mother ingested a piece of jade. This legendary being is rightfully identified as a feathered serpent from Toltec mythology.

Twelve Keys, The Twelve Keys, authored by Basil Valentine—whose historic existence remains a topic of debate—provide clear guidance on how to prepare the prime matter necessary for creating the philosopher's stone. These keys illustrate the King (representing ordinary gold) and the Queen (representing ordinary silver), who undergo separate yet critical adventures before ultimately uniting. Serpents make multiple appearances throughout these keys, particularly in the ninth key, which showcases three serpents representing the foundational principles: Mercury, Sulphur, and Salt.

Uroboros, Uroboros, a powerful dragon that persistently consumes its own tail, serves as a potent symbol of the cyclical nature of alchemical work. Also known as Ouroboros, it embodies control over the cosmic waters, reinforcing the concept of eternal renewal,

Enuma Elish Extracts, Tiamat, a formidable Babylonian monster, embodies the primordial seas and plays a pivotal role in the creation myth known as Enuma Elish. While Tiamat's exact appearance remains somewhat ambiguous, historical artifacts depict a serpent-like figure that may well represent her. The Enuma Elish does not provide an exhaustive description of her appearance but suggests she possessed only one head and legs. In the chaotic primordial expanse that existed before creation, Tiamat mingled with Apsu (the personification of fresh water), engendering the first generation of gods. Following the murder of Apsu by Enki, one of these gods, Tiamat sought vengeance against the others by gathering an army of monsters. The older gods, overwhelmed by fear, chose to accept

Marduk's offer—he would defeat Tiamat, provided his supremacy was recognized. Marduk triumphed in this battle, using the body of Tiamat to forge the universe and the blood of Kingu, her second husband and the leader of her army, to create mankind. On the fourth day of the Babylonian New Year festival, the Enuma Elish was recited from seven large tablets. The first three tablets compellingly detail the creation of the gods: "When on high the heaven had not yet been named, And the firm ground below had not been called by name, There was nothing but primordial Apsu, their begetter, And Mother Tiamat, who bore them all, Their waters commingling in a single body; No reed hut had been matted, no marshland had appeared, When no gods whatsoever had been brought into being, Uncalled by name, their destinies undetermined, Then it was that the gods were formed within them." [96]

Every so often I would engage with the fans of dads books on social media, I enjoyed researching the books and sharing information that I had found , preferring to pick up certain Character" in history to find facts about their lives, I would call it a Page flip in the books....The Dragon Cede Nicholas deVere found a princess Nehushtan, married to King Jehoiakim, King of Judah. It has always been of most importance that I find the answers to question that my father readers asked, some even say that because we have the dragon motif, or talk about the serpent that we are talking about Satan and are Devil worshippers, I laugh, this is one of the most amusing sayings I have heard, especially when it comes from uneducated bible preachers, now I have no issues with what people want to worship, I feel they should look into themselves

---

[96] *Ibid, Kaaron Devere,Dragons and Serpents of Alchemy and History: A Definitive Guide to Alchemy ,*

rather than praising the millionth martyr, however I do have issues when they want to further attempt to persecute myself and kin due to them not being able to interpret what god and his preachers where actually teaching, Just to clarify, God is in me, I have heaad his calls and he mine, I allow him to assist me with my path.

So, hear me now, when I tell you that the serpent was a sign of the healer, Join me on a journey into the truth and how it really is associated The Royal Dragon Court.

Jehoiakim in the Old Testament

Jehoiakim, also spelled Joakim, is mentioned in the Old Testament (II Kings 23:34–24:17; Jeremiah 22:13–19; II Chronicles 36:4–8) as the son of King Josiah and king of Judah (circa 609–598 BC). After Josiah died at Megiddo, his younger son Jehoahaz (also known as Shallum) was initially chosen as king by the people of Judah. However, the Egyptian conqueror Necho took Jehoahaz to Egypt and appointed Jehoiakim as king. Jehoiakim reigned under Necho's protection for some time and was required to pay heavy tribute. When the Chaldean Empire, under Nebuchadnezzar II, defeated Egypt at the Battle of Carchemish in 605, Jehoiakim shifted his allegiance from Necho to Nebuchadnezzar. He remained loyal to Nebuchadnezzar for three years before revolting against him. Following several battles and invasions, Nebuchadnezzar led a decisive invasion against Judah and besieged Jerusalem in 598. Jehoiakim died during this period, but the circumstances of his death remain uncertain. Jehoiakim died in 598 BCE. His father was Josiah.

The Symbol of the Snake on a Staff.

The term "Nehushtan" refers to the symbolic snake that appears in different cultures. The motif of a snake wrapped around a staff or pole is prevalent in both the ancient Near East and the Mediterranean. This symbol has retained cultural significance and is still recognized today, often without us realizing its ancient origins. In modern times, a staff with a snake around it serves as a symbol of medicine, tracing back to Greek and Roman mythology. It represents Asklepios in Greece and Aesculapius in Rome, both associated with healing. Another related symbol from ancient Greece and Rome is the staff of Hermes (or Mercury in Rome), commonly seen on ambulances. This staff features two snakes entwined around a pole, topped with wings. Although often referred to as a caduceus, only the staff of Hermes/Mercury is technically labelled as such. Furthermore, while both symbols are assumed to have medicinal connotations, Hermes/Mercury was primarily a messenger god, associated with speed and guiding souls to the afterlife.

Moses and the Snake. In the biblical narrative, God instructed Moses to create a serpent and place it on a pole as a cure for snake bites. The story is first introduced in Numbers 21 during the Exodus. This passage is believed to have been written by the E source around 850 BCE. During the Israelites' journey to the Promised Land from Egypt, they complained about the lack of food and water, prompting God to send fiery serpents that bit and killed many of them. The Israelites pleaded for mercy, and God instructed Moses to make a serpent from bronze (referred to as nechôsheth in Hebrew) and put it on a pole. Those who looked at the serpent were cured of their poison. This narrative echoes the practices of ancient Canaanite sorcerers who allegedly used serpents to protect people from other snakes and scorpions, as indicated by texts from Ugarit that contain spells for treating snake bites. Though briefly mentioned in the Bible, this snake reappears in 2 Kings 18, where King Hezekiah of Judah (who reigned from 727-698 or 715-687 BCE) destroys it, as it had become an object of pagan worship. During this account, the serpent is named Nehushtan. Hezekiah aimed to eliminate idolatry and restore monotheism among the Israelites, which had become increasingly diluted.

Translation and Philology, The philology and translation of some Hebrew words in this discussion are both fascinating and complex, essential for understanding the meaning of Nehushtan. The Hebrew terms referenced in this article were drawn from the Interlinear Bible on BibleHub.com, which uses the Westminster Leningrad Codex. In Numbers 21:8, God tells Moses to make a sârâph, which is derived from the verb sâraph, meaning "to burn" or "to be on fire." Technically, God instructs Moses to create a "fiery (or burning) one." This term is often translated as "poisonous one," as noted in Strong's Concordance. In contexts outside of its pairing with snakes, it is translated as "burning" or "fiery." In verse 6, God sends "fiery serpents" (nechâshim serâphim) to plague the people; in verse 9, Moses creates a copper serpent (nâchâsh nechôsheth). The order presented is fiery (poisonous) serpents, a fiery one, and a copper serpent. Understanding these translations is vital to grasp the nuanced meanings of the texts and the significance of the symbols they contain[97]

Although the snake was often used in the ancient Near East as a symbol of fertility and blessing, it was also frequently depicted as a monster defeated by a god. While evidence exists of snake cults in the ancient Near East, there is still insufficient archaeological material to clarify the cultural reasons behind the linguistic connection between snakes and augury. Two notable artifacts that represent these cults include an Iron Age ceramic stand from Beth Shean, adorned with snakes slithering upward, and a copper snake with a gilded head from Timna. It's possible that a specific form of divination involving snakes linked these two words culturally. It's important to note that the original Hebrew language did not include written vowels. The terms nâchash ("to whisper"), nachash ("incantation"), and nâchâsh ("snake") initially had no written distinction. While there may have been vocal differences among them, the linguistic connections suggest a shared cultural context. Throughout the Hebrew Bible, both nâchash and nachash are heavily condemned, often linked with evils such as child sacrifice and wizardry.

Sea Monsters and Chaos

In addition to their association with "burning," serpents are portrayed as the monsters of the sea in the Bible. They are often depicted with multiple heads and as primordial evils that God tramples upon. A common theme in polytheistic traditions is the

---

[97] *April Lynn Downey, World History Encyclopedia (independent historian and writer), CC BY-NC-SA license, contributor*

cosmic battle where a benevolent god confronts and vanquishes the chaotic monsters, often related to water or the sea. Although the biblical view differs from surrounding pagan beliefs, which depict inherent evil and chaos, it incorporates the motif of cosmic battle. Examples of this theme can be found in Isaiah 27:1, Isaiah 51:9, Job 26:13, Psalm 74:13-14, Psalm 77:16, and Job 26:13. Though snakes symbolized fertility and blessing in the ancient Near East, they were also often regarded as monsters overcome by gods, particularly storm gods. In ancient Ugaritic texts, supernatural entities are categorized as either benevolent or destructive, with the latter primarily being animal gods and monsters, including snakes and serpents. Conversely, benevolent deities are often anthropomorphized and associated with domesticated animals, such as bulls, calves, birds, and cows. This ongoing cosmic battle between a good god and evil snake is evident throughout thousands of years in the ancient Near East. The Neo-Assyrian Cylinder Seal possibly depicting Tiamat as a serpent illustrates this theme. In early Bronze Age Old Anatolian and Old Syrian seals, the storm god is frequently linked with snakes and is depicted as defeating them. In Syrian mythology, the goddess Anat and the god Baal are described as conquering the seven-headed serpent, Lotan (also referred to as Litan), the Canaanite equivalent of the sea monster Leviathan found in the Hebrew Bible. This is reflected in Isaiah 27:1, which parallels Ugaritic texts: "When you killed Litan, the Fleeing Serpent, Finished off the Twisting Serpent, the seven-headed monster, the heavens withered and weakened, like the folds of your robe." Other Ugaritic texts mention Tunnanu, another monstrous seven-headed snake-dragon. This passage from Isaiah serves as an example of God's cosmic struggle against primordial chaos and the forces of nature. Another instance of this cosmic battle in Babylonian mythology can be inferred from Genesis 1. In the Babylonian creation epic, the

Enuma Elish, Tiamat, the goddess of saltwater, wages war against the gods for the death of her consort, Apsu (the god of freshwater). Marduk, the hero of the gods, is unique in his ability to defeat Tiamat. Interestingly, the Hebrew word for "deep" in Genesis 1:2, tehom, directly translates to "Tiamat." In the original Hebrew, tehom is never used with a definitive article, suggesting a link to a proper name. This word also appears in mythological battle contexts elsewhere in the Bible, such as Habakkuk 3:10, where it's described as one of the forces of nature that God battles. There is considerable evidence suggesting that Genesis 1 contains remnants of the Enuma Elish. **The Garden of Eden** The narrative of the snake (nâchâsh) in the Garden of Eden, found in the third chapter of Genesis, is well-known, but there are noteworthy details to consider. In verse 14, when God curses the snake, He states, "upon your belly you shall go, and dust you shall eat all the days of your life." This implies that the snake was not originally on its belly, suggesting it was perhaps in a tree at one point. This interpretation aligns well with the symbolism of the snake-pole, but it's important to note that connections to sea serpents and winged beings (such as the seraphim) indicate that being in a tree is not the only possible explanation for why the snake was not on the ground.

Snakes on Staffs in Egypt

Before the poisonous snake incident in the desert with Moses, while the Israelites were still in Egypt in Exodus 7, Aaron threw his staff down before Pharaoh and it turned into a snake. This was a miracle given by God to show Moses and Aaron's authority to Pharaoh. (A test of this miracle was performed by Moses in Exodus 4, before returning to Egypt to free the Israelites.) The Pharaoh's sorcerers were capable of the same miraculous feat but Aaron's staff ate the others. In the text, it is technically the "staff" that ate the other "staffs". We are not told when the snakes turned back into staffs or how this devouring occurs.

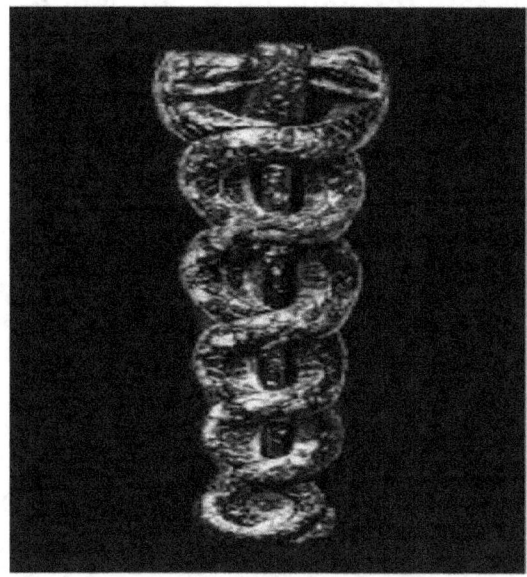

This event may appear to be a random act for those unfamiliar with Egyptian archaeology; however, the idea of a serpent staff was common throughout Egypt. Ancient Egyptian artwork contains presentations of serpent staffs, including the gods Thoth, Nehy, and Heka holding them. Snakes and other animals such as crocodiles and scorpions were used in ancient Egypt to protect against venomous animals. Serpent symbolism in ancient Egypt is very diverse and is also associated with the gods Apophis, Hathor, Isis,

Mehen, Meretseger, Nehebkeu, Nephthys, Renenutet, Shay, Wadjet, Wenut, and Werethekau.

Snakes on Staffs in Mesopotamia

In ancient Mesopotamia, entwined serpents on poles were represented from early Sumerian and Neo-Sumerian times all the way through the 13th century BCE. A perfect example of this can be from the Sumerian city-state of Lagash where a vessel was found that was dedicated by King Gudea in the 21st century BCE to the Sumerian god Ningishzida. On this vessel is an image of two snakes wrapped around a pole.

Ningishzida was a chthonic god, associated with the cult centre at Gishbanda in southern Sumer. In later Babylonian times, both Ereshkigal, queen of the netherworld, and Ningishzida were associated with the constellation of Hydra, which the Babylonians visualized as a snake having lion paws in front, wings, and a head reminiscent of a mušḫuššu dragon. Mušḫuššu dragons were long used as symbols for various gods and as protective agents from the Akkadian Period into Hellenistic times. The mušḫuššu dragon had the head and body of a snake with horns, lion feet in the front, and bird feet in the back.

Ninazu, father of Ningishzida, was known as" King of the snakes" in Old Babylonian incantations and the father-son pair shares the mušḫuššu dragon, the same way the god Marduk and his son Nabû share the same dragon in later texts. On Gudea's vessel mentioned above, beside the snakes on either side are dragons. This type of dragon was called a bašmu and was similar to a mušḫuššu. The bašmu figure in ancient Mesopotamian art and mythology was modelled after the real-life horned viper and was represented in a range of places and times including as Assyrian protectors, on Kassite kudurrus stones (which were inscribed with land grants), on Neo-Assyrian seals and figurines, and in Akkadian artwork (with forelegs).

Perhaps these representations of Ningishzida are the origin of Nehushtan. While separated by a large expanse of time, the common symbolism is uncannily striking. One more piece of evidence potentially connecting the two is the etymology of the name Ningishzida, which means "Lord of the Good Tree". In addition to the visual similarities, there is also this linguistic connection between the snake god and a tree, as seen in Genesis. If it were proven that Ningishzida has a direct link to Nehushtan, we would still have to wonder whether this snake-staff motif in Numbers was used because of previous knowledge of Ningishzida at the time of Moses or if the evolution of the snake-staff into the deity Nehushtan in two Kings was influenced from the Ningishzida myth possibly known to the Israelites at that later time.

Conclusion

There is a patchwork of connectedness across the ancient Near East that gives context to the mystery of Nehushtan, although few definitive answers. The peoples of the ancient Near East were diverse, but they frequently embraced similar motifs. While correlations are easily presented, there may always be a mystery about how snakes, staffs, copper, fire, and sea monsters became intertwined.[98]

---

[98] *April Downey, "Nehushtan,"* World History Encyclopedia, *last modified August 20, 2020, https://www.ancient.eu/nehushtan/.*

² Alberto R. W. Green, *The Storm-God in the Ancient Near East* (Winona Lake, IN: Eisenbrauns, 2003).

³ Michael D. Coogan and Cynthia R. Chapman, *The Old Testament: A Historical and Literary Introduction to the Hebrew Scriptures* (New York: Oxford University Press, 2017).

⁴ Jeremy Black and Anthony Green, *Gods, Demons and Symbols of Ancient Mesopotamia: An Illustrated Dictionary* (Austin: University of Texas Press, 1992).

⁵ Piotr Bienkowski and Alan Millard, *Dictionary of the Ancient Near East* (Philadelphia: University of Pennsylvania Press, 2000).

⁶ Oded Borowski, "Animals in the Religions of Syria-Palestine," in *History of the Animal World in the Ancient Near East*, ed. Billie Jean Collins (Leiden: Brill, 2001).

⁷ Emily Teeter, "Animals in Egyptian Religion," in *History of the Animal World in the Ancient Near East*, ed. Billie Jean Collins (Leiden: Brill, 2001).

⁸ Michael D. Coogan and Mark S. Smith, *Stories from Ancient Canaan*, 2nd ed. (Louisville, KY: Westminster John Knox Press, 2012).

⁹ Richard Elliott Friedman, *The Bible with Sources Revealed* (San Francisco: HarperOne, 2005).

¹⁰ Mark S. Smith, *The Origins of Biblical Monotheism* (New York: Oxford University Press, 2003).

¹¹ Nahum M. Sarna, *Understanding Genesis*, vol. 1 (New York: Jewish Theological Seminary of America, 1966).

¹² Walter J. Friedlander, *The Golden Wand of Medicine: A History of the Caduceus Symbol in Medicine* (New York: Praeger, 1992).

¹³ Sarah Carr-Gomm, *The Hutchinson Dictionary of Symbols in Art* (Oxford: Helicon, 1995).

¹⁴ Miranda Green, *Symbol and Image in Celtic Religious Art* (London: Routledge, 1992).

¹⁵ *Power of Nehushtan: Medicine's Impact on God's Story* (Scripture Through the Lens of Science), author unspecified, title inferred.

A Spiritual Journey

My connection to spirituality began during a turbulent time in my life. I encountered the Book of Thomas—a collection of sayings attributed to Jesus—and it immediately struck a chord with me. I listened to it countless times, often falling asleep with the audio playing, allowing the words to embed themselves in my subconscious. I believe Jesus was not only a divine teacher but also one of the most profound spiritual practitioners—what some might even call a form of sacred magician or energy worker. His words, like "Seek and ye shall find," resonate deeply with me, especially when I speak with others who haven't yet explored paths outside conventional thought. In my view, Jesus was teaching principles that align with what we today call the Law of Attraction—a spiritual law that, when used with integrity, carries powerful transformative potential.

Before 2015, I had never formally practiced witchcraft or consciously employed the Law of Attraction. Yet, there were always signs: visions, vivid dreams, daytime premonitions—all of which manifested in real life. I could sense energy and outcomes before they materialized. These abilities, though unrefined at the time, were my compass.

When my father passed away in 2013, I was left without familial support, grappling with grief and a broken support system. That's when I first encountered "The Secret" by Rhonda Byrne. At first glance, it felt overly commercialized, almost cultish. But beneath the glitzy promises of instant wealth and abundance, I sensed a fundamental truth about energy, intention, and focus. I knew my journey would be different—less about acquiring material wealth and more about reclaiming personal power.

I began with vision boards. I pinned images of places and things that brought me joy and symbolized freedom: Hedingham Castle, a white horse, a stack of money (as I was financially controlled), and a white Peugeot, my dream car. During full moons, I would speak my affirmations aloud, infuse my crystals with intention, and draw images of a life I dreamed of living. In one particularly painful moment, after a traumatic argument, I sat upstairs with my young daughter. We drew pictures together—a cozy cottage, horses in the field, hens and ducks pecking in the yard. It was a whimsical dream of a simple, peaceful life.

Years later, that dream took root. I began a small business to reclaim my independence. At a local community event, I met a clairvoyant named Kim King—a striking woman with red hair and a silver streak. When we met, there was an unspoken recognition between us. She took my hand and said, "You'll work in care, or as a nurse. Has it started yet?" At the time, I had no such plans. She also asked about a baby in spirit—a painful truth I had never shared. A year earlier, amidst the emotional breakdown after my father's death and an abusive relationship, I had made the hardest decision of my life. I chose not to bring another child into a loveless, unsupported situation. My partner sent me to the hospital alone for the procedure and told others I was having dental work done. Kim didn't need to know the details—she saw the truth.

She told me I would need strength for the year ahead but refrained from specifics. Everything she predicted began to unfold I became a carer and started training in health and social care. When I saw Kim again, it was at a spiritual church she belonged to. That community became a sanctuary for me. They spoke of legal entanglements—represented by the scales of justice—and said I would overcome them. These insights echoed truths I hadn't even spoken aloud.

One man at the church offered to test whether I had spiritual gifts. During one session, I noticed a book on a shelf: "Genesis of the Grail Kings" by Laurence Gardner. My heart stopped. My father's name was inside. He had contributed extensively to Gardner's research. That moment confirmed so many synchronicities.

When I visited a university open day in hopes of studying nursing, I was told I lacked the formal qualifications. The following year, inspired by my father's will and legacy, I returned—but this time for a law degree. I wanted to study copyright law to protect his work and also defend myself in ongoing legal battles with my ex-partner. I remember finding a white feather that day. I took it as a sign. Despite having no new credentials, I was accepted onto the course and granted student finance. This allowed me to hire a barrister to help with my case.

I started the law degree in 2018, and by 2020, I was in court defending my rights. On the same day I was supposed to travel to Parliament with my university cohort, I won that legal case. After another year of delays, I finally sold the house to my ex-partner in 2021. I then viewed a plot of land I'd admired for years. I placed crystals along its path, whispered affirmations at my favourite river, and said aloud that it would be mine. A week later, the agent called: my offer was accepted. That land was in the exact village I had longed to live in all those years ago.

Now, four years later, I live in a cottage that leads onto those four acres. I own two horses—one of them white—and keep hens, ducks, and goats. I've manifested the very life I once drew in that notebook with my daughter. My dreams have taken physical form. For anyone who doubts the Law of Attraction, I am living proof.

I share this not to boast, but to inspire. The Law of Attraction works—but only when wielded with pure intentions. Speak your desires aloud. Think carefully, intentionally. Let your breath carry your affirmations into the universe. When trauma breaks us, healing must come from within. I combined spiritual practice with religious exploration. Buddhism, in particular, offered refuge—its teachings on mindfulness and self-observation helped me view myself not as a broken woman but as an evolving soul.

Understanding our emotions, learning to detach from harmful thoughts, and recognizing the body's stress responses allowed me to slow down, breathe, and respond rather than react. Through forgiveness and acceptance, I began the process of shadow work—confronting my pain, acknowledging the people I had harmed, and releasing burdens I had carried for too long.

This spiritual and emotional excavation led to profound transformation. With mindfulness, dietary awareness, and energy alignment, I reclaimed authority over my life. One pivotal moment came when I met a teacher of Vedic Kundalini Tantra Yoga. This practice, rooted in ancient traditions, combined physical movement, breathwork, mantra, and meditation to awaken dormant energy within me. It's a powerful system that clears emotional blockages and facilitates spiritual awakening. For me, it was life changing.

Kundalini Tantra Yoga opened my chakras, released repressed trauma, and empowered me to live consciously and authentically. I encourage everyone—even sceptics—to try it. Coupled with the teachings in my father's books and the wisdom I've accumulated through clairvoyants, affirmations, and lived experience, I've shaped a life aligned with my highest self.

This is my truth. This is my offering. May it inspire you to walk your own path—with courage, with clarity, and with the unwavering belief that your dreams are waiting for you to arrive.

"The concept of dimension is entirely subjective, as is any concept of reality, which to the greatest extent in humans, is manipulated not only by their internal constitutions, but also and largely by external environmental conditioning and attachment. This training forces humans to subdue and modify their internal constitutions in order to align themselves with arbitrary social expectations. The consequence of this is to create a dichotomy—an endlessly chattering, self-flagellating, hateful monkey in the human forebrain whose ceaseless din, which humans call reality, prevents the individual from entering any other form of perception or, if you like, stops them from changing their dimension.

Humans cannot perceive the monkey. However, by virtue of a different chemical constitution, the Fairies could, quite naturally, and were able to put it in its correct perspective. Once silenced, the monkey which creates the illusion of time and substance is unable to keep the doors to other dimensions, so securely locked.

The Fairies were Dragons and this means that they "saw clearly", they saw subtler emanations than man could. In order to be able to do this the Fairies would have to have their senses tuned into a higher frequency than man. Therefore, the Fairies were tuned to a higher frequency of perception and activity generally"[99].

---

[99] *Nicholas De Vere, The Dragon Legacy (San Diego, CA: The Book Tree Publishing, 2004), 22.*

I continued on this path for a very long time, I still now go back to visit certain texts that ease such pains and stop me from taking on the Victim persona of all things that have happened to me, I say that I am the luckiest person alive, even though I have only my two children as close family, I have been put on a path where my associates that I have met over the years have help guide me with their wisdom.

Spiritual Conciousness

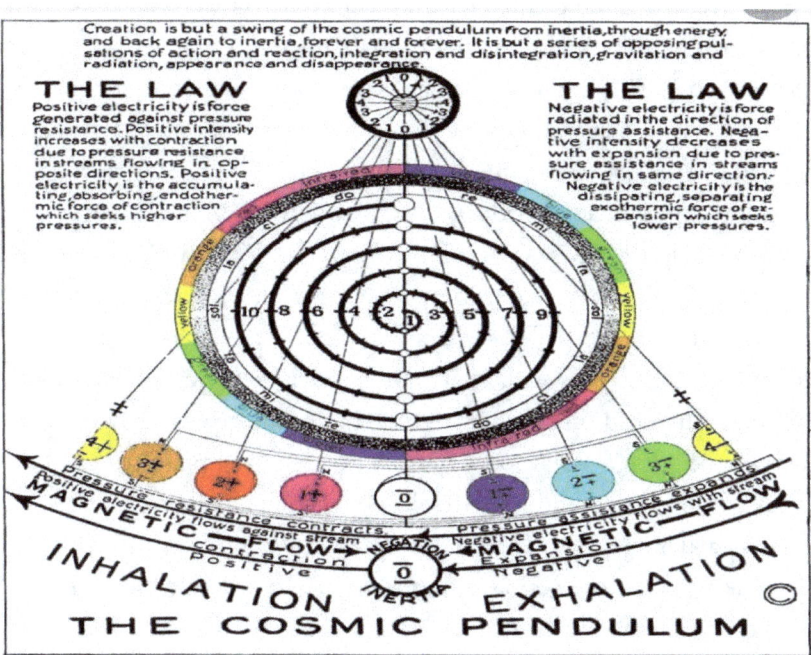

ALL EFFECTS OF MOTION ARE ORDERLY AND PERIODIC. THE COSMIC PENDULUM UNFAILINGLY RECORDS AND ADJUSTS ALL PERIODICITIES

"I have come to realize that the notion of "plots" against us, perpetrated by hidden individuals in high positions, is a common perspective. However, through my own self-initiations, I have transformed my understanding. The higher one climbs the seven-step ladder of awareness, the clearer it becomes that both the Lords of the Dark Tower and the Keepers of the Lighthouse are fundamentally in service to Natural Law and the Universal Order, which comprises both Light and Dark, maintaining a crucial balance. Moe Bedard, The Gnostic Warrior, accurately articulates this when he states, "The Grand Architects of CHAO (Hell on Earth) become the Masters of ORDO (Heaven on Earth). The torchbearers who carry the light in the dark will now be the light

bearers who usher in the new dawn of a new day." It's essential to recognize that extreme challenges are necessary for spiritual growth. There must be individuals who act as instruments for these challenges on Earth, and they are sanctioned by Universal Law to fulfil this role. This is simply how the system operates. Each person, along with the entire world, must descend into the Pit of Tartarus (the hellish experience) in order to rise through the Gates to their Heaven. During the Precession of the Equinoxes, the world experiences 4,000 years of darkness in every cycle, and it is crucial that someone plays the role of the antagonists during these dark periods. This is not personal; viewing it as such only perpetuates a victim mentality and distracts from the larger picture. As articulated in the Law of One, "The most efficient way to bring peace to the world is to find peace within yourself." We achieve balance when we refuse to participate in conflict. From this standpoint, we can truly rise. Speaking from the centre requires us to avoid taking sides and instead embrace the entirety of existence as part of ourselves".
. -- Scott Maurer
"Whatever is rejected from the self, appears in the world as an event"."[100]
-- Carl Jung

Body Wisdom & Natural Senses

Coagulation is the operation of turning something into earth--spirit manifesting as substance, so it often equated with creation. When psychic substances become earth, they take on a particular, localized form, promoting ego development and solidifying personality,

---

[100] *Scott Maur. July 2020 from a facebook post he shared with me. Moe Bedard, The Gnostic Warrior,*

connecting the ego with the Self. Here it is represented by the substantive reception of physical impulses via the sensory organs, which is also the confinement within the limits of our own personal reality, but with the capacity for redemption. Psychic development is a process of coagulation--the images of dreams and active imagination coagulate, connecting outer and inner worlds and relationships.

The pre-existent totality, the Self is first incarnated, then assimilated through the living efforts of the individual. Then spirit inhabits body. The blue background of this piece is composed of closeups of actual sensory apparatus, the various sensory receptors. In the center, the incubation of the divine child continues within the realm of the anima--active imagination.

The spiritual sense, and even the symbolic sense of balance interact to produce a quickening of the transmutive process. Images of sexual sense, chastity, pregnancy, even dreamsex amplify the definition of the natural senses, the basic substance of existence and embodiment, without which consciousness cannot interact with the environment.

The illuminative brain/mind is the center of the revealed truth of a living Universe, a process/goal of evolution, which is overseen here by the celestial hierarchy and the Absolute. The anima media natura corresponds to Sophia caught in the embrace of Physis and is equated with Divine Wisdom, the feminine counterpart of God. This gnostic Sophia is the alchemical mother. Our own belief in the light means the spirit draws the soul to itself from its imprisonment in the body.

"Problems are places where love is hidden," writes James Hillman, and the "oracle" thrust of each "cure" consists in animating and re-animating "together," bringing souls to places of care and relationships. After all, if Gods love to hide, he wants to look and

not to become the "salvific" place of the disease in the extreme."[101]
--Eldo Stellucci

The psychological path is a middle way. Spiritual paths tend to encourage the glorification of the spirit (ascent) over the body and instincts (descent) we need to keep us grounded. We cannot merely drop the body and soar infinitely skyward, even metaphorically.

We are neither solely 'ascenders' or 'descenders.' Soul connects the two movements if we pay attention and engage with it. There is even a shadow-side to the god-image. Meaning is about connectivity and interdependence with everything else out there: self, others, and cosmos. As Hillman notes in Re-Visioning Psychology, "The soul loses its psychological vision in the abstract literalisms of the spirit as well as in the concrete literalisms of the body."

We cannot deny the body's role in our complete being as we confront the autonomous aspects of our transpersonal nature. Our wounds and blocks are expressed as psychic or somatic symptoms. So, to come 'full circle' we need to make both upward and downward spiralling movements which are expressed in imagery and embedded in our innate physical nature. Thus, we circulate among the aspects of our unfolding sacred and natural being.

"We see, therefore, that possession by a breath-like being is a primeval conception of a spiritual condition.

The man who unexpectedly speaks from an exalted or peculiar state is mana or tabu, if he speaks paradoxically then he is surely a sorcerer.

All this shows us that the psychological phenomenon of the spirit is an exalted condition of life, or at least an unusual one, or, to formulate it still more carefully, it is a change in the personality. You see it is something very different to the modern use of the word

---

[101] *Miller, Iona. Drakenburg.weebly.com. Edited for the Royal Dragon Court Website. Public Domain. Eldo Stellucci.*

"Geist", and I am convinced that these original forms are far nearer to its real nature.

We can only speak of it as a human condition; what it is in and for itself is a question which cannot be answered, we can only know how it is experienced. This is equally true of the concept of matter or body.

We must say here that the body has nothing to do with matter. Matter is an abstraction, nowadays it has become a philosophical and scientific concept, whereas body is the direct psychic experience of the body.

Here again there is danger of a misunderstanding. If we ask modern man what is body?, he describes the anatomical structure which he can see with his eyes. But that is no psychic experience, it is scientific experience of the body. Psychic experiences is the image of the body which is reflected in the psyche.

How I experience the body from within is a totally different question. I am inside the body as a psyche. If we investigate carefully what that means we come on a lot of extremely peculiar experiences which have given rise to many of the strangest symbols. If you want to know how the body can be experienced psychically you must turn to eastern Yoga; medieval philosophy also knew something of the matter. If you contemplate the body from the point of view of the psyche, you will be able to locate a mental sphere of consciousness in the head, another centre of consciousness in the heart and one in the abdomen. Our medieval philosophers discovered these, and such centres are highly differentiated in India.

Anatomical knowledge does not tell us how we fill our own bodies, but psychic experience does give us information on this point. We fill our bodies as if through inner streams. The Indian teaching of Prana formulates this, it makes people aware that they can, so to speak, stream into certain limbs and, if one experiments on these lines, one finds it is possible to achieve very peculiar results.

One can, for instance, warm cold limbs in this way and enervate certain muscles. Yogins have many stunts of this kind which are based on psychological Prana experience and have nothing to do with mysticism."[102]

"Probably in absolute reality there is no such thing as body and mind, but body and mind or soul are the same, the same life, subject to the same laws, and what the body does is happening in the mind. The contents of the neurotic unconscious are strange bodies, not assimilated, artificially split-off, and they must be integrated in order to become normal."[103] (Jung, 1984, p.20)

---

[102] Jung, Carl. *The ETH Lectures.* Pages 225–226.
[103] Jung, Carl. *Collected Works.* 1984, 20

The Relativity of Body and Soul

We are not concerned here with a philosophical, much less a religious, concept of the soul, but with the psychological recognition of the existence of a semiconscious psychic complex, having partial autonomy of function, [anima].
--C.G. Jung, TWO ESSAYS...

The soul loses its psychological vision in the abstract literalisms of the spirit as well as in the concrete literalisms of the body. --James Hillman, RE-VISIONING PSYCHOLOGY

Psychic and somatic symptoms express the soul's painful wounds and obstructions. The rational mind is incapable of deciding what is best for the soul. The mind can discover what is needed only by listening to and reflecting upon the subtle movement of the soul as it expresses itself in bodily sensations, feelings, emotions, images, ideas, and dreams.[104]

---

[104]Stein, Robert M. *Body and Psyche: Psyche and Soma in the Perception of the Middle Ages*. New York: Routledge,

We are not engaging in a philosophical or religious discussion about the soul; we are focusing on the psychological recognition of the sacred Kundalini energy. Kundalini is your life force energy. In those who are unawakened, this potent energy remains coiled at the base of the spine. When an awakening event occurs, individuals become conscious of their true selves, and the energy spirals upward, activating each chakra. This transformation elevates them to the status of Enlightened Masters or Ascended Masters. The term "Kundalini" signifies the vital force inherent in all of us. Often referred to as the "Sleeping Goddess," Kundalini is a Sanskrit word that translates to "snake." It is known as "serpent power" because this dormant spiritual force lies coiled at the base of the spine in every individual. Kundalini embodies the power of the Divine present within each person. It has two fundamental aspects: one sustains the entirety of our body, mind, and spirit, while the other, considered dormant, represents the power of consciousness to recognize the Divine in its infinite nature as the Self. This potential power, which is intrinsic to all of us, can propel our awareness beyond the limitations of individual existence—along with all its wants, needs, and deficiencies—toward Unity Consciousness. This is the sublime awareness of our Divine Self, which is infinite and all-encompassing. Symbolized by a coiled serpent at the center of earthbound consciousness, this aspect of Kundalini eagerly awaits the Great Awakening, a momentous event in the soul's long journey, which encompasses countless cycles of physical birth and death. It's important to recognize that both Krishna and Christ are powerful symbols of Kundalini. In Greek, "Christ" translates to "Christos," which is also the term for "Krishna." Christos represents the anointing oil, or Prana, that ascends the Sushumna, known as the Tree of Life. This process unifies male and female energies, as well as the sun and moon within, opening the Third Eye and revealing the divinity and oneness of the Godhead, each manifesting as an expression of the God and Goddess. Kundalini is recognized in India as the life force, in Egypt as Uraeus, and in Mesoamerica as Quetzalcoatl. Collectively referred to as NAGAS, this energy is renowned for its transformative power in self-development and spiritual growth. Kundalini awakening is not only a process but also a definitive goal of spiritual development, leading to the profound union of personal consciousness with divine consciousness[105]..

It is only when you have managed to heal yourself that you are able to give knowledge to others so that they can also heal themselves, I never pertain to be a self-healing guru, far from it. I never pertain to be anything I am not. I just share my experiences with those I feel it would benefit.

Creation of False Self

"We create the illusions we need to go on. And one day, when they no longer dazzle or comfort, we tear them down, brick by glittering brick, until we are left with nothing but the bright light of honesty. The light is liberating. Necessary. Terrifying. We stand naked and emptied before it. And when it is too much for our eyes to take, we build a new illusion to shield us from its relentless truth." -- Libba Bray
"We are not a Self-living within a body; we are a body, heart and mind living within a Self. Our body, heart and mind all exist within

---

[105] *Miller.Iona. The relativity of Body and Soul, Edited by Abbe de Vere 2017www.drakenberg.weebly.com 1992..*

the field of our Self. The "I" that we think we are is not who we really are. Unless we are Self-realised or enlightened, we are "asleep" to our true nature – we have forgotten who we truly are. We live from a self-created (false) centre of consciousness which is known as the ego-self. When we were born, our personal consciousness was undeveloped and inexperienced, and we had very little understanding of the world outside of us. As we learned about the world, we gradually constructed a mental model of how we believed things were out there. The more we learned about the outer-world, the more complex our inner-world model became. Over time, it developed into a meticulously detailed virtual representation of reality. The virtual-reality world inside our mind was a near-perfect representation of the real world, but it was (and still is) coloured by our beliefs and distorted by our misconceptions. Our interactions with other people helped us to fit them into our inner model, and their interactions with us helped us to develop our own concept of self and fit that into our inner model. The concept of self that we developed through our interactions with others was that we are a separate individual contained within a physical body. This was very different to our inherent sense of true-Self, which is pure, radiant, infinite and one-with-everything. So, at this early stage of life we had a sense of two different selves – our true-Self and our "false" mental concept of self. The two selves were so different that we didn't know which one to go with – we didn't know who we were. Our parents related to us as if we were a separate individual in a physical body (our false-self); not as if we were an infinite radiant being (our true-Self). They interacted with our false-self and pretty much ignored our true-Self. Only our false-self got validated, so we eventually went with that one. Essentially, the false-self came into being because we were not seen for who we truly are. Our false-self became our identity, and our virtual inner-world became our home.

Obviously, we can't live solely in our virtual-world because we have to eat, drink and interact with the real world in order to survive. We have to maintain a connection between our virtual-world and the real-world, so we project our virtual-world and virtual-self out onto the real-world. This gives us the impression that we (false-self) are living in the real-world. We perceive the real-world with our virtual world seamlessly projected over it. This virtual-world overlay is what makes an anorexic person believe they are fat, or a tone-deaf person believe they are a great singer. When our two images of "reality" don't match up; when our real-world experience clashes with our inner-world expectations, our inner-world and our (false) sense of self are de-stabilised. This makes us anxious, so we feel compelled to reinforce our (false) sense of self and our model of reality by justifying, denying or blaming someone else. Our false-self is in control in its virtual inner-world, but it has very little influence on the real outer-world, so we often get frustrated when things don't go our way. Our virtual world provides the added benefit of distancing us from the confusing, distressing and traumatic situations of the real-world. As a young child we learned how to use our virtual world as a psychological buffer to soften the impact of real-world distress. It allowed us to block out or distort certain aspects of our reality, paint a rosier picture of our life and justify the other people's negative behaviour towards us. It allowed our innocent and immature personal consciousness to cope with the sometimes harsh realities of the real world. Over time we stopped perceiving the real world directly because it felt safer to perceive life indirectly, through the intermediary of the mind. Over time we became so identified with our false-self and our virtual-world that we fell asleep to objective reality and forgot who we truly are." [106]

---

[106] *Scott Maur https://esotericscience.org/articlea.htm*

The Memory Beneath the Veil

Across these pages, I have not attempted to build a new belief system, nor to rewrite history with a single voice. Instead, I have uncovered, compared, and threaded truths — from old trails walked by Romani families and wandering tradesmen, to the blood-soaked soil of witch trial sites where ordinary women and men were branded with extraordinary fear. I have turned the stone over on topics many avoid: the genetic consequences of inbreeding, the false prestige of so-called "pure bloodlines", and the very real human cost of inherited arrogance.

For too long, people have been told their worth begins and ends with a surname, a place in the social hierarchy, or a strand of royal blood. But the truth is far more intricate. There is no one origin. Bloodlines cross oceans. Cultures blend by force and by fate. What we inherit is not only physical — it's spiritual, psychological, and ancestral. And it is often hidden in plain sight.

The Witch, in popular imagination, has been reduced to a character — cloaked, brewing, casting — but the real Witch was often a grandmother, a blacksmith, a dreamer, or a healer. Sometimes not even named, not self-aware, not practiced — and yet carrying memory in their very bones. What we now frame as "occult" or "esoteric" was once ordinary knowledge, passed down through craft, land, silence, and blood. In many cases, it was never written — it lived in dreams, compulsions, talents, and second sight. And for some, it still does.

The Romani and so-called gypsy families — scorned, romanticised, misunderstood — carried knowledge in music, metallurgy, herbalism, and movement. They were the keepers of memory not stored in books. Their migration is not just a map of exile; it's a map of diffusion. Bloodlines carried east to west, north to south, exchanging with native populations and leaving behind traces that remain in modern DNA.

Every family, no matter how simple or forgotten, carries roots that reach far beneath the soil of nations. Even the so-called noble houses often originate from wandering warlords, adopted sons, priest-kings, or outsiders who rose to power and cloaked themselves in legitimacy. No line is untouched. All are mingled. And all are sacred — not because of title or tradition, but because of survival, knowledge, and soul.

Elitism blinds us. Whether in De Vere's writings or modern royalist mysticism, there is danger in believing only the titled or the chosen carry the light. Many of the brightest lights were born in mud. Some came from trades long gone — cobblers, spinners, boatmen — whose work encoded knowledge the elite could never reach. I have seen it in the faces of ordinary people, in rural families who speak of dreams they can't explain and know things they never studied.

The modern spiritual seeker often searches outward — for a title, a system, a teacher. But much of what they're seeking is already within. As I've shown, many people adopt frameworks that are closest to hand — New Age, Witchcraft, Paganism — but their blood is already whispering truths older than any label.

This book is not an instruction manual. It is a mirror and a reminder. The blood remembers. The land remembers. And you, too, carry something the world tried to burn, silence, or forget. That is why this work matters.

It is not about being special., It is about remembering who we were — so we can reclaim who we are.

This book has been a journey through time, blood, land, and spirit. I have explored the forgotten and often ridiculed bloodlines of Europe — those marked by the red hair gene, the Rh-negative trait, and the deep psychic memory that pulses through certain veins. These traits are not random. They are echoes of an ancient people who once walked as gods, who lived by the dragon standard, and who left their imprint not just on history, but on human DNA.

Through the blood of my mother, I have shown our descent from noble lines — the de Courtenay's, Cobham's, and Seyliard's — names woven into the fabric of English aristocracy and Norman conquest. Through the blood of my father, I have upheld the Dragon Court legacy — a line forged in mysticism, royalty, and mythic memory. And through my own feet returning to the lands of Torquay and Combeinteignhead, I have done more than study this past — I have lived it.

I now walk among the hills and stones where my ancestors once ruled, prayed, and bled. This isn't just history — it is home. The bloodlines that once shaped the courts of Europe now return through me to the soil they emerged from. In buying back this land, I do more than reclaim property — I restore a legacy interrupted, a cycle closed. What was hidden is now seen. What was scattered is now gathered. And what was denied is now declared: the Royal

Dragon Court lives, and I, Princess Abbe de Vere von Drakenberg, stand in full sovereignty of both lineage and land.

Alongside facts and documents, I have faced myths, distortions, and impostors. I have challenged pseudohistory not to dismiss legend, but to reveal the deeper truths obscured beneath it. We are not merely products of empire or accident — we are the descendants of tribes who crossed the mountains, sailed the seas, and shaped civilization. From the Scythians to the Tribe of Dan, from Phoenicians to Merovingians, their blood runs in the rivers of France, Spain, and Britain.

And yet, in the end, the greatest truth I've uncovered is that we are all connected. All families intertwine. All stories cross paths. But some of us carry the fire more consciously — the memory more vividly — and the responsibility more heavily. It is for those souls, like my father, and now myself, that this work was written. To reclaim, restore, and remember what was never truly lost — only buried.

This is not mythology. This is memory. This is the return of the Dragon.

A message from the author, Thank you dad, may you now rest in peace knowing that you have passed on your legacy to the right person. I will continue to preserve your work, the best way I can in your honour.

THE GOAT

Appendix

This appendix highlights groundbreaking information and research that has never before been synthesised in this way to fully represent the truth of who we are, where we come from, and how our social behaviours have fundamentally shaped the way we are governed today. No other author has integrated anthropology, genetics, sociology, and history to present this new perspective on human society and leadership structures. It also helps the reader understand why certain elements have been given their own section- The information is enables constructive conclusions to stop further confusion of the many narratives available on the internet.

Discussion to separate fantasy and fact, where titles land, and laws are concerned

Page 29- Footnote 11

1. *Erskine May, Parliamentary Practice, "Peerage claims" section (UK Parliament, 2024 update), detailing process via the Lord Chancellor and Crown Office.*

2. *G.H. White, "The Household of the Norman Kings," Transactions of the Royal Historical Society, 5th Series, vol. 28 (1948), pp. 111–129; H.A. Davis et al. (eds.), Regesta Regum Anglo-Normannorum, vol. II (Oxford: Clarendon Press, 1914–1968), no. 1685 (grant of the chamberlainship to Aubrey de Vere II, June–July 1133).*

3. *G.E. Cokayne, The Complete Peerage of England, Scotland, Ireland, Great Britain and the United Kingdom, vol. 10: "Oxford (Earl)" (London: St. Catherine Press, 1945 reprint), pp. 199–206, for Aubrey de Vere III's creation as Earl of Oxford during the Anarchy.*

4. *A.C. Fox-Davies, A Complete Guide to Heraldry (London: T.C. & E.C. Jack, 1909), pp. 453–454; Cokayne, Complete Peerage, vol. 10, heraldic description of the Earls of Oxford, noting the mullet and quarterly gules and or arms, and later crest of a blue boar.*

5. *Journals of the House of Lords, vol. 3 (1620–1628), pp. 777–780 (May–June 1626), decision awarding the hereditary office of Lord Great Chamberlain to Robert Bertie, Lord*

Willoughby de Eresby; G.E. Cokayne, *Complete Peerage*, vol. 7: "Lindsey (Earl)," pp. 681–683.

6. Royal Household, "Lord Chamberlain's Office," official website of the British Monarchy (accessed August 2025), describing the appointed Lord Chamberlain of the Household; UK Parliament Glossary, "Lord Great Chamberlain," defining the hereditary office and its current division among co-heirs.

7. William Page (ed.), *A History of the County of Northampton: Volume 3* (London: Victoria County History, 1930), pp. 141–147, "Parishes: Great Addington," detailing the medieval church fabric, de Vere associations, and later manorial transfers; Great Addington History Society, parish archives (accessed August 2025).

8. Maria Tatar (ed.), *The Oxford Companion to Fairy Tales*, 2nd ed. (Oxford: Oxford University Press, 2015), s.v. "Mélusine"; Jean d'Arras, *Roman de Mélusine*, ed. and trans. Donald Maddox and Sara Sturm-Maddox (University Park, PA: Pennsylvania State University Press, 2012), on the Lusignan legend and its later association with the House of Vere in family lore.

9. Government Legal Department, "Bona Vacantia" (Crown's right to ownerless property in England and Wales), GOV.UK (accessed August 2025); Government Legal Department, "Unclaimed Estates (Bona Vacantia)" public notice list, GOV.UK (accessed August 2025).

10. Land Registration Act 2002, Schedule 6 (Adverse possession of registered land); HM Land Registry, *Practice Guide 4: Adverse possession of registered land* (updated 2024), outlining the 10-year possession requirement and counter-notice procedure.

11. College of Arms, "Grants of Arms" (process and eligibility), official website (accessed August 2025); Court of the Lord Lyon, "Petitioning for Arms" (process and fees), official website (accessed August 2025).

12. Erskine May, *Parliamentary Practice*, "Peerage claims" section (UK Parliament, 2024 update); House of Lords Debate, "Peerages in Abeyance" (Hansard, 2 February 1927), detailing principles for termination of long-standing abeyances.

13. Bill of Rights 1689 (1 Will. & Mar. c. 2); Act of Settlement 1701 (12 & 13 Will. 3 c. 2); Succession to the Crown Act 2013 (c. 20), as published on legislation.gov.uk, confirming Parliament's statutory control over the royal succession.

14. S.B. Chrimes, *Henry VII* (London: Eyre Methuen, 1972), pp. 38–42, on Lambert Simnel's 1487 rising; Michael Hicks, *Warwick the Kingmaker* (Oxford: Blackwell, 1998), pp. 312–315, on Simnel's coronation in Dublin and defeat at Stoke.

15. Ian Arthurson, *The Perkin Warbeck Conspiracy 1491–1499* (Stroud: Alan Sutton, 1994), pp. 188–194, detailing Warbeck's capture, imprisonment, and execution; S.B. Chrimes, *Henry VII* (London: Eyre Methuen, 1972), pp. 168–170.

16. ABC News (Australia), "Queensland man claiming to be Charles and Camilla's secret son loses latest court bid," 7 March 2023; Supreme Court of Queensland registry records in *Dorante-Day v State of Queensland* (2022–2023) confirming absence of judicial recognition of royal status.

17. Richard Askwith, "The man who would be king," *The Independent*, 6 November 2005; Guy Stair Sainty, "Self-Styled Orders of Chivalry," Heraldica.org, section on Michel Roger Lafosse ("Prince Michael of Albany"), detailing lack of legitimate documentation.

18. Courts and Tribunals Judiciary (UK), "Judicial Review" overview page, accessed August 2025; *Administrative Court Judicial Review Guide* (London: HM Courts & Tribunals Service, 2024), ch. 1, clarifying judicial review as a public law remedy not applicable to private property or title recovery.

19. College of Arms, "Registers of Grants and Confirmations of Arms" (access via College enquiries), accessed August 2025; Court of the Lord Lyon, *Public Register of All Arms and Bearings in Scotland* (Edinburgh: Lyon Office, ongoing), for verification of arms held by relatives.

20. HM Land Registry, *Practice Guide 22: Manors* (updated 2024), distinguishing manorial lordships from ownership of the land itself; The National Archives, "Manorial documents and lordships" research guide (accessed August 2025).

21. Companies House (UK), "Sovereign Grand Duchy of Drakenberg: Political and Legislative Administration in Exile Ltd," current registration: company no. **16644372**, incorporated **12 August 2025**, status: Active. Previous registration: company no. **07236272**, incorporated **27 April 2010**, dissolved **10 November 2015**. Both entries confirm the name's legal use in the UK as a registered company, rather than as a recognised sovereign state.

Due to its unique and pioneering nature, this research is accompanied by a separate footnote and bibliography system. This approach ensures the work receives the focused recognition it deserves, while maintaining rigorous acknowledgement of all authors and scholars whose studies have provided essential insights. This appendix serves both as a scholarly resource and as an emphasised statement on the importance of this research to modern anthropologists, geneticists, sociologists, and historians with a vested interest in this interdisciplinary field.

The Origins of Humanity, Hybridization, and the Foundations of Social Structure.

Page 85 - Footnote 30

1. Royal Dragon Court archives and research.
2. G. Nickelsburg, *1 Enoch: A Commentary*, Fortress Press, 2001.
3. Ibid.
4. M. Kramer, *Sumerian Mythology*, University of Pennsylvania Press, 2010.
5. Prüfer et al., "The complete genome sequence of a Neanderthal from the Altai Mountains," *Nature*, 2014.
6. Sankararaman et al., "The genomic landscape of Neanderthal ancestry in present-day humans," *Nature*, 2014; Reich et al., "Denisova admixture and the first modern human dispersals into Southeast Asia and Oceania," *Am J Hum Genet*, 2011.
7. Slon et al., "A fourth Denisovan individual," *Science*, 2017.
8. Villanea & Schraiber, "Multiple episodes of interbreeding between Neanderthal and modern humans," *Nat Ecol Evol*, 2019.
9. Liu et al., "The earliest modern humans outside Africa," *Nature*, 2017.
10. Dannemann & Kelso, "Neanderthal contribution to phenotypic variation," *Am J Hum Genet*, 2017.
11. Ji et al., "Harbin cranium morphology," *Nature*, 2021.
12. Chen et al., "Proteomic and genomic analyses of the Harbin skull," *Sci Adv*, 2022.
13. Ibid.
14. Détroit et al., "New Homo species from the Philippines," *Nature*, 2019.

15. Ibid.

16. Brown et al., "Homo floresiensis discovery," Nature, 2004.

17. Ibid.

18. Foster, "Island dwarfism in hominins," J Hum Evol, 2017.

19. Détroit et al., "Homo luzonensis," Nature, 2019.

20. Berger et al., "Homo naledi," Elife, 2015.

21. Ibid.

22. Higham et al., "Extinction of Neanderthals," Nature, 2014.

23. Ibid.

24. Ibid.

25. Johanson & Edey, Lucy: The Beginnings of Humankind, 1981.

26. White et al., "Ardipithecus ramidus," Science, 2009.

27. Rightmire, Homo erectus, 1990.

28. Bennett et al., "Kenya fossil footprints," Nature, 2009.

29. Hublin et al., "Modern humans emergence," Science, 2017.

30. Mallory, In Search of the Indo-Europeans, 1989.

31. Davis-Kimball, Warrior Women, 2002.

32. Ibid.

33. Ruff, "Human stature variation," Am J Phys Anthropol, 2018.

34. Prüfer et al., "Neanderthal genome," Nature, 2014.

35. Foster, "Evolutionary aspects of dwarfism," J Hum Evol, 2017.

36. Prüfer et al., 2014.

37. Dunbar, Grooming, Gossip and the Evolution of Language, 1996.

38. Al-Shamahi, "The social life of Neanderthals," Nat Ecol Evol, 2019.

39. Pettitt, The Palaeolithic Origins of Human Burial, 2011.

40. d'Errico, "Origins of Symbolic Thought," *Philos Trans R Soc Lond B Biol Sci*, 2003.

41. Ibid.

42. Turner, *The Forest People*, 1965.

43. Barstow, *Witchcraze*, 1994.

44. Ibid.

45. Fuhlrott & Schaaffhausen, 1856.

46. Watson & Crick, *Nature*, 1953; Pääbo, *Proc Natl Acad Sci USA*, 1989.

47. Green et al., "Neanderthal genome," *Science*, 2010.

48. Krause et al., "Denisova genome," *Nature*, 2010.

49. Slon et al., 2018.

50. Brown et al., 2004.

51. Ji et al., 2021.

52. Reich, *Who We Are and How We Got Here*, 2018; Meyer et al., *Science*, 2012.

53. Prüfer et al., 2014.

54. Hawks et al., "Fossil record incompleteness," *Science*, 2000.

55. Huerta-Sánchez et al., "Altitude adaptation," *Nature*, 2014.

56. Ridley, *The Origins of Virtue*, 1996.

57. Weber, *Economy and Society*, 1922.

58. Barstow, 1994.

59. Foster, *Picts, Gaels and Scots*, 2014.

60. **Ibid**

It 's a Family Affair, pg 199 footnote 56

William Dugdale, *The Baronage of England*, vol. I (London, 1675), pp. 180–185.

Victoria County History, *A History of the County of Somerset: Volume 2* (London: Archibald Constable, 1911), pp. 98–101.

Charles Worthy, *Devonshire Wills* (London: Henry Sotheran, 1896), pp. 45–49.

G.E. Cokayne, *The Complete Peerage*, vol. 9: "Neville" (London: St. Catherine Press, 1936), pp. 491–508.

G.E. Cokayne, *Complete Peerage*, vol. 10: "Oxford (Earl)" (London: St. Catherine Press, 1945 reprint), pp. 199–206.

H.F. Brown, *The Venetian Republic* (London: Fisher Unwin, 1902), pp. 372–376.

Francis William Blagdon, *A Brief History of the Grimaldi Family* (London, 1810), pp. 14–21.

Friedrich Heer, *The Holy Roman Empire* (London: Phoenix House, 1950), pp. 252–257.

William Stubbs, *Select Charters* (Oxford: Clarendon Press, 1913 ed.), pp. 440–443.

J. Horace Round, *Studies in Peerage and Family History* (London: Archibald Constable, 1901), pp. 114–118.

S.B. Chrimes, *Henry VII* (London: Eyre & Spottiswoode, 1948), pp. 38–42. Ibid., pp. 220–223.

G.E. Cokayne, *Complete Peerage*, vol. 1 (London: St. Catherine Press, 1910), Introduction, pp. xix–xxii.

Friedrich Heer, *The Holy Roman Empire* (London: Phoenix House, 1950), pp. 300–304.

A Witches Craft page 247 footnote 68

Giovan Battista della Porta, De Miraculis Rerum Naturalium (1558), Bk. II, ch. xxvi.

Joseph Ennemoser, The History of Magic, vol. II (London: Henry Colburn, 1854), pp. 67–72.

Jacob Grimm, *Teutonic Mythology*, vol. III *(London: George Bell & Sons, 1883), pp. 1056–1061*.

Montague Summers, *The Geography of Witchcraft (London: Kegan Paul, 1927), pp. 184–190*.

The CIA Files

I am inspired to explore the reasons behind the CIA's experiments on consciousness and to uncover how some individuals—possibly all—have the extraordinary potential to achieve higher states of spiritual and self-awareness. For many years, discussing out-of-body experiences, forms of psychic telepathy, and connections to other worlds has been taboo. Those who spoke about such topics were often ridiculed or labelled as mentally ill, and they risked being taken to an asylum, shamed, or accused of being schizophrenic. I ask why conversations about these subjects have been discouraged when the CIA has conducted its own experiments in this area. Perhaps what we were told was false, and what we were led to believe was wrong is actually right. Is this something that is a capability of those of the bloodline or is it forgotten skills that all of the human race once had, now wiped out, censored, persecuted for having the knowledge much like pagan and druid practices.

DEPARTMENT OF THE ARMY US ARMY OPERATIONAL GROUP US ARMY INTELLIGENCE AND SECURITY COMMAND FORT GEORGE G. MEADE, MARYLAND 20755 Freedom of Information Act disclosure.

AGPC- 9 June 1983

SUBJECT: Analysis and Assessment of Gateway Process

TO: Commander US Army Operational Group Fort Meade, MD 20755

1. You tasked me to provide an assessment of the Gateway Experience in terms of its mechanics and ultimate practicality. As I set out to fulfil that tasking it soon became clear that in order to assess the validity and practicality of the process I needed to do enough supporting research and analysis to fully understand how and why the process works. Frankly, Sir, that proved to be an extremely involved and difficult business. Initially, based on conversations with a physician who took the Gateway training with me, I had recourse to the biomedical models developed by Itzhak Bentov to obtain information concerning the physical aspects of the process. Then 1 Found it necessary to delve into various sources for information concerning quantum mechanics in order to be able to describe the nature and functioning of human consciousness. I had to be able to construct a scientifically valid and reasonably lucid model of how consciousness functions under the influence of the brain hemisphere synchronization technique employed by Gateway. Once this was done, the next step involved recourse to theoretical physics in order to explain the character of the time-space dimension and the means by which expanded human consciousness transcends it in achieving Gateway's objectives. Finally, I again found it necessary to use physics to bring the whole phenomenon of out-of-body states into the language of physical science to remove the stigma of its occult connotations and put it in a frame of reference suited to objective assessment.

2. I began the narrative by briefly profiling the fundamental biomedical factors affecting such related techniques as hypnosis,

biofeedback and transcendental meditation so that their objectives and mode of functioning could be compared in the reader's mind with the Gateway experience as the model of its underlying mechanics was developed. Additionally, that introductory material is useful in supporting the conclusions of the paper. I indicate that at times these related techniques may provide useful entry points to accelerate movement into the Gateway Experience,
; neanscencdtntal Meditation. On the other hand, transcendental meditation works in a distinctly different fashion. In this technique, intense and protracted single-minded concentration on the process of drawing energy up the spinal cord ultimately results in what appears to be creation of acoustical standing waves in the cerebral ventricles which are then conducted to the gray matter in the cerebral cortex on the right side of the brain. As a result, according to Bentov, these waves "will stimulate and eventually 'polarize' the cortex in such a way that it will tend to conduct a signal along the homunculus, starting from the toes and on up." The Bentov bio-medical model, as described in a book by Lee Sannella, M.D., entitled: Kundalini-Psychosis or Transcendence, states that the standing acoustical waves are the result of the altered rhythm of heart sounds which are occasioned by prolonged practice of meditation, and which set up sympathetic vibrations in the walls of the fluid filled cavities which comprise the third and lateral ventricles of the brain. In addition, according to Bentov: "The states of bliss described by those whose Kundalini symptoms have completed the full loop along the hemispheres may be explained as a self-stimulation of the pleasure centers in the brain caused by the circulation of a 'current! along the sensory cortex." Bentov also notes, "that most of the described Symptoms start on the left side of the body means that it is mostly a development occurring in the right hemisphere." Although normally a period of meditation

involving intense concentration and practice for five years or some is required to "bring up the Kundalini," Bentov states that exposure to mechanical or acoustical vibrations in the range of 4-7 Hertz(cycles per second) for protracted periods may achieve the same effect. Bentov cites as an example "repeated riding in a car whose suspension and seat combination produce that range of vibrations or being exposed for long periods of time to these frequencies caused, for instance, by an air conditioning duct." He also notes that: "The cumulative effect of these vibrations may be able to trigger a spontaneous physio-Kundalini sequence in susceptible people who have a particularly sensitive nervous system."

Consciousness and Energy. Before our explanation can proceed any further, it is essential to define the mechanism by which the human mind exercises the function known as consciousness, and to describe the way in which that consciousness operates to deduce meaning from the stimuli which it receives. To do this, we will first consider the fundamental character of the material world in which we have our physical existence in order to accurately perceive the raw stuff with which our consciousness must work. The first point which needs to be made is that the two terms, matter and energy tend to be misleading if taken to indicate two distinctly different states of existence in the physical world that we know it. Indeed, if the term matter is taken to mean solid substance as opposed to energy which is understood to mean a force of some sort, then the use of the former is entirely misleading. Science now knows that both the electrons which spin in the energy field located around the nucleus of the atom and the nucleus itself are made up of nothing more than oscillating energy grids. Solid matter, in the strict construction of the term, simply does not exist. Rather, atomic structure is composed of oscillating energy grids surrounded by other oscillating energy grids which orbit at extraordinarily high speeds. In his book, Stalking the Wild Pendulum, Itzhak Bentov gives the following figures. The energy grid which composes the nucleus of the atom vibrates at approximately 1022 Hertz(which means 10 followed by 22 zeros). At 70 degrees Fahrenheit an atom oscillates at the rate of 1015 Hertz. An entire molecule, composed of a number of atoms bound together in a single energy field vibrates in the range of 10? Hertz. A live human cell vibrates at approximately 103 Hertz. The point to be made is that the entire human being, brain, consciousness and all is, like the universe which surrounds him, nothing more or less than an extraordinarily complex system of energy fields. The so-called states of matter are actually variances in the state of energy, and human consciousness is a function of the interaction of energy in two opposite states(motion vs rest).

Out-of-Body Experience. Although human consciousness can, with enough practice, move beyond the dimension of time-space and interface with other energy systems in other dimensions, the entire process is appreciably enhanced if that consciousness can be detached in large measure from the physical body before such interface is attempted. Once an individual becomes proficient in the technique of out-of-body movement and then reaches the point where he is able to break out of time-space while out of his body, he gains the advantage of "clicking out" part of his enhanced consciousness while starting from a base located much closer to the dimensions with which he wishes to communicate. In other words, since he is starting from a point much "higher up", to use an analogy from the time-space context, that part of his consciousness involved in "clicking out" will have that much more time to interact in dimensions beyond time-space because less time is required to traverse the intervening layers. Moreover, once the individual is able to project his consciousness beyond time-space, that consciousness would logically tend to entrain its frequency output with the new energy environment to which it is exposed, therein greatly enhancing the extent to which the individual's altered consciousness may be further modified to achieve a much-heightened point of focus and a much refined oscillating pattern. As a result, a self-reinforcing process should ensue whereby the farther consciousness in the out-of-body state can be projected beyond the time-space dimension, the more its level of energy output would be enhanced, thus promoting the potential for still further travel. The tentative conclusion to be drawn is that the out-of-body state may be regarded as an extremely effective way of accelerating the process of enhancing consciousness and of interfacing with dimensions beyond time-space. If the practitioner of the Gateway technique has a choice of concentrating on achieving and exploiting the out-of-body experience as opposed to concentrating his full efforts on expanding his consciousness exclusively from a physical base, the former would appear to promise much faster and more impressive successes than does the latter.

There is a sound, rational basis in terms of physical science parameters for considering Gateway to be plausible in terms of its essential objectives. Intuitional insights of not only personal but of a practical and professional nature would seem to be within bounds of reasonable expectations. However, a phased approach for entering the Gateway Experience in an accelerated mode would seem to be required if the time needed to reach advanced states of altered consciousness is to be brought within more manageable limits from the Standpoint of establishing an organization-wide exploitation of Gateway's potential. The most promising approach suggested in the foregoing study involves the following steps:

A. Begin by using the Gateway Hemi-Sync tapes to achieve enhanced brain focus and to induce hemisphere synchronization.

B. Then add strong REM sleep frequencies to induce left brain quiescence and deep physical relaxation.

C. Provide hypnotic suggestion designed to enable an individual to induce deep autohypnotic state at will.

D. Use autohypnotic suggestion to attain much enhanced focus of concentration and motivation in rapidly progressing through Focus 12 exercises.

E. Then repeat steps A and B following use of the autohypnotic suggestion that an out-of-body movement will occur and be remembered.

F. Repeat step E to achieve facility in gaining out-of-body state under conscious control. Alter hypnotic suggestion to stress ability to consciously

control out-of-body movement and maintain it even after REM sleep state ends.

G. Approach Focus 15 and 21 objectives (escape from time-space and interact

26 within new dimensions) from the out-of-body perspective.

H. Use multi-focus approach to solve problem of distortion in terrestrial information gathering trips. This approach involves the use of three individuals in the out-of-body state, one viewing the target object here, in time-space, one viewing it at Focus 15 as it slips into the immediate past, and one viewing it at Focus 21 as it slips from the immediate future. Debrief all three and compare data gathered from the three points of view. If care is taken to ensure that the three all go out-of-body together, in the same environment, their consciousness energy systems should resonate in sympathetic oscillation. They can tune in to the same target on different planes(dimensions) with greater effectiveness.

I. Encourage pursuit of full self-knowledge by all individuals involved in the foregoing experiments to enhance objectivity in out-of-body observation and thinking, and to remove personal energy blockages likely to retard rapid progress.

J. Be intellectually prepared to react to possible encounters with ~* intelligent, non-corporal energy forms when time-space boundaries are exceeded.

K. Arrange to have groups of people in Focus 12 state unite their altered consciousness to build holographic patterns around sensitive areas to repulse possible unwanted out-of-body presences.

L. Encourage more advanced Gateway participants to build holographic patterns of successful attainment and rapid progress for advanced colleagues to assist them in progressing through the Gateway system.

If these experiments are carried through, it is to be hoped that we will truly find

a gateway to Gateway and to the realm of practical application for the whole system of techniques which comprise it[107]

Bibliography

BOOKS:

Alter, Robert. New York: W. W. Norton, 2004. His commentary on Genesis 3:20 discusses the linguistic relationship between the Hebrew and , and mentions the alternative folk etymology linking the name Eve with serpent imagery.

Bannerman, J. (1974). Studies in the History of Dalriada. Scottish Academic Press.

Barrow, G. W. S. (2005). Robert Bruce and the Community of the Realm of Scotland. Edinburgh University Press.

Bienkowski, Piotr & Millard, Alan. Dictionary of the Ancient Near East. University of Pennsylvania Press, 2000.

Black, Jeremy & Green, Anthony. Gods, Demons and Symbols of Ancient Mesopotamia. University of Texas Press, 1992.

Borgeaud, Philippe. Chicago: University of Chicago Press, 1988.

Borowski, Oded. "Animals in the Religions of Syria-Palestine." History of the Animal World in the Ancient Near East, edited by Billie Jean Collins. Brill, 2001.

---

[107] *United States Department of the Army. Analysis and Assessment of Gateway Process. Fort George G. Meade, MD: U.S. Army Operational Group, U.S. Army Intelligence and Security Command, June 9, 1983. https://archive.org/details/CIA-RDP96-00788R001700210016-5.*

Brommer, Frank. "Pan." In , edited by Georg Wissowa and August Friedrich Pauly, suppl. vol. 8, 949–1008. Stuttgart: Metzler, 1893–1980.

Broun, D. (1999). The Irish Identity of the Kingdom of the Scots in the Twelfth and Thirteenth Centuries. The Boydell Press.

Budge, E. A. Wallis. Vols. I & II. London: Methuen & Co., 1904. Discusses the origins and usage of the title "pharaoh" as well as serpentine symbolism in ancient Egypt.

Burke's Landed Gentry (1965 edition), s.v. "Scrope of Danby". This is the most recent entry for the family, which has not been updated in the online editions.

Cartwright, Mark. "Quetzalcoatl," , describing name origin and its cultural importance in Toltec/Aztec contexts.

Cartwright, Mark. "Quetzalcoatl." Accessed 2025. Describes the god's origin and etymology in Nahuatl and situates the figure within Toltec and Aztec religious cosmology.

Chrimes, S. B. Yale University Press, 1999.

Cokayne, George Edward. Vol. X. St. Catherine Press, 1945.

Coogan, Michael D. & Chapman, Cynthia R. The Old Testament. Oxford University Press, 2017.

Coogan, Michael D. & Smith, Mark S. Stories from Ancient Canaan, Second Edition. Westminster John Knox Press, 2012.

Cressy, D. (2004). Gypsies: An English History. Oxford University Press.

Douglas, David C. University of California Press, 1964.

Edward Foss. The Judges of England (9 vols., London, 1848–1864)

Fraser, A. (1995). The Gypsies. Blackwell.

Friedlander, Walter J. The Golden Wand of Medicine. Praeger, 1992.

Friedman, Richard Elliott. The Bible with Sources Revealed. HarperOne, 2005.

Gantz, Timothy. Baltimore, MD: Johns Hopkins University Press, 1993.

George Edward Cokayne. Complete Peerage, vol. vii. (London, 1896), the most complete but not infallible reference for families that have ever held a peerage.

George Julius Poulett Scrope. History of the Manor and Ancient Barony of Castle Combe, Wiltshire (London, 1852).

Gods, Demons and Symbols of Ancient Mesopotamia: An Illustrated Dictionary.

Green, Miranda. Symbol and Image in Celtic Religious Art. Routledge, 1992.

Hard, Robin. 8th ed., 392–417. New York: Routledge, 2020.

Harper, Douglas. Retrieved from https://www.etymonline.com.

Hollister, C. Warren. Yale University Press, 2001.

Holmyard, E. J. London: Penguin Books, 1957. A classic history of alchemy including dragon, green lion, and caduceus as symbols.

J. H. Wylie. History of England under Henry IV. (4 vols., London, 1884–1898)

Jost, Madeleine. "Pan." In , 4th ed., edited by Simon Hornblower et al., 1072. Oxford: Oxford University Press, 2012.

Jost, Madeleine. Paris: Vrin, 1985.

Kenrick, D. (2004). Romani Origins and Migration Patterns. Journal of the Gypsy Lore Society, 5th Series, Vol. 14.

King, L. W. London: Luzac & Co., 1902.

Lakshmi, Rama (2015). "Indians invented planes 7,000 years ago." The Washington Post.

Linden, Stanton J. Cambridge: Cambridge University Press, 2003.

Matras, Y. (2002). Romani: A Linguistic Introduction. Cambridge University Press.

Nahum M. Sarna. Understanding Genesis Vol. 1. Jewish Theological Seminary of America, 1966.

Needham, Joseph. Vol. 5, Part 2. Cambridge: Cambridge University Press, 1974.

Nicholas Harris Nicolas. The Scrope and Grosvenor Controversy (2 vols., London, 1832).

Oman, Charles. Vol. 2. Methuen, 1924.

Sarah Carr-Gomm. The Hutchinson Dictionary of Symbols in Art. Helicon, 1995.

Strickland, Agnes. Longmans, 1864.

Teeter, Emily. "Animals in Egyptian Religion." In History of the Animal World in the Ancient Near East, ed. B. J. Collins. Brill, 2001.

The Victoria History of Cambridgeshire.

Thompson, M. W. Cambridge University Press, 1987.

Thompson, Tony. Hodder & Stoughton, 2011.

Valentine, Basil. Translated and edited in the 17th century. Alchemical keys using serpent/dragon metaphors.

Ward, Jennifer C. Essex Record Office, 1980.

Wernicke, Konrad. "Pan." In , edited by W. H. Roscher, vol. 3, 1347–1481. Leipzig: Teubner, 1897–1902.

Woolf, Rosemary. The English Religious Lyric in the Middle Ages. Oxford: Clarendon Press, 1968.

Written by Coogan, Michael D. & Chapman, Cynthia R., published by Oxford University Press (2017).

Youings, Joyce. Devon Monastic Lands: Calendar of Particulars for Grants 1536–1558. Devon & Cornwall Record Society, 1955.

— Etymonline entry for Hebrew and Latin roots of "Eve" and serpent etymology.

Anderson, Dr. James – Royal Genealogies or The Genealogical Tables of Emperors, Kings and Princes from Adam to These Times (1732)

Anderson, Verily – The Veres of Hedingham Castle

Baring-Gould, Rev. Sabine – Myths of the Middle Ages

Black, Dr. George Fraser – The Surnames of Scotland: Their Origin, Meaning, and History (1946)

Burke, John – Burke's Peerage (1826–1947)

Burke, John – Burke's Irish Landed Gentry (1897)

Carpenter, David – Magna Carta (Penguin Classics, 2015)

Cary, Ernest. Cassius Dio Roman History

Cokayne, George Edward – The Complete Peerage of England, Scotland, Ireland, Great Britain and the United Kingdom (1887–1898)

Coke, Edward – The Second Part of the Institutes of the Lawes of England (1642)

Dalrymple, Sir James – The Collections Concerning Scottish History Preceding the Death of King David I (1705)

De Loche, Thomas & Mortimer, Jean de – The Plantagenet Chronicles (1130–1173)

De Vere, Nicholas & Gardner, Sir Laurence – Bloodline of the Holy Grail (Element Books, 1997)

De Vere, Nicholas & Gardner, Sir Laurence – Genesis of the Grail Kings (Bantam Press, 1999)

Ellis, Ralph – Jesus: Last of the Pharaohs

Gardner, Sir Laurence – Scythian King Lists (Privately compiled for the House of Vere)

Green, Prof. Vivian – The Madness of Kings

Heroditus – Histories (Scythian Martial Customs and Practices)

Holt, J.C. – Magna Carta (Cambridge University Press, 1992)

Hubner, Johann – Genealogische Tabellen (Leipzig, 1719)

Korablev, Leonid – The True Elves of Europe (Essay)

Leland, Rev. John – The Itinerary (Compiled between 1535–1543, ed. Lucy Toulmin Smith, 1906–1910)

Linebaugh, Peter – The Magna Carta Manifesto (University of California Press, 2008)

Macaulay, Thomas Babington – Histories of England (1849–1855)

Mathieson, Ian et al. – Genome-wide Patterns of Selection in 230 Ancient Eurasians (Nature, 2015)

Matthew Paris – Chronica Majora (13th Century)

Mendizabal, Isabel et al. – Reconstructing the Population History of European Romani from Genome-wide Data (Current Biology, 2012)

Murray, Prof. Margaret – God of the Witches

Murray, Prof. Margaret – The Witch Cult in Western Europe

Platts, Beryl – The Scottish Hazard

Platnauer, Maurice Claudian. London : William Heinemann (Loeb Classical Library), 1922

Plucknett, Theodore F.T. – A Concise History of the Common Law (Butterworths, 1956)

Reich, David – Who We Are and How We Got Here: Ancient DNA and the New Science of the Human Past (Oxford University Press, 2018)

Smith, Prof. Morton – The Secret Gospel of Mark

Stephen, Sir Leslie & Lee, Sir Sidney (Eds.) – The Dictionary of National Biography (1882–1917)

Stow, John – The Workes of Geoffrey Chaucer, Summary of English Chronicles, Survey of London, Chronicles of England

Toulmin Smith, Lucy – The Itinerary (Ed. version of Leland's work, 1906–1910)

U.S. National Archives. "The Influence of Magna Carta on the U.S."

Vincent, Nicholas – Magna Carta: A Very Short Introduction (Oxford University Press, 2012)

Woolf, Alex – From Pictland to Alba, 789–1070 (Edinburgh University Press, 2007)

DICTIONARIES
Bernard Burke. A Genealogical and Heraldic Dictionary of the Landed Gentry of Great Britain and Ireland "Scrope of Danby" p. 1346–1347 (1863).

Bienkowski, Piotr & Millard, Alan. Dictionary of the Ancient Near East. University of Pennsylvania Press, 2000.

Chambers Biographical Dictionary.

Dictionary of National Biography.

For terms like , , , , , and, we can similarly source from or historical dictionaries and scholarly articles pre-2025.

Gods, Demons and Symbols of Ancient Mesopotamia: An Illustrated Dictionary.

Harper, D. Online Etymology Dictionary. Covers transmission from Old French ← Latin ← Greek ("serpent"), PIE root *derk-, development of diminutive forms "dragonet" and obsolete "drake," and medieval usage for Hebrew .

Harper, D. Online Etymology Dictionary. Defines origins in Late Latin/Greek, from Hebrew ("it burned"), first English singular use c. 1667 as back-formation by Milton; also covers interpretive link to "fiery flying serpent."

Sarah Carr-Gomm. The Hutchinson Dictionary of Symbols in Art. Helicon in Association with Duncan Baird Publisher, 1995.

WEBSITES

23andMe, Ancestry and DNA research for Abbe de Vere. 2020.

Adrian Francis Harding, Godalming Photographer – Godalming Museum. https://www.facebook.com/GodalmingMuseum/videos/2321583594812143/

Ancestry.com

Banebdjedet: Exploring the Enigmatic Egyptian God – Of One Tree.

Baphomet | Occult Deity, History, & Facts | Britannica.

Bede, Historia ecclesiastica gentis anglorum – Internet Archive.

Ballyhealy Castle – The Norman Way. https://thenormanway.com/ballyhealy-castle/
Borgen, Carl The Bock Saga: An Introduction to the World's Oldest Unbroken Oral Tradition (Amsterdam: Blue Dolphin Publishing, 2019), https://www.carlborgen.com/what-is-the-bock-saga.

Cumnock History Group – Country Houses, Villas and Castles.

Clan MacDonald: History, Tartan & Battles. www.highlandtitles.com/blog/clans-scotland-macdonald

Clan Weir Origins & History – Rowan Displays. rowandisplays.com

Clan Donald: An Introduction into History – High Council of Clan Macdonald. https://highcouncilofdonald.com/clan-donald-an-introductory-history/

Cartwright, Mark. "Quetzalcoatl." World History Encyclopaedia. https://www.worldhistory.org

De Vere, Abbe. The Royal Dragon Court. www.royaldragoncourt.com

Digital South Asia Library: Manipur. https://digital.library.upenn.edu/.../manipur/manipur.html

Dragon Family Tree – DRAGON Labyrinth 2012–2014. https://drakenberg.weebly.com/dragon-family-tree.html

Electric Scotland. (n.d.). The Story of Leith – The Logans. https://www.electricscotland.com/history/leith/5.htm

Electric Scotland. www.electricscotland.com

Fiona Sinclair Genealogy. (n.d.). The Sinclair's of Greenland and Rattar. https://fionamsinclair.co.uk/genealogy/Caithness/Rattar.htm

Geni.com – various genealogy references.

Georgian Era History Blog. "Absalom Smith, King of the Gypsies." https://georgianera.wordpress.com/tag/king-of-the-gypsies

Godalming Museum Facebook Page. https://www.facebook.com/GodalmingMuseum/

Harper, Douglas. Online Etymology Dictionary. https://www.etymonline.com

Highland Titles. (2024). Clan MacDonald Overview. https://www.highlandtitles.com/blog/clans-scotland-macdonald

Historic Environment Scotland. https://www.historicenvironment.scot

History of Richard Earl of Cornwall.

History of Tintagel Castle | English Heritage.

Iona Miller on behalf of Nicholas De Vere. https://drakenberg.weebly.com/dragon-family-tree.html

King Tut was a Celt. http://wn.com/King_Tut_was_a_Celt

Matthew Paris, Chronica Majora, c. 1250. (cited from web-accessed digitized manuscripts)

Mytrueancestry.com

New World Encyclopaedia. Rosslyn Chapel. https://www.newworldencyclopedia.org

Óláfs saga helga. http://vsnrweb-publications.org.uk/Heimskringla%20II.pdf

Online Etymology Dictionary entries: "dragon", "seraphim", "Quetzalcoatl", "Eve", and others.

Pan – Mythopedia. https://mythopedia.com/topics/pan

Rosslyn Chapel Trust. St Clair Family. https://www.rosslynchapel.com

RootsChat Forum. Smith Family and Romany Burials in Leicestershire. https://www.rootschat.com/forum/index.php?topic=857434.0

Royal Archives: Queen Victoria's Household Staff.

Royal Red Dragons. http://www.youtube.com/watch?v=OnYpMcaHCFI&feature=related

San Diego Scottish Highland Games. "The History of the Clan Weir."

ScotClans. www.scotclans.com

ScotlandShop – Clan Weir entries and merchandise. https://www.scotlandshop.com

Stirnet – genealogical tree references.

Study.com. "Tuatha De Danann | Origins, Symbols & Significance." http://study.com/.../tuatha-de-danann-origin-symbols.html

The Douglas Archives. https://www.douglashistory.co.uk

The Queen's Hidden Cousins – Channel 4 / Daily Mail Online.

The Rose and The Thistle. (2019). Rosslyn Chapel Feature. https://theroseandthethistle.com

Theoi Project. "Pan." https://www.theoi.com/Georgikos/Pan.html

Tuatha De Danann. https://www.connollycove.com/tuatha-de-danann/

U.S. National Archives. "The Influence of Magna Carta on the U.S. Constitution."

Wikipedia – multiple pages including on the Weirs, Seraphim, Pan, and Clan histories.

YouTube – Fellowship of Isis: Lady Olivia Robertson.

YouTube – TIPI VALLEY TV FIRST TUESDAY (1985).
YouTube – The ROYAL DRAGON COURT.

OTHER WEBSITES CONSULTED

Bibliotheca Polyglotta. Polyglotta Volume Search Portal. University of Oslo. Accessed August 14, 2025. https://www2.hf.uio.no/polyglotta/index.php?page=volume.

"Olaf Geirstad-Alf." Scribd. Accessed August 14, 2025. https://www.scribd.com/document/188728450/Olaf-Geirstad-Alf.

"Dökkálfar and Ljósálfar." Wikipedia. Accessed August 14, 2025. https://en.wikipedia.org/wiki/D%C3%B6kk%C3%A1lfar_and_Lj%C3%B3s%C3%A1lfar.

"Light Elves: Myths, Legends, and Modern Interpretations." Viking.Style. Published July 16, 2025. https://viking.style/light-elves-myths-legends-and-modern-interpretations/.

"Elves in Norse Mythology." Skjalden. Published September 24, 2020. https://skjalden.com/elves/.

"Elves." Norse Mythology for Smart People. Accessed August 14, 2025. https://norse-mythology.org/gods-and-creatures/elves/.

"Celtic Mythology." The Tolkien Forum. Accessed August 14, 2025. https://www.thetolkienforum.com/threads/celtic-mythology.

"Document 0." OnTheMarket. Accessed August 14, 2025. https://media.onthemarket.com/properties/612487423/document-0.pdf.

Royal Collection Trust. Explore the Royal Collection Online. Accessed August 14, 2025. https://www.rct.uk/collection/search.

"Hecate." Encyclopaedia Britannica. Last modified August 2, 2025. https://www.britannica.com/topic/Hecate.

"Hekate — Greek Goddess of Witchcraft, Magic & Ghosts." Theoi Greek Mythology. Accessed August 14, 2025. https://www.theoi.com/Khthonios/Hekate.html.

Vitelli, Romeo. "The Case of Thomas Weir." Providentia. Published December 21, 2014. https://drvitelli.typepad.com/providentia/2014/12/the-case-of-thomas-weir.html.

ACADEMIC JOURNALS

"A genomic view of the peopling of Europe." *Current Opinion in Genetics & Development*, 53, 21–27.

"A major Y-chromosome haplogroup R1b Holocene era founder effect in Central and Western Europe." *European Journal of Human Genetics* 19.1 (2011): 95–101.

"Forensic Science International: Genetics* 17 (2015): 91–98.

"Genomic ancestry of North Africans supports back-to-Africa migrations." *PLoS Genetics* 8.1 (2012): e1002397.

"How to Map Your DNA with DNA Painter." *Journal of Genetic Genealogy*, 10(1), 2020.

"Sequencing Y chromosomes resolves discrepancy in time to common ancestor of males versus females." *Science* 341.6145 (2013): 562–565.

"The American Journal of Human Genetics* 84.6 (2009): 740–759.

"The great migration and African-American genomic diversity." *PLoS Genetics* 12.5 (2016): e1006059.

"Tracing the route of modern humans out of Africa by using 225 human genome sequences from Ethiopians and Egyptians." *The American Journal of Human Genetics* 96.6 (2015): 986–991.

Ancient human genomes suggest three ancestral populations for present-day Europeans. *Nature* 513.7518 (2014): 409–413.

Gresham, David et al. "Origins and Divergence of the Roma (Gypsies)." *American Journal of Human Genetics*, vol. 83, no. 2 (2008): 285–294. https://doi.org/10.1016/j.ajhg.2008.07.002

Inferring ancestral origin using a single autosomal microhaplotype set: comparison with ancestry-informative SNP panels.

Lazaridis, I., et al. "Ancient human genomes suggest three ancestral populations for present-day Europeans." *Nature* 513.7518 (2014): 409–413.

Matisoo-Smith, E. A., & Gosling, A. L. (2017). "The human genetic history of Oceania: Near and Remote views of dispersal." *Current Opinion in Genetics & Development*, 47, 93–98.

Myres, Natalie M., et al. "The American Journal of Human Genetics* 84.6 (2009): 740–759.

Pagani, L., et al. "The great migration and African-American genomic diversity." *PLoS Genetics* 12.5 (2016): e1006059.

Phillips, C., et al. "Inferring ancestral origin using a single autosomal microhaplotype set: comparison with ancestry-informative SNP panels."

Schiffels, S., & Haak, W. (2018). "A major Y-chromosome haplogroup R1b Holocene era founder effect in Central and Western Europe." *European Journal of Human Genetics* 19.1 (2011): 95–101.

MANUSCRIPTS AND ARCHIVES
Abbe deVere von Drakenberg, The Restoration of Redonda's Crown: From Prince Nicholas de Vere to Princess Abbe deVere von Drakenberg (London: Dragon Publishing Ltd, 2025). UK Statutory Declarations Act 1885, c. 55, https://www.legislation.gov.uk/ukpga/Vict/48-49/55.

Margaret Parry, "Statutory Declaration of Hereditary Claim to the Crown of Redonda," 1993. Private archive of the Dragon Court.

UK Home Office Passport Entry for Nicholas de Vere von Drakenberg, OBTO observation, issued c. 1990s. Copy held by Princess Abbe deVere von Drakenberg within the Dragon Archives.

Nicholas de Vere, The Dragon Legacy and associated genealogical records. Craig Brewin, How Prince Nicholas de Vere made the Queen of Redonda a Legal Title (Part 1), March 16, 2025. (livinginmontserrat.wordpress.com)

Declaration of Legal Succession to the Throne of Redonda, Craig Brewin, March 2025.

"Find My Past Parish Register Collection," 2017, https://rtfhs.org.uk/2017/01/leicestershire-or-rutland-interests-find-my-past-launch-new-parish-register-collection

Fellowship of Isis – Lady Olivia Robertson. (n.d.). YouTube Archives.

Macalister, R. A. S. (1938). *Lebor Gabála Érenn: The Book of the Taking of Ireland*, Volumes I–V. Irish Texts Society.

Marquis de Ruvigny. *The Plantagenet Roll of the Blood Royal: Clarence Volume*, pp. 457–458 (1905), reprinted 1994. (Limited availability online via Google Books)

Needham, Joseph. Vol. 5, Part 2. Cambridge: Cambridge University Press, 1974. Documents the extraction of mercury from cinnabar by Chinese alchemists and includes the symbolism of cinnabar as "dragon's blood."

"Rajasthan minister". Hindustan Times. 16 January 2017. Archived from the original on 27 April 2019.

Scrope of Danby family papers archive.

The Douglas Archives. (n.d.).

Valentine, Basil. Translated and edited in the early 17th century. Widely circulated in manuscripts and later printed in English. The keys use allegorical symbolism to describe alchemical processes, including serpent and dragon metaphors representing Mercury, Sulphur, and Salt.

Ward, Jennifer C. Essex Record Office, 1980.

Royal Archives: Queen Victoria's Household Staff.

U.S. National Archives. "The Influence of Magna Carta on the U.S. Constitution."

Essex Record Office (ERO). Chelmsford, Essex.

Original Text Inclusion, "Magna Carta 1215" – Clause 61 Analysis.

The Victoria History of Cambridgeshire.

Domesday Book to Magna Carta.

ADDITIONAL READING SOURCES

Alter, Robert. . New York: W. W. Norton, 2004. His commentary on Genesis 3:20 discusses the linguistic relationship between the Hebrew -mentions the alternative folk etymology linking the name Eve with serpent imagery.

Barrow, G. W. S. (2005). Robert Bruce and the Community of the Realm of Scotland. Edinburgh University Press.

Behar, D. M., et al. (2006). The matrilineal ancestry of Ashkenazi Jewry. , 78(3), 487–497.

Black, Jeremy & Green, Anthony. Gods, Demons and Symbols of Ancient Mesopotamia. University of Texas Press, 1992.

Borgeaud, Philippe. . Chicago: University of Chicago Press, 1988.

Borgen, Carl The Bock Saga: An Introduction to the World's Oldest Unbroken Oral Tradition (Amsterdam: Blue Dolphin Publishing, 2019), https://www.carlborgen.com/what-is-the-bock-saga.

"Ior Bock," Wikipedia, last modified July 2024, https://en.wikipedia.org/wiki/Ior_Bock.

Eli London, "The Strange Story of Ior Bock, the Man Who Claimed to Reveal the World's Oldest Mythology," InsideHook, May 19, 2021, https://www.insidehook.com/culture/strange-story-ior-bock.

BockSaga.info, "Ior Bock and the Bock Saga," accessed August 4, 2025, https://www.bocksaga.info/ior-bock.

Borowski, Oded. "Animals in the Religions of Syria-Palestine." History of the Animal World in the Ancient Near East, edited by Billie Jean Collins. Brill, 2001.

bringer").

Brommer, Frank. "Pan." In , edited by Georg Wissowa and August Friedrich Pauly, suppl. vol. 8, 949–1008. Stuttgart: Metzler, 1893–1980.

Broun, D. (1999). The Irish Identity of the Kingdom of the Scots in the Twelfth and Thirteenth Centuries. The Boydell Press.

Budge, E. A. Wallis. , Vols. I & II. London: Methuen & Co., 1904. Discusses the origins and usage of the title "pharaoh" as well as serpentine symbolism in ancient Egypt.

Burke's Landed Gentry (1965 edition), s.v. "Scrope of Danby". This is the most recent entry for the family, which has not been updated in the online editions.

Cartwright, Mark. "Quetzalcoatl," , describing name origin and its cultural importance in Toltec/Aztec contexts.

Cartwright, Mark. "Quetzalcoatl." . Accessed 2025. Describes the god's origin and etymology in Nahuatl and situates the figure within Toltec and Aztec religious cosmology.

Chambers Biographical Dictionary.

Citations

Cowan, Ian B. The Parishes of Medieval Scotland. Scottish Record Society, 1967.

Craig, F. W. S. British Parliamentary Election Results 1832–1885. Macmillan, 1977.

Crawford, Barbara E. The Northern Earldoms: Orkney and Caithness from AD 870 to 1470. Birlinn, 2013.

Davidson, H. R. Ellis. Gods and Myths of Northern Europe. Penguin Books, 1964.

Dictionary of National Biography.

Dictionary of the Ancient Near East. Edited by Piotr Bienkowski and Alan Millard. British Museum Press, 2000.

Domesday Book to Magna Carta.

Duffy, Seán. Ireland in the Middle Ages. Macmillan, 1997.

Duffy, Seán. The Concise History of Ireland. Gill & Macmillan, 2005.

Egeria. Diary of a Pilgrimage. Translated by John Wilkinson. SPCK, 1999.

Eliade, Mircea. Patterns in Comparative Religion. Sheed & Ward, 1958.

Enuma Elish: The Seven Tablets of Creation. Trans. L. W. King. London: Luzac & Co., 1902.

Essex Record Office (ERO). Chelmsford, Essex.

Gantz, Timothy. Early Greek Myth: A Guide to Literary and Artistic Sources. Johns Hopkins University Press, 1993.

Harper, D. Etymology of "Quetzalcoatl", Online Etymology Dictionary. Explains the Nahuatl derivation from quetzalli ("plumage, tail-feather") and coatl ("snake"), and the English usage dating to the 1570s. Ellen G. White Writings+2English Language & Usage Stack Exchange+2Nahuatl Studies+2mythosanthology.com+6Etymology Online+6Etymology Online+6

Harper, D. Etymology of "dragon", Online Etymology Dictionary. Covers transmission from Old French dragon ← Latin draco ← Greek drákōn ("serpent"), PIE root *derk-, development of diminutive forms "dragonet" and obsolete "drake," and medieval usage for Hebrew tannin. Etymology OnlineEtymology Online

Harper, D. Etymology of "seraphim", Online Etymology Dictionary. Defines origins in Late Latin/Greek seraphim, from Hebrew saraph ("it burned"), first English singular use c. 1667 as back-formation by Milton; also covers interpretive link to "fiery flying serpent." en.wikipedia.org+6Etymology Online+6Etymology Online+6

History of Richard Earl of Cornwall.

History of Tintagel Castle | English Heritage.

King, L. W. Enuma Elish: The Seven Tablets of Creation. London: Luzac & Co., 1902.

Lazaridis, I., Patterson, N., et al. (2014). Ancient human genomes suggest three ancestral populations for present-day Europeans. Nature, 513, 409–413.

Lebor Gabála Érenn: The Book of the Taking of Ireland. Translated by R. A. Stewart Macalister. Irish Texts Society, 1938–1956.

Lindahl, Carl, John McNamara, and John Lindow, eds. Medieval Folklore: A Guide to Myths, Legends, Tales, Beliefs, and Customs. Oxford University Press, 2000.

MacKillop, James. Dictionary of Celtic Mythology. Oxford University Press, 1998.

Myres, N. M. (1969). The English Settlements. Oxford University Press.

Oppenheimer, Stephen. The Origins of the British. Constable & Robinson, 2006.

Óláfs saga helga http://vsnrweb-publications.org.uk/Heimskringla%20II.pdf.

Original Text Inclusion, "Magna Carta 1215" – Clause 61 Analysis.

Pagani, L., Ayub, Q., et al. (2016). Genomic analyses inform on migration events during the peopling of Eurasia. Nature, 538(7624), 238–242.

Royal Archives: Queen Victoria's Household Staff.

Schiffels, S., et al. (2016). Iron Age and Anglo-Saxon genomes from East England reveal British migration history. Nature Communications, 7, 10408.

Schrijver, Peter. Language Contact and the Origins of the Germanic Languages. Routledge, 2014.

Schroeder, H., et al. (2019). Unraveling ancestry, kinship, and violence in a Late Neolithic mass grave. PNAS, 116(22), 10705–10710.

Sinclair, Fiona. "The Sinclair's of Greenland and Rattar." fionamsinclair.co.uk

St Neots Local History Magazine 30.

Sturluson, Snorri. The Prose Edda. Translated by Jesse Byock. Penguin Books, 2005.

The Victoria History of Cambridgeshire.

Tuatha De Danann. https://www.connollycove.com/tuatha-de-danann/

Ultimate_grimoire_and_spellbook_of_real_ancient_Witchcraft_anglais__ws1034133243.pdf

U.S. National Archives. "The Influence of Magna Carta on the U.S. Constitution."

Witches the history of a persecution. NIGEL CAWTHORNE

Woolf, Rosemary. The English Religious Lyric in the Middle Ages. Oxford: Clarendon Press, 1968.

FURTHER READING FOR SOURCES FOR THE DRAGON LEGACY

Arbroath Abbey MSS

Arden, St. George and Glover Rolls of Arms, ref: College of Arms,

London, England.

Bain I, 174.

The Bloodline of the Holy Grail – Sir Laurence Gardner: Research assisted by Nicholas deVere. Element Books, 1997.

The Book of the Surnames of Scotland: Their Origin, Meaning, and History – Dr. George Fraser Black. New York Public Library, 1946.

British Government's Home Office Identity and Passport Agency
Burke's Irish Landed Gentry – Published 1897.

Burke's Peerage – A Genealogical and Heraldic History of the Peerage and Baronetage of the United Kingdom, 1826–1947.

The Charter "De Decimus Episcopatus," 1100 AD, Moray
Classical Sources:

Sumerian Anunnaki King Lists – Library of Ninevah, northern Iraq.

The Library of King Nebuchadnezzar of Babylon

Egyptian Hyksos King Lists – Manetho of Egypt.

Egyptian Kings Lists – Dr. David Rohl.

Scythian Martial Custom and Practice – Herodotus, 400 BC.

Scythian Mittani King Lists for Syria – researched for the House of Vere by Sir Laurence Gardner.

Scythian Pictish King Lists for Scotland and France – researched for the House of Vere by Sir Laurence Gardner.

Colne Priory MSS

The Collections – Sir James Dalrymple. Collections concerning the Scottish history, preceding the death of King David the First, 1705.

Complete Peerage of England, Scotland, Ireland, Great Britain and the United Kingdom – George Edward Cokayne, 1887–1898.

The Dictionary of National Biography – Designed and published by George Smith, 1882–.

The Family Archives of the House of Vere – Oxford, Lanark, Fermanagh, and Clare.

Genealogische Tabellen – Johann Hubner. Leipzig, 1719.

Genesis of the Grail Kings – Sir Laurence Gardner: Research assisted by Nicholas deVere. Bantam Press, 1999.

The God of the Witches – Prof. Margaret Murray. Rider and Co.

Griffith's Valuations for Tyrone – Public Records Office, Belfast, Northern Ireland.

The Historia Britonum – Nennius, 800 AD.

Histories of England – Lord Macaulay of Rothley Temple, 1849–1855.

The Itinerary – Reverend John Leland. First published 1710–12; later editions 1906–10.

Jesus: Last of the Pharoahs – Ralph Ellis.

Kelso Abbey MSS

Lady Pembrokeshire's Genealogies – Reference Section, City of Brighton Library.

The Library of King Nebuchadnezzar of Babylon

The Madness of Kings – Prof. Vivian Green.

Medieval and Post-Reformation Sources:

Family Archives of the House of Vere

Collison Royal Genealogies, House of Vere, Co. Clare, Ireland.

The Plantagenet Chronicles – Thomas de Loche and Jean de Mortimer.

Transcript of the trial of Major Thomas Weir, Edinburgh, April 10th, 1670.

Sir Randolph Crew's summary – House of Lords Archives.

Roll of Arms of the Lord Lyon King of Arms of Scotland – Lyon Court, Edinburgh.

Medieval Scottish Manuscripts:

Bain I, 174.

Panmure II, 126.

Colne Priory MSS

Kelso Abbey MSS

Paisley Abbey MSS

Arbroath Abbey MSS

Charter "De Decimus Episcopatus," 1100 AD, Moray.

Myths of the Middle Ages – Rev. Father Sabine Baring-Gould, Lord of Lew Trenchard.

Official Government Documentary Proofs of Identity and Title:

British Government's Home Office Identity and Passport Agency.

Government Register of Electors (West Sussex and Carmarthenshire) up to 2009.

Department for Work and Pensions (National Insurance Identity Division).

Department of Transport (Licensing and Identity Agency).

European Union Health Services Department (Medical Identity Card Division).

Republic of Ireland Financial Services Department (Identity Card Division).

Department of Genetics and Haematology, London University, UK.

Paisley Abbey MSS

Panmure II, 126.

Parish Records and Census Returns for County Tyrone – PRO Belfast.

Parish Records and Census Returns for Wigtonshire – Scottish Records Office, Edinburgh.

Parish Tithe Records for County Tyrone – P.R.O. Belfast.

Post Great War Government Documents:

Parish Records and Census Returns for Wigtonshire.

Post Second World War Government Documents:

Registry for Births, Marriages and Deaths – Cumbria, Kent, East Sussex, Hertfordshire, West Sussex.

The Royal Genealogies – Dr. James Anderson, 1732.

Royal Genealogies: Holding Library – Cambridge University.

Scythian Martial Custom and Practice – Herodotus, 400 BC.

Scythian Mittani King Lists for Syria – Sir Laurence Gardner.

Scythian Pictish King Lists for Scotland and France – Sir Laurence Gardner.

Secondary Sources for Genealogies

The Scottish Hazard – Beryl Platts. British Library.

Stow MSS – John Stow (1525–1605). Published 1720, 1908 editions by Strype and Kingsford.

Sumerian Anunnaki King Lists – Library of Ninevah, Iraq.

The True Elves of Europe – Leonid Korablev.

The Veres of Hedingham Castle – Miss Verily Anderson.

The Witch Cult in Western Europe – Prof. Margaret Murray. Rider and Co.

www.ingramcontent.com/pod-product-compliance
Lightning Source LLC
Chambersburg PA
CBHW052007070526
44584CB00016B/1658